Conversations on Canaanite and Biblical Themes

Conversations on Canaanite and Biblical Themes

Creation, Chaos and Monotheism

Edited by
Rebecca S. Watson and Adrian H. W. Curtis

DE GRUYTER

ISBN 978-3-11-061086-4
e-ISBN (PDF) 978-3-11-060629-4
e-ISBN (EPUB) 978-3-11-060524-2

Library of Congress Control Number: 2021940389

Bibliographic information published by the Deutsche Nationalbibliothek
The Deutsche Nationalbibliothek lists this publication in the Deutsche Nationalbibliografie;
detailed bibliographic data are available on the Internet at http://dnb.dnb.de.

© 2024 Walter de Gruyter GmbH, Berlin/Boston
This volume is text- and page-identical with the hardback published in 2022.
Cover: "Judgment on Mt. Carmel (sketch)" by Rembrandt. Image from the Städtische
Wessenberg-Galerie Konstanz, used with permission.

www.degruyter.com

Acknowledgements

There are many people without whom this book would not have been possible, beginning with the SOTS members who heard our dialogue, "Churning the Mighty Waters: A Dialogue on Habakkuk 3", at the Society's winter meeting in January 2012 and were generous with their comments and encouragement to take the project forward. Our thanks are also due to John Barton for his comments on the proposal and to Aaron Sanborn-Overby, the content editor for theology and religion and the ancient Near East at De Gruyter, for his unfailing patience and support. We would also like to acknowledge our long-suffering families, and particularly Rebecca's mother, who very kindly offered to help with the tedious job of trying to impose a uniform style on the earliest draft of the book. Any errors that remain are our own.

Finally, though, but by no means least, we would like to thank the other contributors for their willingness to be involved in this project and their commitment to it despite its long gestation. To enable dialogues such as these to function successfully requires in each participant openness to the other's point of view, real engagement with their partner's work, and readiness not only to give criticism but to receive it and to have the results—even when some of the comments received are quite sharp—shared with the wider world in print. Not everybody would be willing to make themselves vulnerable in this way, and we are grateful to them both as willing participants and for seeing the book through to its conclusion. We hope that they will feel they have genuinely gained something from the experience and that our readers will find observing the process of debate through these pages equally enjoyable, challenging and illuminating.

Abbreviations

AB	Anchor Bible
ABD	*Anchor Bible Dictionary*, edited by David Noel Freedman. 6 vols. New York: Doubleday, 1992
ALASP	Abhandlungen zur Literatur Alt-Syrien-Palästina
AOAT	Alter Orient und Altes Testament
ARMT	Archives royales de Mari, transcrite et traduite
ASOR	American Schools of Oriental Research
ATS	Arbeiten zu Text und Sprache im alten Testament
AuOr	*Aula Orientalis*
AuOrS	Supplements to *Aula Orientalis*
BASOR	*Bulletin of the American Schools of Oriental Research*
BBB	Bonner biblische Beiträge
BBRSup	Bulletin for Biblical Research, Supplements
BDB	F. Brown, S. R. Driver and C. A. Briggs, eds. 1906. *A Hebrew and English Lexicon of the Old Testament*. Oxford: Clarendon
BETL	Bibliotheca Ephemeridum Theologicarum Lovaniensium
BHS	*Biblia Hebraica Stuttgartensia*, edited by Karl Elliger and Wilhelm Rudolph. Stuttgart: Deutsche Bibelgesellschaft, 1983
BibOr	Biblica et Orientalia
BibSem	The Biblical Seminar
BKAT	Biblischer Kommentar, Altes Testament
BS	*Bibliotheca Sacra*
BS	The Biblical Seminar
BWANT	Beiträge zur Wissenschaft vom Alten und Neuen Testament
BZAW	Beihefte zur Zeitschrift für die alttestamentliche Wissenschaft
CAD	*The Assyrian Dictionary of the Oriental Institute of the University of Chicago*, edited by I. J. Gelb *et al*. Chicago: Chicago Oriental Institute. Glückstadt: J. und J. Augustin Verlag, 1956–2011
CAT	*The Cuneiform Alphabetic Texts from Ugarit, Ras Ibn Hani and Other Places*, edited by M. Dietrich, O. Loretz and J. Sanmartín. Münster: Ugarit-Verlag, 1995
CBQ	*Catholic Biblical Quarterly*
CBQMS	Catholic Biblical Quarterly Monograph Series
CC	Continental Commentaries
CD	Cairo Genizah copy of the Damascus Document
CDA	*A Concise Dictionary of Akkadian*, edited by J. Black, A. George, and N. Postgate. SANTAG 5. Wiesbaden: Harrassowitz, 2nd edition, 2002. See http://www.trin.cam.ac.uk/cda_archive/ for online updating facility ("Addenda, corrigenda, and supporting bibliography")
CHANE	Culture and History of the Ancient Near East
COS	*The Context of Scripture*, edited by W. W. Hallo. 3 vols. Leiden: Brill, 1997–2002
CRAI	*Comtes rendus de l'Académie des inscriptions et belles-lettres*

CTA	*Corpus des tablettes en cunéiformes alphabétiques découvertes à Ras Shamra-Ugarit de 1929 à 1939*, edited by Andrée Herdner. Paris: Geuthner, 1963
CUP	Cambridge University Press
CUSAS	Cornell University Studies in Assyriology and Sumerology
DCH	*Dictionary of Classical Hebrew*, edited by David J.A. Clines. 9 vols. Sheffield: Sheffield Phoenix Press, 1993–2014
DDD	*Dictionary of Deities and Demons in the Bible*, edited by Karel van der Toorn, Bob Becking, and Pieter W. van der Horst. Leiden: Brill, 2nd edition, 1999
DULAT	*A Dictionary of the Ugaritic Language in the Alphabetic Tradition*, edited by Gregorio Del Olmo Lete and Joaquín Sanmartín. Handbuch der Orientalistik 67. Leiden: Brill. 2003
DUL³	*A Dictionary of the Ugaritic Language in the Alphabetic Tradition*, by G. del Olmo Lete and Joaquín Sanmartín. Edited, revised and translated by Wilfred G.E. Watson. Handbook of Oriental Studies. Section 1, The Near and Middle East 112. Leiden: Brill, 3rd edition 2015
EBC	Earth Bible Commentary
ECC	Eerdmans Critical Commentary
EQ	*The Evangelical Quarterly*
ErIsr	*Eretz-Israel*
ESHM	European Seminar in Historical Methodology
ESO	Editions Sankt Ottilien
ET	English Translation
ExpTim	*Expository Times*
FAT	Forschungen zum Alten Testament
FOTL	Forms of the Old Testament Literature
FRLANT	Forschungen zur Religion and Literatur des Alten und Neuen Testaments
GKC	*Gesenius' Hebrew Grammar*, edited by Emil Kautzsch. Translated by Arthur E. Cowley. Oxford: Clarendon, 2nd edition, 1910
GUS	Gorgias Ugaritic Studies
HALOT	*Hebrew and Aramaic Lexicon of the Old Testament*, by Ludwig Koehler and Walter Baumgartner. Revised by Walter Baumgartner and Johann Jakob Stamm. Translated and edited by M.E.J. Richardson. 5 vols. Leiden: Brill 1994–2000.
HBM	Hebrew Bible Monographs
HOS	Handbuch der Orientalistik
HS	*Hebrew Studies*
HSM	Harvard Semitic Monographs
HTR	*Harvard Theological Review*
ICC	International Critical Commentary
IEJ	*Israel Exploration Journal*
IJCS	*International Journal of Comparative Sociology*
IOSOT	International Organization for the Study of the Old Testament
IVP	Inter-Varsity Press
JANER	*Journal of Ancient Near Eastern Religions*
JANES	*Journal of the Ancient Near Eastern Society*
JAOS	*Journal of the American Oriental Society*
JBL	*Journal of Biblical Literature*
JDS	Judean Desert Studies

JHebS	*Journal of Hebrew Scriptures*
JRS	*Journal of Religion & Society*
JSJSup	Journal for the Study of Judaism Supplement Series
JSOT	*Journal for the Study of the Old Testament*
JSOTSup	Journal for the Study of the Old Testament Supplement Series
JSQ	*Jewish Studies Quarterly*
JSS	*Journal of Semitic Studies*
KAT	Kommentar zum Alten Testament
KTU	*Die Keilalphabetischen Texte aus Ugarit, Ras Ibn Hani und anderen Orten = The Cuneiform Alphabetic Texts from Ugarit, Ras Ibn Hani and Other Places*, edited by Manfred Dietrich, Oswald Loretz, and Joaquín Sanmartín. 3rd, enlarged edition. AOAT, 360/1; Münster: Ugarit-Verlag, 2013
KUSATU	*Kleine Untersuchungen zur Sprache des Alten Testaments und seiner Umwelt*
LHBOTS	Library of Hebrew Bible / Old Testament Studies
LSAWS	*Linguistic Studies in Ancient West Semitic*
MARI	*Mari: Annales de recherches interdisciplinaires*
NABU	*Nouvelles assyriologiques brèves et utilitaires*
NCB	New Century Bible
NIBCOT	New International Biblical Commentary on the Old Testament
NICOT	New International Commentary on the Old Testament
NIDOTTE	*New International Dictionary of Old Testament Theology and Exegesis*, edited by Willem A. VanGemeren. 5 vols. Grand Rapids: Zondervan, 1997
OBO	Orbis Biblicus et Orientalis
OTL	Old Testament Library
OTS	Oudtestamentische studiën/Old Testament Studies
OUP	Oxford University Press
PEQ	*Palestine Exploration Quarterly*
RA	*Revue d'assyriologie et d'archéologie orientale*
RIA	*Reallexicon der Assyriologie*, edited by Erich Ebeling *et al.* Berlin: de Gruyter, 1928–
RS	*Religious Studies*
RSO	*Rivista degli studi orientali*
RSO	Ras Shamra-Ougarit
SANTAG	SANTAG Arbeiten und Untersuchungen zur Keilschriftkunde
ŚB	*Śatapatha Brāhmaṇa*
SBAB	Stuttgarter biblische Aufsatzbände
SBE	Sacred Books of the East
SBL	Society of Biblical Literature
SBLMS	Society of Biblical Literature Monograph Series
SBLWAW	Society of Biblical Literature Writings from the Ancient World
SBTS	Sources for Biblical and Theological Study
SD	*The Sumerian Dictionary of the University of Pennsylvania Museum*, edited by Åke W. Sjöberg. 4 vols. in 2. Philadelphia, PA: University Museum, University of Pennsylvania, 1984–98
SJOT	*Scandinavian Journal of the Old Testament*
SJT	*Scottish Journal of Theology*
SNTMS	Society for New Testament Studies Monograph Series

SOTSMS	Society for Old Testament Study Monograph Series
SSS	Semitic Study Series
SWC	*Studies in World Christianity* (*Edinburgh Review of Theology and Religion*)
TBN	Themes in Biblical Narrative
TOTC	Tyndale Old Testament Commentaries
TS	*Theological Studies*
TWOT	*Theological Wordbook of the Old Testament*, edited by R. Laird Harris, Gleason L. Archer Jr., and Bruce K. Waltke. 2 vols. Chicago: Moody Press, 1980
UBL	Ugaritisch-biblische Literatur
UBS	United Bible Societies
UCOP	University of Cambridge Oriental Publications
UF	*Ugarit-Forschungen*
VKAWA	Verhandelingen der Koniklijke Akademie van Wetenschappen te Amsterdam (Afdeeling Letterkunde)
VAT	Vorderasiatische Abteilung Tontafel. Siglum of tablets in the Vorderasiatisches Museum, Berlin
VT	*Vetus Testamentum*
VTSup	Vetus Testamentum Supplement Series
WBC	Word Biblical Commentary
WMANT	Wissenschaftliche Monographien zum Alten und Neuen Testament
ZABR	*Zeitschrift für altorientalische und biblische Rechtsgeschichte*
ZA	*Zeitschrift für Assyriologie*
ZAW	*Zeitschrift für die alttestamentliche Wissenschaft*

Table of Contents

Rebecca S. Watson and Adrian H. W. Curtis
Introduction —— 1

First Conversation

Habakkuk 3: Canaanite Chaos and Conflict?

Part I: Engagement

Adrian H. W. Curtis
"Churning the Mighty Waters": Opening a Dialogue on Habakkuk 3 —— 13

Rebecca S. Watson
"Was your Wrath Against the Rivers?" Focusing the Debate in Habakkuk 3 —— 29

Part II: Continuing the Dialogue on Habakkuk 3

Rebecca S. Watson
Response to Adrian Curtis —— 75

Adrian H. W. Curtis
Response to Rebecca Watson —— 85

Part III: Final Reflections

Adrian H. W. Curtis
Some Observations on Rebecca Watson's Response —— 95

Rebecca S. Watson
Some Observations on Adrian Curtis's Response —— 99

Adrian H. W. Curtis and Rebecca S. Watson
Some Joint Concluding Reflections on Habakkuk 3 —— 107

Rebecca S. Watson
Appendix. Occurrences of *hă ... 'im* **in the Hebrew Bible** —— 109

Bibliography —— 127

Second Conversation

Did Josiah Enact a Monotheistic Reform? Debating Belief in One God in Preexilic Judah Through 2 Kings 22–3

Part I: Engagement

Richard S. Hess
2 Kings 22–3: Belief in One God in Preexilic Judah? —— 135

Nathan MacDonald
Did Josiah Enact a Monotheistic Reform? —— 151

Part II: Continuing the Dialogue on Monotheism

Nathan MacDonald
Response to Richard S. Hess —— 171

Richard S. Hess
Response to Nathan MacDonald —— 177

Part III: Final Reflections

Richard S. Hess
Some Observations on Nathan MacDonald's Response —— 185

Nathan MacDonald
Some Observations on Richard S. Hess's Response —— 189

Richard S. Hess and Nathan MacDonald
Some Joint Concluding Reflections on Monotheism —— 191

Bibliography —— 193

Third Conversation

Creation and Chaos in Biblical Thought

Part I: Engagement

Nicolas Wyatt
Distinguishing Wood and Trees in the Waters: Creation in Biblical Thought —— 203

David Toshio Tsumura
Chaos and *Chaoskampf* in the Bible: Is "Chaos" a Suitable Term to Describe Creation or Conflict in the Bible? —— 253

Part II: Continuing the Dialogue on Creation and Chaos

David Toshio Tsumura
Response to Nicolas Wyatt —— 285

Nicolas Wyatt
Response to David Tsumura —— 299

Part III: Final Reflections

Nicolas Wyatt
Some Observations on David Tsumura's Response —— 315

David Toshio Tsumura
Some Observations on Nicolas Wyatt's Response —— 325

Bibliography —— 329

Index of Hebrew words and phrases discussed in the text —— 345

Biblical reference index —— 347

Index of Ancient Near Eastern Texts and Inscriptions —— 353

Index of authors —— 355

Subjects Index —— 357

Rebecca S. Watson and Adrian H. W. Curtis
Introduction

The stimulus for the present volume was a sense of dissatisfaction with the way scholarship is currently conducted insofar as it operates, in the main, within a competitive and combative ethos, in which points of view are "argued" and "opposed", often from "entrenched positions", and differences between standpoints are exaggerated in the interests of rhetoric and the pursuit of "originality". Now at last the gender imbalance is easing in the current generation of younger scholars, it is time to re-evaluate the assumptions and practice of past centuries, and to ask if a more open and collaborative approach may not be devised, in which value is placed on consensus and a more open acknowledgement of the strengths and weakness of different positions. This is far from an abandonment of the goal of advancing research: rather it is to acknowledge that traditional argumentation, with its tendency towards artificial polarisation, can only progress so far before it ends in a stalemate and the iteration of established views. What is required is an open re-examination of a more fundamental level of presuppositions, definitions, methods and conflicting or uncertain evidence, and a recognition of points of commonality where differences have previously been emphasized, in order to build greater clarity and understanding and hence a firm foundation for further developments.

Rarely are the methodological limitations of traditional forms of academic writing exposed more clearly than in respect of the debate over the relation between Israelite religion and that of Canaan more broadly, and indeed between the religion of Israel and that of the Hebrew Bible. Notwithstanding a tendency towards over-polarisation in the interests of "originality", most published views fall at different points on a spectrum rather than at either extreme. It is not uncommon to read two articles which claim to offer highly contrasting perspectives, when in fact their differences are in essence those of definition, and fundamentally the interpretations they offer are not far removed from each other at all. Elsewhere, huge edifices of scholarly argument are set at conflict with each other over issues of detail, when the real point of difference actually lies within the presuppositions or methodologies undergirding everything else, yet these may be scarcely acknowledged, still less worked through in dialogue. In another common scenario, the evidence may be genuinely contradictory and impossible to reconcile satisfactorily, yet scholars toil away to argue one way or the other, and to remove any obstacles to their chosen perspective, but rarely openly acknowledge the points where the opposite case may be stronger. In many other instances, a multi-layered approach to exegesis is possible, with varied possibil-

https://doi.org/10.1515/9783110606294-003

ities of interpretation arising as different values for the plethora of "unknowns" in the presumed context or setting of use are modelled. In some publications, a deliberate hermeneutical decision is made to explore the variety of possible readings, usually without prejudice as to which should be preferred, but more often the attempt is made to find "the" meaning in contrast to and to the exclusion of others. This enterprise is not illegitimate, but again a conscious exploration of presuppositions and variables, and of the uncertainties in such judgments, including "both-and" and "either-or" options rather than artificially imposed "this not that" scenarios, is warranted. Even an "historical" reading of a text can include its pre-history, composition history and history of interpretation and use within its ancient community or communities. These layers may not in practice be accurately distinguished—or distinguishable—but awareness of possible stratifications of meaning should at least caution against infelicitous exclusivism.

Particularly inimical to a deep exploration of these important underlying issues is the reality that much scholarly debate is conducted on a "tip of the iceberg" basis. We contrast our conclusions and the immediate basis for them with others', but in a brief exegesis of a particular passage, for example, there is insufficient space, and it is not felt to be appropriate, to delve beneath the visible tip and to uncover all the varieties of method, presupposition, definition and even cultural and educational background that divide us but which underpin all our work. Often, debates are conducted within a subculture in which, say, archaeologists wrangle over the interpretation of their data, but engage little with texts, while textual scholars discuss the fine details of redaction and exegesis, but with little engagement with the archaeological material—even when both are attempting to address the same questions. In some cases, we are restricted by our personal competence in one methodology or another, but in others there is a tacit preference for one form of approach, which sees alternatives as of lesser relevance but which rarely makes the justification for this explicit.

The aim of this book, then, is to engage with these deeper sub-surface issues that underpin much visible and explicit debate. The intention here is to understand the fundamental bases for opposing positions, to seek to evaluate whether there is any means of objectively adjudicating between the claims and fitness of different methodologies and presuppositions, and to find common ground between them, as well as fresh avenues for exploration. More importantly, our hope in initiating this project is to prompt a cultural change in scholarly practice. It seeks to engender a new, consciously collegial and collaborative, approach, whereby scholars of contrasting views might seek to bridge or reflect on their differences in what might be a more productive way than is customary.

This exercise is not attempted in a vacuum or in relation to a miscellaneous assembly of topics. Rather, it engages with the issue of the relation between Canaanite and biblical religion, one where, more than in almost any other case, it may clearly be said that the details of various debates are so much less important than the deeper, and often less explored, issues that lie below the surface. The approach taken is one of a collection of "conversations" between scholars paired according to their contrasting perspectives and shared expertise in a particular topic encompassed within the overarching theme. Each member of a pair here offers a study of exactly the same issue as their partner, even to the point of beginning on the same exegetical springboard. However, once they have presented their exegesis and reflections on the implications of the chosen passage for the issue under debate, each will offer a response to the other's contribution, resulting in an engaged dialogue and, as far as possible, the forging of a shared perspective together with the clarification of points of difference and agreement.

The ensuing "conversations" engage with some of the most elusive and challenging areas of debate within the sphere of relations between Canaanite religious belief and practice, and that presented in the Hebrew Bible: first, Adrian Curtis and Rebecca Watson grapple with the apparent application of Canaanite mythical "divine warrior" and "chaos" symbolism to Yahweh in Habakkuk 3; in the following "conversation", Nathan MacDonald and Richard Hess tackle the question of whether there is evidence for "monotheism" in preexilic Judah, with reference to 2Kings 22–3; whilst in the third main section of the book, Nicolas Wyatt and David Tsumura debate evidence for the understanding of creation in the Bible, asking, from different perspectives, whether there was, in this worldview, *creatio ex nihilo* or an antecedent "chaos", and how far biblical thought went beyond other ancient Near Eastern thinking. They explore whether it is meaningful to describe the biblical view as "demythologised" and to what degree we should regard the biblical tradition as a wholly new departure in ancient Near Eastern literature, or conversely how far it should be seen within the broader context of tradition. They will focus on Genesis 1 and Psalm 74 as providing the most accessible entrée to the discussion.

The "conversations" presented here will provide a forum for presenting fresh research from some of the leading scholars in the sphere, as well as consolidating much of what has already been achieved and suggesting further avenues for dialogue and progress. As such, it should be of interest to academics working at the forefront of this area. However, the book should, in a unique and explicit way, also lay bare for graduate students and others new to the subject of the relation of Canaanite religion to that presented in the Old Testament, not only the state of the debate, but the fundamental issues at stake, whether of presuppositions, definitions, methods or the balance of evidence, and the processes by which such research is conducted.

One issue that emerges very strongly from these "conversations" is that of methodology: if you take an archaeological approach or a literary one to the same question (such as that of Josiah's reform), the results will be very different. Likewise, if the question of *creatio ex nihilo* is addressed from a comparative mythological perspective, it can lead in a very different direction from an examination of linguistic and etymological data. However, this obviously begs the question of why one methodology should be preferred to another, and in which order they might be employed. Is it right to adopt only one methodological perspective, or a limited range of approaches, or should every form of critical interpretation be brought to bear? What happens when one is given priority over another, and does the first form of approach in any case become determinative? Can or should we seek to escape this?

However, the insight of the influence of methodology on interpretation leads to another, more fundamental, question. Is our choice of methodology already primarily influenced by our prior perceptions of the text: our sense of the relative validity of archaeological or textual data, our instinct as regards the distinctiveness of much biblical material or conversely our view on how it sits within a broad spectrum of Canaanite and wider ancient Near Eastern or Mediterranean belief and practice?

A further issue besets the debates embodied in the present essays, and this is one of definition. What do we mean when we speak of creation, or chaos, or monotheism, to name but a few of the central terms wrestled with here? Sometimes an argument over whether "creation", for example, is the subject of a particular passage can seem deeply divided at first glance, but under closer examination seems to derive more from a different definition of terms. In this case, must "creation" only refer to an initial originating act "in the beginning", or may *creatio continua* also be understood as encompassed within this definition? Can broader "creative" activities, like temple-building, also be understood within the same frame, or is this to stretch the definition too far?

However, perhaps one of the most striking elements of the "conversation" enterprise is its intra-human aspect. A dialogue between two scholars over a very specific question and texts magnifies the process of engagement and response, the complexity of communication, and the importance yet fragility of the process of hearing and being heard. One contributor emailed when reflecting on his partner's response to his initial contribution,

> I'm finding it hard to be entirely eirenic, where I wanted to be constructive, since he misrepresents me on a large number of points, accusing me of crimes against humanity, when I

have been exceedingly careful in the words I have chosen. He often seems to have read me *à l'envers*, as though programmed to react negatively on an instinctive basis, and so to assume that I have the opposite view to the one I have expressed.

From an editorial point of view, we could not discern a greater tendency for this contributor to be misread by his partner than *vice versa*—certainly wilfully—though the myth of editorial omniscience does not mitigate our own subjectivity. Inevitably we are all guilty at times of failing to communicate what we wish as effectively as we might, and conversely of not picking up the intended nuances of what someone else has said—especially when we have already decided what we expect them to say next. It is a common experience for scholars at times to feel misread by a reviewer or others responding to their work, but this hardly imputes any deliberate ill intention, and perhaps for every such incident there might have been more that could have been done to guard against such "misreadings".

Nonetheless, the speed with which we identify a piece of writing, or an individual scholar, as belonging to a particular school, or as being associated with a certain position or tendency, inevitably means that there is a propensity to anticipate a point of view even before it is expressed (or contradicted), and thereby the subtleties of their interpretation, or its points of congruence with or difference from other perspectives, can be missed. Moreover, like siblings or old friends falling back automatically into long-established patterns of interaction, scholarly dialogue can at times be typified by habituation and predictability. This is well epitomised by Nick Wyatt's opening gambit about David Tsumura's paper, one that is by no means particular to this particular scholarly relationship, but resonates with many such engagements:

> I have a feeling of inevitability about the paper submitted by David Tsumura. I suspect that he has the same feeling with regard to mine. The feeling is that a scholar, he or I, or any other, shapes his or her arguments precisely to end up in a predetermined position. He is determined to maintain two positions: the reality (the truth) of the doctrine of *creatio ex nihilo*, and the inappropriateness of seeing in Genesis 1 even a hint of the idea of chaos. I am determined, it would appear, to maintain the opposite position on both points. Can this *impasse* be resolved, or should we shake hands and agree to differ?
>
> So far as I am concerned, I must make a plea in my own defence. This is that, when I begin to write on a given topic, I often have no idea where my nose will lead me. At times I surprise myself and end up a long way from where I expected to be. The same is true in the present instance. In my earlier work I have admittedly argued along the familiar lines, as those who know my work will agree. But as I remarked to Rebecca Watson as I began to read Tsumura 2005 as a starting point for my discussion above, ... it seemed that he and I agreed rather more than I expected. But when I put finger to keyboard, things loosened up considerably. As opponents of my views might argue, my old prejudices kicked in.

As is often the case, however, these "prejudices" can apply not just to previous experience of the writings of that particular dialogue partner, but to "others like them". Nick himself, in a later private communication, admitted that some of his responses may be governed by personal experience of bruising encounters with a particular colleague who would regularly critique his papers along predictable lines determined by his outlook. We all have such ghosts, from whichever perspective we come, and our noses, objective as we would like them to be in sniffing out the truth of a particular scholarly question, take us in many different directions.

If prejudice besets the scholarly enterprise, personality is no less a factor in determining the outcome of interactions. Out of these three dialogues, it would be fair to summarise that one resulted in a warm acknowledgment that, despite some remaining differences, the dialogue partners found, after debating together, that their positions were closer than at first appeared. It is perhaps not coincidental that these partners were the editors, those most committed to (and convinced of) the value of such discussions and of the possibility of obtaining a wider consensus than is generally acknowledged. Despite talk of prejudice, Nick Wyatt and David Tsumura maintained an impressive balance between agreement and difference, amicably agreeing to differ whilst conceding what they could. However, it is striking that their most fundamental disagreement concerned the meaning of language, and whether it should best be resolved in terms of etymology or myth and metaphor.

The issue of understanding and being understood was tested most in the second of the dialogues here, which provided a challenge to the ideal of conciliation and consensus. Areas of apparently irreconcilable difference were exacerbated by the reality that the participants were, in a sense, speaking different languages, since one addressed the research question by historical means, while the other adopted a text-analytical approach, limiting the possibility of direct interchange between the two. It provided a salient reminder of the reality that scholars are effectively only asking the same question if they approach it through similar, or compatible means, and that dialogue is a fundamentally intra-human process. While this conversation provides an example of a more confrontational approach, it also serves as a vital reminder of the variable outcomes of the dialogic process.

A hidden aspect of the genesis of this book is the process of editing and of progressing from draft to final form, which itself comprised an important element of the discussion. The contributors exchanged their first papers only once both were complete, and likewise penned their final reflections after both had shared their contributions to the continued dialogue in part two. However, it would be misleading to imply that the contributors did not feel an impulse to respond to criticism, in some cases wishing to buttress and strengthen their case further by drawing up further lines of defence or attack, but in others instead moderating their initial claims or carefully rewording statements that their interlocutor had questioned (or which were simply too harsh to remain) and therefore moving towards a more central position. Much as such endeavours might have been motivated by the intention to erode any opposing case, they provided evidence in motion of the benefits of dialogue and of the enrichment that another's perspective can bring to all our work and to our collective endeavours. Although, in the end, this process needed to be brought to a close, what remains is a testimony to a lively, and very much continuing, debate as well as to the real differences that still remain.

We have found participating in this project stimulating, revelatory and enjoyable, enabling a fresh appreciation both of the common ground between apparently opposing positions and of the issues that divide us. We hope that you will have a similar experience in reading these conversations.

First Conversation
Habakkuk 3: Canaanite Chaos and Conflict?

Part I: **Engagement**

We have chosen Habakkuk 3 as a topic for discussion partly because it is germane to our common interest in the relation of the Bible to religious motifs known from Ugarit and elsewhere in the ancient Near East; and partly because through its compact 19 verses it presents a clearly defined, discreet unit for examination whilst also bristling with points of contention and debate, so it should offer an ample opportunity for us to test the "conversation" format. Moreover, Habakkuk provides possibly the most sustained and varied example of apparently "archaic" Hebrew poetry that is replete with imagery echoing motifs familiar from the wider ancient Near Eastern context. Most notable among them are the themes of warrior and storm god, cosmic conflict and combat with chaos, besides possible minor allusions to the sun god and gods of plague and pestilence. Habakkuk 3 thus demands in microcosm answers to questions that are fundamental to our understanding of such language and of its wider religious context. In particular, this poem invites an exploration of the force and purpose of "chaos" and divine warrior imagery and of the degree in which it stands in continuity or discontinuity with other, seemingly related, examples, whether biblical or from the broader ancient Canaanite or Near Eastern context.

Adrian H. W. Curtis and Rebecca S. Watson

Adrian H. W. Curtis
"Churning the Mighty Waters": Opening a Dialogue on Habakkuk 3

A paper I presented to the Society for Old Testament Study in December 1976 was entitled, not very catchily, "The 'Subjugation of the Waters' Motif in Ugarit and Israel, and some implications for the themes of kingship, creation and the seasonal pattern". An abbreviated version was subsequently published with a rather more focussed title, "The 'Subjugation of the Waters' Motif in the Psalms: Imagery or Polemic?"[1] I chose to refer to "subjugation", rather than "conflict" in these titles, as a term which could embrace a wider range of possibilities in describing Yahweh's control of the waters. But I certainly did not rule out the likelihood that some passages reflected the idea of a conflict. I also commented on the possible relationship between this motif and creation, defending the view that the establishment of order might legitimately be regarded as a sort of creation, albeit not to be confused with *creatio ex nihilo*. In the published version, I was particularly concerned to question what I perceived as a tendency to dismiss such language as merely "imagery", and to suggest that there was at the very least implicit polemic in such descriptions of Yahweh.

My "dialogue" with Rebecca Watson began when I examined her DPhil thesis, a revised version of which was subsequently published as *Chaos Uncreated: A Reassessment of the Theme of "Chaos" in the Hebrew Bible*.[2] Here she suggested a "...tendency to force ... Hebrew material into a '*Chaoskampf*' straitjacket, and in particular to place disproportionate emphasis on comparisons with Babylonian and Canaanite (especially Ugaritic) mythology..."[3] This, she argued, had given rise to "...numerous references to Yahweh's battling with the waters of chaos and thereby bringing the cosmos into being, without there being any clear statement or account of such an idea in the Hebrew corpus..."[4] Therefore, she proposed, "... the association of chaos with each of these motifs—a battle and an act of creation—must now be contested, the former in every supposed instance, the latter in the majority".[5] A survey of past scholarship in preparing this paper has certainly revealed a number of situations in which it has been over-easily assumed that

---

[1] Curtis 1978, 245–56.
[2] Watson 2005.
[3] Watson 2005, 2.
[4] Watson 2005, 2.
[5] Watson 2005, 2–3.

the presence of the motif of conflict with, or subjugation of, the waters will automatically go hand in hand with the idea of creation. I am happy to agree that it is right to distinguish conflict from creation and not simply assume any link. I also accept that not every reference to the waters must imply chaos, albeit that frequently the waters do constitute a threat to order, both in nature and, figuratively, in society, as is succinctly summed up in Psalm 93.

For present purposes, it may be appropriate—indeed important—to distinguish between the "battle" and "act of creation" mentioned above. Divine warrior and cosmic creator need not necessarily go hand in hand, something which may be an important contribution of the extant mythology from Ugarit regarding Baal. Baal's battle with Yam/Nahar does not seem clearly to be associated with any act of creation of the cosmos, even if it might be understood as paving the way for the establishment of seasonal order or for the creation of the phenomenon of lightning. In the context of this dialogue, it may be more important to focus on the figure of the divine warrior. The image of a divine warrior, who presumably would actually or potentially have engaged in conflict, and among whose activities might be a subjugation of the waters, could well have been important to those threatened by enemies—particularly enemies whose god was believed to be a divine warrior with similar powers!

However, I wonder whether Rebecca Watson can at least be questioned over the validity of the following suggestion:

> ...nowhere in the Old Testament, still less the Psalter, is the sea manifested as a personal being, and nowhere does Yahweh engage in conflict with it. So great is his sovereign mastery over his creation, that sometimes he stirs up the sea so that its waves roar, but elsewhere stills it; he both "cleaves open springs and brooks and dries up overflowing streams".[6]

The focus of this paper is an attempt to challenge those opening claims. With regard to the sea being a personal being, even in the above quotation she accepted that it (or its waves) roar(s) and later acknowledged that the waters join in joyful praise of their maker. In addition to using their voices (e. g., Pss 69:35; 96:11; 98:7) the waters clap their hands (Ps 98:8). Are not Leviathan and Rahab personifications, even if not anthropomorphic? And does not the crushing of Rahab in Ps. 89:11 imply conflict? The powerful description of Yahweh as storm-god at the end of Ps 77 not only has the waters "seeing", "fearing" and "trembling", but likens the lightning to his arrows, implying a picture of conflict. So there seems to be room for dialogue here.

---

[6] Watson 2005, 4.

In order to pursue this conversation, and since we had previously discussed it with particular reference to the Book of Psalms on which her doctoral thesis focussed, it was decided to look at Habakkuk 3. This immediately invites the reaction that the chapter is presented very much in the form of a psalm with a title, a title-like postscript, and a couple of *Selah*s! But its present literary context is in the Prophets, and more specifically within the Book of the Twelve. The issue of whether it was original to the Book of Habakkuk or a later addition to it will be touched upon in our survey of treatments of the chapter. But it is perhaps not a major issue, since what really matters is that it was felt to be appropriate by the book's originators or editors to incorporate this material in conveying their message.

There have been differences of opinion as to the chapter's date. W. F. Albright saw "no valid reason why the book should not be treated as a substantial unit and dated between 605 and 589".[7] P. L. Redditt described the Hymn as undatable, but noted that the reference to "your anointed" in verse 13 seems to have the king in mind and therefore to suggest a date pre 586.[8] As we shall see, Theodore Hiebert saw the Hymn itself as very ancient, but later inserted into the Book of Habakkuk in the postexilic period.[9] But again, whether we regard it as containing early material *per se* or reflections of early material is not particularly important. What is more significant is that its key themes may have had an earlier origin but they could speak to a later period or periods.

Any discussion of the significance of the references to the waters in Habakkuk 3 must take into account the extent to which it contains possible resonances with ancient Near Eastern, particularly Canaanite, mythological motifs—something which has come to be widely accepted. It may therefore be relevant briefly to highlight the salient features of some significant earlier treatments, in order to assess the basis and the validity of such views. An appropriate starting point is that of W. F. Albright,[10] though he referred to an earlier study by Cassuto in 1938 as having "showed convincingly that Habakkuk iii. contains reminiscences of the myth of the conflict between Yahweh and the primordial dragon Sea or River".[11] Albright commented on the importance of the discovery of the Ugaritic texts for the understanding of Hebrew philology and epic poetry and noted the "striking agreement in style" between some Hebrew triumphal songs (including Habak-

---

7 Albright 1950, 2.
8 Redditt 2008, 294.
9 Hiebert 1986.
10 Albright 1950, 1–18.
11 Albright 1950, 2–3 (referring to Cassuto 1938).

kuk 3) and Canaanite epic poems of the early fourteenth century BCE which, he felt, could not be "accidental".[12]

His treatment of the Psalm argued that it should be divided into four parts "of quite heterogeneous origin, though all were probably rearranged and in part reworded by the author".[13]

> Part III (i.e., verses 8–15) now appears in the light of Ugaritic and other parallels as adapted from an early poem or poems of Canaanite origin, celebrating the triumph of Baal over Judge River, Prince Sea and Death, all apparently serving as variant names of a single primordial dragon of chaos. Tehom, Shemesh and Yareah are all personified, as in the underlying Canaanite mythology... This part of the Psalm reflects the theophany of Yahweh in the north-west thunderstorm, with its torrents of water, which stands in sharp contrast to the disease-laden sirocco of Part II.[14]

Albright had no reason to doubt that the Book of Habakkuk was substantially the work of one author, whom he described as "not an original spirit" but one who "possessed a considerable amount of literary appreciation" and who "lived in a strongly archaizing period".[15]

Another important treatment of Habakkuk 3 was that of John Eaton.[16] Immediately noteworthy is that in his translation he gave capital letters to Rivers, Sea (v. 8) and Deep (v. 10), as he did to Plague and Fever (v. 5), but not to "rivers" in v. 9. He translated the beginning of v. 4 as:

> And a glitter as of lightning appears,
> Twin prongs which project from his hand

In his notes he commented, "Surely Yahweh is holding (but not yet using!) the weapon of double-lightning, characteristic of Semitic 'storm' deities".[17] Eaton argued that Habakkuk 3 originated as a liturgical text in the context of the Autumnal Festival and suggested that it is in that light that the meaning of God's warfare becomes plain. "All this makes sense" he argued, "only as a renewal of Creation, poetically presented as the drama of combat between God the Creator-King and the embodiment of Chaos".[18] He saw a similarity with Psalm 144,

---

12 Albright 1950, 5.
13 Albright 1950, 8.
14 Albright 1950, 8–9.
15 Albright 1950, 9.
16 Eaton 1964, 144–70.
17 Eaton 1964, 148.
18 Eaton 1964, 161.

where he took the speaker to be the king, praying for Yahweh's appearance to rout hostile forces with fiery missiles, and commented: "He needs deliverance both from *Mayim Rabbim* and from *Benê Nekar*, foreign enemies".[19] This is perhaps an example of the bringing in of the creation element unnecessarily, but his noting of the juxtaposition of mythological and earthly enemies is significant.

Picking up on the contrasting imagery of rainstorm and sirocco noted by Albright, Eaton suggested that the two are linked together in the Palestinian climate at the beginning of the rainy season.

> It is not therefore surprising if the theology of the Autumnal festival, understanding the giving of rains as the saving work of God the victorious King, should picture it in the two aspects,—the sirocco implying his advent from the Sinai deserts with escort of plague and fever, while the torrential Mediterranean storms display the climax of his battle with the primeval foe.[20]

In considering why such a psalm is to be found in the context of a prophetic book, Eaton noted (but tended to discount) the suggestion that it was a "retrospect, recounted to incite God to action and to stimulate the faith of the hearers".[21] He preferred to envisage Habakkuk's description of a theophany as corresponding to "a 'coming' of God experienced by faith in the process of the worship—a *present* event, but signifying both the renewal of *ancient* salvation and the promise of a *future* outworking of the victory".[22] Whether the psalm had been composed in advance or was the spontaneous product of the inspiration of the act of worship was unclear, though Eaton did not rule out the latter.

Frank Cross (in *Canaanite Myth and Hebrew Epic*) saw the presentation of Yahweh as a divine warrior who led the cosmic forces of heaven alongside Israel's armies as an important motif in the context of a holy war ideology and noted that this theme "is found in the archaic tradition preserved in a part of the hymn in Habakkuk 3".[23] He suggested that, "The collapse of the cosmos in response to the battle of the divine warrior is well known in biblical lore", citing Habakkuk 3:5–12 as an example.[24] He included Habakkuk 3:3–15 among a group of ancient poems which mention the "event at the Reed Sea as part of the Conquest march" (of the divine warrior), along with Exod 15:1–18, Psalm 77:15–20, and Psalm 114, whereas other early poetic material (preserved in Judges 5, Psalm 68 and Deu-

---

[19] Eaton 1964, 162.
[20] Eaton 1964, 163
[21] Eaton 1964, 164.
[22] Eaton 1964, 165.
[23] Cross 1973, 70.
[24] Cross 1973, 150.

teronomy 33) only mention the march from Sinai northward.[25] But particularly noteworthy for our present discussion is his comment on the parallelism of River and Sea in Habakkuk 3:8.

> These verses stand much closer to the myth of Yamm/Nahar and the Cloud Rider than those of Psalm 114.[26]

A couple of general points can appropriately be noted from Baruch Margulis's detailed study of the text of Habakkuk 3.[27] He is one who seems almost automatically to have linked the divine-warrior storm-god motif with creation, because he saw the chapter as including:

> a hymnal description of the storm-god Yahweh which portrays the terror-inspiring, world shaking effects of His march to do battle and His victory over the enemies of His chosen people and their king, in what amounts to a historicization of the creator-god's primordial conflict with the personified forces of chaos.[28]

He noted that, in the "hymn within a hymn", as he described the theophany-description (vv. 3–15), realia mix freely with mythic personages (Resheph, Yam, Nahar, Tehom) "all well-known from ancient Near Eastern, specifically 'Canaanite' mythology", and that "it is here that the poet makes most frequent use of traditional 'formulaic' language and motif-stereotypes of ancient—and epic—vintage".[29] It is beyond the scope of the immediate purpose of this summary to discuss Margulis's suggestions for the *Sitz im Leben* of the theophany passage (a cultic procession) or the psalm as a whole (a Communal Lament), but it may be relevant to note his description of vv. 3–15 as "elaborating this call for—and recollection of—Divine intervention via reiteration of 'former' (i.e. 'typic' acts) of *national* salvation ... The fact that this reiteration is couched in mytho-historical language is almost incidental".[30]

John Day (in *God's Conflict with the Dragon and the Sea*)[31] saw echoes of Canaanite mythology in Habakkuk 3, and suggested that the conflict with the powers of chaos depicted there "clearly involves their identification with a hostile political power which has invaded Judah ... which in view of the probable date of Ha-

---

[25] Cross 1973, 157.
[26] Cross 1973, 140.
[27] Margulis 1970, 409–41.
[28] Margulis 1970, 437.
[29] Margulis 1970, 437.
[30] Margulis 1970, 438.
[31] Day 1985.

bakkuk, is presumably the Babylonians".[32] He noted a hint at the connection between Yahweh's control of the waters and his ability to send rain and bring about agricultural fertility in vv. 17–18. He took the force of v. 2 to be that the present conflict is the renewal of Yahweh's earlier victory which he linked with the time of creation, though it might be suggested that that is not a necessary corollary. He too saw Plague and Pestilence as being personified, and the latter reflecting the plague-god Resheph, here "demoted to a kind of demon in Yahweh's entourage".[33] He felt that v. 11 makes it clear that the theophany is in the form of lightning.[34] Day also suggested some additional mythological echoes which could be argued to be more speculative, but he felt it possible to conclude that, in the light of the specific parallels in the chapter, together with what he described as "the Canaanite background of the Old Testament chaos and chaos monster imagery generally", Habakkuk 3 should be seen as deriving from Canaanite rather than Babylonian mythology. But I wonder whether it is unwise to see this as entirely an "either/or" situation. The use of motifs ultimately deriving from Canaanite mythology may have been particularly appropriate precisely because of resonances with Babylonian mythology.

The year after Day's book appeared, Theodore Hiebert's monograph entitled *God of My Victory: The Ancient Hymn in Habakkuk 3* was published.[35] Its title and sub-title highlight one of its major suggestions: the psalm is an ancient Hymn of Triumph, "composed in the premonarchic era as a recitation of the victory of the divine warrior over cosmic and earthly enemies", but eventually "reinterpreted as a prophecy of God's eschatological victory".[36] It therefore sheds light on Israel's earliest religious thinking but also on the expectations of the postexilic period. Some of Hiebert's arguments for the antiquity of the poem have rightly been questioned.[37] But this does not invalidate his belief that the poem preserves ancient motifs, some of which it is relevant to mention here. As have others, he saw Deber and Resheph as divine beings who form part of the divine warrior's entourage.[38] He saw the vivid description of the divine warrior's preparations and march as "drawn from the traditional picture of the storm god in Semitic

---

32 Day 1985, 105.
33 Day 1985, 106.
34 Day 1985, 108.
35 Hiebert 1986.
36 Hiebert 1986, 1.
37 See for example the review by Williamson (1989, 509–10).
38 Hiebert 1986, 92.

mythology", noting that the closest example at hand is Baal at Ugarit, but that Marduk is similarly pictured.³⁹ He stated with confidence that:

> All modern interpreters acknowledge connections between Habakkuk 3 and the ancient conflict myth in which the storm god goes out as a warrior to do battle with the sea.⁴⁰

But he went on to note that there has been disagreement as to whether Habakkuk 3 actually describes the "mythological" battle or a battle with a historical enemy. He believed that vv. 12–13a place the battle in a more historical context.

> It is clear from these verses that Yahweh's battle with the dragon is not viewed as purely mythical or cosmic but as a battle for the salvation of God's people in which the nations are trampled down.⁴¹

His conclusion represented something of an amalgam of the possibilities. The recital of the cosmic battle functions as a way of celebrating Yahweh's victory in earthly wars, and the defeat of Sea/River would evoke in the listener's mind the traditions of the defeats of the Egyptians at the Reed Sea and the Canaanites at the River Jordan.⁴²

With regard to the psalm's antiquity, Hiebert stated:

> The manner in which mythological language is employed in Habakkuk 3 also fits appropriately into the early days of Israel. The vivid parallels between the Ugaritic myth ... and Habakkuk 3 ... suggest a setting in Israel's early religious life when its own religion was emerging from its Canaanite context.⁴³

However, he did acknowledge that motifs such as that of the battle of the divine warrior were employed at later periods. He found it difficult to think that the prophet Habakkuk would himself have personified the sun and moon, given contemporary concern about their worship (as, e. g., in Jeremiah 8:2).⁴⁴ (But it could be countered that they are here personified along with mountains and the deep as part of the whole of nature being discomforted by the theophany of Yahweh.) Although he saw the psalm's origins as ancient, he did accept that its incorpo-

---

39 Hiebert 1986, 97–8.
40 Hiebert 1986, 101.
41 Hiebert 1986, 106.
42 Hiebert 1986, 108.
43 Hiebert 1986, 123
44 Hiebert 1986, 123.

ration may have been prompted by events which followed shortly after Habakkuk's career, i.e. the fall of Jerusalem and the Babylonian captivity.

> The addition of Habakkuk 3 to the writings of Habakkuk is to be understood as having occurred in just such a setting. Among the disciples of the prophets, including those preserving the writings of Habakkuk, arose the apocalyptic fervor of the late sixth and early fifth centuries.[45]

The hymn was to be understood eschatologically rather than historically and as reflecting an *Urzeit—Endzeit* characteristic of myth in Israel which has long been noted.[46]

If we are to retain chronological sequence in this survey, it is appropriate here to note some cautionary remarks made by David Tsumura in his article "Ugaritic Poetry and Habakkuk 3", published in 1988,[47] though his arguments were subsequently reinforced in more general treatments of the *Chaoskampf* motif. Tsumura was at pains to warn of the methodological problems which are confronted in relating ancient Near Eastern texts to the Hebrew Bible. Perhaps inadvertently he alluded to one such problem in quoting a comment of Kenneth Kitchen[48] that "it is necessary to deal individually and on its own merits with each possible or alleged case of relationship or borrowing", but he did not immediately indicate the significant difference between "relationship" and "borrowing". He went on to note that comparison between Ugaritic literature and the Hebrew Bible "is basically between different genres of literature",[49] but without comment as to whether that necessarily makes such comparisons inappropriate. Rather, he noted:

> It has become almost customary in modern scholarship to hold that Habakkuk 3 was *influenced* by Ugaritic poetry. It may be questioned whether this pays due attention to the difference in their literary genre.[50]

Note the new word "influenced"! (The emphasis is Tsumura's.) But he did proceed to underline the importance of the careful use of words like "allusion" and "reference" and then to suggest that:

---

45 Hiebert 1986, 137.
46 Hiebert 1986, 138.
47 Tsumura 1988, 24–48. See his subsequent comments in Tsumura 2005, and Tsumura 2007, 473–99.
48 Kitchen 1966, 88.
49 Tsumura 1988, 25.
50 Tsumura 1988, 25.

> In comparative studies of Ugaritic mythology and Old Testament Literature in general too much emphasis has been given to similarity or "fact" of sameness in form and no clear distinction has been made between the synchronic and the comparative–diachronic approach.[51]

He argued that it is almost always in poetic texts that such "similar" materials appear, "and they usually constitute a group of words or phrases, never sentences or discourses".[52]

Tsumura then considered in detail some specific examples. He examined the suggested use of the Sea/River word-pair in v. 8 in light of some Ugaritic usages, and concluded:

> Hence if Habakkuk 3:8 is a *direct* transfer of the Ugaritic pair of the conflict scene, *yām // nāhār* would have been expected. The fact that Habakkuk has a rather unusual pair *nəhārîm // yām*—which corresponds to the Ugaritic word pair *ym // nhrm* of the non-conflict scene—may suggest that the author used it on purpose for describing an entirely different reality from the Baal-Yamm mythology.[53]

He went on to note the possibility, *inter alia*, that Habakkuk had "borrowed" (another new word) from some thought-world other than the Ugaritic. But surely borrowing suggests something rather more specific than, e.g., alluding.

In commenting on some of the military language, in particular that connected with horses and chariots, Tsumura noted:

> storm gods such as Ninurta, Enlil and Adad ride in a chariot and the sound of the wheels of the storm-god's chariot refers to thunder. Therefore, it would not be surprising if Baal the storm god of Ugaritic mythology rode a chariot and the sound of his wheels symbolized thunder. But there is nothing in the present texts to suggest this was the case.[54]

(This is perhaps an overstatement, as the epithet "rider of the clouds" could at least be said to *suggest* it, even if it does not prove it.) More generally, he proposed that the martial imagery of Habakkuk 3 may derive from "metaphorization of a normal usage of military activities of a human king in the ancient Near East", and went on to suggest:

---

51 Tsumura 1988, 27.
52 Tsumura 1988, 28.
53 Tsumura 1988, 30.
54 Tsumura 1988, 32.

Since Yahweh is not a storm god, his chariot and the sound of his wheels do not automatically represent or *refer* to thunder or cloud, though his divine action may be described as "thunder-like" by metaphor.[55]

But it can be countered that if Yahweh is not a storm god he is certainly likened to one! And presumably much language about the gods would ultimately derive from descriptions of human kings, as he later noted:

> the image of Yahweh in Habakkuk 3 may be compared with "an image of Assur, raising his bow, riding in his chariot ... with the deluge" as described in the Annals of Sennacherib. Habakkuk also, in depicting his God, uses here a metaphor based on a normal practice of a human king in war time.

This at least suggests that comparison with ancient Near Eastern texts *can* be informative!

It is possible to agree with Tsumura in his criticism of some suggestions of a literary relationship between Habakkuk 3 and the Ugaritic Baal/Yam myth, though it is noteworthy that his language shifts from literary relationship, to the preservation of a literary tradition, to literary connection.[56] His reference in fact seems to be to *direct literary borrowing*, which is something very different and which issues of chronology and language would tend to rule out.

Since it appears prominently in discussions of the chapter, it is also appropriate to note Tsumura's comment on the possible mention of Resheph in Habakkuk 3.

> Certainly, the god Resheph served as a warrior and also the god of plagues, like Apollo in the Greek world and the god Nergal in the Mesopotamian world. They are all connected with heavenly bodies, mainly with falling stars (meteors) which shoot like arrows. Therefore it is no surprise if Resheph as a warrior god participates in the divine conflict as described in the Ugaritic myth ... However, in Habakkuk 3 *rešep* as well as *deber* are the symbols of Yahweh's destructive power rather than appearing as archers.[57]

He was doubtless correct in his conclusion that "a metaphorization of an ordinary word should be carefully distinguished from a demythologization of a divine name".[58] But surely this need not mean that there would not have been any connection in the mind of the hearer.

---

55 Tsumura 1988, 33.
56 Tsumura 1988, 40–1.
57 Tsumura 1988, 46–7.
58 Tsumura 1988, 48.

Let us now look at some points mentioned in two commentaries, firstly that by J. J. M. Roberts in the Old Testament Library series.[59] He noted that the archaic features of Habakkuk 3 are concentrated in vv. 3–15 and suggest the adaptation of an archaic hymn depicting Yahweh's march to destroy his people's enemies. However he argued that this is not a later addition but rather that it contains the vision to which 2:2 looks forward.[60] (He therefore disagreed with Hiebert on both counts.) In his translation he gave capital letters to Plague, Fever, River, Sea and Deep;[61] and saw Plague (*dbr*) as a demon who travels in Yahweh's royal entourage, and Fever as Resheph, the West Semitic god of pestilence.[62] Noting a suggestion that *nhrt* in v. 9 should be understood as "lightnings" rather than "rivers" because rivers are Yahweh's enemies but not weapons, he defended the traditional understanding, noting parallels in Psalm 74:15 and in *Enuma Elish* V, 54–5, where Marduk created the water courses from the body of Tiamat. He also argued that in v. 10 the subject of "raised" must be the Deep (not, e.g., the Sun as in the NRSV), pictured as raising up its waves against Yahweh "as in the primordial cosmogonic battle".[63] Like Eaton, as noted earlier, he saw a reference to lightning bolts in v. 4 and noted the iconography of storm-gods holding lightning bolts.[64] In connection with v. 6 ("he looked and made the nations tremble"), Roberts pointed to an analogy in *Enuma Elish* IV 67–8 where Marduk's glance confuses the plans of Kingu. Underlying v. 8, he saw the "paradigmatic mythical pattern borrowed from the Baal cycle of Canaanite mythology",[65] albeit that the implied enemy here is Babylon. In v. 9, Yahweh is depicted as the typical charioteer armed with a bow.

> Yahweh's splitting open of the earth with rivers recalls the motif in which the cosmogonic warrior, after having subdued the waters of chaos, reorders them as manageable sources of water for the benefit of his structured world.[66]

And with regard to v. 13 he commented:

---

[59] Roberts 1991.
[60] Roberts 1991, 148–9.
[61] Roberts 1991, 128–9.
[62] Roberts 1991, 135.
[63] Roberts 1991, 140.
[64] Roberts 1991, 152–3.
[65] Roberts 1991, 155.
[66] Roberts 1991, 155–6.

> Just as Baal in the Ugaritic myth …, Yahweh smites first the back and the head of his opponent … and just as Marduk in the Babylonian myth … Yahweh splits his opponent open from bottom to top.[67]

V. 15 identifies the enemy with the personified Sea of ancient mythology and offers "a clear promise that God would destroy the Babylonian oppressor, the contemporary embodiment of those ancient powers of chaos".[68]

We may also note the Abingdon Old Testament Commentary by Julia O'Brien.[69] She proposed that Habakkuk 3 looks both backward and forward to the appearance of the divine warrior, Yahweh, who will put things right.[70] The portrayal of Yahweh as the cosmic divine warrior is done in "bold mythic terms", and "drawing from the well of ancient Near Eastern mythological motifs".[71]

> In both Canaanite and Babylonian mythologies, the world was formed as the result of combat between gods. In the Canaanite account, the god Baal fought and defeated Yamm (Sea) to create order in the world; in the Babylonian myth, the god Marduk slew the chaos monster, Tiamat, and created the heaven and the earth from her body.[72]

As did Roberts, O'Brien saw this chapter as providing the answer to the prophet's complaint and the contents of the vision alluded to in 2:1–5.

> In its current form, the march of the Divine Warrior is now the assurance of God's power and will to save. Although Yahweh may be described in terms akin to those of other ancient Near Eastern deities, Hab 3 insists that Yahweh—not Baal or Marduk—rules the cosmos.[73]

What seems to emerge with some level of consensus from this survey is that the chapter certainly describes a theophany—probably one rather than two. The primary image is that of the Divine Warrior. The chapter may contain some archaic language and certainly some mythic language. There are allusions to mythological motifs other than "waters" which might be referred to as "Canaanite", a possibility which might make it more likely that references to the waters might reflect Canaanite ideas. And what about a *conflict* with the waters?

This brings us back to direct dialogue with Rebecca Watson. She proposed:

---

67 Roberts 1991, 156–7.
68 Roberts 1991, 157.
69 O'Brien 2004.
70 O'Brien 2004, 80.
71 O'Brien 2004, 81–2.
72 O'Brien 2004, 82.
73 O'Brien 2004, 84.

So, to the question, "Was thy wrath against the rivers, O Yahweh? Was thy anger against the rivers, or thy indignation against the sea?" we must answer resoundingly with Habakkuk: no. Rather, the anguish of the waters at the divine theophany is one in which they participate with the whole of creation, just as elsewhere, they join in joyful praise of their maker.[74]

It is not clear whether it is the Hebrew or the context which led her to make this statement, but I am not sure that the former could be supported. The opening question is introduced by *hă* with the two subsequent questions introduced by *'im*. According to GKC § 150 e 2(b), disjunctive questions are usually introduced by *hă—'im*, but such double (and presumably also triple!) questions need not be mutually exclusive, but "frequently the disjunctive form serves (especially in poetic parallelism ...) merely to repeat the same question in different words, and thus express it more emphatically". Gibson (§ 153) also noted that the disjunctive or alternative question is indicated by *hă* in the first clause and *'im* in the second, and commented, "The second half of the alternative is often merely the first in a varied form".[75] Neither authority suggests that there is necessarily any indication of the expected answer. Rather, in poetry, we should expect this to be repetition, perhaps with emphasis.

So, what about the context? In Habakkuk 3 it seems difficult to avoid the conclusion that God's activity is at least *likened* to a conflict with the waters, even if here the actual enemy is "historical". This certainly seems to be the implication of v. 8, with its indication of anger against the sea juxtaposed with reference to driving horses and chariots to victory. And in v. 15, this example of the Divine Warrior's activity is associated with trampling the sea with horses (presumably war horses or those pulling chariots) and thereby churning the mighty waters. If the anger was not actually against Sea/River in this instance, the use of such language suggests that the motif was well known and meaningful and could be used in a nuanced way to allude to an actual enemy, in all probability the Babylonians. God's hoped-for coming in the here and now will be just like his other warrior-like theophanies. In particular it will be just like when, according to the old, old story, he confronted the waters.

Redditt, in his *Introduction to the Prophets*, commented, with regard to Habakkuk 3:

---

[74] Watson 2005, 4.
[75] Gibson 1994, 184.

One may surely ask how a hymn associated with Israel/Judah's past got pressed into service in a chapter of a prophetic collection dealing with Judah's future.[76]

His question perhaps implies that he believes, like Hiebert, that an old poem or hymn is being re-used here. This may well be to go beyond the evidence, and it is perhaps better to think of the ongoing use of ancient motifs. And the possibility of some conscious archaising need not be ruled out. That said, a possible answer to such a question may be that this language offered an assurance that Yahweh could do the very things that the Babylonians believed Marduk could do. It has to be accepted, with particular reference to Habakkuk 3, that there is no clear reference to creation, so *that* aspect of Marduk's activity may not be in mind here. As acknowledged earlier, conflict and creation do not necessarily go hand in hand. And it could be argued that the focus of *Enuma Elish* is not on creation *per se*, even though it is often referred to as the Babylonian Epic of Creation, but on the exalting of the power of Marduk and justifying his supremacy as patron god of Babylon. The hearers or readers of Habakkuk 3 may not have needed assurance that Yahweh had created the world, but rather that he could defeat powerful enemies. That seems to be the key point at issue in this chapter.

With regard, then, to this particular chapter, does it contain imagery ultimately derived from or shared with Canaanite or Babylonian mythic thought? My answer would still be: "Yes, reasonably certainly!" Does it contain polemic? "Probably!" Why is it presented as a psalm? The use of material from a different *Sitz im Leben* or genre for effect is a well-known feature of prophetic literature.

And with regard to some more general issues, it is to be hoped that we have perhaps moved away from a past over-emphasis on direct (literary) borrowing. It seems much more likely that we should think of concepts and motifs which take on a life of their own but which continue to convey meaning. Similarly, we should beware of the suggestion that it is only appropriate to compare material of the same genre. Recent studies of intertextuality invite us to consider a much wider and more nuanced range of possibilities—allusion, echo, resonance etc—both within and across genres and thought-worlds.

---

76 Redditt 2008, 299.

Rebecca S. Watson
"Was your Wrath Against the Rivers?" Focusing the Debate in Habakkuk 3

Since Adrian has helpfully surveyed the state of the debate with Habakkuk 3, the present chapter will instead concentrate on its exegesis, taking much of the foregoing discussion of genre, date and structure for granted and simply clarifying my own view where necessary.[1] Limitations of space here prohibit exploring the full panoply of textual and interpretative questions raised by this complex and often perplexing chapter, so our attention will have to be restricted to the key aspects of the poem pertaining to the core focus of our dialogue. Fortuitously, verse 8 seems to bring us to the heart of the interpretation of Hab 3—or at the very least it tightly encapsulates the issue at stake in the present dialogue: that of its relation to Canaanite antecedents. Here, the verse poses the rhetorical question: "Was thy wrath against the rivers, O Yahweh? Was thy anger against the rivers, or thy indignation against the sea?"[2] As is evident from Adrian's survey in the previous chapter, it is most commonly maintained or indeed assumed) that the answer to this question must be affirmative,[3] and in particular that the use of the word pair *yām / nāhār* indicates an allusion to the *Chaoskampf*. However, I think this conclusion is highly contestable, both on the grounds of the Hebrew and of the context in which this disputed verse occurs.

In order to navigate this contentious issue, therefore, I propose first of all to consider the broader context for this verse, and then to examine the more immediate one, and finally to analyse very carefully the evidence from the Hebrew employed. Once the force of the questions in v. 8 has been established, then this will form a basis for the interpretation of the rest of the poem in which it sits.

---

[1] For further surveys of research, see Jöcken 1977, 290–313, and Andersen 2001, 350–5.
[2] I have here followed the NRSV translation, and will do so throughout unless otherwise indicated.
[3] See e.g. van Bekkum 2017, 58, Haak 1992, 93, Ortlund 2012, 211–2 n. 50, Hiebert 1986, 102–4, and the summary of scholarship in Watson 2019, 450–2.

1 Habakkuk 3:8

1.1 Habakkuk 3:8 in Context: Its Place Within the Psalm of Chapter 3

Taking the broad context first, namely the place of verse 8 in the psalm of chapter 3, it probably first of all needs to be stated that Adrian and I are (I think) in general agreement with each other and with the majority of commentators in recognising vv. 2, 16–9 as providing a first-person frame to the main theophany, and we also concur in identifying signs that vv. 3–7 and 8–15 should on some level be distinguished, though not necessarily in origin. It is notable that Yahweh is referred to in the third person in vv. 3–7,[4] but in the second person in vv. 8–15.[5] The former section in many ways provides a classic expression of the theophany motif, being focused on the coming of the deity from the southland[6] in glory,[7] brightness,[8] and might,[9] and the concomitant reaction of the world, which is epitomised by the distress and trembling[10] of the earth/nations

---

[4] The first person perspective with which the psalm commenced (v. 2) recedes but for a possible appearance in v. 7a, where the Hebrew is very uncertain. There are some cola with contentious content (chiefly in v. 5, where there is debate over the status of *dāber* and *rešep*) and others exhibiting corrupt and difficult Hebrew (notably in v. 4 and vv. 6e, 7a).

[5] The first person, as an object suffix, may feature in v. 14c, in perhaps the most difficult and obscure verse of this poem, but this reading is uncertain.

[6] In v. 3a, as in Zech 9:14, from Teman / the south (*têmān*); and in v. 3b, like Deut 33:2, from Mount Paran (which is paralleled with Sinai and Seir, also in the south). The linguistic and thematic correlations with Zech 9.14 are especially close: note the reference to Yahweh's arrow (*ḥēṣ*, cf. Hab 3:11) and to lightning (*bārāq*, cf. Hab 3:11) and whirlwinds (*saʿărôt*, cf. the verbal form, again from the root *sʿr*, in Hab 3:14).

[7] *hôd*, v. 3c; cf. Isa 30:30. This quality is often associated with Yahweh as king, in the sanctuary: Ps 96:6, 1Chr 29:11, or as God of the heavens/sky (Ps 104:1, Job 37:22, 1Chr 16:27, 29:11, cf. Ps 148:13).

[8] *nōgah*, v. 4a: see 2Sam 22:13 // Ps 18:13 [Eng 12], cf. Isa 4:5, 60:2–3, 19–20, Ezek 1:4, 13, 27–8, 10:4, Am 5:20.

[9] *ʿōz* (v. 4c), the classic expression of Yahweh's redemptive intervention: Exod 15:13, Isa 51:9, 62:8, Ps 66:3, 68:29 [Eng 28], 74:13, 77:15 [Eng 14], 89:11 [Eng 10]; but also experienced in divine kingship and the sanctuary: Ps 63:3 [Eng 2], 36 [Eng 35], 93:1, 96:6, 7, 99:4, 132:8, 1Chr 16:27–8; in storm and thunder: Ps 29:1, 68:34–5 [Eng 33–4], cf. 1Sam 2:10; indeed, in heavens and temple simultaneously: Ps 150:1, Ps 68:34–6 [Eng 33–5], and cf. Ps 29:1 with Ps 96:7.

[10] *rgz*, Hab 3:7b, Exod 15:14, Isa 64:1 [Eng 2], Ps 77:19 [Eng 18] (and in v. 17 [Eng 16] of *mayim* and *tehōmôt*, cf. Ps 99:1 (in response to Yahweh enthroned) and Job 9:6 (the cosmic warrior god); also 2Sam 22:8 / Ps 18:8 [Eng 7] (foundations of heaven/the mountains, in an act of personal deliverance), and in judgment, on the day of Yahweh, Isa 13:13, Joel 2:1, 10, cf. Isa 5:25.

(v. 6ab), mountains/hills (v. 6ce),[11] the tents of Cushan and pavilions of the land of Midian (v. 7).[12] The proximate occurrence of the trembling of the peoples and of the earth or mountains is familiar from elsewhere,[13] but another common combination—the distress of both earth and sea—is not in evidence in vv. 3–7.[14]

Verse 5 is of interest to our discussion, insofar as Resheph is the name of a well-attested early northwest Semitic deity.[15] hence were this force intended here it could be seen as sympathetic to seeing reference to the sea god Yam in verse 8. Obviously, the commonality of a word across the northwest Semitic linguistic continuum and its usage to denote both natural forces and their eponymous gods (*ym, mwt, šmš*, and so on) is no guarantee of deity in any specific instance. Rather, such language can at most only offer this interpretative possibility, rather than specifically commending it unless there are contextual indications in its favour. In fact, evidence is lacking that the parallel figure "Deber" was viewed as a divine being,[16] which in itself should prompt caution before "parallelomania"

---

11 Both are very common pairings, with the earth (and its inhabitants) and mountains being especially frequently described as trembling. For the earth, see 1Sam 14:5, Isa 14:16, Joel 2:10, Am 8:8, Ps 77:19 [Eng 18], Job 9:6, Prov 30:21 (*rgz*), Ps 99:1 (*nwṭ*), 2Sam 22:8 // Ps 18:8 [Eng 7] (*gʿš, rʿš*), Isa 13:13, Ps 68:9 [Eng 8] (*rʿš*), Ps 114:7 (*ḥwl*); cf. Joel 2:1 (of *kōl yōšəbê hāʾāreṣ*) and Jer 33:9 (of *kōl gôyê hāʾāreṣ*). For the mountains, see Isa 5:25 (*rgz*), Ps 46:3–4 [Eng 2–3] (*rʿš, mwṭ*), 6, 114:4, cf. 29:6 (*rqd*).

12 There is no precise parallel elsewhere to the tents/pavilions of Cushan/Midian shaking, and indeed this is the only extant mention of the former, which from the parallelism appears to be proximate or equivalent to Midian. However, a more general comparison may be made to human trembling in Exod 15:14[–16], Ps 99:1, Isa 64:1 [Eng 2] and Joel 2:1, all of which use the form *yirgəzû[n]* and concern a response before Yahweh, his actions or kingship, or in the case of Joel, to the coming day of Yahweh. Indeed, such fear may be shown even by the worshipping community (Ps 96:9, cf. Exod 19:16, 18), for it is the fundamental response of creation to the divine presence.

13 Ps 99:1, Isa 63:19cd–64:1–2 [Eng 64:1–3], Nah 1:5, cf. Ps 46:7 [Eng 6], Ps 97:3–5; indeed the earth seems at times to represent its inhabitants as much as to stand for itself (e.g. in Ps 96:9). Note especially the prose account in 1Sam 14:15, in which the earth nonetheless participates fully in the panic of the people: "There was a panic ["trembling", *ḥărādâ*] in the camp, in the field, and among all the people; the garrison and even the raiders trembled [*ḥărədû*]; the earth quaked [*tirgaz*]; and it became a very great panic [*ḥerdat ʾĕlōhîm*]".

14 Contrast Ps 77:17, 19 [Eng 16, 18], 114:3–6, Nah 1:4–5; and cf. the celebratory response to the coming of Yahweh in Ps 96:11, 98:7–8. Consonant with the storm phenomena manifested in theophany, water provision is another theme closely related to the shaking of the earth: Ps 68:9–10 [Eng 8–9], 114:7–8, Judg 5:4–5.

15 See, e.g. *KTU* 1.14.i 19, 1.15.ii 6, 1.100.31. Some have seen this kind of undertone in Deut 32:24, where the parallel word *rāʿāb* could be interpreted as an epithet of Mot.

16 Indeed, the most cogent argument in favour of regarding *deber* as the name or epithet of a deity is its parallelism with *rešep* in the present verse (Del Olmo Lette 1999, 232).

takes hold. The accompaniment of the great God by the attendants who go before, or surround, him occasions no surprise, since it is also familiar from Deut 33:2–3 (of the host of holy ones, en masse) and Ps 89:15 [Eng 14] ("steadfast love and faithfulness go before you"), as well as from the throne visions of Ezekiel (especially Ezek 1:4–28) which in turn find later expression in the four living creatures around the throne in Rev. 4:6–11. Indeed, we already see in verse 3 how the attributes of the deity, glory and praise, expand beyond him to cover and fill heaven and earth (v. 3cd). Here, *dāber* (*deber*) and *rešep* signal aspects of the devastation which accompanies the coming of Yahweh, though—congruent with the focus of this poem—they are features which impact directly on humanity (and perhaps their livestock). *Deber* is especially associated with divine intervention in judgment[17] and often with the experience of war, whilst Ps 91:6 furnishes a further example of its personification or conceptualisation as a personal being.[18] *Rešep* may be associated with fire or burning, most evidently in Song 8:6 (re the "flames" of love or jealousy; NRSV "flashes of fire, a raging flame") and this may also explain its association with plague (fever?, Deut 32:24[19]), and "flashing" weapons of war (Ps 76:4 [Eng 3]) or (according to a common interpretation) sparks (Job 5:7) and storm phenomena (thus probably Psalm 78:48). As such, it is highly appropriate to the current context, as the imagery of fire and brightness features here prominently (v. 4; cf. vv. 3c, 11bc), but the aspect of weaponry (cf. vv. 4b, 9ab, 11bc, 14a) and even plague or fever (paralleling *deber*) are equally apt. However, the context does not permit us to discern whether it might be more appropriate to interpret the reference as personification or, more literally, in reference to Yahweh's heavenly attendants.[20] As such, it cannot provide clear direction for the interpretation of verse 8, except insofar as it constitutes a further aspect of the theophanic approach of Yahweh as warrior God.

The imagery in the ensuing section, vv. 8–15, in part bears close resemblance to other theophanic appearances, most notably in remarkably close ver-

---

17 See Exod 5:3, Lev 26:25, Deut 28:21, 2Sam 24:13, Ezek 14:19, 28:23, 33:27, 38:22, Am 4:10, 2Chr 7:13.
18 On its parallel, *qeṭeb*, see *DDD*. In Ps 91:3, *deber* is something from which God provides deliverance, in parallel, though, to a snare; comparison has also been made with Hos. 13:14c, "O Death, where are your plagues (*dəbārêkā*)?"
19 Here again in judgment.
20 For quite an elaborate development of this possibility, see Andersen 2001, 300–7. Xella's assessment of Resheph in the Hebrew Bible is helpful here: he (or it) is a "decayed demon" or "decayed deit[y]", appearing with "different levels of demythologization: sometimes ... as a personalized figure, more or less faded, sometimes ... as a pure metaphor" (Xella,1999, 702, 703); cf. Day 1985, 106–7: "Plague and Pestilence are clearly personified and behind the latter ... lies the Canaanite plague-god Resheph".

bal parallels between v. 10 and Ps 77:17–8 [Eng 16–7]. However, its strong warlike colouring, with much emphasis on the anger and weaponry of the deity, is evoked not simply through the storm but in anthropomorphic terms, in relation to military hardware: horses and chariots[21] (v. 8), bow and javelins or spears (*maṭṭôt*)[22] (v. 9), arrows (*ḥiṣṣîm*) and spear (v. 11) and *maṭṭôt* again (v. 14), so much so that weather phenomena (clouds, thunder and lightning) are nowhere unequivocally in view. This is in marked contrast to many other theophanies of the Hebrew Bible,[23] where the deity's own arrows occur only in parallel to lightnings[24] and instead natural spectacles are uppermost: storm-wind,[25] tempest,[26] fire,[27] rain,[28] thunder,[29] lightning,[30] hail,[31] quaking earth[32] and melting[33] or smok-

---

[21] For heavenly horses and chariots, compare 2Ki. 2:11, 6:17, Isa 66:15, Zech 10:3, 1Chr. 28:18, cf. 2Kgs 7:6 (auditory only) and 2Kgs 23:11 (chariots of the sun); whilst in Ps 68:18 [Eng 17], God's chariotry is described as numbering tens of thousands. There may be another instace of the theophanic intervention of Yahweh's horses and chariots in Judg 5:22. (Most interpreters suggest that the horses here may be those of the Canaanite kings, but the masc. sing. suffix, "his steeds" may suggest otherwise). Note also Ps 104:3, where Yahweh rides his chariot "on the wings of the wind".

[22] The Hebrew term *maṭṭeh* normally refers to some kind of staff or rod, hence something with a shaft. Given the parallelism with the bow, the translation "arrows" might seem appropriate, but this is not supported by the use of the term elsewhere. Given that the language employed suggests something more substantial than arrows and the fact that acting at the divine command is more appropriate to a projectile than something wielded by hand, I have assumed the translation "javelin" here; both bows and javelins were weapons used from chariots and entailed shooting from a distance into the enemy, and according to Yadin, the javelin was "like a large arrow", with a wood or reed body and metal tip, with several being carried together in a quiver (1963, 10), so the pairing seems more apt than that of bow and spear, though this, too, is possible. Yadin describes the spear as "a replica of the javelin in shape", though larger and made of stouter construction and designed to be thrusted by hand (1963, 10). Probably *maṭṭeh* is a generic term to encompass two or more of these shafted weapons, hence another type (e.g. spear) might be more apt in v. 14, though this is not clear; cf. Tsumura 1996, 355, who (on the basis of Akkadian comparisons) concludes that it is a mace.

[23] I draw for comparison here on the passages identified in Jeremias 1965.

[24] Ps 18:15 [Eng 14] // 2Sam 22:15, Ps 144:6; similarly Ps 77:18 [Eng 17] (again, in the eye of the storm, parallel to clouds pouring out water and skies thundering, and, in the next line, thunder, lightnings and earthquake).

[25] Nah 1:3.

[26] Nah 1:3, Ps 50:3.

[27] Ps 18:13 [Eng 12] // 2Sam 22:12, 50:3, 97:3.

[28] Pss. 68:9–10 [Eng 8–9], 77:18 [Eng 17].

[29] Ps 77:18, 19 [Eng 17, 18].

[30] Ps 18:15 [Eng 14] // 2Sam 22:15, 144:6 (both parallel with arrows), Ps 77:19 [Eng 18], Ps 97:4.

[31] Ps 18:13 [Eng 12] // 2Sam 22:13.

ing³⁴ mountains. Any weaponry mentioned in such passages, apart from the lightning-arrows, is most often instead that of the king whom the deity equips and saves.³⁵ A distinctive aspect of Hab 3:8–15, then, is the extent of the listing of armaments and the receding on an overt level of many of the typical features of the storm, despite the prominence of "cosmic" distress seen through mountains, waters, sun and moon, and the strong sense of dynamic action on the part of the deity. Here in Hab 3:8–15 it is Yahweh himself who comes as warrior, personally acting in targeted wrath and judgment against his adversaries, with the combination of his anger and chariotry found in v. 8 being echoed also in Isa 66:15. In this, therefore, we recognise the prophetic tone of the passage, despite its apparent affinities to the Psalms, and already gain a sense of the intense focus on the shattering of the enemy, which must have been of deep concern to the first audience of this composition.

As Adrian has already indicated, it is often claimed that vv. 8–15 as a whole concerns a battle between Yahweh and the forces of chaos epitomised by the *yām* and *nəhārîm* of v. 8 and by *yām* and *mayim rabbîm* in v. 15, as well as by *təhôm* in v. 10, though it is most widely suggested that there is a dual reference understood throughout the passage, and that the political struggles of the time are also strongly in view. According to the most common interpretative line, therefore, the chaos battle conveys reassurance of Yahweh's victory over Babylon or whichever other oppressor concerned the writer of the Psalm.³⁶ Verse 8 therefore opens this section by explicitly addressing the issue of the object of Yahweh's anger: "Was thy wrath against the rivers…thy indignation against the sea?".

---

32 Nah 1:5 (here quaking earth and heaving moutains), Pss 68:9 [Eng 8], 77:19 [Eng 18], 97:4; cf. Hab 3:6.
33 Nah 1:5, Ps 97:5.
34 Ps 144:5.
35 Ps 18:3, 35 [Eng 2, 34] // 2Sam 22:3, 35, noting the thrust of Ps 18:30–51 [Eng 29–50] // 2Sam 22:3–51, Ps 144:1–2; compare the focus on divine protection in Ps 18:4, 18–20 [Eng 3, 17–9] // 2Sam 22:4, 18–20, Ps 97:10, Nah 1:7–8; and cf. Ps 68:2–4, 12–5, 18–20 [Eng 1–3, 11–4, 17–9], where the same themes are evident though the structure of the psalm is less clear. A partial exception might be the mention of chariotry in connection with Adonai's progress from Sinai to the holy place in Ps 68:18 [Eng 17], yet this is somewhat divorced from the main theophany section notwithstanding the apparent reference to the march from the southland here, and of course chariots are regular aspects of the storm god riding through the sky (cf. Ps 104:3).
36 Hiebert argues, more specifically, that it is the foe of vv. 13b–14 which is conceived in draconic terms and hence the chaos metaphor is here perceived as a battle with a monster (Hiebert 1986, 104). This is despite the fact that he recognises the negative force of the questions of verse 8 (1986, 101–2) and that vv. 12–13a have "a definite historical orientation" (1986, 104).

However, as Adrian observed, whether this question implies the answer "Yes" or "No" may only be resolved by reference to the themes and imagery of the immediate context and then by closely examining the language employed in the verse itself. These shall now therefore be examined in turn.

1.2 Habakkuk 3:8 in Context: Focus, Themes and Imagery

The fundamental historical focus of the present passage is unmistakable. Thus, verse 8 directly follows a description of the affliction of the earth and nations (not the sea or other elements of the cosmos)[37] at the divine epiphany (vv. 6–7) and in v. 12, Yahweh is said to tread/trample the earth/nations in fury. More specifically, he has "come forth to deliver your people, to deliver your anointed" (v. 13ab). The following portrayal of the destruction of the enemy (vv. 13c–14) has been subject to much debate and emendation, but again, despite questions over the imagery employed, the essential implication that there is a present enemy of Israel who will be destroyed, remains firmly established. This is an "evil one" (*rāšāʿ*) who has "warriors"[38] who delight to do harm to the petitioner (14bcd), and if this were not clear enough, v. 16 anticipates that "a people" will "come to attack us", though the Psalmist looks forward to God's deliverance (v. 18). The clear signals that this object of his wrath is a human enemy also tally with the practical and political concerns of chapters 1–2, and, more subtly, with the imagery of vv. 3–7. The march of Yahweh from

---

[37] This combination features also in Ps 99:1, 97:3–5, 46:7; and Am 9:5 (in which latter passage, the earth trembles and those who dwell in it mourn), though at times just the nations will be involved: see Exod 15:14[–16], Isa 63:1–6, Zech 9:15. Conversely, the trembling of the earth in Ps 68:8–9 and Judg 5:4–5 is merely accompanied by dripping skies rather than immediate distress among the peoples (though such distress and/or the victory of Yahweh/Israel is clearly in view in the wider context: see Ps 68:2, 13, 15 and cf. Judg 5:13 and the narrative flow of the latter poem in particular); and in Mic 1:4, the mountains and valley melt/ burst open like wax or cascading water in more volcanic mode, again without a direct human parallel (though again this is implied: note vv. 2, 6[–16], especially *ngr*, vv. 5, 6).

[38] The exact translation of this *hapax legomenon* is uncertain, though its general force is not. *Pərāzāhôt* (Ezek 38:11, Zech 2:8, Esth 9:19) are unwalled villages, hence, *pərāzî* (1Sam 6:18, Deut 3:5, Esth 9:19Q) are their inhabitants and a similar sense (though less clear) is assumed for *pərāzôn* in Judg 5:7, 11 (NRSV "peasantry"). The versions for Hab 3:14 assume either "leaders" (Greek [Syriac] *dunastōn*) or "warriors" (Targ *wgjbrj* [*rjšj*], Vulg *bellatorum eius*). Possibly we should think of conscripted or mercenary forces drawn from the villages in the service of the prince(s)/leader(s) (*rōʾš*, vv. 13c, 14a; 14a Greek (Syriac) *kephalas*; Barb. *archēgous*), but despite the obscurities of the ensuing cola, it seems that a formidable fighting force is intended rather than *ad hoc* local militia.

the south (as in vv. 3–7) is typically with the purpose of the salvation of his people, either triumphing in battle on their behalf against their enemies (see Zech 9:14 [Teman / the south]; also Ps 68:17 [Sinai], Judg. 5:4 [Seir and Edom]) or bestowing blessing (Deut 33:2 [Sinai, Seir, Mount Paran][39]). The common theme of the distress of the cosmos at his terrible theophany here is expressed through the trembling of the earth and nations (earth, nations, mountains, hills [v. 6], tents/pavilions of the Cushan/the land of Midian [v. 7]), not the sea,[40] which again suggests a focus on land and peoples, and hence a primarily political interest.

Moreover, looking at the broader context, it is nowhere else in the Hebrew Bible said that Yahweh showed anger towards the sea or river/s (or to təhôm[ôt]),[41] whereas there is clear evidence for the eradication or muting of such implications and the construction of alternative understandings, asserting Yahweh's uncontested power and/or the lack of marine threat, within this corpus. Examples include the absence of a combat with the sea or deep in Genesis 1;[42] the exalting of Yahweh in Psalm 93 as far more powerful than nəhārôt and mišbərê-yām since, as a result of his kingship which was established from of old, the world will never be moved;[43] and the swaddling of baby sea in Job 38:8–11.[44] By contrast, human adversaries, commonly either enemy nations (Ezek 21:36 [Eng 31], Ps 7:7 [Eng 6]) or especially Israel / Judah or segments of their populations (e.g. Josh 7:1, Isa 5:25, Hos 8:5, Ezr 8:22) are frequent recipients of God's anger. In Hab 3:8 the question of whether Yahweh's wrath was against the rivers and sea is explicitly raised as an important question at issue, and not just alluded to in passing. An exegetical approach which seeks to understand the final form of the text as we have it, rather than detecting the underlying pre-literary tradition-history of some of its motifs, is—by a simple matter of probability,

---

39 Note also in this connection the frequent theme of rain and pouring water, which finds expression also in Hab 3:10: Judg 5:4, Ps 68:8–9, Zech 10:1.
40 See p. 35 n. 37 above.
41 bərûaḥ 'appêkā (Exod 15:8) refers to the "blast of your nostrils" at which the "waters" (mayim // nōzəlîm // təhōmōt) were made into a heap at the Re[e]d Sea crossing; if there were any anger, it is directed at the Egyptian foe, not at the waters, which are compliant here. A similar expression in Ps 18:16 [Eng 15] // 2Sam 22:16, minnišmat rûaḥ 'appô/e[y]kā, is only of tangential relevance since the imagery concerns the underworld and "rivers" are not mentioned in this passage and nor, in Ps 18:2–20 [Eng 1–19], is the sea; the phrase likewise refers to the impact of the divine breath, this time exposing the water [/sea] channels // foundations of the world before Yahweh plucks the psalmist to safety from his "strong enemy" and imminent death (cf. vv. 5–6 [Eng 4–5]; see further Watson 2005: 80–1).
42 Tsumura 1989, van Wolde 1998, Smith 2004, 97, Watson 2005, 14–9, Habel 2011, 29–31.
43 Watson 2005, 13–135.
44 Watson 2005, 274–8, Newsom, 2003, 244, Alter, 1985, 99–100, Fuchs, 1993, 200.

and without prejudging the matter—more likely to result in a reading which accepts that the divine wrath was not actually against the waters. This is not by any means to deny other possible answers that may be implied (though rejected with some rhetorical force) by the very raising of the question itself, or to underestimate the probable disparity between the Yahwistic faith presented in its ideal form in the Hebrew Bible and common Israelite religious practices for much of the "biblical period".

Adrian says in regard to the contextual interpretation of v. 8: "It is difficult to avoid the conclusion that God's activity is at least *likened* to a conflict with the waters even if here the actual enemy is 'historical'". On the surface, this sounds like a moderate claim to make. However, one has to ask whether the questions of v. 8 most naturally pertain to what Adrian terms the "actual enemy" or to something to which the enemy is "likened". It seems to me that, whatever Hab 3:8 may mean, the significance of *nəhārîm* and *yām* was absolutely clear to the author and his audience. These aquatic entities might be distinct from human enemies,[45] or alternatively, it may be that the present political foe/s, such as Babylon, are here *equated* with the watery "forces of chaos", such that the two cannot be distinguished.[46] However, the rhetorical force of the questions and of their implied answers seems to require clarity in the relationship between the waters and the political enemies, and therefore apparently excludes an ambiguous and similitudinous connection between them such as Adrian advocates. He rightly compares v. 15, where an allusion to the chaos struggle has also been seen, but again claims no more than that the "use of such language suggests that the motif... could be used in a nuanced way to allude to an actual enemy". However, although it is possible that the waters might be identified with the enemy (antici-

---

[45] In which case, the implied answer is either: "Yes, and therefore (a) you can crush our comparatively petty enemies with ease, or (b, and unlikely) you are not concerned about our present conflict"; or (c) "No, because you are concerned with events in the historical, political realm instead".

[46] In this case, the answer is either, "Yes, your wrath was against the great forces of chaos and evil in the world, including both cosmic chaos and the perpetrators of military and political threats", or "No, it was not against the great powers we thought you were attacking, it was against something else instead" (e.g., not the empire we thought God was opposed to and which we took to epitomise the forces described in aquatic terms, but another one instead, e.g. Egypt instead of Babylon, or *vice versa*). This last option is somewhat questionable, since according to the perspective which sees cosmic and political "chaos" as part of the same larger whole, the forces described as *nəhārîm* and *yām* would surely be perceived to be embodied in any military power posing a threat to Judah–Israel at a particular time, rather than always being manifested exclusively in the same specifc army or nation regardless of the particulars of the situation.

pating an affirmative answer: yes, your wrath was against the rivers and the nations/s they represent) or distinguished from it (anticipating a negative answer: no, your wrath was not against the rivers but against our human foes) it seems intrinsically improbable that an affirmative answer to the rhetorical question, "Was your wrath against the rivers and your anger against the sea?", might only mean, "Metaphorically speaking, probably so, but a real historical enemy is actually in view".

1.3 Habakkuk 3:8

There are two main aspects to the understanding of the Hebrew of verse 8. First is the question whether of itself the use of the word pair Yam/Neharim necessarily indicates an allusion to the *Chaoskampf* as is commonly supposed, and, second, it needs to be determined whether the structure and form of expression of the questions themselves offer a particular implied answer, as I have claimed.

1.3.1 Yam and Nahar in Habakkuk 3

Any claim that reference to Yam and Nahar must imply cosmic conflict clearly overstates the evidence and should therefore be met with methodological rigour and restraint. Obviously, the combat between Baal and Yam is (and was in ancient times) well-known, so an association with theomachy should not automatically be precluded. However, nor should this correlation simply be assumed, since it must be recalled that in the majority of instances of the poetic pairing of "sea" and "river" in the Hebrew Bible no *Chaoskampf* allusion has been identified, e.g., Isa 19:5, 48:18, Pss. 66:6, 72:8, 80:12. 98:7–8.[47] Moreover, the particular form of the poetic pairing in Hab 3:8 is unique in the Hebrew Bible, since *nāhār* here does not occur in the singular or with a feminine plural ending, as is much more common elsewhere in combination with *yām*, but with the masculine plural. Intriguingly, in all the instances where the masculine plural *nəhārîm* occurs in the Hebrew Bible (except the dubious one in Job) a connection with

---

47 All but the most die-hard *Chaoskampf* enthusiast would similarly agree on the absence of the conflict motif in Isa 11:15, 50:2, Ezek 32:2, Ps 24:2, and a further cluster of such pairings occurs in connection with the delineation of borders, e.g. in Exod 23:31, Deut 11:24, Josh 1:4, Zech 9:10, cf. Mic 7:12. Nor, in Ugaritic, is the pairing unique to the appellatives "Prince Yam // Judge Nahar": see *KTU* 1.3.vi.5–6, 1.4.ii.6–7, and the discussion below, pp. 39–40.

Egypt is evident.[48] We therefore know that the context for use outside Hab 3:8 is (geo-)political; a possible (though not by any means certain) futher implication of the known occurrences in biblical Hebrew is that the use of *nəhārîm* in Hab 3:8 may suggest reference to the waters of Egypt, possibly hinting at an allusion to the exodus as the subject of past recollection, even though a present threat is likely to be the more immediate, if unstated, concern. If so, *yām* in this context might also denote the Nile[49] or even the Re[e]d Sea.[50]

Though unusual, the combination *ym / nhrm* does find a parallel in Ugaritic (in reverse order), in *KTU* 1.3.vi.5 – 6 and 1.4.ii.6 – 7, but there the reference is not to Prince Sea/Judge River, or to any form of conflict, but in the first case as part of a route to Memphis[51] and in the second to the water in which Athirat washes her

---

48 This form is confined to the phrase *naʿărê-kûš* Isa 18:1 and Zeph 3:10, which is followed in Isa 18:2 by mention of *yām* in reference to the Nile (as is evident from the context, and is thus translated by NRSV and REB, in accordance with usage elsewhere, e.g. Isa 19:5) and in vv. 2, 7 to the people "whose land the rivers (*nəhārîm*) divide"; it recurs again in 33:21 in the distinctive phrase *məqôm- nəhārîm yəʾōrîm raḥăbê yādāyim*. A final instance, in Job 20:17, in the rather strange tautology *biplaggôt naʿărê naḥălê dəbaš wəḥemʾâ*, seems to be the product of a scribal error and should probably be deleted (thus BHS, *DCH*).

49 See the previous note re Isa 18:2. The term is more often used of the Euphrates so in theory the reference may potentially be to the two major foreign powers which might present a threat— *yām* as representing Mesopotamian (Babylonian or Assyrian) forces and *nəhārîm*, Egyptian— but, given that a specific historical crisis must on some level be in view, allusion to both of the prime (and potentially opposing) contenders seems unlikely here; moreover, the frequent synonymous pairing of *yām* and *nāhār*[*îm*], especially as combined in the rhetorical question form (which again requires close equivalence), weighs similarly in this direction. Cf. Gen 15:18, where reference is made to both the Nile and Euphrates but they are clearly distinguished, and likewise Isa 11:15.

50 I refer throughout this chapter to the "Re[e]d" Sea since "Red" is the traditional nomenclature, but "Reed" is often thought to be a more appropriate translation (Hoffmeier 2005, 83 – 5); as the issue is not relevant to the present discussion of Habakkuk 3, there is no need to resolve it here and "Re[e]d" is a suitably non-committal form.

51 Wyatt (1998, 88 n. 77) suggests that the route outlined here, which "describes Qadesh-and-Amurr's forthcoming journey", is expressed in "cosmic as distinct from geographical imagery", i.e. in reference to the world-encircling river. If he is correct, this "cosmic" perspective is not unexpected in the context of myths of the divine, but more importantly, mythological perceptions of the world should not be conceived as separate from more realistic counterparts: the circumfluent ocean/river was simply part of an ancient conception of the world. The presence of "geographical" elements here is clear from the mention of Byblos in the following line and the goal of the journey (again!) in Egypt in lines 13 – 5. (On this, see notes 48 and 49 above and Gibson's observation that the syntax provides caution against identifying *Kptr* with Caphtor [1977, 55 n. 2]). In any case, a "cosmic" perspective may very well be present in Hab 3:8 too; the issue under discussion is whether the word pairing here must entail combat, and this Ugaritic example suggests not.

clothes, but which may nonetheless be situated also in Egypt.⁵² Finally, the normal Ugaritic parallelism places Yam first, but here the order is reversed, thus again resisting any assumption of a close identity with combat narratives from Ugarit. "[Prince] Yam" is the primary name of the god of the sea and "[Judge] Nahar" an accompanying attribute placed in a secondary position.⁵³ As a result, there are strong reasons for not jumping to overhasty conclusions.

Thus, although, logically speaking, where the question is asked, "Was your anger against the rivers, your wrath against the sea?", it is hard to resist the corollary that the writer may have been well aware of traditions of a battle with Prince Yam/Judge Nahar, at the same time it is also unmistakable how far removed its expression is from traditional formulae. We can conclude, then, that the form of Hab 3:8 reflects a widespread pairing not solely associated with a particular narrative pattern or content and that in the form here employed it may deliberately be resisting that pattern.⁵⁴ Quite possibly the author may consciously have dropped the titles, reversed the order and used the masculine plural in order to signal the undercutting or reshaping of prior mythic traditions. That in itself suggests a lack of assent to the idea that Yahweh's wrath might be against Yam. A further possibility is that the intention could also have been to make specific reference to the rivers of Egypt as not being the object of Yahweh's anger, and to indicate its focus elsewhere (either, then, on the human foe itself or, more probably, on an alternative enemy from the north) instead.

1.3.2 The Question Form of Habakkuk 3:8

As Yam and Nahar are a synonymous word pair, we can be confident that the only possible answers to the questions the verse poses must be "yes" or "no",

---

52 Note Gibson's description of the "scene [as] a homely one", comparing *Odyssey* vi.91 (1977, 56 n. 8); thus also the majority of more recent commentators. (For a survey of research, see Wyatt 1998, 93 n. 100.) In the *Odyssey*, there is a specific geographical location for this activity, Phaeacia, most commonly identified with Corfu or Crete. Although the top of *KTU* 1.4.ii is damaged, it seems likely that the context for Athirat's ablutions may be Egypt, given that this is the destination of Qodesh-and-Amrur, the "fisher of Athirat" (*KTU* 1.3 vi 10, 1.4.ii 31) as described in *KTU* 1.3.vi 13–6, and taking into account also the Akkadian labelling of Memphis as *(al)Ḥi-ku-up-ta-aḫ*, "the city of Ptah", the Egyptian god of craftsmen (Gibson 1977, 55 n. 1).
53 E.g. *KTU* 1.2.i.7–8, 16, 21, 21–2, 23; only Yam is discernible in line 12, where the text is highly fragmented, so although Nahar features in Wyatt's reconstruction, this remains conjectural.
54 Another possibility is that Canaanite traditions of the battle with Yam were transmitted in a wider variety of forms than that for which we currently have documentary evidence.

not "Yam" or "Neharim". At the same time, I would like to argue that one of the clearest aspects of this challenging chapter is that the answer is negative: Yahweh's anger is not directed against Yam and Neharim. The reason for this is that the evidence from the grammatical construction of this verse is, I think, overwhelmingly strong. The construction employed, *hă...'im*, has been identified by M. Held as that of the "double rhetorical question";[55] it is essentially equivalent, as BDB states, to a "rhetorical *Num?*",[56] to which "the answer *No* is usually expected".[57] In fact, all instances of *hă...'im* fall into one of three categories:[58]

1) Where the two terms are not parts of the same interrogative construction. Occasionally this occurs where the questions are placed in the mouth of different speakers and so function independently of each other. More often, an initial question is followed by another form introduced by *'im*, such as an oath (as in 2Sam 19:14 [Eng 13][59]) or an exceptive clause, e.g. in Am 3:3 "Do two walk together unless they have made an appointment?" These can be discounted for the present purposes.

2) The construction can be employed to present mutually exclusive alternatives, for example in Judg 20:28, "Shall we go out once more to battle ..., or shall we desist?"[60] or in the sequence of questions about the land in Num 13:18–20, whether it is "good or bad,... unwalled or fortified,... rich or poor". In this type of context, the phrases *hă...'im-lōʾ*[61] or *hă...'im 'ayin*[62] are often used to express the alternatives "[whether ...] is ... or

---

55 Held 1969, 71–9.
56 BDB, *'im*, 2.a.(b)(a). This is entirely congruent with the LXX *mē* and Vulgate *numquid* employed in the opening clause of the verse (hence, "Were you not angry ...?"), in each case implying that a negative answer is expected.
57 BDB, *hă* 1.d. This is now also the position taken by Thomas Renz in his forthcoming NICOT commentary on Habakkuk (private communication).
58 I would like to acknowledge my indebtedness to my late colleague Elizabeth Harper, who helped me to conduct an exhaustive digital search for all instances of this combination in the Hebrew Bible. These are listed in the appendix, according to type, first as they appear in the NRSV and, second, with the Hebrew idiom more clearly brought out in an adapted translation. In several instances, the following (or, occasionally, preceding) clause has been quoted in order to illustrate the rhetorical context, which is often tangibly indignant or even, in some cases, aggressive.
59 "[And] say to Amasa, 'Are you not my bone and my flesh? So may God do to me, and more, if you are not the commander of my army from now on, in place of Joab'".
60 See likewise Josh 5:13, Judg 20:28 1 K. 22:6,15 // 2Chr. 18:5,14; compare *hă ... 'im ... wəʾim* in 2Sam 24:13.
61 Examples of the construction *hă ... 'im-lōʾ* ("Is .... or not?") include Gen 24:21, 27:21, 37:32, Exod 16:4.
62 As indeed in the last interrogative pair in Num 13:20: "whether there are trees in it or not".

not?" Again, this can be discounted in respect of Hab 3:8 because of the pairing of Yam and Neharim.

3) In all the remaining sixty-three instances that I have managed to identify, the same oratorical force is evident:[63] the answer expected is always: No;[64] and the repetition intrinsic to the disjunctive form serves for emphasis[65] so that a combative or incredulous tone is often apparent. E.g.,

> [Then] Abraham fell on his face and laughed and said to himself, "Can a child be born to a man who is a hundred years old? Can Sarah, who is ninety years old, bear a child?" Gen 17:17

> Did I conceive all this people? Did I give birth to them, that you should say to me, "Carry them in your bosom ...?" Num 11:12

> "Will you contend for Baal? Or will you defend his cause? Whoever contends for him shall be put to death by morning". Judg. 6:31

> Have you not known? Have you not heard?
> Yahweh is the everlasting God,
>   the creator of the ends of the earth ... Isa 40:28[66]

> Do you work wonders for the dead?
>   Do the shades rise up to praise you? Ps 88:11[Eng 10]

> Are your days like the days of mortals,
>   or your years like human years,
> [that you seek out my iniquity...?] Job 10:5[–6]

Hence, to interpret Hab 3:8 affirmatively would not merely be inappropriate to the context: it would also impart an unparalleled nuance to the prophet's questions.

---

[63] GKC, 475 §150 h; see also Gibson, 1994, 184 §153. For a discussion of Jer 31:20 (possibly the only instance, but for Hab 3:8, where there is any scope for uncertainty over the interpretation), see my article, "אִם ... הֲ: A Rhetorical Question Anticipating a Negative Answer" (Watson 2019).
[64] Besides Hab 3:8, this is the case in Gen 17:17, 37:8; Num 11:12, 22; Judg 6:31, 11:25; 2Sam 19:36, 43; Isa 10:9, 15, 27:7, 40:28, 49:24, 50:2, 66:8, 9; Jer 2:14, 31, 3:5, 5:9, 22, 29; 8:4, 19, 22, 9:8 [Eng 9], 14:19, 22, 18:14, 22:28 [Q; not in LXX, Peshitta or Targ], 31:20 (see previous note), 49:1, Ezek 15:3, 22:14; Joel 1:2, Amos 6:2, 12; Mic 2:7, 4:9; Pss 77:10, 78:20, 88:11, 94:9; Job 4:17, 6:5, 6, 30, 7:12, 8:3, 10:4, 5, 11:2, 7, 13:8, 9, 22:3, 34:17, 37:20, 38:33, 39:9, 10, 40:27; cf. Job 21:4 (hă ... wə'im-maddûaʿ).
[65] *GKC*, 475 §150 h.
[66] In other words, the implied answer to the negative questions of Isa 40:28 is: "No—I do not not know and I have not not heard (i.e. I do know and have heard)". Compare similarly Jer 5:29 ("Shall I not punish ...? Shall I not bring retribution ...?"), Job 11:7, 13:8, 9; and (with hă ... wə'im) Job 8:3, 11:2, 22:3, 34:17, Joel 1:2.

So far, though, we have not considered the impact of the *kî* clause with which the question ends. This is clarified by the recognition that it comprises the final element of what van Selms has identified as a "motivated interrogative sentence",⁶⁷ taking the form *hă...'im...['im]* ... *kî*, with the last of these elements to be translated "that" (not "when", as in the NRSV) and comprising the apodosis. As van Selms recognises from his survey of instances of this structure,

> The putting of the question implies that both the speaker and the person listening know that what has been asked is not a reality... [T]he question ... is motivated by the apodosis and in that apodosis there is something which justifies the putting of the question...It is an attempt to bring the person addressed to reason...The situation arises in a situation of conflict and is an utterance of anger, impatience and indignation.⁶⁸

There may be two aspects to this indignant questioning. One is the obvious one, characterised by van Selms as "pok[ing] mild fun at people who might understand the Lord's action in terms of Canaanite mythology".⁶⁹ However, the other aspect is that of the power and devastating nature of Yahweh's manifestation as a warrior. Surely from this display (and analogously to Job 7:12, another motivated interrogative sentence) it would appear that he were embarking on theomachic combat against a mighty divine power or natural force, not merely human enemies! Yet, as is asserted in verse 17, he "came forth to save [his] people".

2 Habakkuk 3:8–15 in the Light of 3:8

If according to v. 8, Yahweh's wrath is not (or was not) against Yam and Neharim, how does this cohere with the rest of the passage? In answering this question, there are several issues which merit further attention, namely the continued references to water in vv. 9, 10 and (especially) v. 15, the significance of the difficult imagery in vv. 13–4, and finally the evocation of Yahweh as a divine warrior throughout the poem, not least because the repeated references to wrath and weaponry have at times been understood as necessarily invoking the idea of a battle with chaos. I shall deal with each of these in turn.

---

67 Van Selms 1971/2. The other examples identified by van Selms are Num 11:12, 16:13, 1Sam 17:43, Jer 22:15, 48:27, Job 7:12, 10:4–6, 13:25–6, 16:3, cf. Job 6:11, Jer 31:20.
68 Van Selms 1971/2, 143–4.
69 Van Selms 1971/2, 146.

2.1 Verses 9–10

Vv. 9–10 blend images of the divine warrior with that of the storm theophany. Key cola for our purposes are v. 9c ("you split the earth with rivers") and v. 10bc ("a torrent of water swept by; the deep gave forth its voice"). The first two of these cola, vv. 9c and 10b, concern gushing, flowing water, though what is described in the former seems to be something done to the earth by Yahweh: he brings forth rivers by cleaving the earth, cutting it open. As such, it provides an apt parallel to the trembling of the mountains in the following colon with which it is paired. By contrast, the aquatic movements of v. 10bc are not explicitly connected with any terrestrial effect.

2.1.1 Verse 9c

As v. 9b is possibly the most difficult colon in this chapter, it cannot be used with any confidence as a basis for interpreting v. 9c. However, it is reasonable to suppose that v. 9c continues to evoke the manifestation of the divine warrior in the thunderstorm, in continuity with v. 9a and most likely in a manner compatible, though not synonymous, with v. 10. Though the Hebrew of v. 9a is awkward, it seems secure that weaponry (*qaštekā*, "your bow", now unsheathed and ready for action) is involved (cf. vv. 8de, 11bc, and possibly 14a) and this too seems probable for v. 9b (*maṭṭôt*). Key elements of v. 10 are the distress of nature at the theophany, as shown by the rocking of the mountains even at the sight of the deity and by the crying out[70] of the deep, as well as the characteristic pouring out of water, which in such contexts, though ultimately beneficial, is presented in the most extreme way.

Torrential rain is an ancient motif associated with the thunderstorm theophany (Judg 5:4, Deut 33:28, Ps 68:9–10 [Eng 8–9], 77:18 [Eng 17], cf. Ps 18:12 [Eng 11] // 2Sam 22:12, Ps 114:8) and it is likely that what is envisaged in vv. 9–10 is the gushing of water out of the earth in v. 9c (cf. Ps 114:7–8; also Joel 3:18, following the theophany of v. 16) and from above, as rain, in v. 10b[71] (cf. Judg. 5:4; Ps 68:9–10 [Eng 8–9]; 77:18a [Eng 17a; "heavens dripping dew", Deut 33:28; cf. Ps 18:12 [Eng 11]). This can be beneficent, as in Deut 33:28, Ps

---

70 See the discussion below, pp. 49–51.
71 Hebrew *zerem* is "rain, a rainstorm": besides Hab 3:10, see Isa 4:6, 25:4, 28:2, 30:30, 32:2, Job 24:8; cf. the verb in Ps 77:18 [Eng 17], 90:5.

68:9–10[72] and probably Ps 114:8, and indeed it is most probably rain and groundwater that are conceptualised as the "blessings of heaven above, blessings of the deep that lies beneath" in Gen 49:25.[73] However, the aspect of overpowering divine manifestation is uppermost in Ps 77:18 [Eng 17], Judg. 5:4[74] as indeed in Hab 3:9–10, whilst the two are juxtaposed in Ps 68:9–10 [Eng 8–9]. The use of thunderstorm phenomena, including precipitation, as weaponry, is less common, but occurs in Ps 18:13–5 [Eng 12–4] and (as seems likely from the parallelism) Ps 77:18 [Eng 17]; cf. Ezek 13:11, 13. Though on one level, rivers may seem of a different order from rain, creating a duality of water from earth and sky, the two are also closely related in a climate where the dry season was broken by heavy rain and by the transformation of dry riverbeds to rushing torrents; hence it is possible that they could be viewed as part of the thunderstorm phenomena and drawn from the deity's panoply of meteorological weaponry. In this light, it is worth noting that the form of the verb employed here in Hab 3:9c, the piel, suggests more forceful action than the Qal: the earth is cut open ($bq^ʿ$) by the divine warrior in a way that reveals his power and effectiveness, possibly even violence.[75] However, there is more to v. 9c than this, as $bq^ʿ$ is the verb most commonly used of the division of the sea at the exodus,[76] hence hinting at Yahweh's ability to deliver his people from their overpowering enemies, and, more pertinently, echoing the provision of water in the wilderness, as especially in Ps 78:15.[77] This is also congruent with *nəhārîm* as possibly referring specifically to Egyptian waters in the previous verse. It should also be noted that although some commentators have suggested that it should be the rivers or

---

[72] For the "dropping, dripping" (*nṭp*) of rain, compare not only contexts where water is bestowed, as in Judg 5:4, Ps 68:9 [Eng 8], but also where the verb conveys great luxury (hyperbolically, the mountains dripping sweet wine, as in Joel 3:18, Amos 9:13) or sensual allure (Prov 5:3, Song 4:11, 5:5, 13). It is also used of preaching, the "dropping" of words, hence Job's claim that his word "dropped upon them like dew" (Job 29:22) plays on both senses of this term.
[73] Cf. also Deut 33:13.
[74] Note, though, the use of *nṭp* (i.e. "dropped, dripped", not "poured" as the NRSV would overdramatically have it; see note 72 above).
[75] It is used in a variety of contexts, ranging from cutting wood for a fire (Gen 22:3) to ripping open pregnant women (2 Kgs 8:12, 15:16; likewise Am 1:13 in the Qal) or, in the case of Elisha's bears, young boys (2Kgs 2:24; cf. Hos 13:8, of a bear tearing someone open to reveal their heart), as well as breaking through a wall (Ezek 13:11), cutting channels for mining (Job 28:10, *yəʾōrîm*) or even hatching from an egg (Isa 59:5). Probably most pertinent here, though, is the splitting open of rocks in the wilderness in Ps 78:15, clearly a blessing in that context. A common thread is splitting or cutting through.
[76] In the most prosaic accounts! See Exod 14:16 and (in the niphal) v. 21; Neh 9:11, Isa 63:12, Ps 78:13.
[77] Where the piel is used, as here. Compare also Judg 15:19, Isa 48:21, Ps 74:15.

even "rivers of the earth" that are split,[78] the import of this idiom scarcely differs from the splitting of the earth with rivers: compare Gen 7:11 (*kol-ma'yənōt təhôm*), Isa 35:6 (*mayim*), Job 26:8 (*lōʾ +ʿānān*), Prov 3:20 (*təhômôt*) (all niphal), Ps 74:15 (*ma'yān wānāḥal*) (qal), Job 28:10 (*baṣṣûrôt yəʾōrîm*) (piel) with Judg. 15:19 (*maktēš*), Isa 48:21 (*ṣûr*) (both qal), Ps 78:15 (*ṣurîm*) (piel).[79]

2.1.2 Verse 10

The aspect here of the blending of thunderstorm and weaponry is highlighted especially by comparison with Ps 77:17–8, with which Hab 3:10 stands in close relation (see Table 1), and in the light of which some scholars have attempted to reconstruct this prophetic passage.

Table 1: Comparison of Ps 77:17–8 with Hab 3:10

Ps 77:17ab	*rāʾûkā mayim ʾĕlōhîm rāʾûkā mayim yāḥîlû*	Hab 3:10a	*rāʾûkā yāḥîlû hārîm*
Ps 77:18a	*zōrəmû mayim ʿābôt*	Hab 3:10b	*zerem mayim ʿābār*
Ps 77:18b	*qôl nātənû šəḥāqîm*	Hab 3:10c	*nātan təhôm qôlô*
cf. Ps 77:17c	*ʾap yirgəzû təhômôt*		
Ps 77:18c	*ʾap-ḥăṣāṣêkā yithallākû*	Hab 3:11b	*ləʾôr ḥiṣṣêkā yəhallēkû*

As Ps 77:17–20 [Eng 16–9] also shows correspondences with Ps 18:8, 12–7 [Eng 7, 11–6] but the only point of contact between the verses from the latter psalm and Hab 3 is the common phrase *nātan qôl*, it seems probable that Ps 77 has drawn on these two passages, or sources underlying them, rather than the other way round. As a result, any attempt to reconstruct Hab 3:10 on the basis of Ps 77 or even to interpret it too closely in its light, should be treated with caution. Nonetheless, these close linguistic connections do illustrate the vital force and familiarity of this language in evoking Yahweh's intervention in the thunderstorm, in both cases, it seems, for the deliverance of his people. Having noted the resonance of the verb *bqʿ* in v. 9c with the exodus and wilderness traditions, it is striking that the theophany of Ps 77:17–8 [Eng 16–7] (which in turn seems to be dependent on Hab 3:10) leads to the same explicit train of thought in vv. 20–1, though this is not developed further in Habakkuk.

---

78 Lortie 2016, 113, 114.
79 Even a storm can "break": Ezek 13:11, 13 (piel).

2.1.2.1 Verse 10ab

I have already observed how in the first section of the portrayal of the divine theophany (in Hab 3:3–7), Eloah's presence causes affliction to the earth and nations, and this idea is continued to v. 10a, where it is the mountains which writhe, a phrase which in Ps 77:17 is applied to the waters. The notion of seeing and trembling is attested elsewhere in Ps 97:4,[80] whilst the verb *ḥîl* is prevalent in theophany portrayals.[81] However, *ḥîl* is also indicative of the distress accompanying warfare, especially as due to Yahweh's violent intervention;[82] so strong is the reaction this verb conveys that it is frequently applied to the anguish of childbirth[83] and can even be used of a fatal wounding.[84] The aspects of this response of the earth as agonised but as typical of theophany portrayals will be important in assessing the timbre of less familiar phrases in the surrounding verses.

We have already seen how v. 10b tallies with the frequent theophanic feature of rainfall, and how it corresponds closely to Ps 77:18a [Eng 17a] *zōrəmû mayim ʿābôt*.[85] It is not impossible that the thought continues from that of v. 9c, and that run-off from rainfall sweeping by in a torrent is envisaged, but there is no evidence for the use of *zerem* other than to indicate falling rain, so this seems unlikely. Its frequent employment not simply to indicate rain in general but a "downpour, rainstorm",[86] often in association with judgment,[87] invites this con-

---

[80] See similarly Ps 114:3 ("looked and fled"); one might also compare the response to hearing in Exod 15:14.
[81] Cf. Ps 97:4 (of the earth), 114:7 (the earth); 1Chr 16:30 ("all the earth"); Jer 5:22 ("you", i.e. Jacob/Judah).
[82] In anticipation: Jer 51:29, Joel 2:6; in actuality: Ezek 30:16, Isa 13:8; in response to a report, Isa 23:5, Zech 9:5. Cf. the reaction of Jeremiah in 4:19, and of another individual to his enemies in a psalm of lament, Ps 55:5. It is likewise applied by extension to the fear and dread of the nations at Israel's invincible reputation under the protection of Yahweh (Deut 2:25).
[83] Isa 13:8 and often.
[84] 1Sam 31:3.
[85] Some have sought to emend this colon, to bring it into line with Mur 88, Targ and Ps 77:18a (Anderson 2001, 329; Hiebert 1986, 6–7, 30 nn. 42, 43), but as Lortie (2017, 45) aptly states, "It seems more likely that a scribe would have harmonized the text to make it easier to understand, rather than created an entirely new text that is difficult to interpret"; the MT is supported by the Naḥal Ḥever, Symmachus, Vulg. and (more loosely) Barberini, whilst LXX seems to assume Hebrew *zōrēm mayim ʿēber*, thus suggesting the broad veracity of MT but with the verbal root reappearing in nominal form and the nominal root now as a verb (Gelston, 2010, 124, following Rudolph, 1975, 236; cf. Nah. 1:8).
[86] Thus *DCH*. This force seems always to apply in the extant Hebrew texts. See Isa 25:4, 28:2, 30:30, 32:2; it is also seen primarily as something from which shelter is needed in Isa 4:6, Job 24:8, while it is described as causing a wall to collapse in 4Q424 1:4.
[87] See Isa 28:2, 30:30.

nection here and amply suits the context: the "storm of water" passes over (or sweeps by) as a feature of the dramatic theophany and as another instrument in the hand of Yahweh as he intervenes against his enemies.[88]

2.1.2.2 Verse 10c

The two main issues here in determining the force of the colon are the identification of *təhôm* and the assessment of the import of *nātan qôl* in order to ascertain whether this utterance is one of distress or aggression.

Təhôm seems most fundamentally to denote subterranean water, usually the nourishing fresh water which quenches thirst and bestows blessing and fertility.[89] This sense of *təhôm* as water from beneath is famously encountered in respect of the flood narrative where its fountains are opened together with the (superterrestrial) windows of heaven,[90] but the counterbalancing of *təhôm* and the heavens or sky is especially evident in Gen 49:25, where "blessings of heaven above" are paralleled with "blessings of the deep that lies beneath", and similarly by Deut. 33:13, where the "choice gifts" of each are paired; Prov 8:(27–)28, and 3:20 (in this latter reference in the plural) have a similar force. The plural can have a wider sphere of reference, since although *təhômôt* may relate to the nourishing subterranean water that feeds the springs,[91] most often they are associated with the sea.[92] However, in the singular (which is all that need detain us here), the sense of subterrestrial water seems secure.[93] As such, here in Hab 3:10c the deep (beneath) provides a counterbalance to the torrential rain (from above) of the preceding colon. This would come across even more clearly were the text of Ps 77:18a [Eng 17a] ("the clouds poured out water") adopted in Hab

---

[88] Compare 4QpIsa^c 25:3, [*nps̱ w*]*zrm kly mlḥmh hmh*, "cloudburst and downpour are weapons of war". The context of warfare is evident also in 1QM 12:10 and 1QH^a X 27.
[89] Gen 49:25; Deut 33:13; Ezek 31:4 (probably also v. 15) and context; Deut 8:7 (in the plural); Am 7:4; Ps 78:15; Prov 8:24 (in the plural); cf. Prov 3:20 (plural). The exact identification of "the deep" in Job 38:30 is not clear from the context, though the mention of its "face", or "suface" and of the "womb" in the previous verse (cf. Job 1:21, Eccl 5:14 [Eng 15], Jonah 2:3 [Eng 2], besides the pairing of the "fruit of the womb" and "fruit of the ground" in Deut, e. g. 7:13, 28:4) seems to support a subterranean understanding. Gen 1:2 and Ps 104:6 both seem to antedate the separation of the waters, so cannot be related to the post-creation status quo.
[90] Gen 7:11, 8:2; compare also Job 38:16, where the "springs of the sea" are paralleled with the "recesses of the deep".
[91] See Deut 8:7: "... a good land, a land with flowing streams, with springs and underground waters [*təhōmōt*] welling up in valleys and hills"; similarly Prov 8:24.
[92] Exod 15:5, 8, Ps 33:7, 106:9, 135:6, 148:7, Isa 51:10, 63:13.
[93] For a fuller exploration of the meaning and use of *təhôm*, see Watson 2005, 97–8.

3:10b,⁹⁴ though in Ps 77:18, by contrast, the parallel lines retain a celestial focus throughout.

Although water was one of the three primary sources of loud noise known in the ancient world, besides warfare and thunder,⁹⁵ the imagery of the deep calling or roaring occurs only in one other place in the Hebrew Bible, in Ps. 42:8 [Eng 7]: *təhôm-'el- təhôm qōrē' ləqôl ṣinnôrêkā*. The near silence of the texts on this matter is understandable, insofar as *təhôm* denotes underground water or submarine water reserves: it was not therefore usually audible. In Ps 42 the deep appears to be reactive, vocalising in response to the sound of another form of moving water, so this might be considered as a possibility in Hab 3:10bc. The import of this is not self-evident, not least as the apparent allusion to Sheol in Ps 42 may not apply here. Therefore, careful attention to the context will be necessary for the interpretation of this colon.

It appears that here the response of the deep, together with the torrents of water from above, fittingly expresses the effect of the storm theophany on waters both above and below, whilst the earth is gashed with rivers in between. But is the "crying out" of the deep an expression of distress, or does it reflect a role as an instrument of the deity in making known his theophanic presence, thus possibly also impacting on the earth/nations which are the more direct object of his attention in the majority of this passage?

Lifting the voice (*nātan qôl*) can be used in a variety of ways, so it is difficult to interpret with certainty, but it seems that noise is the key idea expressed thereby, rather than any specific kind of sound. Most often Yahweh appears as the subject, in reference to his thunder,⁹⁶ but the "roaring" of lions,⁹⁷ "sounding" of a tambourine⁹⁸ or even "call" of birds⁹⁹ might all be described thus. Such diverse spheres of reference suggest convergence of terminology regardless of agent, and hence an obvious applicability to moving water, and indeed it might invite comparison with the "thundering, roaring" (*r'm*) of the sea in Pss 96:11, 98:7.¹⁰⁰ This does not answer the more important question of why the

---

94 See p. 47 n. 85 above.
95 Ezek 1:24, cf. Isa 17:12, Ps 93:4.
96 Exod 9:23, 1Sam 12:17, 18, 2Sam 22:14 // Ps 18:14 [Eng 13], Jer 10:13 // 51:16; cf. *ntn bəqôl*, Pss 68:33 [Eng 32], 46:7. The divine voice also features where other storm features are less in evidence: Joel 2:11 (on the day of Yahweh, accompanied by earthquakes and darkness); Jer 25:30 (from on high // his holy habitation); Joel 4:16 [Eng 3:16], Am 1:2 (both from Zion // Jerusalem). In Ps.77:18b [Eng 17b] it is the clouds or skies (*šəḥāqîm*) that thunder.
97 Jer 2:15 (*'l*, "against"), Am 3:4.
98 Ps 81:3 [Eng 2].
99 Ps 104:12.
100 Cf. *šə'ôn*, "roar", Ps. 65:8 [Eng 7], *nś' qôl*, Ps 93:3.

deep "gives voice" here. However, given the possible personification operative in this verse, as implied by the writhing mountains and the sun raising its hands, the semantic rage of the phrase as applied to human subjects can perhaps provide some illumination. In fact, with a human subject, most often *nātan qôl* is expressive of distress and wailing,[101] and this would also be congruent with the impression of anguish derived from the first colon of verse 10 and hence would comprise an apt counterpart to it.[102]

Also in support of this interpretation is the "trembling" of *təhōmôt* in Ps 77:17c [Eng 16c]. This in turn follows on from the notion that the waters saw Yahweh and trembled (*rā'ûkā mayim 'ĕlōhîm rā'ûkā mayim yāḥîlû*) in the first two cola of this tricolon, where Hab 3:10 has the mountains doing so. Moreover, Ps 77:17c provides the only other occurrence of *təhôm* in connection with a theophany appearance in the Hebrew Bible (there in the plural), so, given the predictable and formulaic nature of the responses of the constituent elements of the cosmos, the trembling of the deep there should be given significant consideration in assessing the probable nuance of its reaction in Hab 3:10.[103]

At the same time, distress and instrumentality are not necessarily mutually exclusive: compare, for example, Ps 114, where the fleeing of the sea and Jordan is both a fear response before the presence of Yahweh and the one required to enable the Israelites' crossing. Both cosmic distress and the use of natural phenomena to signal the presence of the deity and to act on his behalf are characteristic of theophany portrayals and we see both at work in Ps 77:17–20 [Eng 16–9], with distress in vv. 17, 19c [Eng 16, 18c] framing the manifestation of the warrior-god in the storm in the intervening cola. Here we note the echoing of Hab 3:10c (*nātan təhôm qôlô*) in Ps 77:18b [Eng 17b], where it is the clouds which "give forth their voice" (*qôl nātənû šəḥāqîm*), clearly reflecting Yahweh's agency in the thunderstorm to deliver his people. Obviously, the very difference of Ps 77:18b from the present colon, not least in the subject of the verb, invites attention to the distinctions between the two. Nonetheless, although it seems likely that distress at

---

101 Gen 45:2, Num 14:1, Jer 22:20, 48:34; possibly also Lam 2:7 (cf. vv. 5, 10).
102 Some uses, such as calling out with a message (Prov 1:2, 8:1; cf. 2:3; 2Chr 24:9 [of a proclamation]), are not apposite to the context (cf. also Lam 2:7, apparently in celebration on the day of a festival), whilst the phrase seems only to indicate antagonism where it is followed by *'al* plus the object (Jer 4:16, 12:8), so this interpretation should probably be rejected, much as thundering may be an expression of the power of the storm-god.
103 Other occurrences of the deep in connection with divine action most often pertain to the Re[e]d Sea crossing, where it is congealed (Exod 15:8) or dried (Isa 51:10, 63:13, Ps 106:9). Otherwise, the main action of the deep towards other agents, and in accordance with Yahweh's purpose, is to cover them (Exod 15:5, Ezek 26:19, 31:15, cf. Jonah 2:6 [Eng 5]), most often as they go down to Sheol (though contrast Ps 104:6).

the theophany is uppermost, an instrumental view of the response of the deep as signalling the appearance of the divine warrior and effecting his purpose is also possible, probably as a secondary nuance. The sounding of the deep is indeed an aspect of the theophany but its main import is as part of the turmoil caused by the coming of the deity, comparable with the anguish of the mountains in v. 10a.

2.1.2.3 Verse 10d

Of course, v. 10d, the following colon, should in theory also assist in ascertaining the nuance of v. 10c. However, the MT is here uncertain, as is its interpretation. *Rôm* is a hapax legomenon, usually taken to mean "on high", whilst the rest of the verse reads "he/it lifted its/his hands", i.e. (most naturally) "the deep[104] lifted its hands on high".[105] The situation is complicated by the problematic state of the following colon, v. 11a, since sun and moon (*šemeš* and *yārēaḥ*) stand in juxtaposition without the expected conjunction and are then followed by a singular verb (*'āmad*). Many commentators therefore transfer *šemeš* to v. 10d, thus rendering v. 11a grammatically intelligible without repointing.[106] There would then also be some level of symmetry between these two cola, with sun and moon both being mentioned in the context of elevation, the former with its raised hands and the latter in its "exalted place".

But if this gesture were by the sun, what might it signify? If this is a response to or aspect of the theophany, it is without clear parallel, although there is solar imagery already in v. 4, and the brightness of Yahweh is mentioned in other theophany passages.[107] The interpretation of this section is complicated by the fact that there are various possible significations of hand-lifting within the Hebrew corpus, most of which—such as swearing,[108] blessing[109] or signalling[110]—are

---

[104] Which is feminine eight times in the Hebrew Bible, and masculine six times, plus other indeterminate occurrences; it is masculine in the previous colon (*qôlô*).

[105] Thus MT, Old Greek, Vulg., Syriac, Targum, followed by Eaton 1964, 152, Avishur 1994, 178–82.

[106] Thus the majority of modern commentators, among them Haak (1992, 97–8) Hiebert (1986, 30–1) and Lortie (2016, 46). LXX apparently transposes the verb *nś'* from v. 10d to verse 11, making the sun its subject; cf. Barberini, which however defies attempts to map onto the Hebrew and seems to be missing the last two words of verse 10.

[107] Besides Hab 3:4, see Deut 33:2; cf. also Isa 10:17, 60:1, 19, Ezek 43:2, Ps 18:29 [Eng 28]. Cf. also reference to the brightness of the thunderstorm phenomena through which Yahweh is manifested, e.g. Ps 18:9, 13 [Eng 8,12] // 2Sam 22:9, 13, Ps 77:19b [Eng 18b], 97:4.

[108] This is probably the most common application of the phrase *nāśā' yād*, but in each case in the Hebrew Bible Yahweh is the subject (though we might assume that humans would do the

self-evidently not applicable here. However, Ps 10:12 offers one possible nuance for the phrase *nāśā' yād* which should be considered:

> Rise up, O Yahweh; O God lift up your hand;
> do not forget the oppressed.

Obviously, in this case, Yahweh is the subject, and the idea that he might "rise up" (*qûm*) is especially associated with the going out of the Ark (Num 10:35, Ps 68:2 [Eng 1], 132:8), whilst his hand (often together with his arm or right hand) is another marker of strength that is much celebrated (cf. Exod 3:19, 13:3, 32:11, Deut 4:34, 5:15 and often, Ps 136:12, Neh 1:10, Dan 9:15). Nonetheless, since the hand of Yahweh is most frequently distinguished in such passages as "strong, mighty" (*ḥăzāqāh*; cf. Ps 132:8), it is reasonable to conjecture that the phrasing of Ps 10:12 might also be employed to convey power and readiness by others,[111] especially if acting on his behalf. If applied here to the sun, it might compare with the claim in Judg 5:20, "The stars fought from heaven, / from their courses they fought against Sisera" and it would also have intriguing resonance with the following verse in which the torrent (*naḥal*) Kishon participated in the action against the enemies, as well as with the ensuing reference to horses. However, it is difficult to reconcile this active role for the sun with the moon simply "standing" in the following colon, or indeed with the metaphors of distress in the earlier part of verse 10, so it should most probably be rejected.

The lifting of hands is therefore often understood in this instance distinctively in reference to rays, possibly reaching up over the horizon during the deity's early intervention.[112] The moon standing in its "lofty place" has been explained in terms of its visibility being obscured by the sun's glare.[113] However, the moon's response is instead to the flashing of Yahweh's arrows and gleaming spear (v. 11),

---

same): Exod 6:8, Num 14:30, Deut 32:40, Ezek 20:5, 5, 6, 15, 23, 28, 42, 36:7, 44:12, 47:14, Ps 106:26, Neh. 9:15.

109 Thus Lev. 9:22 (Aaron, the people); Ps 134:2, 63:5 (human subjects, Yahweh/God), all with *'el*, of the person blessed. Compare also with the same preposition Ps 119:48 [*'eśśā'-kappay 'el-miṣwōtêkā*], which is hard to categorise, but suggests blessing, reverence or turning towards, parallel with "meditate on your statues".

110 Thus Isa 49:22, plus *'el*, of the nations signalled to.

111 Cf. the sense of "rising up" against someone (2Sam 18:28, 20:21, both of which entail a man or men "lifting up their hand against" king David); in the extant instances this necessitates the preposition *bĕ* and an indirect object, but it does suggest that the nuance of active involvement in Yahweh's intervention might at least be possible here.

112 Ps 46:6 [Eng 5], cf. Zeph 3:5. Alternatively, both luminaries might function to illuminate the battle scene; cf. Exod 17:12 for a weak comparison.

113 Lortie 2016, 115.

just as the theme of solar brightness introduced already in v. 4 is in respect to Yahweh only by analogy with the sun. As a result, it seems more likely that these luminaries are both outshone and awed by the brilliance of the theophany[114] than that the moon should be rendered ineffective by the sun. If so, the raising of hands, if applied to the sun, would be a gesture of supplication[115] or even submission.[116] This may also cohere with the reality of a rainstorm, which is accompanied by darkened skies, against which the lightning may be the more clearly seen and makes such a striking contrast.[117] Congruent with such a reading is that the hands should be stretched towards the deity (rôm, in this instance)[118] and, in view of the previous colon, that such gestures are accompanied by "crying out" to him. (Although the verbs employed differ in each case, one might compare qôl in Ps 28:2 with nātan qôl in Hab 3:10c).

Despite the complexities of verse 10 and the uncertainties around varying aspects of its interpretation, it therefore seems to be consistently expressive of distress, with the likelihood of this reading of each part in turn being confirmed in turn by the cumulative effect of the whole. The impact of the theophany on (or maybe manifestation through) both celestial and subterrestrial waters emerges in v. 10bc, with a concomitant implied effect on the inhabitants of the earth. However, it is also possible that v. 10d, like 10bc, simultaneously evokes disturbing storm phenomena, with the sun and deep each contributing, from their respective sub-marine or subterranean positions, to the intervention of Yahweh.[119]

---

114 Possibly this understanding might underlie the Barberini text, which has so confused commentators. For "brightness" as a feature of the theophany, compare also Ps 18:13 [Eng 12] // 1Sam 22:13 and Ezek 1:13. For the brightness of Yahweh's lightning, cf. Ps 77:19 [Eng 18].
115 Ps 28:2, Lam 2:19; or worship, Ps 134:2.
116 This is not attested in Hebrew, but since it is a gesture indicating that a person is unarmed and vulnerable (exposing their vital organs unshielded) it may have had universal currency; cf. the cross-cultural prevalence of raising the hand in oath or blessing.
117 Day refers here specifically to a hailstorm (Day 1985, 109), deferring to Westermann's form-critical comparison of Hab 3:3–15 and Ps 18:8–16 [Eng 7–15], in which Hab 3:11a corresponds to Ps 18:13 [Eng 12], but this seems unneccesarily precise. His comparison of the darkness accompanying the storm in *KTU* 1.4.vii 52–60 (Day 1985, 147) may be more apposite, but is complicated by the poor state of the tablet, giving rise to considerable variation in the translations, with Smith (1997, 138) notably losing the reference to darkness and rendering ym as "sea", not "day".
118 'El-dəbîr qodšekā, in Ps 28:2, 'ēlâw in Lam 2:19; cf. Ps 134:2.
119 Should the deep be taken as the subject of nāśā' yād, as favoured by a minority of interpreters, many of the same considerations would apply to the interpretation of the colon, though obviously it would leave the difficulty with v. 11a unresolved. The most plausible interpretation, again, would be that it is a gesture of supplication made from a position of extreme need. This would aptly fit the context, with indisputable distress of the mountains at the theophany in v. 10a and the crying out (nātan qôl) by the deep in v. 10c then immediately being followed by

2.2 Verses 12, 15, 19

2.2.1 "Treading" and "Trampling"

Supposed *Chaoskampf* language is often claimed for v. 15, since it resonates with the "trampling" motif already exposed in v. 12 and iterated in the final verse, v. 19, and also refers to the deity's horses which are mentioned in connection with *nəhārîm* and *yām* in v. 8. However, care has to be exercised here, as the language employed in v. 12 is actually quite distinct from that of vv. 15 and 19, even though this is often not discernible in the English translations. V. 12 has *dûš* and *ṣā'ad* (translated "trod" and "trampled" respectively in the NRSV), whereas both v. 15 and v. 19 use *dārak* (which in the NRSV is rendered with exactly the same verbs: "trampled" in the former verse and "tread" in the latter). Possibly English is simply more impoverished in its range of alternative vocabulary appropriate to this semantic sphere, but it is important to try to ascertain the nature of the distinction made in Hebrew, as it doubtless has some significance.

2.2.1.1 "Tread" and "Trample" in Verse 12

The harshness of the reference in v. 12 can scarcely be missed, since this footwork is done "in fury" and "in anger". In fact the first verb, *dûš*, literally means trampling underfoot in threshing[120] but it is often used of crushing a foe in military contexts, where devastating brutality is implied.[121] *Ṣā'ad* with a human subject can signify little more than "walking,"[122] but with Yahweh as the subject, it is closely connected with his "march" from the southland with accompanying spasms in nature (the trembling of the earth and pouring down of rain, Judg. 5:4, Ps 68:8–9 [Eng 7–8]) as already manifested in vv. 6, 10 in re-

---

its supplicatory efforts, if the MT for this colon were retained. The same analogy with Judg 5, in this case with the participation of the torrent Kishon to fight Yahweh's cause, could be applied here, but the anguish of nature which we have seen in the earlier part of the verse and the emphasis in Hab 3:8–15 on military action by the deity alone, without reference to his host or other participants, makes this unlikely in the present context. However, the suggestion, which is occasionally made, that the lifting of the waters of the exodus into heaps is envisaged here, is belied by the vocabulary employed, as neither *rôm* nor *yād* would be apposite.

[120] As in Jer 50:11, Isa 28:27–8, Hos 10:11, cf. 2Kgs 13:7 where threshing provides a simile for military destruction. There is in addition, a reference to a wild animal "trampling" ostrich's eggs in Job 39:14.

[121] See Judg 8:7, 16, and where the agricultural imagery is retained, Am 1:3, Mic 4:13, Isa 41:15; cf. in the niphal Isa 25:10.

[122] Thus Prov 7:8, Jer 10:5, 2Sam 6:13, cf. Gen 49:22.

sponse to his coming in v. 3.[123] Also of interest is Isa 63:1, where Yahweh is "marching"[124] to save and vindicate his people from the nations whom he has trodden (*dārak*) in his anger (*'ap*, Isa 63:3, cf. Hab 3:8b, 12b) and trampled (*rāmas*; not in Hab 3) in his fury (*ḥēmāh*; also absent from Hab 3). In this late articulation of the warrior-god tradition, the distress of the cosmos has receded but the aspect of divine vengeance on his foes comes to its fullest and most brutal expression; hence there are aspects of continuity with Hab 3 but the imagery is more extreme.

More immediately, in picking up on the language of wrath which was already emphasised so intensely in verse 8, here at the midpoint of vv. 8–15, verse 12 offers a clear statement of the target of divine fury: it is the earth (*'ereṣ*) and nations (*gôyim*), bodies which have already displayed their terror in verse 6 (cf. also v. 9c), just as the path of anger has already been established at the outset in vv. 2–3 when Yahweh marched forth to save his people. Here, too, further linguistic ties binding and setting in tension different threads of the psalms come into play, for in verse 8d, straight after the tricolonic exploration of divine wrath, comes the statement that he drove his chariots of or to victory / salvation (*yəšû'â*), thus expressing exactly the same concern (and language) that is now developed in v. 13ab (*yš'*) in succession to the wrath against the nations. Here, though, in contrast to v. 8d, the aim to save "your people, ... your anointed" is made explicit. The forceful treading of verse 12, then, is not an attempt merely to adorn the poem with the aesthetics of word play and structural ties decoratively arching through the whole, but a clear statement of the focus of wrath, anger, and violent treading and trampling on the nations, in distinction to the activity of verses 15 and 19 and even indeed to verses 3a (*bw'*) and 6a (*'md*) and to the trembling steps of the psalmist in verse 16d.[125] Yahweh had set out in anger (v. 2), but now the target is made explicit before it is resolved through the slaying of the enemy in the ensuing verses (vv. 13–4) and in the establishment of the speaker securely on the heights (v. 19).

---

123 Certain affinities of Hab 3 with these passages have already been noted, especially in relation to the march from the southland (above, pp. 30–1) and torrential rain in v. 9c (above, pp. 44–5).
124 Here the Hebrew *ṣō'eh* ("stooping, bending, inclining") should probably be emended to *ṣō'ēḏ* in line with Sym. *bainōn* and Vulg. *gradiens*.
125 Reading *yirgəzû 'ăšurāy* with BHS notes; cf. LXX.

2.2.1.2 "Trampled" in Verse 15

Dārak, the Hebrew term operative here, has a varied semantic range, in which the meaning is largely determined by the context and proximate vocabulary and by the use (or not) of certain key prepositions. Where the preposition *bə*, indicating place ("in, on"), is employed, there is no implication of mythological combat outside this passage. Most commonly it is used of land "on which" someone walks, e. g., Deut 1:36 refers to the land *'ăšer dārak-bāh* and there are a number of Deuteronomic allusions to "all the land on which you set foot" (*kol-hā'āreṣ'ăšer tidrəkû-bāh*, Deut 11:25) or "every place on which you shall set foot" (*kol-hammāqôm'ăšer tidrōk kap-ragləkem bô*), Deut 11:24, Josh. 1:3, or similarly, Joshua 14:9: *hā'āreṣ'ăšer dārəkah ragləkā bāh*. One might compare Mic 5:4–5 [Eng 5–6], which makes reference to "tread[ing] in our palaces" (*yidrōk bə'armənōtênû*)[126] and "in our border" (*yidrōk bigbûlēnû*), whilst Isa 59:8 talks about walking in metaphorical paths, again using the phrase *drk b*. It is clear that in all of these cases *drk b* is not about aggression towards that which is walked on underfoot, but in all but the last of these references, there is a perceived connection between "walking on" land and possessing it (to which one might compare the old English laws of possessory title).[127] Walking in or on the sea, then, is not a matter of subjugation but a divine act, to be compared with the dramatic theophanic evocation of the exodus crossing in Ps 77:20ab [Eng 19ab]:

bayyām darkekā ûšəbîləkā[128] *bəmayim rabbîm*

(NRSV: Your way was through the sea, [and] your path through the mighty waters).

---

[126] Probably to be emended to "on our soil" (*bə'admātēnû*) in line with LXX, Syriac and v. 5.
[127] The only other instances of *drk b* are either in reference to time (treading wine presses on the sabbath, *dōrəkîm-gittôt baššabbāt*, Neh 13:15), to an emotional state (treading in anger—"I trod them in my anger" *'edrəkēm bə'appî*, Isa 63:3), to a direction in life (walking in truth, *'ĕmet*, Sir 51:15[B], or uprightness, *mîšôr*, 11QPs*ᵃ*) or to treading in a wine-press, in Isa 63:2 (*dōrēk bəgat*). However, it is clear from a comparison with other passages, e.g., Isa 16:10 (where it is said that no-one treads wine in the presses, *yayin bayqābîm lō'-yidrōk haddōrēk*), that the press is the indirect, not direct, object of the verb. In the hiphil, the emphasis of the verb is commonly on leading or guiding in the right paths, most often metaphorically, in moral behaviour (*ba'ămittekā*, Ps 25:5; *bammišpāṭ*, Ps 25:9; *bintîb miṣwōtêkā*, Ps 119:35; *bəma'galê-yōšer*, Prov 4:11; *bəderek tēlēk*, Isa 48:17; *bdrk lbw*, CD 1:11), but also more literally (*bəderek yəšārâ*, of delivering those lost in the desert, Ps 107:7); there's also, slightly tangentially, an instrumental case, "in/with shoes, on foot", in Isa 11:15 (NRSV "and make a way to cross on foot"), re the exodus crossing.
[128] Thus Qere and many manuscripts; Kethib, supported by Gk, Syr, Jer, reads *ûšəbîlêkā*.

In Ps 77:20, the nominal form, *drk*, is employed instead of the verb, but the objects, *yām* and *mayim rabbîm*, are the same as in Hab 3:15. The dominant aspects here are Yahweh's theophanic power and deliverance of his people, as well the clear evocation of the exodus event. In Hab 3:15, any echo of the exodus is much less apparent, as the verse and its immediate context is lacking clear accompanying allusions, although some level of resonance cannot be excluded.[129] However, as in other uses of *drk b*, it should be read as meaning "walk on/in/through" rather than the more vigorous "tread/trample on" (*drk 'al*),[130] and as carrying possible theophanic or possessory connotations.

In discussions of this verse, reference is often made to ancient Near Eastern images of foes being trampled underfoot, and of course, this is an understandably prevalent motif, echoed at times also in the Hebrew Bible, including Hab 3:12. Reference to ancient Near Eastern iconography can be illuminating in illustrating the wider cultural environment and the ideas with which certain biblical images may be in dialogue, and this has been a huge gain. However, just as there are important differences between the tenor of Mesopotamian and north west Semitic myths and images, so we must also be attentive to the nuances of each manifestation of such imagery, including points where a particular example diverges from commonly attested features; and sensitivity to the import of each instance of "treading" language is vital if it is to be interpreted correctly. A careful examination of the context and of all other examples of the expression *drk b* in classical Hebrew indicates that although it may be associated with ownership the vocabulary employed in v. 15 does not imply combat. Lest it be thought that this is to relegate comparative sources to an unduly subordinate place, it is worth quoting Keel's perspective on "Dualistic Features" in ancient Near Eastern iconography, as pertaining to lordship over the waters in connection with the Psalms in particular:[131]

---

129 See above on vv. 8, 9c, and cf. vv. 10a – 11b with Ps 77:17a – 18c [Eng 16a – 17c], where the allusion to the Re[e]d Sea crossing is unmistakable.
130 *drk 'al* occurs in the phrase "tread on the high places [of the earth]", Hab 3:19, Am 4:13, Mic 1:3, and the related expressions in Job 9:8 (*'al-bāmŏtê yām*) and in Deut 33:29 in reference to treading on the backs of enemies; and also re trampling the young lion and serpent underfoot, Ps 91:13. The other biblical occurrence in the Qal is in reference to people avoiding treading on the threshold of the house of Dagon (1 Sam. 5:5), whilst in 1QM 9:11 (*'al drwk m't*, "when it advances a little") the preposition has temporal force. Hiphil + *'al* is confined to Hab 3:19 and to Sir 9:2, where *hdrykh 'l bmwtyk* relates to a husband causing his wife to tread on his *bmwt*—something he will clearly wish to avoid!
131 Keel 1997, 47 – 53.

because the power of Yahweh was seen to be all-encompassing and overwhelming, that independence [of the Chaos powers] could no longer imperil the world (Pss 93:3–4; 109:9). The sea, having lost all its threatening power, is demythologized. Its dark, salt floods and its flashing foam are nothing more than water. Once Yahweh, with his mighty, sovereign word, has displaced the hard-fighting Baal, the sea loses every representative aspect (Pss 46:2–3; 65:6–7; 77:16–9; 93; 104:5–6).[132]

Personally, I would hesitate to use the term "demythologized" because denial of power to the sea is an aspect of according Yahweh a superlative authority and supremacy, and hence this could almost be interpreted as an extension and exaggeration of the myths that preceded it. However, if Keel can come to such a conclusion after sustained immersion in iconographic evidence, then this certainly lends weight to hesitation before automatically assuming a close identity between psalmic texts and specific Semtic visual images.

2.2.2 *Mayim Rabbîm* in Verse 15

Another common assumption in scholarship affecting the interpretation of verse 15 is that *mayim rabbîm* is almost a technical term to refer to "cosmic", chaotic waters, and that this vocabulary of itself evokes the notion of a chaos battle. This is due in large part to widespread dependence in the secondary literature on a highly influential but little-critiqued article by H. G. May, "Some Cosmic Connotations of Mayim Rabbîm, 'Many Waters'", which was published in *JBL* in 1955.[133] The present chapter does not afford the space to discuss this term in depth or to consider all the occurrences in the Hebrew Bible.[134] However, to summarise my earlier findings briefly, a careful consideration of its use shows that, despite the diverse contexts in which this term is employed, it essentially denotes "much/abundant water". Most often this is associated with plenty as the fertile water which encourages growth and quenches thirst. One might compare then the characteristic theophanic feature of the heavens dropping dew, or rain pouring down from heaven. However, there is also sometimes a more fearsome aspect to large volumes of water,[135] so that *mayim rabbîm* are themselves often under-

---

132 Keel 1997, 49.
133 May 1955.
134 For a more detailed treatment, readers are referred to my earlier study of this language (Watson 2005, 57–9).
135 Cf. allusions to the "sound" or "roaring" of "mighty waters" in Ezek 1:24, 43:2, Isa 17:12–3, Jer 51:55, Ps 93:4 and to the "rush[ing] (*šēṭep*) of mighty waters" in Ps 32:6.

stood as the sea,[136] and this dynamism may be reflected in the phrase *ḥōmer mayim rabbîm* in Hab 3:15 as well as in the parallelism of the verse, being highly in keeping with its intense and dramatic theophanic colouring. These are the great, foaming waters through which the deity passes. That said, it is not certain whether the location is terrestrial or celestial, since at times Yahweh is envisaged as driving a cloud-chariot through the sky, at others as riding to victory at the head of (or on behalf of) his people,[137] but although here there are both celestial (vv. 3c, 4) and terrestrial (vv. 3d,6–7, 12–4, 16–9) elements in this passage, the latter seems more likely from the immediate context—especially from the emphasis on direct action against the human foe, using the usual accoutrements of battle—and indeed from its close echo of Ps 77:20ab [Eng 19ab], though of course the reference does not have to be exclusively to the one or the other.

The mention of *mayim rabbîm* straight after the overcoming of the enemies may also appear reminiscent of Pss. 18:17 [Eng 16] // 2Sam 22:17 and 144:7. In these psalms, reference to the underworld is evident, most overtly in Ps 18:5–6 [Eng 4–5 // 2Sam 22:5–6], hence this seems to be the implied location of the psalmist during his rescue in Ps 18:16 [Eng 15 // 2Sam 22:16], suggesting that deliverance from the enemies is simultaneously liberation from death.[138] However, it is not clear at all that the underworld is alluded to in Hab 3, much as the language of battle, enmity, oppression and rescue is ever-present and hence, in that sense, cannot entirely be dissociated from a risk of death. Moreover, the individual language of personal rescue which is so prominent in Ps 18 is absent from Hab 3. The collective ("people", "us") is foremost in vv. 13–4, just as the reference here to "nations" (vv. 6, 12, cf. 7) contrasts with the personal nature of the "enemy" and "those who hated me" depicted in Ps 18:18 [Eng 17] // 2Sam 22:18. Most likely, therefore, is that that the aquatic language of Ps 18 // 2Sam 22 and its later echo in Ps 144 represents a particular merging of the theophany and distress of nature theme with the imagery of Sheol, but that this particular combination should not necessarily be assumed here in Habakkuk, and nor should the very personal experience of the enemy and its merging with the waters.

An important aspect of verse 15 is its place at the end of the psalm proper (vv. 3–15) but also more narrowly of the section beginning with verse 8. As a result, many scholars have recognised the inclusio operative in the iteration of mention of the waters. However, this encourages v. 15 to be read in dialogue

---

136 As in Ps 107:23, Isa 23:3, Ezek 26:19, 27:26, Exod 15:10, Neh. 9:11, Ps 77:20.
137 See above, p. 33 n. 21.
138 See further Watson 2005, 78–83; also 2005, 83–4 re Ps 144.

with verse 8, which, as we have established, emphatically denies that Yahweh's wrath is against the sea and rivers. We find a corrective to this idea in the trampling of the earth // nations in the heart of this section (v. 12) and the affirmation of that focus both in the intervening lines (vv. 13–4) and in the succeeding verses (vv. 16–9, noting especially v. 16ef), culminating with the speaker's confidence in the strength bestowed in him by Yahweh, enabling him to tread (hiphil) upon the heights (*weʻal bāmôṯay yadrikēnî*, v. 19).

2.2.2 Verse 19

Structually, verse 19 falls outside the section comprising vv. 8–15 on which our attention has been placed. However, given the iteration of the trampling theme here and its structural importance as the last word in this chapter, and indeed in the book of Habakkuk as a whole, it merits brief consideration, particularly insofar as it might illuminate verse 15. In attempting to understand this verse, its close similarity with Ps 18:33–4 [Eng 32–3] // 2Sam 22:33–4 may be of assistance. There are minor differences between the parallel texts, but the Psalm 18 version is as follows:

33	*hāʼēl hamʼazzərēnî*[139] *ḥāyil*	the God who girded me with strength
	wayyittēn[140] *tāmîm darkî*[141]	and made my way safe.
34	*Məšawweh raglay*[142] *kāʼayyālōt*	He made my feet like the feet of deer,
	wəʻal bāmōtay[143] *yaʻămîdēnî*	and set me secure on the (lit. "my") heights.

whilst Hab 3:19abc reads:

---

[139] Ps 18:33 [Eng 32], and 2Sam 22:33 4QSamª; similarly 2Sam 22:33 in Lucian, Syriac, and Vulgate. 2Sam 22:33 MT reads *māʻûzzî*.
[140] Thus Ps 18:33 [Eng 32], followed by the Syriac and Greek manuscripts of 2Sam 22:33; 2Sam 22:33 Hebrew has *wayyattēr*.
[141] Some manuscripts of Ps 18 and 2 Sam 22:33 kethib read here *darkô*, "his way", which seems less probable in this context (note the 1s sf in v. 33a; 34a of Ps 18 and 2Sam qere; and twice in Ps 18:34b, plus 2Sam 22:34b qere). The majority witness for Ps 18 Heb, as well as 2Sam qere, many Hebrew and Greek manuscripts, Syriac, Targum and Vulgate, favours the first person suffix.
[142] 2Sam 22:34 kethib has a ms suffix here, *raglâw*, "his feet", but the versions, qere, a few kethib, and Ps 18 favour the first person. See the previous note.
[143] Greek, Syriac, Jerome and 2Sam 22:34 Greek and Vulgate omit the suffix here; 2Sam 22:34 Heb agrees with Ps 18 in having the 1 sing suffix through the 3 ms suffix occurs in some manuscripts.

Yahweh 'ăḏōnāy ḥêlî	Yahweh Adonai is my strength;
wayyāśem raglay kā'ayyālôt	he makes my feet like the feet of deer,
wəʿal bāmôtay yadrikēnî	and makes me tread upon the heights.

Common points are: God (El or Yahweh Adonai) as a source of "strength" (ḥayil) for the speaker; "my feet like the feet of deer" (raglay kā'ayyālôt); the immediately following phrase weʿal bāmōtay ("on my [the?] heights"), accompanied by a 3ms hiphil with 1s sf, "he makes me (either stand or walk)"; and the root drk, either nominal (Ps 18:33b [Eng 32b] // 2Sam 22:33b) or verbal (Hab 3:19c). The sequencing is also the same in both, but for the inclusion of an extra colon in Ps 18:33b [Eng 32b] // 2Sam 22:33b, the content of which is not reproduced in Habakkuk 3:19, except for the use of the root drk.

The context in each case is the deity's personal protection of the psalmist, bestowing strength (ḥayîl) and security ("like the feet of deer"), following on from a powerful evocation of his appearance in the theophany, wielding his storm weapons and securing victory for his people. Trampling down "the heights" underfoot would not be compatible with the image of the nimble-footed deer (especially as these are does). However, "walking" or "treading" "on the heights" does fit with the impression that early Israelite warriors were at their strongest in ad hoc raids and guerrilla tactics in their home territory, the hills, where being fleet of foot and confident in that environment were vital skills.[144] This is reflected in 1Kgs 20:23, where the servants of the king of Aram are quoted as saying "Their gods are the gods of the hills, and so were stronger than we; but let us fight against them in the plain, and surely we shall be stronger than they".[145] However, it is particularly relevant to the Judean situation, since its settlements were chiefly in the highlands and Shephelah, rather than on the coastal plain dominated by Philistine cities.[146] This ties in also with the possessory connotations of drk. In Ps 18, the preceding verses focus on Yahweh's protection, loyalty and again conferral of skill and power (prowess) on the psalmist; though there is no mention of loyalty in Habakkuk 3, the aspect of equipping and protecting do seem most compatible with the context.[147]

A further possible association is provided by the other two occurrences of ʿal-bāmôt being accompanied by a causative verb giving Yahweh as the subject

---

[144] Cf. also reference to hiding in the hills, 1Sam 14:22, though also to Jonathan "slain upon your high places" (ʿal-bāmôtêkā ḥālāl), 2Sam 1:25.
[145] A similar impression is given by Josh 17:16,18, Judg 1:19.
[146] See, e.g. Faust 2013, 203–19.
[147] The following verses of Ps 18 similarly attribute to Yahweh giving the psalmist military skill, strength, salvation, protection, victory, and destruction of enemies.

and Israel as the direct object expressed as a suffix. These are found in the promise, "I will cause to ride/mount on the heights of the earth" in Isa 58:14 and Deut 32:13, each of which seem to be associated with the ample provision of food, which is elaborated in detail in the latter passage. Given the preceding affirmations about continuing trust in Yahweh even in the face of agricultural failure in Hab 3:17, this is a possible aspect of v. 19 which is not often considered.

Finally, Deut 33:29 may also be relevant to the understanding of Hab 3:19, since here Israel is promised that it shall tread on its enemies' backs in the only instance of the qal of *dārak* with a human subject together with *'al-bāmôt* (in this case, rather peculiarly, *'al-bāmôtêmô*). However, as Hab 3:19 specifically concerns "my heights" rather than "theirs", it might be thought to indicate freedom within one's own territory (a defensive aim) rather than incursion on others' (an offensive aim). In this respect, the sense of "enable me to make my stand / hold my ground"[148] proposed for the hiphil *ya'ămîdēnî* in Ps 18:34b [Eng 33] // 2Sam 22:34b might be suggestive as a possible nuance for the verb *yadrikēnî*, which stands in an equivalent position in Hab 3:19c, and it would also be compatible with the use of the personal suffix, "my heights". As in the other passages here discussed, such as Ps 18, in Deut 33:29 the context is one of protection and deliverance, though also triumph and domination.[149] Once again, theophanic features closely precede this allusion (in vv. 26–7) together with the highlighting of agricultural plenty (v. 28), so there is much here that offers suggested resonances with the present verse, Habakkuk 3:19.

Overall, then, Habakkuk 3:19 carries connotations of military strength and skill, accompanied by divine protection. The concern is not with crushing and trampling enemies, as has sometimes been thought, but rather with freedom and flourishing within one's own territory and the ability to 'hold one's ground' defensively. Associations with Yahweh's theophany and agricultural plenty may also be detected.

---

148 Briggs and Briggs 1906, 159; cf. (Qal) Am 2:15, 2Kgs 10:4, Mal 3:2, Judg 2:14. Briggs and Briggs suggest the meaning "battlefield" for *bāmāh*, but "heights" are not the most likely spot for whole armies to engage, despite the miltary context of 2Sam 1:19, 25. Rather, a natural elevation seems more likely, as something held and defended.

149 Cf. Sir 9:2 (Heb) where the aspect of interrelational (marital) power-dynamics seems to be foremost, though presumably without any suggestion of violence. For both the wife and the speaker of Hab 3:19, any attainment of dominance might be unexpected and contrary to the current order of things, but whether this is typical of this construction (hiphil *drk* + *'al bmwt* [+ possessive suffix]) or coincidental cannot be discerned from the two examples available.

2.3 Verses 13 – 4

2.3.1 Parallels to Ancient Near Eastern Combat Myths in Verses 13 – 4?

A distinctive feature of Habakkuk 3 is the density of language relating to warfare, with much reference to anger and weaponry, hence the idea that this is a divine warrior song. The aspect of direct combat with a specific foe comes especially to the fore in verses 13 – 4. Of course, this is seen by some as evidence that a *Chaoskampf* is depicted here, but closer inspection reveals that elsewhere when the language of wrath appears in connection with the theophany there is in many cases an evident human object,[150] whereas there is no instance where there is a clear expression of the *ḥārāh*, *'ap* or *'ebrāh* of God against the rivers or sea.[151] Likewise, although lightnings and arrows are common features of theophany appearances,[152] more detailed reference to weaponry (or less infrequently, warfare) is rare, but again characteristically has an explicitly mentioned human object.[153] More importantly, that the divine fury and anger was against the earth and nations has already been explicitly stated in verse 12.

Perhaps then, the Ugaritic texts can offer support in echoing the use of similar implements in divine combat? In fact, the evidence is not as favourable to this as one might expect. For example, *mṭ*, the Ugaritic equivalent to *maṭṭeh* "staff, shaft", is employed in about half a dozen instances, but only once clearly

---

[150] See Isa 30:27, 30; 59:17 – 8; 63:3 – 6, Jer 23:19, 30:23.
[151] In two cases the wrath of Yahweh is proximate to mention of water, in Nah 1:6 and Ps 18:8 [Eng 7], cf. Nah 1:2, Ps 18:9, 16 [Eng 8, 15]. However, in both the direction of his anger against human enemies is clear: see Watson 2005, 78 – 83, 373.
[152] As in Pss. 77:17 – 8, 18:14 [Eng 13] // 2Sam 22:14 (plus fire in vv. 8, 12), 144:6; lightnings and fire, Ps 97:3 – 4, cf. Ps 29:7.
[153] As in Isa 30:30 – 3, following the theophany especially in v. 27, 30, where the enemy is named as Assyria. Ps 68 again uses militaristic language of God, though without reference to named weapons, in combination with theophanic imagery, and the human nature of the foe is especially evident in vv. 12 – 5, 19. In Isa 59:17 Yahweh dons metaphorical armour against "his foes//his enemies// distant lands", which again indicates a human foe in the shape of foreign nations, but any theophanic colouring is quite slight. The violent imagery of Isa 63:1 – 7 similarly eschews reference to named weapons, yet again "peoples" are the object of his wrath (v. 6). One might compare also Ps 46:9, where he destroys (human) weaponry in the earth, although whether this is an aggressive or pacifist act is unclear. Finally, there is militaristic language, without reference to named weapons, in Deut 33:27, where some have seen mythological overtones in a possible reference to the "ancient gods"; however, this is not the only possible interpretation, as one might translate, e. g., with JPSA, "the ancient god is a refuge", as would suit the interest in dwelling "untroubled" in the land (v. 28) and prevailing over their enemies (v. 29).

as a weapon, and then by Anat towards people (*KTU* 1.3.ii 15);[154] the term also occurs once in the Baal-Yam cycle (*KTU* 1.2.ii 9) but as the sole intelligible word in the line, so it is difficult to draw any inference from it, especially as it is not later used in combat between the two main protagonists. Likewise, although the term *qšt* (equivalent to Hebrew *qešet*), "bow", does occur a number of times in the Ugaritic corpus, most of them are in the Aqhat texts, which is hardly a basis for assuming an innate (or even quite remote) connection with theomachic combat. This is not to deny that Baal was depicted as armed, most probably with the implements of the storm, not least on the famous Baal stele in which he appears to be carrying a lightning-spear and thunder-club, nor that theomachic combat was envisaged at times as potentially involving weaponry (though his struggle with Mot is depicted in theriomorphic terms[155]). However, it does indicate the importance of not assuming that mention of weapons—even those associated with the storm—necessarily implies reference to theomachic combat.

Notwithstanding this, it is sometimes claimed that the language of vv. 13cd–14ab in particular reflects the motif of God's battle with the chaos dragon.[156] The text here is very difficult, the versions do not always agree with the MT and numerous emendations have been proposed, some of which have allowed free expression of certain scholars' expectations of a *Chaoskampf* allusion here. However, the chief arguments are that the verbs *mḥṣ* and *nqb* and mention of certain body parts, especially the head, reflect traditions also seen in *Enuma Elish* and the Ugaritic Baal cycle,[157] and that *rāšāʿ* also echoes a description of Tiamat in *Enuma Elish* 4:83–4.

Against this, although Tiamat is accused of "wickedness" and "seeking evil", she is not referred to as the (or an) evil one, and Tsumura finds a better Akkadian parallel in the description of the goddess Anunitu as:

---

[154] Most of the occurrences are in relation to sexual behaviour in the Shachar and Shalim texts (*KTU* 1.23:37–8, 40, 44, 47), and there is a further example of relating to "a staff in/for his hand" (thus Wyatt, Gibson) apparently in readiness for a journey (*KTU* 1.19.iii 49, 56, iv 7).

[155] *KTU* 1.6.vi 16–22. Strikingly, in his combat with Yam it appears that it is Kothar-and Khasis who takes the initiative in supplying Baal with clubs and commissioning them to strike Yam once they had left his hand (and indeed, even in instructing Baal to fight) (*KTU* 1.2.iv.8–15,18–23). Clearly, though, his victory results in his kingship and in celebration and acclaim.

[156] Hiebert 1986, 103–5; Andersen 2001, 337–8.

[157] Hiebert 1986, 103; Irwin 1942, 29–30.

the lady of warfare, who carries the bow and the quiver, ... who annihilates the enemy, who destroys the evil one.[158]

In any case, *rāšāʿ* in Habakkuk 1:4, 13 clearly applies to a group of people, as opposed to the "righteous", and this is consistent with the use of the term elsewhere in the Hebrew Bible. (The singular can, of course, be used in a collective sense, as perhaps in Hab 1:4, 13; cf. also, e. g., Eccl 9:2, Ps 9:6, 17 [Eng 5, 16; cf. v. 18 (Eng 17)], 10:2, 55:4 [Eng 3]). Nor are Leviathan or Rahab so described anywhere in the Hebrew Bible, so it would be an otherwise unparalleled way of alluding to a dragon. Likewise, although *mḫṣ* in Ugaritic is indeed sometimes used of theomachic combat,[159] it is not exclusively so (for example, it occurs twice in Aqhat, in *KTU* 1.19.iii 47, iv 34), and Tsumura has pointed out that the Akkadian equivalent appears on monumental inscriptions, with "the head of the enemy" as its object.[160] More importantly, in Hebrew, there is just one instance of this verb being used of Rahab (Job 26:12), as opposed to numerous examples of a human enemy as the object. In particular, smiting the head occurs, outside Hab 3:13, in Ps 68:22, 110:6, whilst similar language is also used in Judg. 5:26 and Num 24:7, all of human enemies. Another passage with which Hab 3:13–4 finds echoes is Jer 23:19 and its near parallel in Jer 30:23:

> Lo, the tempest (*saʿārāh*) of Yahweh goes forth in fury (*ḥēmāh*),
> a whirling (23:19) / raging (30:23) tempest (both use the word *saʿar*).
> It shall whirl down on the head of the wicked (*rōʾš rašāʿîm*)[161]

Again, that the divine judgment is on human adversaries is very evident. It is noteworthy also that, here, as elsewhere,[162] the singular *rōʾš* is used of the heads of a plurality of people, as contrasted with Ps 74:14 where there are a plurality of heads of the singular Leviathan. It is sometimes also claimed that *nqb* (v. 14a) is indicative of theomachic combat, as the dragon is "pierced" in Ps 89:11, Job 26:13, Isa 51:11; however, the verb used in these instances is not *nqb*, but *ḥll*.[163] Finally, it can hardly be assumed that the mention of the "head" of the ad-

---

158 Tsumura 2005, 179; COS 2: 313.
159 Within the Baal and Mot cycles, it features in *KTU* 1.1.iii 27, 2.iv 9, 4.ii 24, 5.i 1, chiefly in speech.
160 He cites Warad-sin in COS 2: 251 (Tsumura 2005, 175 n. 53).
161 I have used my own translation here, to bring out the verbal repetitions in these verses.
162 E.g. Josh 7:6, Judg 9:57, Isa 35:10, 51:11, Jer 14:3.
163 Except in Job 40:24, 26, which may be regarded as the exception which proves the rule, since here the verbs are used in sarcastic questioning of whether it is possible to control and tame Leviathan or Behemoth as one might a less fearsome creature.

versary as the object of the victor's attention is of itself indicative of the chaos battle, since it is almost an inevitability of any attempt to slay someone; this is confirmed by the lack of correspondence with the different verbs used in connection with the head of Tiamat in *Enuma Elish*. Here Marduk "let loose an evil wind" in her face, then after overcoming her, "with his unsparing mace he crushed her skull".[164]

A final parallel has also been suggested between Hab 3:14a and *Enuma Elish* 4.130, since Marduk's "unsparing mace" or "merciless club" is a *miṭṭu*, akin to the Hebrew *maṭṭeh*. As we have seen, the verbs employed in these respective contexts do not correspond, and given the number of weapons referred to in Habakkuk 3, some overlap in terminology should not occasion surprise. The context in Hab 3:14a does not seem to be one of theomachic combat—laying bare in the previous colon has no parallel in combat myth and neither can any readily be extracted from the difficult two cola which follow—and the foe is not described in terms that correlate with a draconic identification.

2.3.2 Explaining the Language of Combat In Verses 13–4 and Beyond

Close dependence on ancient Near Eastern *Chaoskampf* myths cannot be demonstrated in Habakkuk 3:13–4, and even a meaningful relation between them seems doubtful, beyond broad cultural similarities, especially bearing in mind that warfare was an international pursuit. So how can the putative parallels, and especially the reference to the *maṭṭeh*, the head of the enemy, and the use of verbs communicating the idea of crushing or piercing, be explained?

The most straightforward answer is simply that the general correlations between references to combat, whether theomachic or between human enemies, are coincidental and to be expected. Any correspondences are general and loose, rather than indicating close verbal similarities between specific texts and would naturally have arisen through the context of the slaughter of an enemy, as well as being informed by shared practice.

More particularly, conventional language and concepts are almost certainly employed here, for example, involving *maṭṭeh* as the standard weapon of a god or king and reflective of his role and authority. Tsumura[165] cites a number of examples of the "bow" and "mace" being paired in Akkadian, in none of them in connection with the struggle with Tiamat, and the same pairing is used of Anat

---

164 *Enuma Elish* 4.130.
165 Tsumura 2005, 170–1.

in *KTU* 1.3.ii 15–6, again with human victims; Hab 3:9 of course provides another point of comparison. In some Akkadian texts, the mace is said to have 50 heads. This would cohere with its use to crush a skull (v. 13c), if this is what is intended, as well as certain iconographic presentations, but has to be held together with the apparent penetrative power of the Hebrew *maṭṭeh* in Hab 3:14.[166]

An intriguing but persuasive suggestion is that the sequence of weapons in Hab 3:8–15 broadly mirrors the order in which they might be employed in ancient warfare, as depicted on Assyrian and Egyptian reliefs,[167] with the psalm therefore conveying the unfolding of a battle. Long-, medium-, and short-range weapons would each be used in succession as the troops drew closer to each other and the battle unfolded. The principle at work here is encapsulated by the proverb of the Chinese strategist Sun Tzu, "The supreme art of war is to subdue the enemy without fighting" (*The Art of War* 2.2). A hail of arrows would permit the attackers to damage and frighten the enemy from a distance, ideally to the extent that the foe might withdraw, but it also had the advantage of enabling the aggressors to manoeuvre under cover, as the enemy would be ducking behind their shields to avoid the arrows. Next would come chariots, as a way of moving the archers closer for the next level of attack, and, once at medium range, they would also have had spears and javelins to throw. This could also be backed up by archers mounted on horseback. These were nimbler than a chariot, but of limited use in an era before stirrups because of lack of stability,[168] though Assyrian reliefs do show mounted archers working in pairs, with one man taking the reins of both horses while the other was able to focus on shooting arrows. Finally, infantry could attack with hand-weapons such as swords and axes or maces, before the enemy had recovered from the hail of arrows and spears.[169] At the climax might come the decapitation of the enemy.[170] Here in

---

166 "Make a hole in" or "having holes" (niphal, so "holed", i.e. "pierced") is the sense required for *nqb* in 2Kgs 12:10 [Eng 9] and Hag 1:6 respectively, while "cut, pierce" is the expected sense in 2Kgs 18:21 // Isa 36:3, Job 40:26 [Eng 41:2]. The verb in v. 13, *mḥṣ*, does not provide further clarity or corroboration, as it is used of the action of only two named weapons, namely, arrows (*ḥiṣṣîm*, Num 24:8) and the tent peg which penetrated Sisera's temple (Judg 5:26). Despite the difference of mechanism, piercing again may be the common thread. It is something done to the head, besides the latter verse, also in Ps 68:22 [Eng 21], 110:6, but at times seems to imply more general injury (Deut 32:39, Job 5:18) or slaying (2Sam 22:39 // Ps 18:49 [Eng 38], Ps 110:5). Perhaps, then, it has a specific sense, "pierce, penetrate" or "slay/injure by piercing", and a more general one, "injure, slay".
167 Lortie 2017, 125–8.
168 Hobbs 1989, 174.
169 I am immensely grateful to Lieutenant General Richard Nugee for explaining military strategy to me, which has informed this section of the chapter. See also Yadin 1963, 6–13.

Habakkuk 3, Yahweh himself is the sole agent of battle, wielding the full panoply of weapons as he engages with the enemies himself, rather than supporting or enabling his people in their fight. However, a broadly similar sequence may be discernible, as Yahweh's bow (v. 9a, 11b) gives way to his javelin (v. 9b) and spear or other shaft-borne weapon (v. 11c, 14a) and perhaps a mace (v. 13c), by vv. 13–4 apparently in individual combat.

The poem may also mirror the sequence of chariots (v. 8d), cavalry (v. 15) and infantry—or at, least, standing one's ground on the heights (v. 19), which is something evidently achieved on foot. Alternatively, one might think of Yahweh as the supreme king accomplishing his victory chiefly from his chariot. Assyrian reliefs show chariots bearing archers, but with a spear or other long-handled weapon carried vertically at the back of the vehicle, ready for an ensuing stage in the battle.[171] A short-range weapon may also often have been to hand for close combat by the charioteer later still in the battle, as is suggested by a papyrus recording the experience of an Egyptian courier in Canaan:

> A coward steals your bow, your dagger and your quiver. Your reins are cut in the darkness. Your horse is gone and starts to run away over the slippery ground, as the the road stretches out before him. He smashes your chariot …. Your weaons have fallen to the ground…[172]

The account of Caesar invading Britain well illustrates the versatility and importance of chariot-based warfare, albeit from a later era and geographically remote location:

> Their mode of fighting with their chariots is this: firstly, they drive about in all directions and throw their weapons and generally break the ranks of the enemy with the very dread of their horses and the noise of their wheels; and when they have worked themselves in between the troops of horse, leap from their chariots and engage on foot … Thus they display in battle the speed of horse, [together with] the firmness of infantry.[173]

Read as the depiction of a battle, with typical sequences and ranges of weapons, the reference to rivers and churning water might also attain new significance, since battles often took place near rivers.[174] It has to be recalled that, unless they had been channelled by humans (which is only likely near settlements)

---

170 Yadin 1963, 445.
171 Yadin 1963, 380, 386, 388 (from Ashurnasipal II's palace in Nimrud, 883–859 BCE), 402–3 (from the gates of Shalmaneser III, 858–824 BCE).
172 Yadin, 1963, 89.
173 Gallic Wars 4.33.
174 E.g. Judg 5:19, 2Kgs 3:22, 2Chr 20:15, 35:20.

or flowed through rock, most natural watercourses would have had marsh either side of them in this period, as they were not well-defined by man-made boundaries. "Mud is the epitaph of soldiers",[175] so this hazard would have afforded a means of defending an army's position and limiting avenues for attack[176] either as flank protection, or by remaining on the opposite side of a river from the enemy,[177] thus forcing the foe to withold an assault or to make themselves vulnerable in the attempt. Another useful strategy could be to drive the opposing army towards the river, or most effectively, into the mud and marsh, which would slow their escape[178] and ensure that they would be much easier to slaughter. For those fleeing in defeat, once they had crossed, a river could restrict the capacity of the opposing side to continue their pursuit—as, most famously, at the Re[e]d Sea, though this is hardly a typical scenario.[179]

The imagery of horses and torrents is already familiar from the battle scene of Judg 5:2–21, though there the waters, like the stars, fight on Yahweh's side. Here Yahweh alone acts in might, without discernible human involvement and possibly also without active agency from other forces being depicted in a direct way. However, the terror and noise of a charging chariot should be seen as a key aspect of his assault (v. 8d), though in this case, the onslaught is intensified by the addition of the voice of the deep (v. 10c). Splitting the earth with rivers might include a strategic aspect, with water courses restricting the activity of the enemy, cutting them off or limiting their capacity to attack or escape. The horses (and quite plausibly implicitly also chariots) surging through the waters would demonstrate the unique power of Yahweh, able to maintain his assault—or departure in victory—irrespective of the natural barriers that would limit human combatants. This is not necessarily the only aspect of the role of the waters in

---

[175] Richard Nugee, personal communication; cf. Exod 14:25.
[176] Hence, for example, the Hittites' choice of Kadesh, on the Orontes, to engage in battle with Egypt (see Yadin 1963, 104, 109).
[177] For example, a river offered a relatively safe place for encampment the night before battle: see Gen 32:22–3, Exod 14:2 (*'al-hayyām*), Judg 7:1; and compare also Josh 8:11 (*haggay bênâw* [qere]).
[178] Yadin, 1963, 442–3, 444–5, re Ashurbanipal's victory over the Elamaites on the River Ulai (from the southwest palace at Nineveh, c 668–630 BCE); cf. also the battle of Kadesh, where the Hittite infantry were able to cross the river Orontes to safety, but not without leaving the chariots behind, thus limiting their capacity to launch a further attack (Yadin, 1963, 104–5, 108). Hobbs (1989, 170) reconstructs a similar scenario in respect of Judg 4–5, with the Israelites using the terrain to their advantage by descending on their bechariotted enemies from the hill, then driving them into the mud of the flooded Kishon (4:14–6, 5:19, 21).
[179] Cf. also 1Sam 30:10. Hab 3 could be read as a recollection of the Re[e]d Sea event, but this is not certain.

the poem: the common aspect of distress at the theophany and possible involvement of natural forces in the assault have already been discussed, as has the potential for the exodus crossing to have had some influence as the occasion of salvation from a fearsome army par excellence. However, its presence as part of the explicit and tangible portrayal of the battle scene in this composition also needs to be integrated more seriously into the interpretation here, instead of attention being diverted by the question of how or whether the sea might be understood as the foe.

A further military feature of the poem, occurring in verse 19, is the principle that "'dominate the high ground' is the mantra of every soldier throughout the ages".[180] There are three principal reasons for this: first, there is a huge psychological advantage to being higher, as the tall man towering over the smaller. Anyone attacking would have to fight going uphill, thus being placed at a psychological disadvantage in having to "look up" to the army on the dominating higher ground. Second, it is more exhausting fighting uphill. The body is designed to look straight or look down: humans are not built constantly to look up, let alone run with equipment uphill. In addition to the psychological and physical advantage to taking a stand on "the heights", there is also a strategic one. Those fighting from the high ground have the benefit of time, since by stationing themselves at a visual vantage point, they are able to see further and watch what the enemy is doing; it is less easy to be surprised for the same reason, and in practical terms the enemy toiling uphill is an easier target: whereas it is possible to crouch and create a smaller target if you are firing down, the attacking forces would have to expose themselves to shoot up. Particularly important, given the positioning of verse 19 at the end of the poem, is the truism that once an army has attained control of the high ground, it is much harder to dislodge: "once you have won you keep the high ground as you now have all the advantage".[181] The psalmist here looks forward to a time when he (with his people) is not just saved, but secure and in a position of strength, from which any potential future assaults will be less threatening.

However, a crucial aspect of this poem is the central role of Yahweh. Here, he seems to operate as the sole agent against the enemies, yet it should be recalled

---

180 Richard Nugee, personal communiction. Examples are numerous, from Saxon forts to Wellington's position at Waterloo on a high ridge; the battle of Cassino in Italy in WW2 when the Germans stopped the British 8th Army for weeks from the high ground of the monastery; the crusader and Saladin's castles in Jordan (Kerak, Aljoun); the Cathar castle of Queribus in the south of France; the Jews' last stand at Masada. All are on high dominating ground, and this is just a fraction of the examples that could be cited.
181 Richard Nugee, personal communication.

that in the ancient Near East, warrior-kings provided not just functional leadership but also symbolic and patriotic focus for their armies. The inspired their troops by their presence at the head on the battlefield and, conversely, provoked demoralisation and desertion if they were slain.[182] Yahweh, as the divine warrior, then, is the warrior-king *par excellence*, assuring his people of victory (vv. 8e, 13ab), whilst the "head" of the enemy remains a particular focus for attack (vv. 13c, 14a).

Overall, therefore, rather than attempting to read the detail of warfare and strategy, weapons and action displayed in Habakkuk 3 as an attempt to emulate specfic mythical texts and traditions from elsewhere, they are more meaningfully and reliably to be interpreted in the light of broader military practice. As such, they can be understood as communicating Yahweh's status as warrior God fighting on behalf of his people against his enemies, at the end of which they are "secure" (v. 19). If a play on the language of *Enuma Elish* were to be discerned in Hab 3:13, therefore, it might best be construed as an ironic allusion in order to describe Yahweh's destruction of the Babylonians. Marduk was supposed to have slain Tiamat, symbolic of all Babylon's enemies, thus; but actually Yahweh will so treat Babylon. If so, the emblematic expression of victory by Babylonia's god against its enemies is harnessed to communicate its defeat. Such a theological point might attain especial force on the basis of 2:18–20. Here the worship of graven or cast images is dismissed on the basis that they are merely lifeless human products, in contrast to Yahweh, before whom all the earth should keep silence. This assertion immediately precedes the prayer of chapter 3, which looks forward to the destruction of Yahweh's enemies and mocks the idea that his battle should be with the sea.

This last point brings us back conveniently to the very question with which we began, "Was your wrath against the rivers?", to which the author of Habakkuk 3 seems to want us to answer with such a resounding negative. Why is this so? Presumably, this rhetoric is aimed either at those who thought that Yahweh's wrath was against the rivers (or perhaps River, though Yam is not referred to thus except in combination with his primary name), or at others, whether inside Israel

---

[182] This point is well made by Hobbs 1989, 168, citing Thutmosis III's leadership of his troops through the Aruna Pass and Rameses II's personal valour at Kadesh and, negatively, both the death of Ahab in 1Ki 22:29–36 (who, according to 2Chr 18:34, remained propped up in his chariot facing the Arameans all day before dying at sunset, presumably at or after the close of battle) and Ehud's tactic of marching against the Moabites immediately after throwing them into disarray by killing their king (Judg 3). The centrality of the king in war is embodied also in ancient Near Eastern war monuments, in which the king is presented as supreme and "completely self-sufficient" in a way that reflects ideological rather than military reality (Wright 2020, 237–9).

or out, who celebrated (or wished to celebrate) the battle of another deity with the sea. But Yahweh alone is the holy one before whom all the earth should stand in awe (2:20), and as other gods are mere idols, products of human maufacture (2:18–9), then there is no place for theomachic combat.[183] Rather, his action has a thoroughly terrestrial and political focus, for, in the words of vv. 12–3, "you tread the earth in rage and trample the nations in fury. You come forth to deliver your people, to deliver your anointed".

---

183 Without wishing to instigate a debate on the nature of the allusion to Rahab in Isa 51:9, it should at least be uncontroversial to distinguish between the slaying of a draconic figure that is not even attested outside Israel, but has affinities with Leviathan / Ltn, and true theomachic combat with an "active deity" such as Yam (Handy 1994).

Part II: **Continuing the Dialogue on Habakkuk 3**

Rebecca S. Watson
Response to Adrian Curtis

I am grateful to Adrian for his willingness to debate with me on our interpretations of Habakkuk 3, both at a SOTS conference in 2012 and now in the present volume. My sense is that this discussion has revealed not only points on which we concur but also dimensions in which our interpretations are perhaps not as sharply opposed as at first might appear. At the same time, the exercise has also perhaps brought into sharper focus those areas on which agreement is more elusive. I hope in what follows to reflect on these differences with the aim of identifying common ground and ways in which the debate might develop in the future, rather than, in the spirit of *Chaoskampf*, perpetuating the cycle of academic combat.[1]

However, as Adrian began his paper by outlining key areas where he thinks I might be wrong, then it seems apposite for me to respond to these directly. Part of my intention in so doing will be for clarification, defence and persuasion, but it is also exactly in tackling these core points of perceived disagreement that the issues underlying our differences will emerge.

1 Areas of Critique by Adrian Curtis

First, Adrian quotes me as observing a tendency among scholars "to force the Hebrew material into a '*Chaoskampf*' straitjacket, and in particular to place disproportionate emphasis on comparisons with Babylonian and Canaanite (especially Ugaritic) mythology".[2] I'd like to stand by this absolutely, as it is so pervasive. Very often, such putative connections are assumed rather than demonstrated, and passed on through the secondary literature without further examination. A classic example comes in relation to *mayim rabbîm*, since it is common for commentary writers, instead of discussing this phrase, simply to refer to the article by H.G. May, "Some Cosmic Connotations of Mayim Rabbim" with mini-

---

[1] Perhaps such a predisposition is a subconscious influence in my interpretative tendencies, just as battle may be a more natural model for some of my more combative colleagues. There must be a thesis waiting to be written on personality and interpretation, which might subvert (or at least relativise) the "findings" of us all.
[2] Above, p. 13; Watson 2005, 2.

mal further comment.³ However this article makes some dubious assumptions which I have explored in more detail elsewhere.⁴

I would also like to question the wisdom of explaining allusions with reference to comparative material *before* or *instead of* other biblical occurrences of the same language. Nonetheless by some such circularity is virtually elevated to the status of a methodological principle. For example, Mowinckel's working assumption was that: "*A priori*, we could expect Israel … to have a cult whose basic elements would be the same as those of neighbouring peoples … Where the Old Testament texts contain only casual and vague allusions … the picture can be successfully completed by analogies from the cults of neighbouring peoples".⁵ Similarly, Wakeman, in her book *God's Battle with the Monster*, seeks to "read with an eye to *possible* allusions to the myth".⁶ She thinks in terms of a single myth which, despite considerable diversity both in form and content and divergence through space and time, was nevertheless still "felt as the same myth"⁷ since "the various ways of telling the same story all serve the same function—it is basically *the same* story"⁸. Hence, where a particular iteration of "the myth" (e.g., in the Ugaritic or biblical material) diverges from "the pattern derived from the myths summarised earlier", she proposes "using this as a hypothesis, [to] see if an arrangement of the facts to fit it is plausible"⁹ Her aim is for "a level of generalization"¹⁰ that seeks meaning in "the essential structure of the myth",¹¹ not to attend to the specifics of the extant biblical references, to understand their nuances or to plot the subtleties of the interactions with other iterations. Whereas I would contend that the key to intepreting a passage is precisely in identifying what is different and distinctive in its use of tradition and specific to its particular context, without denying the existence of some commonalities within the West Semitic world, Wakeman finds meaning in the general and universal, regardless of the specifics. As a result, any sense of trajectory or dialogue, of traditions having been shaped in the service of a

---

3 E.g., on Ps. 29:3, Dahood 1966, 177, Terrien 2003, 277, Anderson 1972, 236.
4 Watson 2005, 57–9.
5 Mowickel 1951, 1: 16.
6 Wakeman 1973, 65; her italics.
7 Wakeman 1973, 4.
8 Wakeman 1973, 103; her italics
9 Wakeman 1973, 37.
10 Wakeman 1973, 5.
11 Wakeman 1973, 5.

new situation, or of seeking to identify the rhetorical intention and theological message of each passage, is simply ignored.¹²

It hardly needs to be stated that there are a lot of unexamined assumptions in such an approach, not least that Israelite and Judean religion may have been effectively monolithic across time and different social groups (or at least that the differences are inconsequential), and that it may be simultaneously equated with both the wider ancient near Eastern and the narrower biblical tradition. The possibility is not examined that the battle with chaos may in Israel and/or Judah, at least in some circles, have been attributed to a deity other than Yahweh (such as Baal), or reframed in order to present a fresh vision of reality, or even—by some of the groups behind the Bible—polemically denied in anything other than a historicised form; and in fact, the emphasis in such discussions as Wakeman's or Mowinckel's seems to be on the retrieval of a history of religion behind certain texts rather than a careful exegesis of these texts read according to their rhetorical intentions.

In my view, it is much more helpful to recognise the variations in portrayals of the gods' engagement with the waters as revealing important distinctions in the theology, worldview and socio-political experiences of their mythmakers. To read them all collectively as effectively indistinguishable is to abandon oneself to the myopia of hindsight, incapable of recognising this imagery as a form of language in which to express different visions of the world and of the place of order, disorder and various divine powers within it. Obviously, the degree to which this occurs varies between interpreters. Few are as explicit about their working assumptions as Wakeman, yet the habit of adopting a history-of-religions approach to the interpretation of a passage such as Habakkuk 3 is deeply established as a norm, desensitising us to the nuances of its language and to its independent manipulation of earlier traditions. The immediate assumption by the majority of interpreters that the answer to the question, "Was thy wrath against the rivers?" must be affirmative is one example of the subconscious bias in this area which is simply a current norm.

Adrian also quotes me as saying, "the association of chaos with each of these motifs—battle and an act of creation—must now be contested, the former in every supposed instance, the latter in the majority".¹³ In this, I do not think we are as far apart as first appears, since my sense is that our differences are at least in part ones of definition. As I understand it, a battle entails physical conflict

---

12 The ideological and historical, geographical and political specificity of different iterations of conflict myth is something that is increasingly recognised: see especially Ballentine 2015 and Tugendhaft 2013; also Pitard 2013 re the Ugaritic context and Miller 2013 re the Judean.
13 Above, p. 13; Watson 2005, 2–3.

between two or more opponents; hence the domination or control of one power by another does not necessarily involve a battle. Although there are allusions in the Old Testament to waters fleeing or dragons being slain, there is no mention of such agents issuing a challenge, or attempting to assault God, or even acting in self-defence. Their active opposition to God is nowhere unequivocally stated; nor is there any indication that God's destruction or "ordering" of them is a reaction to their behaviour.[14]

Furthermore, if one consults the comparative evidence, it seems that essential to any "combat-myth"—at least outside the Old Testament—are the motifs of the genuineness of the struggle and the real risk of defeat, a particularly vivid example of this being furnished by *KTU* 1.6.vi.16–22:

> They eye each other like fighters,
> Mot is fierce, Baal is fierce.
> They gore each other like buffalo,
> Mot is fierce, Baal is fierce.
> They bite each other like serpents,
> Mot is fierce, Baal is fierce.
> They drag each other like runners,
> Mot falls, Baal falls.[15]

This is not to deny that the sea or a dragon may appear as an "enemy" of God, of the same order as the nations which they often represent; it may also be the case that the waters surrounding the earth have to be restrained by his power. However, it appears that the presence of "combat" themes in such contexts cannot simply be presupposed and in many cases, such a claim is self-evidently inapporpriate. Any attempt to interpret the references concerned according to this pattern must therefore first be justified on the basis of detailed textual support.

What, then, of chaos and creation? Am I right in thinking that a connection should not automatically be assumed? Again, there are issues of definition, as I would wish to distinguish between an originating act of creation (though not necessarily *ex nihilo*) and the maintenance of the created order, as indeed would Adrian. It is also important to attempt to untangle the logical connections

---

14 This has already been recognised by certain scholars in respect of specific passages. For example, Mark Smith remarks of Ps. 104:5–9 that "there is no real battle to speak of"; indeed, "the waters ... are changed from a negative, hostile force into a positive material of creation" (Smith 2004, 96). Similarly, "Genesis 1 evidently transforms creation by conflict into creation by the word ... Accordingly, Genesis 1 omits not only the conflict but also any personification of the cosmic waters. With no hint of conflict or even hostility, God speaks (not even rebukes), and the divine will is achieved " (Smith 2004, 97).
15 Translation from Smith 1997, 162.

between allusions standing in proximity to each other: if a reference to Yahweh's restraint of the sea occurs close to mention of an act associated with creation (whether originating or sustaining), does it mean that the connection is *necessarily* sequential or reverse-sequential (i.e., that bringing creation into being is subsequent to and dependent on the defeat of a chaos-dragon, even where no dragon is mentioned)? May not the link rather be logical and thematic (i.e., may it lie in the idea of acts of divine power and cosmic ordering)? Adrian has already alluded to the lack of any connection between Baal's subjugation of Yam and creation in the extant Ugaritic texts, and in many of the biblical passages where an allusion to a struggle with Chaos is commonly identified, any hint of creation is likewise also missing—not least in Habakkuk 3. What I am calling for, then, is caution before jumping to over-hasty conclusions about references to "the myth" and what it might contain in any particular context.

Adrian also quotes me as saying that "nowhere in the Old Testament ... is the sea manifested as a personal being, and nowhere does Yahweh engage in conflict with it".[16] Hopefully, my reasons for the second part of this statement—the lack of what may truly be defined as "engaging in conflict"—should by now be clear. As regards the first part, the claim that the sea is not manifested as a personal being, first of all, I would wish to distinguish the sea from Leviathan and Rahab and any "dragon" (*tannîn*) which might be *in* the sea. I do not think there are grounds in the Hebrew Bible for equating these different entities, however unclear the distinction may be in many modern minds; and, further, I am not aware of anything in the Ugaritic texts indicating that Yam should be identified with Lotan, still less Rahab, either. The second aspect which needs to be clarified is that personification is not the same as existing as a personal being, though sometimes the distinction may be a difficult one to make and there may be a degree of subjectivity in discerning the force of a particular reference. However, when the sea roars and the mountains or trees sing joyfully together at the presence of Yahweh in Pss. 96 and 98, or the sea/Jordan fled and the mountains/hills skipped when they saw him in Ps. 114, it is very difficult to maintain that the aquatic elements of creation are qualitatively different from the terrestrial in the degree of personification or "personhood" attributed to them.

I suspect, therefore, from Adrian's paper, that we are more in agreement over many of these issues than first appears and that our differences are ones of degree rather than being based on a fundamentally divergent approaches or incompatible presuppositions. My sense is that that we sit at different points along the same spectrum, rather than in opposing camps.

---

16 Above p. 14; Watson 2005, 4.

2 A Response to Adrian's Proposals

As regards Adrian's own proposals, my impression is that he has sought to be moderate and reasonable, often finding a "middle way" between different views and eschewing some of the more exaggerated claims among those he has surveyed. There is therefore much in this consensual approach with which I can concur. Aside from the question of the conflict with the waters, Adrian concludes that "the passage certainly describes a theophany—probably one rather than two. The primary image is that of the divine warrior. The chapter may contain some archaic language and certainly some mythic language".[17] I agree on all of these points.

He also states that "there are allusions to mythological motifs other than the 'waters' which might be referred to as 'Canaanite', a possibility which might make it more likely that references to the waters might reflect Canaanite ideas".[18] Here our differences are more subtle, since I would tend to see the use of traditional "Canaanite" language here as a means of asserting a distinctive message in dialogue with ideas current in the broader North-West Semitic context as well as in Israel and Judah.[19] This could include the possibility of engagement with notions that might, for example, have comprised part of some religious thinking or practice in neighbouring territories, quite possibly including Israel (and even Judah itself),[20] and which may have gained greater currency[21] or

---

[17] Above, p. 25.

[18] Above, p. 25.

[19] For evidence of the worship of Baal in Israel and Judah through to the end of both kingdoms, see, e.g., 2 Chron 28:2, 2 Ki. 21:3 // 2 Chron. 33:3, 2 Ki. 23:4, Jer. 2:8, 7:9, 9:13, 12:16, Zeph. 1:4 and Smith 2002, 75.

[20] For the "convergence" of different divine attributes and functions in to the person of Yahweh during the late monarcy and subsequently, see Smith, 2001, 163.

[21] Albertz, for example, notes an increase in religious pluralism and syncretism in the seventh century (Albertz 1994, 188–94). Factors here, in addition to the theological pressure of impending or actual crisis, might include the influx of exiles from Syria and Babylonia brought into Israel after the fall of Samaria, replacing the local population who were removed elsewhere and bringing with them ideas that may previously have been less prominent in that part of Palestine (2Ki 17:29–31). Further, there was the incorporation of aspects of the Assyrian state cult in the Temple of Jerusalem (2Ki 16.1–16, 25:5,11) and other apsects of Assyrian religion, together with Aramean influences, on popular religious practice (Albertz 1994, 189–90). The possible movement of northern Levitical priests (and others) into Jerusalem in the wake of the same events provides another likely theological influence.

been more under debate in Judah[22] after the fall of Samaria and other cities to the Assyrians (or indeed—given the thrust of Habakkuk[23]—to the Babylonians),[24] but which were later rejected by the Jerusalemite Temple hierarchy.

The tone of religious polemic is already explicit in 2:12–20, which immediately precedes the psalm of chapter 3, and mockery of making offerings to a worthless object of worship is also implicit in 1:16. Whether or not Habakkuk 3 was moulded from a prior composition or simply drew on archaic ideas and motifs, there is no reason to doubt its appropriateness to the context or indeed its perceived consistency with the rest of Habakkuk's message. Therefore, the explicitly and vehemently anti-idolatry sentiment contained in the preceding two chapters provides an illuminating hint of the perspective we should expect to find within it.

Sitting between 1:16 and 2:12–20 is a reference to Death, which, though pointed as *māwet* in the MT, at the very least is personified and behaves in a way that is entirely recognisable of Mot (2:5cd):

> They open their throats wide as Sheol;
>   like Death they never have enough.[25]

Hence, we arguably have already before chapter 3 the presence of imagery and ideas drawn from the traditional North-West Semitic thought-world and repertoire, which are likely to have been a feature of the originator's heritage,[26] maybe drawn from its slightly unorthodox margins or "borrowed" from "Canaan". In its current position, it seems to be a figure of speech, a rhetorical point of comparison, rather than necessarily reflecting the apparatus of divine

---

[22] Of especial relevance are issues expressed in the tradition of Josiah's reform, in which the exclusivity and purity of Yahwistic worship over against practices which had previously been tolerated, either in the worship of other gods or in relation to Yahweh himself, are central; cf. e.g. Jer. 2:26–8 for the apparent shaming of the whole nation for religious practices now felt to be unacceptable. For the disjunction between prophetic religion and actual practice, even on an official level, see, e.g., Smith 2002, 163.

[23] See especially 1:6–11, 2:14–7.

[24] Hess notes the "increase in domestic cultic activity, perhaps reflecting a movement toward the worship of a variety of deities in such cultic contexts" which occurred towards the fall of both kingdoms (Hess 2007, 312) and the appearance of additional cult centres "at village sites, along trade routes, and in alternative nonconformist contexts" during the eighth to sixth centuries BCE (Hess 2007, 314).

[25] The NRSV, quoted here, is misleading, as the subject, the "arrogant man" is described in the singular as opening his throat and, like Death, as not being satisfied.

[26] Cf., for example, the apparently theophoric names *'azmāwet* (2Sam. 23:31, 1Chron. 27:25) and *'ăḥîmôt* (1Chron. 6:10).

conflict with Mot as an immediate article of belief.²⁷ This example may therefore provide an indication of how we might expect to interpret terms occurring in chapter 3 which are both used as the names of specific divine or quasi-divine beings familiar from the Ugaritic texts and as common nouns.

Thus, interpreters of Habakkuk 3 are equipped with clear evidence from the earlier chapters of this book both of anti-idolatrous sentiment of the kind employed by Deutero-Isaiah in the service of arguably the most explicitly monotheistic sentiments in the Hebrew Bible, as well as of the metaphorical employment of a common Northwest Semitic religious motif in the service of the prophet's (or author's) own message. Whether or not this poetic oracle originally comprised, or was moulded from, a separate composition there is no reason to doubt its appropriateness to the context or indeed its perceived congruence with the rest of Habakkuk's message. Therefore, when we encounter similar linguistic features in its verses, we might expect to find a consistent polemic, with prior motifs being moulded to a distinctively—and, most likely, "orthodox"—Yahwistic agenda.

3 "Was thy Wrath Against the Rivers?"

Adrian ends his paper with the question with which I began, and this is perhaps where our differences come into sharpest focus. Adrian quotes GKC and Gibson,²⁸ who comment on the use of *hă ... 'im* for emphasis but do not evaluate the answer which is implied by the framing questions this way, as if this omission settles the question of the force of the structure. However, one only has to turn to BDB to find this combination of particles defined either as (i) "expressing a real alternative" and (ii) "more often, expressing a merely formal alternative, especially in poetry (a rhetorical *Num?*)". In accordance with this, the negative form *hălō'* is also recognised by a number of grammarians and lexicographers as equivalent to the Latin *nonne?*²⁹ However, irrespective of the claims or omis-

---

27 In fact, as observed by Haak (1992, 49), the idea of an enemy "swallowing" his victim is a common metaphor in the Hebrew Bible: Hab. 1:8, 13, 16, 2:4, 5, 13, 16; cf. Jer. 51:34, 44, Prov. 1:12. For the rapacity of Sheol, compare Isa 5:14, Prov. 1:16, 30:16, cf. Ps. 141:7 and see Tromp 1969, 104–7, Johnston 2002, 28–9. The association of Death with swallowing (now reversed) is most apparent in Isa 25:8 (cf. also Odes of Solomon 29:4), but it is personified also in Isa 28:15, 18, Jer. 9:20 [Eng 21], Hos. 13:14, Ps. 18:5–6 [Eng 4–5], 2 Sam. 22:5–6, Rev. 21:4, cf. Odes of Solomon 15:9.
28 Above, p. 26.
29 Thus Joüon 1996, 2: 334; 3: 610; van der Merwe, Naudé and Kroeze 1999, 322; Gesenius and Rüterswörden 1987, 1: 70 (MIa II. 1.).

sions in the secondary literature—even in such established authorities as GKC and Gibson—, when seeking to discern the meaning of this (or any) phrase, it is of far more value to conduct a careful examination of the primary literature than simply to rely without further critical evaluation on whatever has previously been asserted. I have therefore conducted a thorough search of every instance of the construction *hă ... 'im* in the Hebrew Bible and found that the evidence is consistent and unequivocal: this phrase always either indicates real alternatives or anticipates an emphatic negative in response.[30] (It perhaps scarcely needs to be explained that the negative forms *hă ... lō' ... [wə]'im ... lō'* anticipate a double negative, and hence an affirmative, reply.[31]) Although this may come as a surprise to anyone immersed in the commentaries on Hab. 3:8, the wholly consistent use of the question form *hă ... 'im* everywhere else in the Hebrew Bible[32] should weigh very heavily in the effort to discern the force of this verse. In my view, in the absence of overwhelming indications to the contrary, it simply requires that we accept that the implied answer is negative even if this entails a re-evaluation of the interpretation of this verse and hence of the whole passage in which it occurs.

I do not disagree with Adrian's view that the poem displays awareness of the motif of conflict with the waters or that "the motif was well known and meaningful, and could be used in a nuanced way to allude to an actual enemy, in all probability the Babylonians".[33] I also think that he is absolutely correct in affirming that "the hearers or readers of Habakkuk 3 ... needed assurance that Yahweh ... could defeat powerful enemies. That seems to be the key point at issue in this chapter".[34] Where we would differ is that where Adrian would see an overlap between Yahweh's conflict with the sea and his hoped-for deliverance of his people from the Babylonians, I would see a denial of his combat with the sea, at least in this crucial moment for Israel, though possibly also more broadly, and a strong assertion of the deity's focus on his imperial foe. In this activity he is manifested as the warrior God found of old in the march from the southland, causing turmoil in his wake and exhibiting his power in earthquake and storm and casting his arrows as weapons against the enemy. However, the reason for his intervention is stated explicitly in verse 13:

---

[30] Watson 2019, 437–55.
[31] E.g. Jer. 5:9, 22, 29, 8:4, 9:8 [Eng 9]. See also p. 42 n. 66 above and pp. 122–4 of the Appendix.
[32] This includes Ugaritic evidence from the equivalent construction "[] ...*hm* ...": see Held 1969, 71–9.
[33] Above, p. 26.
[34] Above, p. 27.

> You came forth to save your people,
> to save your anointed.

This assertion is framed by mention of Yahweh "in anger ... trampl[ing] nations" (v. 12) and by the piercing of the head of his warriors

> who came like a whirlwind to scatter us,
> gloating as if ready to devour the poor who were in hiding. (v. 14)

The human foe is also directly in view in the prophet's expression of hope:

> I wait quietly for the day of calamity
> to come upon the people who attack us. (v. 16)

As is common with divine manifestations in the storm and as warrior God, this has an effect on the waters, as on the land, but his lordship over watercourses and seas is already established, whereas his power over the hostile nation(s) needs to be (re)asserted. Yahweh split the earth with rivers (v. 9), because is action is on and against the "earth" (v. 9c; cf. vv. 6a, 12a) and the rivers are tools at his disposal, along with other watery forces, in the storm. The mountains writhed in anguish (v. 10a; cf. v. 6cde), but the "rainstorm" passed over as an instrument of the deity in the force of the tempest (v. 10); he marched on/trod (ṣʿd) the earth and trampled/threshed (dûš) the nations (v. 12), but merely trod / walked (drk) on the sea (v. 15). In addition, he smote through/shattered (mḥṣ) the head of the wicked house, laying it bare/slaying (ʿrh) it from base to neck (v. 13), piercing (nqb) ... the head of his warriors (v. 14): for, as is stated within the text itself, the foe against whom the divine warrior marches is human.

Adrian H. W. Curtis
Response to Rebecca Watson

I am very grateful to Rebecca Watson for her comments on this passage. I can certainly agree on some points, in whole or in part, but there are other observations which I find less convincing. Let me pick up on a few points from her argument by way of response. The danger of "parallelomania" is certainly something to be avoided. She is right that it is important not to assume that, just because ideas or concepts stand in proximity to one another, there is necessarily a consequential relationship, for example, between conflict and creation, and it should be stressed that where there is one element common to two traditions, it does not necessarily mean that other elements are also common. Whereas in *Enuma Elish* Marduk's conflict with Tiamat is followed by an account of his creative activity, this is not the case with the Ugaritic myth of Baal's defeat of Yam, and it is more likely that El was believed to be the creator at Ugarit. (It is, of course, important to be clear about the definition of "creation" in any context —*creatio ex nihilo*, creation from a preexisting state, or the establishment of order.) The danger of forcing material into a straitjacket is a real one.

There may be some truth in the suggestion that it is important to prioritise consideration of inner biblical parallels or evidence, rather than those from elsewhere in the ancient Near East. But there is surely also a place for being aware of the possibility of a wider thought-world of ideas in addition to verbal parallels. It seems risky to assume that concepts were necessarily restricted to the religious thought or mythology of a particular people or narrow region. The interchange of ideas may have gone alongside the interchange of, e.g., trade. In this context, I refer again, as I did previously, to Julia O'Brien's reference to the portrayal of Yahweh in Habakkuk 3 as "drawing from the well of ancient Near Eastern mythological motifs".[1] This seems to be an apposite comment, and to allow for the use of such motifs in different genres of material. There may also have been a tendency to over-emphasise the possibility of direct, literary borrowing, implying knowledge of texts in written or oral form, rather than a more general awareness of, and reflection of, such mythological motifs.

Rebecca suggests a tendency to place a "disproportionate" amount of emphasis on comparisons with Babylonian and Canaanite, especially Ugaritic, mythology. There may be an element of truth in this, though it would depend on what is disproportionate! It can hardly be denied that this material has of-

---

[1] O'Brien 2004, 82.

fered new horizons within which to read the biblical texts. The Hebrew Bible was surely the product of a wider culture than the narrow Israelite/Judean, albeit that there must have been local or regional variations. It may be appropriate to refer to a suggestion made half a century ago by Thorkild Jacobsen about the relationship, in terms of priority, between the Canaanite and Babylonian versions of the conflict between the thunderstorm and the sea.[2] He notes that one can readily see how such a motif might have taken shape on the Mediterranean coastline, at somewhere like Ugarit.

> The common sight of a thunderstorm attracted to, and spending its fury as it moved out over, the sea laid to hand a mythopoeic rendering in terms of a battle between the power in the thunderstorm and the power in the sea.[3]

However, he argued that such a motif made less sense as one which might have emerged in Mesopotamia, where the sea was for most people far away and not a feature of everyday experience.

> That he [i.e., a Babylonian] should independently have thought up a myth about a battle between the thunderstorm and the sea and should have made the myth central in his cosmogony is exceedingly difficult to imagine and common sense must preclude it as a probable possibility.[4]

Jacobsen felt it to be easier to assume an origin on the coast of the Mediterranean, whence it spread to Babylon. Marduk was envisaged as a god of thunderstorms, so a story told about a victory of the god of thunder and lightning, might naturally be met with interest and readiness of acceptance. It is not necessarily to agree with all the elements of Jacobsen's view, to see the force in the suggestion that ideas might have been shared and adapted.

Another area of agreement with Rebecca is on the importance of definition (as already mentioned in the context of creation), specifically whether domination or control necessarily involves a battle. This need not be the case, whereas conflict or combat would imply some sort of physical engagement. However, there is quite a lot of reference to weaponry and warlike activity in Habakkuk 3, albeit that the imagery is not restricted to warfare. As Rebecca has noted, in verses 9–10 there is a blend of divine warrior and storm theophany language. It is not unusual for a mixture of images to be used when attempting to describe

---

[2] Jacobsen 1968, 104–8.
[3] Jacobsen 1968, 107.
[4] Jacobsen 1968, 107.

what an appearance of God on earth might be like. Judges 5 includes a clear example of the combining of storm and warrior language.

> LORD, when you went out from Seir,
>   when you marched from the region of Edom,
> the earth trembled,
>   and the heavens poured,
>   the clouds indeed poured water. (Jud. 5:4)

A somewhat different example is in Exodus 19 where the effect of God's descending upon Mount Sinai is described. Arguments as to whether the description demonstrates that Sinai was a volcano rather miss the point! The mention of thunder, lightning, cloud, trumpet blast, smoke, fire, and the mountain shaking represent the attempt to put into words what it would be like if God were to appear on earth, employing a catalogue of awesome phenomena. This is the language of theophany.

Rebecca may well be right, in connection with her claim that nowhere in the Hebrew Bible is the sea "manifested as a personal being",[5] to distinguish "personification" from "personal being" when comparing the sea with figures like Leviathan and Rahab.[6] But it is difficult to think that they are being treated differently in, e.g., Ps 74:13–14a:

> You divided Sea by your might;
>   you broke the heads of the dragons in the waters.
> You crushed the heads of Leviathan …

Perhaps it would be better to speak of "anthropomorphism" rather than "personification" in such instances.

Rebecca notes the association of the pouring out of water with the image of the storm theophany, but suggests that the use of thunderstorm phenomena, including precipitation, as weaponry, is less common.[7] This may be so but, as she acknowledges, it is certainly there in Psalm 77:18–9 [Eng 17–8], in particular in verse 18 [Eng 17]:

> The clouds poured out water;
>   the skies thundered;
>   your arrows flashed on every side.

---

5 Watson 2005, 4.
6 Above, p. 79.
7 Above, p. 45.

The reference to "arrows" suggests that weaponry is in mind here. It can be agreed that there is often a blending of images of the divine warrior with that of storm theophany, and surely what distinguishes warriors is their weapons. Rebecca comments that evidence from the Ugaritic texts for the use of meteorological weapons in divine combat is unfavourable,[8] and there may be some truth in this. The precise nature of the weapons (ṣmdm)[9] used by Baal in his combat with Yam is unclear. The word is often translated "clubs"[10] or "maces"[11]. Here it may be important to take account of available iconographic evidence, notably in this context the famous Baal stele in which the god is depicted as a striding warrior, holding a mace or club above his head, often thought to represent thunder, and in the other hand a weapon whose lower section is clearly a spear and whose upper section has been understood as representing a lightning flash.[12] The imagery of the stele has been widely, though not universally, interpreted, as a depiction of the storm god armed with his weapons of thunder and lightning, and is worthy of consideration in this context. I wonder to what extent it is wise to distinguish the use of language such as that of "wrath" as being appropriate when referring to human rather than divine or mythological objects. Theophany language uses human vocabulary to portray the divine.

With regard to Rebecca's comment on the unusual form of the pairing "rivers" and "sea" in Hab 3:8, and to two possible Ugaritic parallels to the use of the plural "rivers" as a parallel to the singular "sea", she suggests that these are both allusions to geographical locations.[13] I agree that this is the case with *KTU* 1.3 vi 5–6, where they precede references to known places. But this seems less clear in the other instance (*KTU* 1.4 ii 6–7) albeit that it may depend on what is meant by "geographical". (Back to the importance of precise definition!) Although the meaning of the passage is not entirely clear, it seems likely that it is referring to Athirat washing her clothes in the sea/rivers.[14] This seems more convincing than Wyatt's suggestion that her clothes are made "from" the sea/river.[15] Rebecca is, of course, correct that neither passage refers to Yam/Nahar. But it is perhaps

---

8 Above, p. 63.
9 *KTU* 1.2 iv 11.
10 So Gibson 1978, 43.
11 So Wyatt, 2002, 65. In a footnote Wyatt also suggests "clubs", "axes".
12 On the possible meanings of Ugaritic ṣmdm, and on storm-god iconography, including the Baal stele, see Mark Smith 1994, 338–41.
13 Above, pp. 39–40.
14 So e.g. Gibson (1978, 56) who, in a footnote, suggests that here "the scene is a homely one" (n. 6).
15 Wyatt 2002, 93.

less convincing to think that "the author may consciously have dropped the titles, reversed the order and used the masculine plural in order to signal the undercutting or reshaping of prior mythic traditions".[16] The plural *nəhārîm* is less frequent than *nəhārôt* but it is not unique. The suggestion of a connection with the waters of Egypt is interesting but, if so (and to anticipate the next paragraph), would not the questions of verse 8 expect the answer "Yes"? Yahweh did indeed vent his wrath on the Nile and the Reed Sea, according to the traditions of the plagues and the exodus.

Turning to the suggestion that the questions in verse 8 expect the answer "No", BDB suggests that it is the use of *'im* alone which usually equates to *Num?* expecting the answer "No" especially in a rhetorical style, and that this usage is not frequent. Its use is more frequent in disjunctive interrogation where *'im* follows *hă* expressing a real alternative. In *DCH*, it is suggested that *'im* after a clause beginning with *hă* with the sense "is it the case that", means "or" introducing a question similar to that of the first clause. There is no suggestion of the expectation of the answer "No", and this was true of GKC and Gibson as already noted. A number of the instances where Rebecca claims the answer "No" is expected seem at best to be uncertain or equivocal, even if not impossible, for example in Isaiah 40:28:

> Have you not known? Have you not heard?
> The LORD is the everlasting God ...

Here Rebecca suggests the expected answer is "No", but the prophet could be reminding the people of what they do know,[17] or at least should know,[18] from their own tradition, as is suggested a little earlier in the same chapter:

> Have you not known? Have you not heard?
>   Has it not been told you from the beginning?
>   Have you not understood from the foundations of the earth? (Isa 40:21)

I am not convinced by Rebecca's suggestion that verse 28a should be understood as implying a double negative, but, even if she is correct, a double negative often becomes a strong positive.

---

16 Above, p. 40.
17 Childs (2001, 311) comments on Isa 40:28, "The reality of God as creator and redeemer is everywhere present and known. Israel only has to listen, look, and remember".
18 Blenkinsopp (2002, 194), comments, "What they should know is that Yahveh's presence extends over time past, present and future and over the whole world from one end to the other".

In some cases the answer "Yes" seems much more likely. For example, Jer 5:29 (=9:8)

> Shall I not punish them for these things? says the LORD
>   and shall I not bring retribution on a nation such as this?

surely expects the answer "Yes", as do the questions in Jer 8:4:

> You shall say to them, Thus says the LORD:
> When people fall, do they not get up again?
>   If they go astray, do they not turn back?

Here the implied answer is surely "Yes, they usually do" by way of contrast with the behaviour of "this people" outlined in the following verses.

In Ps 94:9,

> He who planted the ear, does he not hear?
> He who formed the eye, does he not see?

it seems likely that the expected response to the questions is "Yes, the creator of ear and eye does indeed hear and see". And Job 6:5 and 7:1 both seem most naturally to expect the answer "Yes", the latter in particular:

> Do not human beings have a hard service on earth,
>   and are not their days like the days of a labourer?

The above are instances where expectation of the answer "Yes" is at least possible. This is not, of course, to suggest that "No" is not sometimes the expected answer, but that it need not be assumed that that is the case. Sadly, Hebrew lacks Latin's clarity with the different interrogatives *Num* and *Nonne*.

To return to the passage under discussion, it is difficult to reconcile questions expecting the answer "No" with Hab 3:15, thought by some to mark the end of a unit which begins with verse 8. It could be argued that it provides the answer to the questions of verse 8:

> You trampled the sea with your horses,
>   churning the mighty waters.

Ralph L. Smith, in the Word Commentary, sees in Hab 3:8–15 the answer to the question "Why is God coming?", and comments, "He is coming to defeat his enemy represented by rivers, water, and sea, and the enemy of his people".[19] He notes the possibility that the prophet may be remembering an earlier occasion when God came from Sinai to rescue his people. J. J. M. Roberts comments, with reference to Hab 3:8,

> The point of the questions is not to suggest that God's anger is really directed to Babylon, rather than the Natural world. The point of the questions is to identify Babylon with the primeval powers of chaos, and thus to suggest that this new march of Yahweh is a fundamental reenactment of Yahweh's primeval victories from which there emerged an ordered world under God's kingship.[20]

It seems highly likely that God's acts are being likened to his conflict with the waters. A belief elsewhere understood mythologically is applied to a historical situation but retaining mythological language. Rebecca's comment on one of the possible implications of Hab 3:13 seems apposite, when she suggests that this type of language is being used ironically, "... to describe Yahweh's destruction of the Babylonians. Marduk was supposed to have slain Tiamat, symbolic of all Babylon's enemies, thus; but actually Yahweh will so treat Babylon". Even if Yahweh's wrath was not actually against the sea in this particular context, the language (perhaps consciously archaising?) reveals knowledge of the underlying myth both by the author and the audience, and conveys the claim about Yahweh's power in a particularly dramatic and forceful way. This language may (to pick up on the paper mentioned at the beginning of my opening piece) move beyond imagery to polemic (at least implicitly) about the relative power of Yahweh when compared with that of the gods of Israel's enemies.

Reflecting on Rebecca's paper has been valuable in terms of sharpening my thinking, in particular about the importance of clarity in the definition of concepts. While there has been some convergence, some areas of difference remain, though in some cases these may be differences of emphasis. An important issue which emerges is whether a narrower "Israelite" or a wider ancient Near Eastern focus is appropriate for the understanding of some of the language and imagery employed in Habakkuk 3. Even if the answer lies somewhere in between, it seems to me that there is no need to deny use of, or at least allusion to, what is a pervasive idea, and that the force of the words of Israel's poets and prophets is enhanced when they are seen from the perspective of the thought-world within which Israelite religious thinking emerged and developed.

---

19 Smith 1984, 116.
20 Roberts 1991, 155.

Part III: **Final Reflections**

Adrian H. W. Curtis
Some Observations on Rebecca Watson's Response

I have found it helpful to reflect on Rebecca's response to my opening contribution to this dialogue, which has clarified some points from her own paper and highlighted several key points for further thought. There are many places where I believe we are basically in agreement, or not far apart, and some where differences may be of emphasis or what should be prioritised in thinking about a text such as Habakkuk 3. I welcome her suggestion that we may in fact be sitting at different points on the same spectrum, rather than in opposing camps. But there do remain some differences and one significant point of genuine disagreement. In these brief additional comments I shall focus primarily on points from her response.

I have earlier indicated my agreement over the danger of parallelomania, and I accept that this may extend into what Rebecca has described as forcing material in the Hebrew Bible into a "'*Chaoskampf*' straitjacket".[1] The example she provides is a valid one. In connection with her questioning of whether it is appropriate to explain allusions in the Hebrew Bible by referring to comparative material "*before* or *instead of* other biblical occurrences of the same language"[2] she may well have a cogent point. But this may perhaps be an issue of priority, and I would not want to rule out the possibility that insights from the wider thought-world of the ancient Near East could help to elucidate a biblical text. Nor, I suspect, would Rebecca, given some of her observations on the chapter. Perhaps it is not just a case of "before" or "instead of", but in addition "alongside" should be an option. Disproportionate emphasis on comparative material is to be avoided, but the wider horizons should not be forgotten. Rebecca envisages the possibility of the use of "Canaanite" language as a means of putting forward a different message in dialogue with ideas current in the wider north-west Semitic context. This certainly implies that those ideas were well known and could be adapted, engaged with, or challenged.

I can envisage the possibility that "Canaanite" language might be used as a means of asserting "a distinctive message in dialogue with ideas current in the broader North-West Semitic context as well as in Israel and Judah".[3] But I have

---

[1] Watson 2005, 2.
[2] Above, p. 76.
[3] Above, p. 80.

more difficulty with the suggestion that this might be in order to engage with notions "which were rejected by the Jerusalemite Temple hierarchy",[4] since I am not sure how we can know for certain who would have constituted such a group and what they would have accepted or rejected. What about allusions in the Psalms to the sort of motif under discussion in Habakkuk 3? Might they not reflect the views of those involved in worship in the Jerusalem temple? I am happy to endorse Rebecca's comment about the presence in the book of Habakkuk, before chapter 3, of "imagery and ideas drawn from the traditional North-West Semitic thought-world and repertoire, which are likely to have been a feature of the originator's heritage".[5] I am less sure about the suggestion that these might be drawn from the "slightly unorthodox margins".[6] Whose orthodoxy and whose margins?

Rebecca makes a valid point about the need for clarity in referring to "the myth". The biblical material and the ancient Near Eastern evidence point to a variety of myths, or variations on the theme of a conflict with a watery opponent. The precise relationship between Yam and Lotan in the Ugaritic texts is unclear. Mark Smith comments: "The two conflicts of Baal against his enemies, Yamm and Leviathan, constituted apparently separate traditions. Each of these stories perhaps served as a prelude to kingship".[7] (Evidence for the former statement is perhaps clearer than for the second!) He goes on to note Frank Cross's suggestion that various conflict stories were variants or "alloforms" of the same cosmogonic story.[8] Perhaps a more cautious word than the "evidently" which Cross uses of this suggestion would have been appropriate.

That these variant traditions were, however, closely connected in these ancient thought-worlds does seem clear. Rebecca may well be correct in questioning whether there is any evidence that Yam should be identified with Lotan in the Ugaritic mythology, but it can be argued that they were closely associated. At the beginning of tablet 5 of the Baal "cycle" we read:

Though you smote Litan the wriggling serpent,
finished off the writhing serpent,
Encircler-with seven heads ... (*KTU* 1.5 i 1–3—Wyatt's translation[9])

---

4 Above, p. 81.
5 Above, p. 81.
6 Above, p. 81.
7 Smith 1994, 34.
8 Cross 1973, 149.
9 Wyatt 2002, 115. Wyatt prefers "Litan" to the more widely used "Lotan".

Here we have an explicit reference to Litan/Lotan. This is not the case in another passage:

> Surely I smote the Beloved of El, Yam?
> Surely I exterminated Nahar, the mighty god?
> Surely I lifted up the dragon,
> I overpowered him?
> I smote the writhing serpent,
> Encircler-with seven heads! (*KTU* 1.3 iii 39–42—Wyatt's translation[10])

However, the same description as in the previous passage, "the writhing serpent, Encircler-with seven heads", suggests that Lotan is being envisaged. Since this is part of a lengthy list of enemies of Baal, it is likely that reference is being made to different beings. But thought of Yam seems to lead naturally to thought of Lotan.

Something not dissimilar is to be found in Psalm 74.13–14a:

> You divided Sea by your might,
>   you broke the heads of the dragons in the waters.
> You crushed the heads of Leviathan ...

There are perhaps grounds for thinking that there might have been variations on a theme, that associations would have been known, and that it would have been taken for granted that readers/hearers would be aware of such interconnected motifs.

Another broad area of agreement lies in the necessity for clear definitions. This is certainly true of what is meant by creation—*creatio ex nihilo* or the establishment or order—and Rebecca may be right to raise the issue of the definition of "battle" and whether it necessarily involves physical conflict. Nowadays it is possible to speak metaphorically of a "battle of words" or "battle of wills" and the word could be applied to gaining dominance in various ways. She describes the encounter between Baal and Mot, described in the Ugaritic texts, as a "combat-myth", and this may be a better term to describe a physical encounter.

A remaining difference is in our interpretations of 3:8. I am willing to accept that the questions *could* expect the answer "no", but I am far from convinced that biblical evidence suggests that questions formed in this way *must* always do so, and I am not at all sure that they do so here. I prefer to see the answer being provided in v. 15 where, after a graphic description of Yahweh as a divine warrior in the preceding verses, it is claimed that he did indeed demonstrate his

---

10 Wyatt 2002, 79.

wrath and anger, and therefore his power, by trampling the sea and churning the waters. The prophet's prayer could be answered by a similar demonstration of power, *mutatis mutandis*.

In an essay on Habakkuk 3 which only came to my attention after I had written my opening piece and my initial response to Rebecca (and to which I would otherwise have given fuller attention), Koert van Bekkum says of verses 8–15:

> The outer parts of the stanza are connected by mentioning the river and sea as the objects of Yhwh's anger and the targets of his chariotry, and by the actual victory over the sea and the many waters (3:8ab, 15ab).[11]

This reading seems to support the contention that verse 15 provides the answer to the rhetorical questions of verse 8.

This engagement has underlined, for me, the value of a dialogical approach. It has shown areas where clarity is needed, particularly in definition of terminology and in the appropriateness of using comparative material for the elucidation of a biblical text, and the checks and balances to be borne in mind. And, in the end, dialogue may involve an element of agreeing to differ, may it not? (Expecting the answer "Yes"!)

---

[11] Van Bekkum 2017, 71.

Rebecca S. Watson
Some Observations on Adrian Curtis's Response

I am very grateful to Adrian for his comments on my discussion of Habakkuk 3. Despite entering into this dialogue because of our perception that we disagreed significantly over the interpretation of this much-debated passage, I have been surprised at quite how close our positions are on many points. In terms of general approach, methodology and working assumptions, we are not as far removed from each other as I anticipated, even if we differ in nuance or in the relative importance we might assign to inner-biblical and comparative evidence. We find common ground in accepting the risk of forcing biblical material into a *Chaoskampf* mould, even if we might set the boundary for this in rather different places, and we concur in recognising the importance of careful use of language and definition when making claims about matters such as the presence (or not) of allusions to creation. Although I do not think that the author(s) of Habakkuk 3 intended to identify the hostile forces threatening Judah with those of the sea ("chaos") I have no disagreement with the principle that knowledge of such myths provided the backdrop to the questions of verse 8 in particular, and that this was therefore an important issue both to writer and audience. On the whole, I find it more helpful to think of the authors of the Hebrew Bible (just like their counterparts elsewhere in the Near East) as finding their own distinctive voice within, or in dialogue with, particular national or local traditions and the wider cultural milieu, rather than merely as a fairly indistinguishable part of a more monolithic whole. Generally, it is the points of difference, more than of commonality, that are most interesting and informative and which might help us understand the distinctive force of each reference or composition, and I believe attentiveness to this will better enable us to honour the intention of the material we are seeking to interpret.[1]

If this is the case with texts, so also it is with interpretations. Despite an unforeseen level of agreement over our basic approach, Adrian and I still differ quite considerably in some of the details of how Habakkuk 3 should be understood. Possibly standing within a common cultural stream within UK universities might, in part, explain our unanticipated level of concurrence, but notwithstanding this—or perhaps because of it—our purpose (like that of any other scholars) in venturing to write was because we intended to offer our own unique perspec-

---

[1] For examples of scholarship which has been influenced by this insight, see p. 77 n. 12.

tives, not because we wanted our offerings to merge nebulously within the wider current of Habakkuk research. As with the ancient texts themselves, the difference is in the detail.

Turning now to specific points where Adrian has highlighted continuing disagreement, I am willing to take on board his suggestion that it might be more helpful to speak of "anthropomorphism" rather than "personification".[2] However, I am not sure this resolves the perceived ambiguity, given that both gods and natural forces might be portrayed anthropomorphically, whereas only something that is not a person (a category which would apply to the sea but not to Yam) can be said to be personified. Possibly, the counterpart to this, "deification", might better enable us to express the distinction we are seeking to identify. The issue is about the extent to which the sea (or waters, rivers or deep) should be viewed simply as an aquatic mass, having personality attributed to it only in a metaphorical and figurative way (personification), or whether there is to some extent at least a residual sense of the sea as a god (deification). The question itself, "Was your wrath against the rivers …?" might already suggest an awareness of the latter possibility as a credible option for some, even if it is vehemently denied by the writer. In this instance, it seems that Adrian and I concur over the difficulty of finding suitable terminology to describe a particular interpretation of a rather ambiguous language feature quite precisely, even if we have not yet resolved the problem to our mutual agreement.

Adrian questions my comment about evidence from the Ugaritic texts being unfavourable[3] to seeing similarities in the implements used in divine combat to those mentioned in verses 13–4. However, my point related to the use of specific weapons, *mṭ* and *qšt*, not to thunderstorm phenomena more generally. I do not disagree that Baal's weapons may also simultaneously have been thought to have meteorological counterparts, nor that the Baal stele may also have been understood in this way. However, since we are dealing with a literary tradition in this instance, then it is relevant to ask whether the terminology used for Yahweh's weaponry in Habakkuk 3 is characteristic of portrayals of Baal's conflict with Yam, as a positive identification could support the sort of interpretation Adrian favours. However, this evidence is lacking. I am not sure I fully understand either Adrian's resistance to noting whether the language of "wrath" is applied to divine or mythological objects as well as human ones. "Theophany language uses human vocabulary to portray the divine"[4] indeed, but that relates

---

[2] Above, p. 87.
[3] For my original comment, see above, p. 63, and for Adrian's response, see p. 88.
[4] Above, p. 88.

primarily to the subject, or agent, of the wrath, Yahweh, not the objects. The frequency of certain objects of a verb can alert the reader to conventional concepts and phrases as well as to nuances or applications that are more or less typical, and this is exactly why they are catalogued at length in dictionaries such as *DCH*.

Our main remaining points of difference concern the interpretation of verse 8. Regarding the phrasing of the first three cola, Adrian first of all takes issue with my tentative suggestion that "quite possibly the author may consciously have dropped the titles, reversed the order and used the masculine plural in order to signal the undercutting or reshaping of prior mythic traditions".[5] However, this also sits alongside another more speculative proposal (which does not necessarily exclude the first one), that the allusion could be to the rivers of Egypt. Either or neither may be correct, but I believe it is right to be curious about why unusual forms of language (the masculine plural *nəhārîm* and the mention of rivers before sea) might be employed, even if this can only be explained conjecturally, rather than not raising the question at all. It is obvious to all interpreters that the forms of expression here in Hab 3:8 differ from more widespread conventional patterns, both in the mention of the rivers before the sea and in the use of the less common masculine plural (though, of course, if there were a direct allusion to a battle with Yam, one would expect the singular instead). This is surely not coincidental, and we cannot reasonably expect the original author/s and readers to be unaware of it. Therefore, any interpretation of the verse should be able to account for this language use, even if only speculatively, and to devise a reading that is consonant with the text we have rather than ideas attributed to its earlier cultural background. Whatever solution is preferred, it is clear that this must be explained in terms of intentional difference and differentiation, and I am not sure that Adrian has come up with a viable alternative to my proposal.

Adrian's suggests in his response to my paper that if verse 8 makes reference to the rivers of Egypt, this should support an expectation of an implied affirmative to the questions it poses. In replying to this, I shall temporarily set aside all efforts to urge my case, in order to make an observation about wider issues of interpretation arising from our discussion. Adrian's remark (and my response to it here) fascinatingly illustrates a key problem that has beset this debate, since it appears that, each of us, having arrived at a certain impression of how a particular text or texts should be read, uses this to inform any ensuing efforts in interpretation. Although this is probably inevitable and even virtuous, insofar as any understanding should be coherent and take account of all the evi-

---

5 For my original comment, see above, p. 40, and for Adrian's response, see p. 89.

dence in a consistent way, it seems that one or both of us—and maybe anyone engaged in the interpretative process—must be guilty of circularity. Adrian states that "Yahweh did indeed vent his wrath on the Nile and the Reed Sea, according to the traditions of the plagues and the exodus". My reading of the plague account contradicts this claim, since, as far as I can see, some of the plagues affected the Nile but they were aimed at the Egyptians, and specifically at the Pharaoh. The Nile might, in some sense, be emblematic of Egypt, but as its lifeblood and the foundation of its health and success, not as a specific target of divine judgment. Similarly, the escape from Egypt happened at the sea rather than to it: the movement of the waters was compliant with and even facilitated the divine will rather than being in conflict with it and occurred in order to facilitate the Israelites' escape and the pursuing Egyptians' demise. This also reflects my understanding of Psalm 77:6[6] (which, as we have seen above, has notable commonalities with Habakkuk 3) and Exodus 15, one of the best-known examples of the celebration of Yahweh as warrior god triumphing over his enemies. However, the interpretation of these passages will in turn, I suspect, be a further substantial area over which Adrian and I differ! We thereby discover that Adrian and I disagree in the understanding of Habakkuk 3, and verse 8 in particular, in part because we diverge in how we approach not only the specific verses we have been debating, but the wider corpus in which they sit, and conversely, our interpretation of each element informs the bigger mental picture on which we draw in seeking to discern the meaning of each constituent part. It is as if we have begun with the same threads of evidence but woven very different garments from them. By pulling at one thread, we may be in danger of unravelling, connection by connection, the whole edifice of understanding, built on a multitude of interwoven motifs and interrelated texts; but the more common pattern in interpretation (and one that is easier to hold psychologically) will be for each of us to continue to inhabit our comfortable and much favoured old garments, living with the holes until we are forced to start anew. So far, each of us can only see the holes in each other's garments—but then in scholarship there is always the danger of each of us proudly cladding ourselves, like the proverbial emperor, in new clothes which everyone else can see through but ourselves.

To return to the debate on Habakkuk 3: by far our most substantive area of disagreement concerns the issue of the rhetorical force of the questions of verse 8. In his response to my initial paper, Adrian cites a number of examples where

---

[6] See further Watson 2015, 147–52; for other poetic passages which have been associated both with the exodus and with divine combat, see also (also in the same volume) 156–68, 173–89, 243–64, 291–301, 38–381.

the pattern *hă-lō' ... (wə)'im-lō'* (or *hă ... lō' ... (wə)'im ... lō'*) occurs in clear anticipation of an affirmative answer. I find it perplexing that he has highlighted these verses, as they absolutely reinforce my point about the significance of the construction *hă ... 'im*. As I seek to illustrate through the appendix and have explained above[7] (but, it seems, should have highlighted more fully) in these instances a double negative should be discerned. For example, in relation to the questions of Isa 40:21a, 28a, "Have you not known? Have you not heard?", the implied answer is "No, I/we have *not* not known and have *not* not heard", or, in other words, "I/we have *most definitely* known and have *certainly* heard". This is entirely consistent with the interpretation of *hă ... 'im* that I have been advancing and applies in every instance. Therefore, Adrian has still not identified any example which calls my observation about the force of this construction into question. In the spirit of continuing our dialogue, I invite Adrian to revisit all the instances of this interrogative construction again and indeed would like to challenge him to find one example where the implied answer falls outside the expected pattern. As verse 8 seems to provide the key to the section which it introduces (vv. 8–15), any revision in his interpretation of this verse will (or should!) have significant ramifications for the rest of the passage and should instigate a modification of the reading he has been advocating.

From the point of view of method and process, this particular disagreement highlights an issue that has occurred also in the other dialogues in this volume, namely, that sometimes differences arise not because of a fundamental clash of opinion but due to misunderstanding (whether arising from clumsy expression or inattentive reading or both) and disparities in the interpretation even of the secondary literature. Usually this problem is obscured in the monovocality of scholarly papers, but the dialogical format employed here has revealed that this phenomenon is relatively common and hence it indirectly illustrates the importance of conversations such as this one.

Turning back again to the specifics of my conversation with Adrian, I agree wholeheartedly with him that we might expect to detect an answer to the questions of verse 8 in the following verses, at the very least on an implicit level. However, much as we agree in seeking coherence in our respective interpretations, because we have read verse 8 in very different ways, this has informed our expectations of the ensuing lines. Having already settled on an implied affirmative answer to the question of whether Yahweh's wrath is against the rivers, it is natural that Adrian would see this corroborated in verse 15, and indeed that he should look for the answer in a verse mentioning the sea and expect to read this

---

[7] P. 42 n. 66 and pp. 122–4.

as implying some level of conflict or control over the waters. Conversely, because my starting point was to establish that verse 8 requires the answer "No", then it is not surprising that I should find the answer in verse 12, which unequivocally confirms that it was the nations whom Yahweh trampled in anger:

> In fury you trod the earth,
>   in anger you trampled nations.

Here, therefore, we expose once again the influence of our working assumptions in interpretation. Although in theory, the apparent meaning of one verse might act as a corrective to the proposed construal of another and encourage us to challenge our initial understanding, very often by expecting one verse to elucidate another, we may instead perpetuate our interpretative biases. In my defence, I would say that I assiduously check alternative contexts for the use of key words and phrases, to try to ensure that I obtain as objective an understanding as I can. As I am sure Adrian does as well, I try to develop a provisional sense of the implied meaning of each component and of the passage more broadly before trying to enforce an over-arching interpretation that, in my view, best honours each of these elements. Nonetheless, that we should end up with, in many respects, quite different readings are a testament to the element of personal judgment in interpretation, despite our best efforts at careful methodology and detailed analysis.

Turning now to Adrian's final reflections, I am inclined to accept many of his critical comments on my response to his initial essay. The draft which I sent him was definitely in need of polishing, and he has helpfully identified a number of instances where I should have rephrased more judiciously what I was claiming. This is a case not merely of differences of definition but of the need for more precise use of language. Had there been more time available for editing, his feedback would have enabled me to improve my response or address instances where my casual use of language required clarification. For example, he takes issue with attribution of the "orthodoxy" of the Hebrew Bible to the "Jerusalemite Temple hierarchy". This is a fair point. I struggle to find appropriate vocabulary to label the tendencies towards certain positions—monotheism, denial of other gods and certain practices which came to be viewed as associated particularly with their worship but as inappropriate to Yahwism—in the Hebrew Bible without implying a greater degree of theological uniformity than I intend or extending the notion of "deuteronomistic" influence beyond reasonable reach. Nonetheless, the currency of such ideas is attributed to the finding of a scroll in the Temple and they are described as having been implemented, through Josiah's reform, from Jerusalem and focused on it as the exclusive centre of the cult. It is also difficult to imagine the hub of postexilic scribal activity as being anywhere else, so the terminology I used has some basis. This does not mean that there was not theological and ideological diversity in Jerusalemite circles, any more than ideas circulating—or debated—in Westminster or Washington fall at only one point on the political spectrum, nor would I wish to imply that nothing could have originated from elsewhere in Judah. However, I would see "Jerusalemite Temple" circles as likely to have provided a primary conduit both for a late preexilic wish for reform and in the postexilic period for the collection and editing of the scrolls that came to comprise the Hebrew Bible, qualifications and exceptions notwithstanding.

A further issue of debate relates to the Ugaritic texts. Although I concur with Mark Smith in seeing the conflicts of Baal with Yam and Lotan as "apparently separate traditions", I also agree with Adrian in recognising that there are hints of association between them, but I do not think this should be overplayed. It should occasion no surprise that both might feature in a list of Baal's conquests. Adrian quotes *KTU* 1.3 iii 39–42, in which the smiting of Yam is followed by mention of the overcoming of "the dragon" in language which echoes the description of Lotan in *KTU* 1.5 i 1–3. However, to put the former passage in context, it continues (using Wyatt's translation again, for the sake of consistency):

> I finished off El's calf, Atik,
> I smote El's bitch, Fire,
> I exterminated El's daughter, Flame.

Although it may be that "Fire" and "Flame", like the pair "Yam" and "Nahar", refer to the same being, it is evident that this is a list of several conquests, rather than variant expressions of the same victory, so there is no justification for attempting to read too much into the mention of the dragon after the sea, especially when Yam had already been paired with Nahar. To add an extra layer of complexity, the speaker making these claims of victory appears to be Anat, not Baal himself, so this again should prompt caution against assertions that over-extend the evidence. In this instance, the differences between Adrian and I are probably quite subtle but highlight again the difficulty of interpreting fragmentary evidence from the distant past with any degree of certainty, even where there is agreement over which source might be relevant to a particular question.

I am grateful to Adrian for his willingness to debate with me and have appreciated his feedback on my work as much as the opportunity to question and comment on his. The process has helped me identify more clearly where our perspectives converge or diverge, and to develop a better understanding of how these differences have arisen. Much as I expected our points of variance to centre around underlying issues, such as our respective approaches, definitions and working assumptions, it transpires that our thinking around the interaction of the biblical writers with the wider Near Eastern cultural context is not as different as might first be assumed. Rather, it seems to be in the interpretation of Habakkuk 3 itself that our divergences are most apparent, in particular, the way each of us, having developed a particular sense of how the writer is interacting with motifs of divine combat, then carries that through to apply it to the whole composition.

My impression—from observing the results of our debate in retrospect, rather than speaking as an advocate for what has apparently happened in the process of exegesis—is that a sense of "what the text is about" has coloured each of our readings and informed the interpretation as much as the interpretation has been informed by something innate in the text. In my defence, I think the evidence for anticipating the answer "no" to the questions posed in verse 8 is unavoidable, and therefore that has to be one of the more "fixed" points of any reading. I also like to think of interpretation as a "spiral" process where attention is constantly shifted from the implications of a particular fragment of the whole to the bigger picture and back again, with each informing the other. No doubt Adrian will equally have a sense of the integrity and consistency of his methodology and of the coherence of his understanding of the poem as a whole. Does this render our debate superfluous? I do not think so. If in developing our individual readings of a particular text we are blind to the forces that lead us each in our own characteristic direction, all the while believing that we are being open to contrary possibilities, then this could rather suggest that exegesis might be better conducted in a collaborative manner from the outset. By the time Adrian and I had written our respective chapters we had each made up our minds about the text. We have engaged with each other, enjoyed the discussion and acknowledged points of commonality, but not shifted in any significant way. I wonder, though, what might have happened, if we had had to work together from the outset, agree each point through open debate and discussion, and develop a coherent picture of the whole together? Maybe we would only have succeeded in churning the waters of debate without any resolution, but perhaps—just perhaps—we might have found a way through the sea, though whether walking, treading or trampling we could not, from this point, possibly say.

Adrian H. W. Curtis and Rebecca S. Watson
Some Joint Concluding Reflections on Habakkuk 3

Overall, we have found that a dialogic approach has resulted in a degree of convergence of opinion rather than an accentuation of difference. Both of us have acknowledged areas where our views are—or could be brought—closer than we had first supposed. For example, although Rebecca has maintained that the rhetorical force of Hab. 3:8 is that Yahweh's wrath was not against the sea, this also recognises engagement with and knowledge of the myth both on the part of the author of this passage and his audience. Conversely, Adrian has been content to acknowledge Rebecca's "anti-*Chaoskampf*" reading as a possible interpretation, as it leaves room for his recognition that there seem to be concrete signs of engagement with the myth in the passage. We have both become aware of the importance of clarity of definition and appreciated some of the potential pitfalls in employing a so-called comparative method. The issue of whether the starting point for interpretation should be narrowly Israelite/Judean or more broadly ancient Near Eastern remains, though we acknowledge that there is room for both.

But although there may be more common ground between us than at first appeared, two essential differences remain. The first is the detailed interpretation of the text before us, especially as regards v. 8, which Rebecca would view as critical to the meaning of the passage as a whole. The other takes us back to the point of divergence with which we began, namely the operating assumptions governing the evaluation of the nature of the allusions to the waters and our contrasting assessments of whether the identification of language and spheres of reference familiar from elsewhere in the extant North West Semitic corpus of literature must imply acceptance, at least to some degree, of the idea of Yahweh's combat with the sea. We believe that our thinking has been sharpened by this exercise, not least in its element of self-examination. The churning continues!

Rebecca S. Watson
Appendix. Occurrences of *hă* ... *'im* in the Hebrew Bible

1 Alternative Structures

1.1 A question introduced by *hă*, plus conditional clause(s) with *'im*

Gen 4:7 If you do well, will you not be accepted? And if you do not do well, sin is lurking at the door; its desire is for you, but you must master it.

Will you *not* (*hălô'*) be accepted *if* (*'im*) you do well? *And if* you do *not* (*wə'im lō'*) do well ...

Gen 13:9 Is not the whole land before you? Separate yourself from me. If you take the left hand, then I will go to the right; or if you take the right hand, then I will go to the left.

Is not (*hălô'*) the whole land before you? ... If (*'im*) you take the left hand then I will go to the right; or if (*wə'im*) you take the right hand, then I will go to the left.

Gen 18:21 I must go down and see whether they have done altogether according to the outcry that has come to me; and if not, I will know.

... whether (*hă*) they have done ... and if not (*wə'im-lō'*)

Gen 18:28 "... Suppose five of the fifty righteous are lacking? Will you destroy the whole city for lack of five?" And he said, "I will not destroy it if I find forty-five there".

"... Will (*hă*) you destroy the whole city for lack of five?" And he said, "I will not destroy it if (*'im-*) I find forty-five there".

Note: The first column represents the NRSV translation of the relevant verses; in the second column this is edited where necessary to bring out the Hebrew structure, even if the resultant translation appears somewhat awkward. In several cases, I have also included material from the succeeding (or occasionally, preceding) line in order to indicate how the *hă* ... *'im* pattern is part of a larger rhetorical structure, in which the affirmative is vigorously denied or a consequence of the answer is made explicit in a further vehemently articulated statements or questions. I have also at times indicated further aspects of the questions' expression in order to highlight other significant language features, for example, the use of negative forms or of the infinitive absolute to add intensity.

https://doi.org/10.1515/9783110606294-011

1Sam 15:17 Samuel said, "Though you are little in your own eyes, are you not the head of the tribes of Israel? The LORD anointed you king over Israel.

Aren't (*hălô'*) you, though (*'im-*) small in your own eyes, head of the tribes of Israel?

2Sam 17:6 When Hushai came to Absalom, Absalom said to him, "This is what Ahithophel has said; shall we do as he advises? If not, you tell us."

"Shall (*hă*) we do as he advises? If not (*'im 'ăyin*), you tell us".

2Sam 19:14 [Eng 13] " ... And say to Amasa, 'Are you not my bone and my flesh? So may God do to me, and more, if you are not the commander of my army from now on, in place of Joab'".

"Are you not (*hălô'*) my bone and my flesh? So may God do to me, and more, if you are not (*'im-lô'*) the commander of my army from now on"

Isa 28:25
When they have levelled its surface,
   do they not scatter dill, sow cummin,
and plant wheat in rows
   and barley in its proper place,
   and spelt as the border?

Do they not (*hălô'*)
When/if (*'im*) they have levelled its surface,
   scatter dill, sow cummin,
and plant wheat in rows
   and barley in its proper place,
   and spelt as the border?

Joel 3:4 What are you to me, O Tyre and Sidon, and all the regions of Philistia? Are you paying me back for something? If you are paying me back, I will turn your deeds back upon your own heads swiftly and speedily.

Are (*hă*) you paying me back for something? If (*'im*) you are paying me back, I will turn your deeds back upon your own heads swiftly and speedily.

Am 3:3–4
Do two walk together
   unless they have made an appointment?

Does a lion roar in the forest,
   when it has no prey?
Does a young lion cry out from its den,
   if it has caught nothing?

Do (*hă*) two walk together
   (*'im-*) unless they have made an appointment?

[Does (*hă*) a lion roar in the forest,
   when (*wə*) it has no prey?]
Does (*hă*) a young lion cry out from its den,
   if (*'im-*) it has caught nothing?

Obad 1:5[1]
If thieves came to you,
   if plunderers by night
   —how you have been destroyed!—

If (*'im-*) thieves came to you,
   if (*'im-*) plunderers by night
   —how you have been destroyed!—

---

1 Properly speaking, this example is not relevant to the present context, since the pattern shown here is *'im-* + *hălô'* twice over, rather than a *hă* + *'im-* construction. However, it is included here for the sake of completeness.

| would they not steal only what they wanted? If grape-gatherers came to you, would they not leave gleanings? | wouldn't (*hălô'*) they steal only what they wanted? If (*'im-*) grape-gatherers came to you, wouldn't (*hălô'*) they leave gleanings? |

1.2 A question introduced by *hă* plus *'im* indicating an oath

1Sam 14:45 Then the people said to Saul, "Shall Jonathan die, who has accomplished this great victory in Israel? Far from it! As the LORD lives, not one hair of his head shall fall to the ground; for he has worked with God today". So the people ransomed Jonathan, and he did not die.

"Shall (*hă*) Jonathan die, who has accomplished this great victory in Israel? Far from it! As the LORD lives, not one hair of his head shall fall to the ground... (*'im-yippōl miśśa'ărat rō'šô 'arṣāh*)"

1Sam 30:15 David said to him, "Will you take me down to this raiding party?" He said, "Swear to me by God that you will not kill me, or hand me over to my master, and I will take you down to them".

"Will (*hă*) you take me down to this raiding party?" He said, "Swear to me by God that you will not kill me (*'im-təmîtēnî*), or hand me over (*wə'im-tasgirēnî*) to my master ..."

2Sam 14:19 The king said, "Is the hand of Joab with you in all this?" The woman answered and said, "As surely as you live, my lord the king, one cannot turn right or left from anything that my lord the king has said. For it was your servant Joab who commanded me; it was he who put all these words into the mouth of your servant.

"Is (*hă*) the hand of Joab with you in all this?" The woman answered and said, "As surely as you live, my lord the king, one cannot (*'im-'îš*) turn right or left from anything that my lord the king has said ..."

Ezek 20:3 Mortal, speak to the elders of Israel, and say to them: Thus says the Lord GOD: Why are you coming? To consult me? As I live, says the Lord GOD, I will not be consulted by you.

Are (*hă*) you coming to consult me? As I live, I will not be consulted (*'im-'iddārēš*) by you, says the Lord GOD.

1.3 A question introduced by *hă* plus *'im* meaning "only, except"

1Kings 22:18 The king of Israel said to Jehoshaphat, "Did I not tell you that he would not prophesy anything favourable about me, but only disaster?"

"Didn't (*hălō'*) I tell you that he would not prophesy anything favourable about me, but only disaster (*kî 'im-rā'*)?"

2Chr 18:17 The king of Israel said to Jehoshaphat, "Did I not tell you that he would not prophesy anything favourable about me, but only disaster?"

"Didn't (*hălō'*) I tell you that he would not prophesy anything favourable about me, but only disaster (*kî 'im-lərā'*)?"

2 Expressing Genuine Alternatives

Gen 24:21 The man gazed at her in silence to learn whether or not the LORD had made his journey successful.

... had (*hă*) the LORD made his journey successful or not (*'im lō'*)?

Gen 27:21 Then Isaac said to Jacob, "Come near, that I may feel you, my son, to know whether you are really my son Esau or not".

Are you (*hă*) really my son Esau or not (*'im lō'*)?

Gen 37:32 They had the long robe with sleeves taken to their father, and they said, "This we have found; see now whether it is your son's robe or not".

Is it (*hă*) your son's robe or not (*'im lō'*)?

Gen 42:16 Let one of you go and bring your brother, while the rest of you remain in prison, in order that your words may be tested, whether there is truth in you; or else, as Pharaoh lives, surely you are spies.

Is there (*hă*) truth in you; or, if not (*wə'im lō'*), as Pharaoh lives, surely you are spies.

Exod 16:4 Then the LORD said to Moses, "I am going to rain bread from heaven for you, and each day the people shall go out and gather enough for that day. In that way I will test them, whether they will follow my instruction or not.

Will ((*hă*) they follow my instruction or not (*'im lō'*)?

Exod 17:7 He called the place Massah and Meribah, because the Israelites quarrelled and tested the LORD, saying, "Is the LORD among us or not?"

"Is (*hă*) the LORD among us or not (*'im 'āyin*)?"

Num 11:23 The LORD said to Moses, "Is the LORD'S power limited? Now you shall see whether my word will come true for you or not".

Now you shall see: will (*hă*) my word come true for you or not (*'im-lō'*)?"

Appendix. Occurrences of *hă ... 'im* in the Hebrew Bible

Num 13:18–20 "... and see what the land is like, and whether the people who live in it are strong or weak, whether they are few or many, and whether the land they live in is good or bad, and whether the towns that they live in are unwalled or fortified, and whether the land is rich or poor, and whether there are trees in it or not. Be bold and bring some of the fruit of the land". Now it was the season of the first ripe grapes.

and the people who live in it, are (*hă*) they strong or (*hă*) weak

or (*hă*) few or (*'im-*) many

and the land they live in, is (*hă*) it good or (*'im-*) bad,

and the towns that they live in, are (*hă*) they unwalled or (*'im*) fortified, and what the land is like, is (*hă*) it rich or (*'im*) poor, and are there (*hăyēš*) trees in it or not (*'im-'ăyin*)?

Deut 8:2 Remember the long way that the LORD your God has led you these forty years in the wilderness, in order to humble you, testing you to know what was in your heart, whether or not you would keep his commandments.

would (*hă*) you would keep his commandments or not (*'im-lō'*)?

Josh 5:13 Once when Joshua was by Jericho, he looked up and saw a man standing before him with a drawn sword in his hand. Joshua went to him and said to him, "Are you one of us, or one of our adversaries?"

"Are (*hă*) you one of us, or (*'im-*) one of our adversaries?"

Judg 2:22 In order to test Israel, whether or not they would take care to walk in the way of the LORD as their ancestors did, ...

Would (*hă*) they take care to walk in the way of the LORD as their ancestors did or not (*'im-lō'*) ...?

Judg 9:2 "Say in the hearing of all the lords of Shechem, 'Which is better for you, that all seventy of the sons of Jerubbaal rule over you, or that one rule over you?' Remember also that I am your bone and your flesh".

"Which (*mah*) is better for you? Shall (*hă*) all seventy of the sons of Jerubbaal rule over you, or (*'im-*) one rule over you?"

Judg 20:28 ... "Shall we go out once more to battle against our kinsfolk the Benjaminites, or shall we desist?" The LORD answered, "Go up, for tomorrow I will give them into your hand".

"Shall (*hă*) we go out once more to battle against our kinsfolk the Benjaminites, or (*'im-*) shall we desist?"

2Sam 24:13 So Gad came to David and told him; he asked him, "Shall three years of famine come to you on your land? Or will you flee three months before your foes while they pursue you? Or shall there be three days' pestilence in your land? Now consider, and decide

"Shall (*hă*) three years of famine come to you on your land? Or will (*'im-*) you flee three months before your foes while they pursue

what answer I shall return to the one who sent me". | you? Or shall (wə'im-) there be three days' pestilence in your land?"

1Kings 22:6 Then the king of Israel gathered the prophets together, about four hundred of them, and said to them, "Shall I go to battle against Ramoth-gilead, or shall I refrain?" They said, "Go up; for the LORD will give it into the hand of the king". | "Shall (hă) I go to battle against Ramoth-gilead, or shall ('im-) I refrain?"

1Kings 22:15 When he had come to the king, the king said to him, "Micaiah, shall we go to Ramoth-gilead to battle, or shall we refrain?" He answered him, "Go up and triumph; the LORD will give it into the hand of the king". | "... shall (hă) we go to Ramoth-gilead to battle, or shall ('im-) we refrain?"

Eccl 11:6 In the morning sow your seed, and at evening do not let your hands be idle; for you do not know which will prosper, this or that, or whether both alike will be good. | ... for you do not know which will prosper: whether this or that (hăzeh 'ô-zeh), or whether (wə'im) both alike will be good.

2Chr 18:5 Then the king of Israel gathered the prophets together, four hundred of them, and said to them, "Shall we go to battle against Ramoth-gilead, or shall I refrain?" They said, "Go up; for God will give it into the hand of the king". | "Shall (hă) we go to battle against Ramoth-gilead, or shall ('im-) I refrain?"

2Chr 18:14 When he had come to the king, the king said to him, "Micaiah, shall we go to Ramoth-gilead to battle, or shall I refrain?" He answered, "Go up and triumph; they will be given into your hand". | "Micaiah, shall (hă) we go to Ramoth-gilead to battle, or shall ('im-) I refrain?"

3 Questions Anticipating a Negative Answer (a Rhetorical "Num")

3.1 Anticipating a simple emphatic negative

Gen 17:17 Then Abraham fell on his face and laughed, and said to himself, "Can a child be born to a man who is a hundred years | [Then Abraham fell on his face and laughed, and said to himself,] "Can (hă) a child be born to a man who is a hundred years old?

old? Can Sarah, who is ninety years old, bear a child?"

Gen 37:8 His brothers said to him, "Are you indeed to reign over us? Are you indeed to have dominion over us?" So they hated him even more because of his dreams and his words.

Num 11:12 Did I conceive all this people? Did I give birth to them, that you should say to me, "Carry them in your bosom, as a nurse carries a sucking child", to the land that you promised on oath to their ancestors?

Num 11:22 "Are there enough flocks and herds to slaughter for them? Are there enough fish in the sea to catch for them?"

Judg 6:31 But Joash said to all who were arrayed against him, "Will you contend for Baal? Or will you defend his cause? Whoever contends for him shall be put to death by morning. If he is a god, let him contend for himself, because his altar has been pulled down".

Judg 11:25 Now are you any better than King Balak son of Zippor of Moab? Did he ever enter into conflict with Israel, or did he ever go to war with them?

2Sam 19:36 [Eng 35] Today I am eighty years old; can I discern what is pleasant and what is not? Can your servant taste what he eats or what he drinks? Can I still listen to the voice of singing men and singing women? Why then should your servant be an added burden to my lord the king?

Or can (*wə'im*) Sarah, who is ninety years old, bear a child?"

"Are you indeed to reign (*hămālōk timlōk*) over us? Are you indeed to have dominion (*'im-māšōl timšōl*) over us?" [So they hated him even more (*wayyôsipû 'ôd śənō'*) ...]

Did (*hă*) I conceive all this people? Did (*'im*) I give birth to them, that (*kî*) you should say ...?

"Are (*hă*) there enough flocks and herds to slaughter for them? Are there (*'im*) enough fish in the sea to catch for them?" [The LORD said to Moses, "Is (*hă*) the LORD's power limited? Now (*'attāh*) you shall see whether (*hă*) my word will come true for you or not (*'im-lō'*).]

"Will (*hă*) you contend for Baal? Or (*'im-*) will you defend his cause?"

[Now are you any better (*hăṭôb ṭôb*) than King Balak son of Zippor of Moab?] Did he ever enter into conflict (*hărôb rāb*) with Israel, or did he ever go to war (*'im nilḥōm nilḥam*) with them? [... why (*ûmaddûa'*) did you not recover them...?]

Can (*hă*) I discern what is pleasant and what is not? Can (*'im*) your servant taste what he eats or what he drinks? Can ([*wə*]*'im*) I still listen to the voice of singing men and singing women? [Why then (*wəlāmmāh*) should your servant be an added burden ...?]

2Sam 19:43 [Eng 42] All the people of Judah answered the people of Israel, "Because the king is near of kin to us. Why then are you angry over this matter? Have we eaten at all at the king's expense? Or has he given us any gift?"

"[... Why then (*wəlāmmāh zeh*) are you angry over this matter?] Have we eaten at all (*heʾākôl ʾākalnû*) at the king's expense? Or has he given us any gift (*ʾim-niśśēʾt niśśāʾ lānû*)?"

Isa 10:15
Shall the axe vaunt itself over the one who wields it,
 or the saw magnify itself against the one who handles it?
As if a rod should raise the one who lifts it up,
 or as if a staff should lift the one who is not wood!

Shall (*hă*) the axe vaunt itself over the one who wields it,
 or (*ʾim*) the saw magnify itself against the one who handles it?
[As if (*kə*) a rod should raise the one who lifts it up,
 or as if (*kə*) a staff should lift the one who is not wood!]

Isa 27:7
Has he struck them down as he struck down those who struck them?
 Or have they been killed as their killers were killed?

Has (*hă*) he struck them down as he struck down those who struck them?
 Or (*ʾim-*) have they been killed as their killers were killed?
[... Therefore (*lākēn*) ...]

Isa 49:24–5
Can the prey be taken from the mighty,
 or the captives of a tyrant be rescued?

But thus says the LORD:
Even the captives of the mighty shall be taken,
 and the prey of the tyrant be rescued;
for I will contend with those who contend with you, and I will save your children.

Can (*hă*) the prey be taken from the mighty,
 or (*wəʾim*) the captives of a tyrant be rescued?

[But thus (*kî-kōh*) says the LORD:
Even (*gam-*) the captives of the mighty shall be taken ...]

Isa 50:2
Why was no one there when I came?
 Why did no one answer when I called?
Is my hand shortened, that it cannot redeem?
 Or have I no power to deliver?
By my rebuke I dry up the sea,
 I make the rivers a desert;
their fish stink for lack of water,
 and die of thirst.

[Why (*maddûaʿ*) was no one there when I came?
 Why did no one answer when I called?]
Is (*hă*) my hand shortened, that it cannot redeem?
 Or haven't (*wəʾim-ʾên*) I power to deliver?

Isa 66:8–9
Who has heard of such a thing?
 Who has seen such things?
Shall a land be born in one day?
 Shall a nation be delivered in one moment?

[Who (*mî*) has heard of such a thing?
 Who (*mî*) has seen such things?]
Shall (*hă*) a land be born in one day?
 Shall (*ʾim-*) a nation be delivered in one

Appendix. Occurrences of *hă ... 'im* in the Hebrew Bible — 117

Yet as soon as Zion was in labour
   she delivered her children.
Shall I open the womb and not deliver?
   says the LORD;
   shall I, the one who delivers, shut the
      womb?
   says your God.

moment? ...
[Yet ...]
Shall I (*ha'ănî*) open the womb and not
   deliver?
   says the LORD;
   shall I (*'im-'ănî*), the one who delivers,
      shut the womb?
   says your God.

Jer 2:14
Is Israel a slave? Is he a homeborn servant?
   Why then has he become plunder?

Is (*hă*) Israel a slave? Is (*'im-*) he a homeborn
   servant?
[Why then (*maddûa'*) has he become
   plunder?]

Jer 2:31
And you, O generation, behold the
   word of the LORD!
Have I been a wilderness to Israel,
   or a land of thick darkness?
Why then do my people say, "We are free,
   we will come to you no more"?

... Have (*hă*) I been a wilderness to Israel,
   or (*'im*) a land of thick darkness?
[Why then (*maddûa'*) do my people say, "We
   are free,
   we will come to you no more"?]

Jer 3:4–5
Have you not just now called to me,
   "My Father, you are the friend of my
      youth—
will he be angry forever,
   will he be indignant to the end?"
This is how you have spoken,
   but you have done all the evil that you
      could.

Will (*hă*) he be angry forever,
   will (*'im-*) he be indignant to the end?"
[This (*hinnēh*) is how you have spoken ...]

Jer 14:19
Have you completely rejected Judah?
   Does your heart loathe Zion?
Why have you struck us down
   so that there is no healing for us?
We look for peace, but find no good;
   for a time of healing, but there is terror
      instead.

Have you completely rejected (*hămā'ōs
   mā'astā*) Judah?
   Does (*'im-*) your heart loathe Zion?
[Why (*maddûa'*) have you struck us down ...?]

Jer 14:22
Can any idols of the nations bring rain?
   Or can the heavens give showers?
Is it not you, O LORD our God?
   We set our hope on you,

Can (*hă*) any idols of the nations bring rain?
   Or can (*wə'im*) the heavens give showers?

for it is you who do all this.

Jer 18:14–5
Does the snow of Lebanon leave
    the crags of Sirion?
Do the mountain waters run dry,
    the cold flowing streams?
But my people have forgotten me …

Jer 22:28
Is this man Coniah a despised broken
    pot,
    a vessel no one wants?
Why are he and his offspring hurled out
    and cast away in a land that they do not
    know?

Jer 31:20[2]
Is Ephraim my dear son?
    Is he the child I delight in?
As often as I speak against him,
    I still remember him.
Therefore I am deeply moved for him;
    I will surely have mercy on him, says the
    LORD.

Ezek 15:3–4
Is wood taken from it to make
    anything?
    Does one take a peg from it on which to
    hang any object?
It is put in the fire for fuel …

Ezek 22:14 Can your courage endure, or can your hands remain strong in the days when I shall deal with you? I the LORD have spoken, and I will do it.

Joel 1:2
Hear this, O elders,
    give ear, all inhabitants of the land!
Has such a thing happened in your days,
    or in the days of your ancestors?

[Is it not you (*hălô 'attāh-hû'*), O LORD our God?]

Does (*hă*) the snow of Lebanon leave
    the crags of Sirion?
Do ('*im-*) the mountain waters run dry,
    the cold flowing streams?
[But (*kî*) my people have forgotten me …]

Is (*hă*) this man Coniah a despised broken
    pot?
[Is he]('*im-*) a vessel no one wants?
[Why (*maddûaʿ*) are he and his offspring
    hurled out
    and cast away in a land that they do not
    know?]

Is (*hă*) Ephraim my dear son?
    Is ('*im-*) he the child I delight in
[*[that]* as (*kî*) often as I speak against him,
    I still remember (*zākōr 'ezkərennû*) him?
Therefore ('*al-kēn*) I am deeply moved for him;
    I will surely have mercy on him, says the
    LORD.]

Is (*hă*) wood taken from it to make anything?
Does ('*im-*) one take a peg from it on
    which to hang any object?
[*[no, rather]* (*hinnēh*) it is put in the fire for
    fuel]

Can (*hă*) your courage endure, or ('*im-*) can your hands remain strong in the days when I shall deal with you?

Has (*hă*) such a thing happened in your days,
    or ('*im-*) in the days of your ancestors?

---

2 On this verse, see Watson 2019, 444–50.

Amos 3:5–7

Does a bird fall into a snare on the
    earth,
  when there is no trap for it?
Does a snare spring up from the ground,
  when it has taken nothing?
Is a trumpet blown in a city,
  and the people are not afraid?
Does disaster befall a city,
  unless the LORD has done it?
Surely the Lord GOD does nothing,
  without revealing his secret
  to his servants the prophets.

Does (*hă*) a bird fall into a snare on the earth,
  when (*wə*) there is no trap for it?
Does (*hă*) a snare spring up from the ground,
  when (*wə*) it has taken nothing?
Is ('*im*-) a trumpet blown in a city,
  and (*wə*) the people are not afraid?
Does ('*im*-) disaster befall a city,
  unless (*wə*) the LORD has done it?
[Surely (*kî*) the Lord GOD does nothing,
  without (*kî* '*im*-) revealing his secret
  to his servants the prophets.]

Amos 6:2

Cross over to Calneh, and see;
  from there go to Hamath the great;
  then go down to Gath of the Philistines.
Are you better than these kingdoms?
  Or is your territory greater than their
    territory ...?

Are (*hă*) you better than these kingdoms?
  Or is ('*im*-) your territory greater than their
    territory ...?

Amos 6:12

Do horses run on rocks?
  Does one plough the sea with oxen?
But you have turned justice into poison
  and the fruit of righteousness into
    wormwood—

Do (*hă*) horses run on rocks?
  Does ('*im*-) one plough the sea with oxen?
[*[that]* (*kî*) you have turned justice into
    poison ...]

Mic 2:7

Should this be said, O house of Jacob?
  Is the LORD'S patience exhausted?
  Are these his doings?
Do not my words do good
  to one who walks uprightly?

Should (*hă*) this be said, O house of Jacob?
  Is (*hă*) the LORD'S patience exhausted?
  Are ('*im*-) these his doings?
[Do not (*hălô*') my words do good
  to one who walks uprightly?]

Mic 4:9

Now why do you cry aloud?
  Is there no king in you?
Has your counsellor perished,
  that pangs have seized you like a woman in
    labour?

[Now why (*'attāh lāmmāh*) do you cry aloud?]
  Is (*hă*) there no king in you?
Has ('*im*-) your counsellor perished,
  [that (*kî*) pangs have seized you like a
    woman in labour?]

Ps 77:10 [Eng 9]

... Has God forgotten to be gracious?
Has he in anger shut up his compassion?
   Selah

... Has (*hă*) God forgotten to be gracious?
Has (*'im-*) he in anger shut up his compassion?

Ps 78:19–20

They spoke against God, saying,
   "Can God spread a table in the wilderness?
Even though he struck the rock so that
     water gushed out
   and torrents overflowed,
can he also give bread,
   or provide meat for his people?"

["Can (*hă*) God spread a table in the wilderness?
Even though (*hēn*) he struck the rock so that
     water gushed out
   and torrents overflowed,]
can (*hă*) he also give bread,
   or (*'im-*) provide meat for his people?"

Ps 88:11 [Eng 10]

Do you work wonders for the dead?
   Do the shades rise up to praise you? *Selah*

Do (*hă*) you work wonders for the dead?
   Do (*'im-*) the shades rise up to praise you?

Job 4:17–8

Can mortals be righteous before God?
   Can human beings be pure before their Maker?
Even in his servants he puts no trust,
   and his angels he charges with error;

Can (*hă*) mortals be righteous before God?
   Can (*'im*) human beings be pure before their Maker?
[Even (*hēn*) in his servants he puts no trust ...]

Job 6:5–6

Does the wild ass bray over its grass,
   or the ox low over its fodder?
Can that which is tasteless be eaten without salt,
   or is there any flavour in the juice of mallows?

Does (*hă*) the wild ass bray over its grass,
   or (*'im*) the ox low over its fodder?
Can (*hă*) that which is tasteless be eaten without salt,
   or (*'im-*) is there any flavour in the juice of mallows?

Job 7:12

Am I the Sea, or the Dragon,
   that you set a guard over me?

Am (*hă*) I the Sea, or (*'im-*) the Dragon,
   [that (*kî*) you set a guard over me?]

Job 8:3

Does God pervert justice?
   Or does the Almighty pervert the right?

Does (*hă*) God pervert justice?
   Or (*wə'im-*) does the Almighty pervert the right?

Job 10:4–5

Do you have eyes of flesh?
   Do you see as humans see?
Are your days like the days of mortals,
   or your years like human years,

Do (*hă*) you have eyes of flesh?
   Do (*'im-*) you see as humans see?
Are (*hă*) your days like the days of mortals,
   or (*'im-*) your years like human years,

Job 11:2
"Should a multitude of words go unanswered,
 and should one full of talk be vindicated?

Should (*hă*) a multitude of words not (*lōʾ*) be answered,
 and should (*wəʾim-*) one full of talk be vindicated?

Job 11:7
"Can you find out the deep things of God?
 Can you find out the limit of the Almighty?

"Can (*hă*) you find out the deep things of God?
 Can (*ʾim*) you find out the limit of the Almighty?

Job 13:8–9
Will you show partiality toward him,
 will you plead the case for God?
Will it be well with you when he searches you out?
 Or can you deceive him, as one person deceives another?

Will (*hă*) you show partiality toward him,
 will (*ʾim-*) you plead the case for God?
Will (*hă*) it be well with you when he searches you out?
 Or can (*ʾim-*) you deceive him, as one person deceives another?

Job 22:3
Is it any pleasure to the Almighty if you are righteous,
 or is it gain to him if you make your ways blameless?

Is (*hă*) it any pleasure to the Almighty if you are righteous,
 or is (*wəʾim-*) it gain to him if you make your ways blameless?

Job 34:17
Shall one who hates justice govern?
 Will you condemn one who is righteous and mighty,

Shall (*hă*) one who hates justice govern?
 Will (*wəʾim-*) you condemn one who is righteous and mighty,

Job 37:20
Should he be told that I want to speak?
 Did anyone ever wish to be swallowed up?

Should (*hă*) he be told that I want to speak?
 Did (*ʾim-*) anyone ever wish to be swallowed up?

Job 38:33
Do you know the ordinances of the heavens?
 Can you establish their rule on the earth?

Do (*hă*) you know the ordinances of the heavens?
 Can (*ʾim-*) you establish their rule on the earth?

Job 39:9–10
"Is the wild ox willing to serve you?
 Will it spend the night at your crib?
Can you tie it in the furrow with ropes,
 or will it harrow the valleys after you?

"Is (*hă*) the wild ox willing to serve you?
 Will (*ʾim-*) it spend the night at your crib?
Can (*hă*) you tie it in the furrow with ropes,
 or will (*ʾim-*) it harrow the valleys after you?

Job 40:27 [Eng 41:3]
Will it make many supplications to you?
　Will it speak soft words to you?

Will (*hă*) it make many supplications to you?
　Will (*'im-*) it speak soft words to you?

Prov 6:27–9
Can fire be carried in the bosom
　without burning one's clothes?
Or can one walk on hot coals
　without scorching the feet?
So is he who sleeps with his neighbour's
　wife ...

Can (*hă*) a man carry fire in his bosom
　And not burn his clothes?
Or can (*'im-*) one walk on hot coals
　without scorching the feet?
[So (*kēn*) is he who sleeps with his neighbour's
　wife ...]

3.2 With *hălô'* and *'im-lō'*, thus anticipating a double negative, i.e. affirmative, response

Isa 40:28
Have you not known? Have you not
　heard?
The LORD is the everlasting God,
　the Creator of the ends of the earth.
He does not faint or grow weary;
　his understanding is unsearchable.

Haven't (*hălô'*) you known? Haven't (*'im-lō'*)
　you heard?
The God of everlasting is the LORD,
　the creator of the ends of the earth ...

3.2.1 With *hă ... lô'* and *'im ... lō'*, or *hă ... 'ên* and *'im ... 'ên*, thus anticipating a double negative, i.e. affirmative, response

Jer 5:9
Shall I not punish them for these
　things?
　　　　　　　　　　says the LORD;
and shall I not bring retribution
　on a nation such as this?

Shall (*hă*), for these things, I not (*lô'*) punish
　them?
　　　　　　　　　　says the LORD;
and shall (*wə'im*) on a nation such as this
　I not (*lō'*) bring retribution?

Jer 5:22
Do you not fear me? says the LORD;
　Do you not tremble before me?
I placed the sand as a boundary for the sea,
　a perpetual barrier that it cannot pass;
though the waves toss, they cannot prevail,
　though they roar, they cannot pass over it.

Do (*hă*) me you not (*lō'*) fear? says the LORD;
　Do (*'im*) before me you not (*lō'*) tremble?

Jer 5:29

Shall I not punish them for these
 things?
 says the LORD,
and shall I not bring retribution
 on a nation such as this?

Shall (*hă*) for these things I not (*lō'*) punish
 them?
 says the LORD,
and shall (*'im*) on a nation such as this
 I not (*lō'*) bring retribution?

Jer 8:4

You shall say to them, Thus says the
 LORD:
When people fall, do they not get up again?
 If they go astray, do they not turn back?

Do (*hă*) people fall and not (*wəlō'*) get up
 again?
Do (*'im*) they go astray, and not (*wəlō'*) turn
 back?

Jer 8:19

Hark, the cry of my poor people
 from far and wide in the land:
"Is the LORD not in Zion?
 Is her King not in her?"
"Why have they provoked me to anger with
 their images,
 with their foreign idols?"

"Is (*hă*) the LORD not (*'ên*) in Zion?
 Is (*'im-*) her King not (*'ên*) in her?"
["Why (*maddûaʻ*) ..."]

Jer 8:22

Is there no balm in Gilead?
 Is there no physician there?
Why then has the health of my poor people
 not been restored?

Is there no balm (*hă ... 'ên*) in Gilead?
 Is there no physician (*'im- ... 'ên*) there?
[Why then has not ([*kî*] *maddûaʻ lō'*) been
 restored
 the health of the daughter of
 my people]

Jer 9:8 [Eng 9]

Shall I not punish them for
 these things?
 says the LORD;
and shall I not bring retribution
 on a nation such as this?

Shall (*hă*) for these things I not (*lō'*) punish
 them?
 says the LORD;
And (*'im*) on a nation such as this
 shall I not (*lō'*) bring retribution?

Jer 49:1

Concerning the Ammonites.
 Thus says the LORD:
Has Israel no sons?
 Has he no heir?
Why then has Milcom dispossessed Gad,
 and his people settled in its towns?

Has (*hă*) Israel no (*'ên*) sons?
 Has (*'im*) he no (*'ên*) heir?
[Why then (*maddûaʻ*) has Milcom
 dispossessed Gad ...?]

Ps 94:9

He who planted the ear, does he not
 hear?

Does (*hă*) he who planted the ear, doesn't
 (*hălō'*) he hear?

He who formed the eye, does he not see?	Or (*'im-*) he who formed the eye, doesn't (*hălō'*) he see?
Job 6:30	
Is there any wrong on my tongue?	Is there (*hăyēš*) any wrong on my tongue?
Cannot my taste discern calamity?	Can (*'im-*) my taste not (*lō'*) discern calamity?

3.2.2 With *hălô' ... hălô' ... 'im-lō' ... 'im-lō'*, anticipating a double negative, i.e. affirmative, response

Isa 10:8–11 For he says:

"Are not my commanders all kings?	"Are not (*hălō'*) my commanders all kings?
Is not Calno like Carchemish?	Is not (*hălō'*) Calno like Carchemish?
Is not Hamath like Arpad?	Is not (*'im-lō'*) Hamath like Arpad?
Is not Samaria like Damascus?	Is not (*'im-lō'*) Samaria like Damascus? ...
As my hand has reached to the kingdoms of the idols	[Shan't I (*hălō'*) do to Jerusalem and her idols what I have done to Samaria and her images?]"
whose images were greater than those of Jerusalem and Samaria,	
shall I not do to Jerusalem and her idols what I have done to Samaria and her images?"	

3.3 Another possible variant: *hă' + hă' + 'im + 'im*, anticipating a negative reply

Amos 3:5–7

Does a bird fall into a snare on the earth, when there is no trap for it?	Does (*hă*) a bird fall into a snare on the earth, when (*wə*) there is no (*ên*) trap for it?
Does a snare spring up from the ground, when it has taken nothing?	Does (*hă*) a snare spring up from the ground, when it has taken nothing (*wəlākôd lō' yilkôd*)?
Is a trumpet blown in a city, and the people are not afraid?	Is (*'im-*) a trumpet blown in a city, and (*wə*) the people are not (*lō'*) afraid?
Does disaster befall a city, unless the LORD has done it?	Does (*'im-*) disaster befall a city, unless (*wə ... lō'*) the LORD has done it?
Surely the Lord GOD does nothing, without revealing his secret to his servants the prophets.	[Surely (*kî*) the Lord GOD does nothing, (*lō' ya'ăśeh*) without (*kî 'im-*) revealing his secret to his servants the prophets.]

3.4 A further possible variant: *hă' + wə'im-maddûaʿ*

Job 21:4

As for me, is my complaint addressed to mortals?
Why should I not be impatient?

As for me, is (*hă*) my complaint addressed to mortals?
Why shouldn't (*wə'im-maddûaʿ lō'*) I be impatient?

Bibliography

Albertz, Rainer. 1994. *A History of Israelite Religion in the Old Testament Period, I: From the Beginnings to the End of the Exile*. Translated by John Bowden. London: SCM.
Albright, William Foxwell. 1950. "The Psalm of Habakkuk". In *Studies in Old Testament Prophecy*, edited by H. H. Rowley, 1–18. Edinburgh: T. & T. Clark.
Alter, Robert. 1985. *The Art of Biblical Poetry*. Edinburgh: T. & T. Clark.
Andersen, Francis I. 2001. *Habakkuk: A New Translation with Introduction and Commentary*. AB 25. New York: Doubleday.
Anderson, A. A. 1972. *Psalms (1–72)*. NCBC. Grand Rapids: Eerdmans / Marshall Pickering.
Avishur, Yitzhak. 1994. *Studies in Hebrew and Ugaritic Psalms*. Publications of the Perry Foundation for Biblical Research, The Hebrew University of Jerusalem. Jerusalem: Magnes Press, The Hebrew University.
Ballentine, Debra Scoggins. 2015. *The Conflict Myth and the Biblical Tradition*. Oxford: OUP.
Bekkum, Koert van. 2017. "'Is Your Rage against the Rivers, Your Wrath Against the Sea?' Storm-God Imagery in Habakkuk 3". In *Playing with Leviathan: Interpretation and Reception of Monsters from the Biblical World*, edited by Koert van Bekkum, Jaap Dekker, Henk van de Kamp and Eric Peels, 55–76. TBN 21. Leiden and Boston: Brill.
Blenkinsopp, Joseph. 2002. *Isaiah 40–55*. AB 19A. New York: Doubleday.
Briggs, Charles Augustus, and Emilie Grace Briggs. 1906. *The Book of Psalms, I*. ICC. Edinburgh: T. & T. Clark.
Childs, Brevard S. 2001. *Isaiah*. OTL. London: Westminster John Knox Press.
Cross, Frank Moore. 1973. *Canaanite Myth and Hebrew Epic*. Cambridge, MA: Harvard University Press.
Curtis, Adrian H. W. 1978. "The 'Subjugation of the Waters' Motif in the Psalms: Imagery or Polemic?" *JSS* 23: 245–56.
Dahood, Mitchell J. 1966. *Psalms: Introduction, Translation, and Notes, I*. Anchor Bible 16. Garden City, NY: Doubleday.
Day, John. 1985. *God's Conflict with the Dragon and the Sea: Echoes of a Canaanite Myth in the Old Testament*. Cambridge: CUP.
Del Olmo Lette, G. 1999. "DEBER דבר". In *DDD*, 231–2.
Eaton, John H. 1964. "The Origin and Meaning of Habakkuk 3". *ZAW* 76: 144–70.
Faust, Avraham. 2013. "The Shephelah in the Iron Age: A New Look on the Settlement of Judah". *PEQ* 145/3: 203–19.
Forsyth, Neil. 1987. *The Old Enemy: Satan and the Combat Myth*. Princeton, NJ: Princeton University Press.
Fuchs, Gisela. 1993. *Mythos und Hiobdichtung: Aufnahme und Umdeutung altorientalischer Vorstellungen*. Stuttgart: Kohlhammer.
Gelston, Anthony. 2010. *Introduction and Commentaries on The Twelve Minor Prophets*. BHQ 13. Stuttgart: Deutsche Bibelgesellschaft.
Gesenius, Wilhelm, and Udo Rüterswörden. 1987. *Hebräisches und Aramäisches Handwörterbuch über das Alte Testament, I*. Revised and edited by Rudolf Meyer and Herbert Donner. 18th edition. Berlin: Springer Verlag.
Gibson, John C. L. 1977. *Canaanite Myths and Legends*. Edinburgh: T. & T. Clark.

Gibson, John C. L. 1994. *Davidson's Introductory Hebrew Grammar: Syntax.* 4th edition. Edinburgh: T. & T. Clark.
Haak, Robert D. 1992. *Habakkuk.* VTSup 44. Leiden: Brill.
Habel, Norman C. 2011. *The Birth, The Curse and the Greening of Earth: An Ecological Reading of Genesis 1–11.* EBC 1. Sheffield: Sheffield Phoenix.
Hallo, William W. (ed.). 1997–2002. *The Context of Scripture. 3 vols.* Leiden: Brill.
Handy, Lowell K. 1994. *Among the Host of Heaven: The Syro-Palestinian Pantheon as Bureaucracy.* Winona Lake, IN: Eisenbrauns.
Held, Moshe. 1969. "Rhetorical Questions in Ugaritic and Biblical Hebrew". In "W. F. Albright Volume", edited by Avraham Malamat, special issue. *Eretz Israel: Archaeological, Historical and Geographical Studies* 9: 71–9.
Hess, Richard S. 2007. *Israelite Religions: An Archaeological and Biblical Survey.* Grand Rapids, MI: Baker Academic.
Hiebert, Theodore. 1986. *God of My Victory: The Ancient Hymn in Habakkuk 3.* HSM 38. Atlanta, GA: Scholars Press.
Hobbs, T. R. 1989. *A Time For War: A Study of Warfare in the Old Testament.* OTS 3. Wilmington, DE: Michael Glazier.
Hoffmeier, James K. 2005. *Ancient Israel in Sinai: The Evidence for the Authenticity of the Wilderness Traditions.* Oxford: OUP. Oxford Scholarship Online. https://doi.org/10.1093/acprof:oso/0195155467.001.000.
Irwin, William A. 1942. "The Psalm of Habakkuk". *JNES* 1/1: 10–40.
Jacobsen, Thorkild. 1968. "The Battle between Marduk and Tiamat". *JAOS* 88: 104–8.
Jeremias, Joachim. 1965. *Theophanie: Die Geschichte einer Alttestamentlichen Gattung.* WMANT 10. Neukirchen Vluyn: Neukirchener Verlag.
Jöcken, Peter. 1977. *Das Buch Habakuk: Darstellung der Geschichte seiner kritischen Erforschung mit einer eigenen Beurteilung.* BBB 48. Köln: Hanstein.
Johnston, Philip S. 2002. *Shades of Sheol: Death and Afterlife in the Old Testament.* Downers Grove, IL: Inter-Varsity Press. Leicester: Apollos.
Joüon, Paul, S. J. 1996. *A Grammar of Biblical Hebrew, Part One: Orthography and Phonetics; Part Two: Morphology; Part Three: Syntax.* Translated and revised by T. Muraoka. Subsidia Biblica 14/I. Rome: Editrice Pontificio Istituto Biblico.
Keel, Othmar. 1997. *The Symbolism of the Biblical World: Ancient Near Eastern Iconography and the Book of Psalms.* Translated by Timothy J. Hallett. Winona Lake, IND: Eisenbrauns.
Kitchen, Kenneth A. 1966. *Ancient Orient and Old Testament.* Downers Grove, IL: IVP.
Lortie, Christopher R. 2016. *Mighty to Save: A Literary and Historical Study of Habakkuk 3 and its Traditions.* ATS 99. Sankt Ottilien: EOS.
Margulis, Baruch. 1970. "The Psalm of Habakkuk: A Reconstruction and Interpretation". *ZAW* 82: 409–41.
May, Herbert G. 1955. "Some Cosmic Connotations of Mayim Rabbîm, 'Many Waters'". *JBL* 74: 9–21.
Miller, Robert D., II. "What Are the Nations Doing in the Chaoskampf?" In *Creation and Chaos: A Reconsideration of Hermann Gunkel's Chaoskampf Hypothesis*, edited by JoAnn Scurlock and Richard H. Beal, 206–16. Winona Lake, IN: Eisenbrauns.
Mowinckel, Sigmund. 1953. "Zum Psalm des Habakuk". *TZ* 9: 1–23.

Mowinckel, Sigmund. 1962. *The Psalms in Israel's Worship*. 2 vols. Revised; translated by D. R. Ap-Thomas. Oxford: Blackwell.
Muilenburg, James. 1969. "Form Criticism and Beyond". *JBL* 88: 1–18.
Newsom, Carol A. 2003. *The Book of Job: A Contest of Moral Imaginations*. Oxford: OUP.
O'Brien, Julia M. 2004. *Nahum, Habakkuk, Zephaniah, Haggai, Zechariah, Malachi*. Abingdon Old Testament Commentaries. Nashville: Abingdon Press.
Ortlund, Eric Nels. 2010. *Theophany and Chaoskampf: The Interpretation of Theophanic Imagery in the Baal Epic, Isaiah, and the Twelve*. GUS 5. Piscataway, NJ: Gorgias Press.
Parker, Simon B. 1997. *Ugaritic Narrative Poetry*. SBLWAW 9. Atlanta, GA: Scholars Press.
Pitard, Wayne T. "The Combat Myth as a Succession Story at Ugarit". In *Creation and Chaos: A Reconsideration of Hermann Gunkel's Chaoskampf Hypothesis*, edited by JoAnn Scurlock and Richard H. Beal, 199–205. Winona Lake, IN: Eisenbrauns.
Redditt, Paul L. 2008. *Introduction to the Prophets*. Grand Rapids, MI and Cambridge, UK: Eerdmans.
Roberts, J. J. M. 1991. *Nahum, Habakkuk and Zephaniah*. OTL. Louisville, KY: Westminster John Knox Press.
Rudolph, Wilhelm. 1975. *Micha—Nahum—Habakuk—Zephanja*. KAT 13/3. Gütersloh: Gerd Mohn.
Scurlock, JoAnn, and Richard H. Beal (eds.). 2013. *Creation and Chaos: A Reconsideration of Hermann Gunkel's Chaoskampf Hypothesis*. Winona Lake, IN: Eisenbrauns.
Selms, Adriaan van. 1971/72. "Motivated Interrogative Sentences in Biblical Hebrew". *Semitics* 2: 143–9.
Smith, Mark S. 1994. *The Ugaritic Baal Cycle, Volume 1: Introduction with Text, Translation and Commentary of KTU 1.1–1.2*. VTSup 55. Leiden: Brill.
Smith, Mark S. 1997. "The Baal Cycle". In *Ugaritic Narrative Poetry*, edited by Simon B. Parker, 81–180. SBLWAW 9. Atlanta, GA: Scholars Press.
Smith, Mark S. 2001. *The Origins of Biblical Monotheism: Israel's Polytheistic Background and the Ugaritic Texts*. Oxford: OUP.
Smith, Mark S. 2002. *The Early History of God: Yahweh and the Other Deities in Ancient Israel*. 2nd edition. Grand Rapids, MI: Eerdmans.
Smith, Mark S. 2004. *The Memoirs of God: History, Memory and the Experience of the Divine in Ancient Israel*. Minneapolis, MN: Fortress Press.
Smith, Ralph L. 1984. *Micah-Malachi*. WBC. Waco, TX: Word Books.
Stonehouse, George G. V. 1911. *The Book of Habakkuk: Introduction, Translation, and Notes on the Hebrew Text*. London: Rivingtons.
Terrien, Samuel. 2003. *The Psalms: Strophic Structure and Theological Commentary*. ECC. Grand Rapids, MI: Eerdmans.
Tromp, Nicholas J. 1969. *Primitive Conceptions of Death and the Nether World in the Old Testament*. BibOr 21. Rome: Pontifical Biblical Institute.
Tsumura, David T. 1988. "Ugaritic Poetry and Habakkuk 3". *Tyndale Bulletin* 40: 24–48.
Tsumura, David T. 1989. *The Earth and the Waters in Genesis 1 and 2: A Linguistic Investigation*. JSOTSup 83. Sheffield: Sheffield Academic Press.
Tsumura, David T. 1996. "The 'Word Pair' *qšt and *mṭ in Habakkuk 3:9 in the Light of Ugaritic and Akkadian". In *"Go to the Land I Will Show You": Studies in Honor of Dwight W. Young*, edited by Joseph E. Coleson and Victor H. Matthews, 353–61. Winona Lake, IN: Eisenbrauns.

Tsumura, David T. 2005. *Creation and Destruction: A Reappraisal of the Chaoskampf Theory in the Old Testament*, Winona Lake, IN: Eisenbrauns.

Tsumura, David T. 2007. "The 'Chaoskampf' Motif in Ugaritic and Hebrew Literatures". In *Le Royaume d'Ougarit de la Crète à l'Euphrate: Nouveaux Axes de Recherche*, edited by J.-M. Michaud, 473–99. Sherbrooke, QC: G. G. C. Éditions.

Tugendhaft, Aaron. 2013. "Babel–Bible–Baal". In *Creation and Chaos: A Reconsideration of Hermann Gunkel's Chaoskampf Hypothesis*, edited by JoAnn Scurlock and Richard H. Beal, 190–8. Winona Lake, IN: Eisenbrauns.

Van der Merwe, Christo H. J., Jackie A. Naudé and Jan H. Kroeze. 1999. *A Biblical Hebrew Reference Grammar*. Biblical Languages: Hebrew 3. Sheffield: Sheffield Academic Press.

Wakeman, Mary K. 1973. *God's Battle with the Monster: A Study in Biblical Imagery*. Leiden: E. J. Brill.

Watson, Rebecca S. 2005. *Chaos Uncreated: A Reassessment of the Theme of "Chaos" in the Hebrew Bible*. BZAW 341. Berlin: Walter de Gruyter.

Watson, Rebecca S. 2019. "אִם ... הֲ: A Rhetorical Question Anticipating a Negative Answer". *JSOT* 44/3: 437–55.

Watson, Wilfred G. E. 1995. *Classical Hebrew Poetry: A Guide to its Techniques*. 2nd, corrected, edition. Sheffield: Sheffield Academic Press.

Williamson, H. G. M. 1989. Review of *God of My Victory: The Ancient Hymn in Habakkuk 3*, by Theodore Hiebert. In *VT* 39: 509–10.

Wright, Jacob L. 2020. *War, Memory and National Identity in the Hebrew Bible*. Cambridge: CUP.

Wolde, Ellen van. 1998. "Facing the Earth: Primaeval History in a New Perspective". In *The World of Genesis: Persons, Places, Perspectives*, edited by Philip R. Davies and David J. A. Clines, 22–47. JSOTSup 257. Sheffield: Sheffield Academic Press.

Wyatt, Nicolas. 1998. *Religious Texts from Ugarit: The Words of Ilimilku and his Colleagues*. BibSem 53. Sheffield: Sheffield Academic Press.

Wyatt, Nicolas. 2002. *Religious Texts from Ugarit*. 2nd edition. London: Sheffield Academic Press/Continuum.

Xella, Paolo. 1999. "RESHEPH רשף". In *DDD*, 700–3.

Yadin, Yigael. 1963. *The Art of Warfare in Biblical Lands in the Light of Archaeological Discovery*. Translated by M. Pearlman. London: Weidenfeld and Nicholson.

—
**Second Conversation
Did Josiah Enact a Monotheistic Reform?
Debating Belief in One God in Preexilic Judah
Through 2 Kings 22–3**

Part I: **Engagement**

This conversation focuses on the question as to whether or not Josiah or anyone before the exile ever believed in a form of monotheism. The discussion will address the issue of whether Josiah carried on a monotheistic "reform" in the late seventh century and whether belief in one god was present in preexilic Judah. So the topic is "Belief in One God in Preexilic Judah" and the text is 2Kings 22–3.

Richard S. Hess and Nathan MacDonald

Richard S. Hess
2 Kings 22–3: Belief in One God in Preexilic Judah?

The purpose of this study is to survey the biblical narrative of 2Kgs 22–3 and to consider its claims regarding religious reform. This will then be evaluated in the light of extra biblical archaeological and textual evidence from the Southern Levant in the late Iron Age. In particular, the issue concerns the reforms of Josiah and the question of belief in a single deity in Judah before the destruction of Jerusalem in 586 BCE.

In terms of definitions and assumptions, I note that this is not an argument for a particular philosophical monotheism in this period.[1] It is not necessary to argue that the Judeans held this or that view of the state religions in the surrounding nations; for example, that they denied the existence of their gods altogether. Nor does it fall to me to argue for a view regarding the deities that one's own neighbours might have worshipped, that these could not have been perceived as spiritual forces on some level. Rather, the emphasis will remain focused on the Judean worshipper and their belief in a deity, in this case Yahweh, whom the worshipper acknowledged to the exclusion of any other deity.

Another area that this paper will avoid has to do with any antecedents to belief in one God in Judah in the period before Josiah. It will not be my concern to argue for a theory on the origins of the practice of worshipping a single deity. Rather, the focus will be on the actual practice of worship in the decades preceding the Babylonian destruction of Judah and Jerusalem.

I will first examine the reforms of Josiah in 2Kgs 22–3. A close examination of their portrayal may invite consideration of a preexilic context. If so, this would reinforce the understanding of the account of Josiah as preserving an authentic record of someone who championed the worship of a single deity, the national deity of Judah, Yahweh.

---

[1] For the term, "philosophical monotheism", cf. Halpern 2009, 13–560, especially p 32. For the idea of monotheism and its appearance in the Hebrew Bible, cf. Moberly 2013, 33–40.

1 2 Kings 22–3

Methodologically, there are different views regarding the witness of 2Kgs 22–3 and the life, reform and death of King Josiah. Many commentators have assumed a substantial historicity to the account, often adding notes where it appears to correlate with the larger historical context of the contemporary ancient Near East in the late seventh century BCE.[2] While commentators sometimes accept a Deuteronomistic redaction to the text, many do not deny its historical kernel as describing a religious reform in the time of Josiah that recognised only Yahweh and rejected other deities.[3] Others have argued against this with a variety of views. For example, Ahlström maintains that what he terms "pure religion" is an exilic creation.[4] Stavrakopoulou has found in 2Kgs 22–3 a "book religion" whose origins lay in the social environment of the postexilic period rather than in late seventh century BCE Judah.[5] More focused on the question of this essay, Niehr asserts that the worship of a single deity, such as Yahweh, did not emerge until the Persian period, and then only gradually.[6] The purpose of this section of the paper will be to examine these recent claims concerning the validity of 2Kgs 22–3 as a narrative whose religious practices might accurately reflect the world of late seventh century BCE Judah. The latter part of this paper will consider the possibility of belief in Yahweh alone at this time in light of the extra biblical evidence.

According to the biblical text, the figure of Josiah looms large over the latter half of the seventh century in the southern Levant. The text informs us of a reign of 31 years, longer than that of his four successors put together. The central feature of this reign occurs in the reforms that Josiah implements. 2Kings 22:1–23:3 describes the discovery of the Book of the Law, the prophecy of Huldah and the

---

[2] Brueggemann (2000, 543–65); Cogan and Tadmor (1988, 277–302); Hobbs 1985, 312–43); G. H. Jones (1984, 607–25); Provan (1984, 270–6); Sweeney (2007, 434–50); Wiseman (1993, 293–306).
[3] The issue of the origins of the "book of the law" and its relationship to the reform itself lies beyond the question addressed in this essay.
[4] Ahlström 1993, 770.
[5] Stavrakopoulou 2010b, 37–58, especially p. 49.
[6] Niehr 2010, 23–36, especially p. 31: "But during the Achaemenid period and even later, the second and third levels of the … polytheistic hierarchy were gradually discarded as increasing emphasis was placed on YHWH as an authoritative deity and on the messengers as YHWH's servants". For a different conclusion regarding the role and evolution of the Israelite "pantheon", one that allows for the presence of a belief in a single deity before 586 BCE, see Smith 2001.

assembly of the people where Josiah promises to follow Yahweh alone. In fact, Yahweh is the only deity mentioned and the only one worshipped by Josiah. The text groups together "other gods" and makes no specific mention of any deity other than the one that Josiah worships. The passage 2Kgs 23:16–30 concludes the story of Josiah's reform, ending with an evaluation of his reign and a description of his death. At no time does it identify any other gods or goddesses by name or suggest that Josiah worshipped any deity other than Yahweh.

In contrast, the middle section of Second Kings' description of Josiah's life, 23:4–15, is filled with many names of deities worshipped in Jerusalem and at Bethel. Taken together the reforms here explicitly identify a major shift at the level of official policy. This testifies to a turn to the worship of a single deity. Those who understand this account as a later and postexilic ideological construct of the religious reform must explain how political concerns of a later time led the writers of this account entirely or largely to recreate it and ascribe it to Josiah. In order to emphasise the reform, in 2Kgs 23:4–15 the authors or editors have made use of many names of gods and goddesses, all of which are known in the preexilic period.[7] They are not attested in the postexilic period in Yehud. In addition to this concurrence in the preexilic period, is there anything in the biblical account that might further betray an authenticity to the witness of the text that Josiah worshipped a single deity?

We can add the evidence of the unexpected absence of some divine names in the list of the elimination of other deities (and their objects) in 2Kgs 23:4–15. Why is it that in one or two places no deity is named? Our argument will be that the absence of a name is intentional and points to a heterodox worship of Yahweh omitted by the author of the account so as to highlight the "Yahweh vs. other gods" opposition present in 1 and 2 Kings. This Yahweh was not the Yahweh that Josiah worshipped. All this would have been clear to a writer in the preexilic religious context, but not in a postexilic environment, where these specific, heterodox forms of Yahweh worship are not attested. Thus this argues for a preexilic origin and authenticity to the account.

2Kings 23:12 makes no mention as to the identity of the deity worshipped on the roof of the palace. Indeed, the identity of various gods and goddesses as reflected in this text invites the possibility that Yahweh is the deity or one of the deities to whom the altars were dedicated. Recent studies in ancient Israelite religions have demonstrated the diverse nature of the worship of deities in the land. There was no single religion that identifies the entire population through-

---

[7] For the identity and Iron Age (as well as Late Bronze Age) attestation of these deities and cult objects, see Cogan and Tadmor 1988, 285–91.

out the Iron Age, but various practices and beliefs are attested in both biblical texts and in the Iron Age cultic remains. The various witnesses provide evidence of both the different religious beliefs and the deities worshipped.[8]

Several lines of evidence converge to suggest that the texts point to Yahweh as the principal recipient of the worship performed by the altars mentioned in 2Kgs 23:12. These include the outline of Josiah's reforms, the context of the rooftop cultic practices of the kings of Judah, and the context of other West Semitic kings as they performed rooftop rituals.

First, we consider the immediate literary environment that describes Josiah's reign. 2Kings 23:12 occurs in the context of Josiah's reforms in vv. 4–14. The verbs and phrases describing the numerous reforms in and around Jerusalem regularly appear with deities named.

Thus Josiah oversees:[9]

> removal from the temple of objects made for Baal, Asherah, and the hosts of heaven (v. 4);
> elimination of *hakkəmārîm* who burned incense on the high places of Judah and around Jerusalem to Baal, the sun and moon deities, the constellations, and all the hosts of the heavens (v. 5);
> removal of the Asherah pole from the temple of Jerusalem (v. 6);
> destruction of the houses of the *haqqədēšîm* in the temple of Yahweh where the female weavers worked for Asherah (v. 7);
> desecration of the Tophet in the Valley of Ben Hinnom where human sacrifice was made to Molek (v. 10);
> removal of the horses and incineration of the chariots dedicated to the sun deity (v. 11);
> desecration of the high places Solomon had built for Ashtoreth, Chemosh, and Molek (v. 13); and
> smashing of the *maṣṣēbôt* and the Asherah poles on those high places (v. 14).

Verse 15 moves the reform north to Bethel where Josiah destroyed the altar and high place, as well as the Asherah pole. Regarding the destruction and removal of cult objects in this list, only the rooftop altars of the kings of Judah in v. 12 and the altar at Bethel in v. 15 have no explicit association with any deity.[10] Yet we know that the authors/editors of Kings had identified Jeroboam's construction of the sanctuary at Bethel with Israel's gods who brought them up out of Egypt (1Kgs 12:28).[11] This connection with Yahweh's epithet (Deut 20:1; Josh

---

[8] See, for example, R. S. Hess 2007a.
[9] See above, n. 7.
[10] For the altars of Manasseh in the courts of the temple of Yahweh and their association with all the host of heaven, see 2Kgs 21:4–5.
[11] The discussion of the prophet's bones in 2Kgs 23:16–8 explicitly relates this passage to 1Kgs 13:1–2, 30–2.

24:17; Judg 2:1; 6:8, 13; 1 Sam 8:8; 10:18; 12:6) suggests that some form of Yahweh was worshipped at Bethel. However unorthodox 2Kings might have regarded this, the Kuntillet ʿAjrud and Khirbet el-Qom connections of Yahweh with Asherah, in the interpretation of most who read these texts, suggests that an Asherah shrine at Bethel should not surprise anyone.[12] This is especially true if Yahweh was in fact the national deity worshipped there.

Why did the writers not give a name to the deity or deities worshipped on the rooftop shrine of 2Kgs 23:12? If, like the reference to the altar at Bethel, this involved an unorthodox expression of Yahweh, then perhaps the writers wished to disassociate the name of Yahweh from any connection with worship outside of the temple of Jerusalem, even if it was only "next door" on the roof of the palace. However, they never explicitly identified the deity as foreign and non-Yahwistic. They simply remained silent in this matter.

A second line of evidence considers rooftop cultic practices of the Judean kings, as recounted in the biblical text. Several commentaries relate 2Kgs 23:12 to other references such as 2Kgs 20:11; 21:3; Jer 19:13; and 32:29.[13] 2Kgs 20:11 associates the *maʿălôt* or "steps" of Ahaz with a shadow that Yahweh uses to demonstrate a miracle. However, we do not know if this is the *hammizbəḥôt ʾăšer ʿal-haggāg ʿălîyat* of 2Kgs 23:12. Even if it is, it indicates nothing about a cultic purpose other than an association with a miracle of Yahweh. 2Kings 21:3 describes how Manasseh built altars to Baal. Are these the altars of Manasseh in 2Kgs 23:12? They are not necessarily located on the roof. Jeremiah 19:13 and 32:29 describe activities of the general populace where they burned incense to the host of heaven and to Baal on their roofs. If these deities were involved, they do not establish a non-Yahwistic rooftop cult among the kings. To the contrary, one might expect the kings of Judah to worship a national or dynastic deity. For Judah, these would both identify Yahweh. The royal worship of Yahweh, perhaps in association with other deities, would have provided part of the rooftop activities for the kings in Jerusalem.

A third line of evidence turns to examine other kings of the West Semitic world.[14] Two Ugaritic texts mention rulers ascending to roofs in order to sacrifice. *CAT* 1.41, the ritual of the new wine festival, requires a specific ceremony that the king must do on the *gg* ("roof") of a building. Although Pardee offers a slightly

---

[12] Aḥituv, Eshel and Meshel 2012, 73–142; Hess 2007b, 13–42; 2007b, 283–90. For connections between Kuntillet ʿAjrud and official (northern) Israelite state-sponsored religion (as at Bethel?), see Naʾaman 2013, 39–51.
[13] Wiseman 1993, 303; Sweeney 2007, 449.
[14] The human sacrifice that King Mesha of Moab offers in 2Kgs 3:27 mentions no deity and so is not directly relevant.

different translation than that of Hutton, they agree that the ritual takes place on a roof where the king sacrifices offerings to a god who, among other things, may be connected with the vineyard.[15] This is likely the roof of the temple of the chief god, Ilu, and thus describes an offering in the context of the chief deity worshipped at Ugarit.[16] The same is true of legendary King Kirta (*CAT* 1.14 iii.52–iv.9a) who, having received a night vision concerning his request for offspring, awakens and goes first to the top of the tower, or the rooftops.[17] Semantically, it may be interesting to note that the Ugaritic *ẓr*, "top, summit", resembles the Hebrew *bāmāh*, "high place", in that both also carry the sense of the back of an animal or a person. Nevertheless, a *gg* or plural *ggt*, "roofs", appears as the place from which Kirta descends after the ritual. In any case, the Ugaritic text explicitly states that King Kirta sacrifices to the chief deity, Ilu.

The evidence points to the chief deity of Judah, Yahweh, as the figure worshipped on the roof of Jerusalem's palace and at Bethel. Why was Yahweh not identified by the biblical writer describing Josiah's reform? In both cases Yahweh had been worshipped inappropriately, whether in conjunction with Asherah, as at Bethel, or in some unorthodox fashion on the palace rooftops. The extra-biblical evidence of Kuntillet Ajrud and Khirbet el-Qom is particularly relevant for the Bethel worship. It suggests that behind 2Kings lay an authentic awareness that an unorthodox form of Yahwism was associated with the worship at Bethel, one that involved Yahweh alongside Asherah.[18] There is no evidence that this form of veneration (Yahweh and Asherah as a couple) remained active in the postexilic period. Yet a writer from that time might have easily added the names of other deities to these "blank spots" in 2Kgs 23:12 and 15. That the writer did not betrays an awareness of an unacceptable form of Yahwistic worship that occurred in the preexilic period. If this knowledge was accurately preserved in 2Kgs 23, might the emphasis on Josiah's worship of Yahweh alone also have been preserved? For this it is necessary to consider the extra biblical evidence during the final generations of the Judean Monarchy.

---

15 Pardee 2002, 65 *CAT* 1.41.50.
16 Pardee 2002, 106 n. 75. See p. 252 for the reference to PRGL-ṢQRN as "an unidentified entity". The location at the temple of Ilu implies an association with this chief deity.
17 *COS* 1: 102, p. 335, translation by Dennis Pardee. The text is *CAT* 1.14 iv. 1–9.
18 This argues against the Bethel account as only a postexilic creation of a redactor, as maintained by Volkmar 2003, 408.

2 Extra-Biblical Evidence

This evidence becomes pertinent in describing Israelite faith and practice because of critical questions regarding the biblical text and because there is useful material for the establishment of a picture of Judean religion during the decades before the fall of Jerusalem to the Babylonian army in 586 BCE. This paper will argue that sufficient evidence exists to posit a belief in a single deity among a significant part of the population of Judah and Jerusalem. There are three areas that provide evidence: material culture, especially iconography; inscriptions that mention deities; and personal names with theophoric elements.

With respect to the material culture, one might not expect any images. If the ban on representations of the divine as found in Exod 20:4 (Lev 26:1; Deut 4:16; 5:8; 7:25) was observed, then we should not expect to find images of Yahweh among those who worshipped him as the sole deity. Perhaps for this reason anthropomorphic figures on seals in the Palestinian region diminish at this time.[19] Archaeologists do, however, find hundreds of clay figurines representing the upper body and sometimes the head of a female. These have been identified with a goddess worshipped in domestic contexts, usually Asherah.[20] More than eight hundred figurines have been uncovered in the territory traditionally ascribed to that of the kingdom of Judah. At Tell en-Nasbeh, to the north of Jerusalem, all but one of the 120 figurines found there were broken, usually at the neck. Were these images of goddesses destroyed in a reform such as that described by Josiah? Or were these figurines serving some other purpose? Often located in domestic contexts (as opposed to sanctuaries), they may have served as good luck charms for conception, birth, or lactation; or as physical expressions of prayers; or as something else.[21] Their crude manufacture and the use of a cheap material such as clay argues against the image of a goddess and in favour of a human or other non-divine figure. In the end certainty is impossible. They cannot be used to argue for or against the worship of a single deity in Judah in the seventh and early sixth centuries BCE.

We turn to the inscriptions. There are many Hebrew inscriptions and more discovered almost annually in Judah. Recent collected studies provide useful resources.[22] Some mention only epithets of deities, such as the ostracon from c.

---

[19] Keel and Uehlinger 1998, 177–281.
[20] Most eloquently by Dever (2005).
[21] Hess 2007a, 308–11.
[22] E.g., Davies 1991, Davies 2004, Renz 1995, Dobbs-Allsopp, Roberts, Seow, and Whitaker 2005, Aḥituv 2008.

700 BCE discovered in the Upper City of Jerusalem and containing the expression, *qn'rṣ* "creator of earth". It is difficult to know to which deity to ascribe this epithet as the fragment does not include an identification.[23]

Those inscriptions that mention deities can be reviewed here. I begin with two of the best known, the small silver scrolls, probably used as amulets, that each contain a blessing of Yahweh to his people similar to that found in Num 6:24–6. Discovered at Ketef Hinnom, in tomb sites from c. 600 BCE, overlooking the Hinnom Valley and west of the City of David, these inscriptions attest to a concern that Yahweh bless and provide deliverance from any evil.[24] The divine name, *yhwh*, occurs seven times. No other deity appears.

The Lachish letters were written on ostraca at the site of Tell ed-Duweir during the period before the Babylonian destruction of Jerusalem. In part, they form official correspondence between the military leaders of the site and others such as Hoshayahu. Ostraca 2, 3, 4, 5, 6, and 9 are preserved well enough to allow reading and understanding of much of their message.[25] They all begin with a blessing invoked to Yahweh for the recipient. Ostraca 3 and 6 invoke the life of Yahweh to emphasise a point the writer wishes to make. Ostracon 2, lines 5–6, may express a wish for Yahweh to make a matter clear (known?) to the recipient. Ostracon 5, lines 7–9, express a wish or prayer for a good harvest from Yahweh. Thus Yahweh has the power to provide fertility.

On the ostraca from Arad, similar to those at Lachish insofar as they contain correspondence and some lists, numbers 16, 18, 21, and 40 invoke Yahweh in blessings.[26] Ostracon 18 concludes the letter with a note that Eliashib is in the house of Yahweh. Ostracon 21 may include a partially preserved oath to Yahweh.

A non-provenanced text that may originate from Makkedah dates to our period of interest and includes a blessing to Yahweh.[27]

Most interesting are four inscriptions found at Khirbet Beit Lei near Lachish. Dating to c. 600 BCE, these texts describe Yahweh as God of Judah and Jerusalem and call on him to absolve and to save.[28] Although there is dispute as to the precise translation of the first two inscriptions, epigraphists are agreed on these general interpretations. The second inscription identifies Yah with Yahweh (as a shortened form of the divine name).

---

[23] Aḥituv 2008, 40–2. Cf. Genesis 14:22.
[24] Barkay et al. 2004, 41–71.
[25] Aḥituv 2008, 56–91.
[26] Aharoni, 1981; Aḥituv 2008, 92–153.
[27] Aharoni 1981,199.
[28] Aharoni 1981, 233–6. These characteristics of Yahweh belie assertions that Yahweh was only a weather god "even until postexilic times", as Niehr 2010, 30.

These examples constitute those Hebrew texts that are generally agreed to date from the seventh or early sixth centuries BCE and originate in the traditional area ascribed to the kingdom of Judah. They mention deities by name. Of course, they mention only one deity, that of Yahweh, or in one inscription his shortened name of Yah. No other deity is mentioned. As far as the inscriptions are concerned Judah at this time worshipped only one deity, Yahweh.

An objection may be anticipated that the inscriptions refer only to the chief deity of the state and that other deities were worshipped by all the people of Judah, including those who wrote these texts. They refer only to the national deity as a matter of special honour and custom, perhaps because they are writing official documents. Is this the case in the surrounding countries of the Iron Age? Do other documents, where there is some degree of abundance in their number, refer only to a single state deity?

The early seventh century BCE inscription from Ekron, one of the cities of the Philistines, was intended as a dedicatory inscription for the temple of PTGYH, a female deity who is called upon to bless the ruler and all that is his.[29] A second dedicatory inscription was found at Ekron.[30] It was composed by King Padi, the father of the king responsible for the first inscription. It is dedicated to Baal. Other deities are mentioned in other inscriptions from seventh century BCE Philistia.[31] Thus it seems that inhabitants of contemporary Philistia, who worshipped various deities, did not hesitate to mention the names of their deities in seventh century BCE inscriptions. This is true even among the kings of Ekron.

The other neighbours with multiple preserved texts from the late Iron Age mentioning one or more deities are the Ammonites. The relevant inscriptions are the Amman Citadel Inscription and the Amman Theatre Inscription.[32] The Citadel Inscription appears as the words of the deity Milkom. The Theatre Inscription, however, mentions Baal. Thus the texts reflect more than one deity. However, their palaeography spans three centuries. The Citadel Inscription dates to the ninth century while the Theatre Inscription dates to the sixth century BCE. Thus the difference in deities cannot be used to demonstrate the worship of multiple deities at a single period.

The comparison with Philistia does remain, however. It suggests that something different may be going on in Judah in the seventh and early sixth centuries BCE, something that is more than the mere recognition of a national deity. All the texts that mention a deity refer to Yahweh alone.

---

29 Gitin, Dothan, and Naveh 1997, 1–16.
30 Gitin and Cogan 1999, 193–202.
31 Gitin and Cogan 1999, 197.
32 Aufrecht 1989, 151–63.

We now turn to consider the single remaining piece of extra biblical evidence, the personal names. In addition to individual Judean seals and bullae that have been discovered in both controlled excavations and otherwise, there are attestations of Judean names both in sources outside Judah, such as the Babylonian Chronicles and other cuneiform documents, and in the burnt archive from the City of David. Various studies have surveyed this evidence and demonstrated the identity of the names, the family relationships, and the occupations of individuals attested in both the biblical sources and these extra biblical texts.[33]

In the larger context of the period of the Monarchy, W. G. Lambert notes that, of the eleven kings of Israel and Judah mentioned in the Neo-Assyrian records, every one of them correlates with the Assyrian rulers and the chronological sequence as suggested in the books of Kings.[34] This is just one of several examples where he demonstrates how biblical narratives may be placed within the context of Assyrian records. Such written narratives could have been preserved on documents transported by deportees during the Judean Exile. Examples can be cited of groups emigrating and taking with them various written texts when moving back and forth across the Levant.[35]

André Lemaire's review of West Semitic inscriptions related to preexilic Israel includes a dozen examples of seals and bullae that he has authenticated. These contain the personal names of name bearers who also appear in the biblical account of preexilic Israel. Most of these come from the decades before the Babylonian destruction of Jerusalem.[36] This has allowed plausible reconstructions of the historical data in the light of the personal names in the biblical and extra biblical texts.[37]

However, the extra biblical attestations of Judean names not only provide additional witnesses to the historical testimony of this period, they also offer direct information about religion of the era. Perhaps the most recent, comprehensive collection and study of these personal names is that of Rainer Albertz in the volume he co-authored, *Family and Household Religion in Ancient Israel and the*

---

[33] E.g., van der Veen 2005.
[34] Lambert 2004, 352–65. See also Jursa 2008/1 (March), 9–10.
[35] E.g., the transport of cuneiform tablets, cf. Eph'al 1978, 84–7. Lambert (2004, 353–4) assumes Judeans may have carried with them scrolls smaller in size than the later Torah scrolls of the synagogue.
[36] Lemaire 2004, 366–85.
[37] E.g. Dearman 1990, 403–21.

Levant.[38] His examination of the personal names and of the religion that they describe is relevant to this study.

Albertz selects his names from epigraphic materials appearing in the standard editions, as well as the materials published by Deutsch, Heltzer, Lemaire, and Yardeni.[39] This yields 675 different Hebrew names and 2,922 individual occurrences of all names. Further, Albertz finds "a considerable degree of correspondence" between the personal names in the Hebrew Bible and those in the inscriptions. He distinguishes nearly all of the Hebrew names in six major groups: thanksgiving, confession, praise, equating, birth, and secular names.[40] He finds a similar distribution among Ammonite, Moabite, Aramaic, and Phoenician names. Albertz maintains the absence of official religious traditions as preserved in the personal names. This supports Martin Noth's study and argues against some of the other onomastic studies.[41] However, it is important to consider the method by which this is argued. For example, the most common verbs used in the Bible to identify the Exodus and the allotments of Joshua do not occur in personal names.[42] Besides the name Noah, which does contain one of these roots and which Albertz does not consider, there are much larger issues. Thus multiple verbs that refer to salvation do appear in personal names. However, in Albertz's view, these cannot refer to national salvation for Israel because the chief verbs used for the exodus and for the allotment of the land of Israel do not appear in personal names. These verbs must refer to personal salvation.

Surely this asserts too much on too little evidence. Albertz may be right but it is more likely that the names reflecting verbs of salvation might refer to national salvation in some circumstances and personal salvation in others. It is precarious to assume precise categorical overlap in name collections, as Dennis Pardee demonstrated in his discussion on personal names from Ugarit in comparison with other religious genres there.[43] Albertz's arguments are not convincing in their attempt to advance his thesis that all personal names have etymologies that reflect personal and family religion.

---

[38] Albertz and Schmitt 2012.
[39] Heltzer and Deutsch 1994, Heltzer and Deutsch 1995, Heltzer and Deutsch 1997, Heltzer and Deutsch 1999, Deutsch 1999, Deutsch 2003a, Deutsch 2003, 45–98, Deutsch and Lemaire 2000, Lemaire 2001, Lemaire 2006, 231–8, Lemaire and Yardeni 2006, 197–223.
[40] Albertz and Schmitt 2012, 253.
[41] Noth 1928.
[42] Albertz and Schmitt 2012, 262–3.
[43] Pardee 1988, 119–51.

That other names might be concerned with family related matters seems entirely plausible. These could include: the distress of infertility (Asaphyahu: "Yahweh has taken away [the distress of childlessness]"), birth oracles (Amaryahu: "Yahweh has spoken"), conception (Jephthah: "[God] has opened / may open [the womb]"), pregnancy (Benaiah: "Yahweh has created [the child]"), confinement (Gemariah: "Yahweh has completed [the birth]"), divine support (Pekah: "[God] has opened [the eyes of the child]"), and others. Many of these names are shortened by the omission of the subject or the object, or both. The assumption that we can be certain of the interpretation remains somewhat speculative. The appearance of many substitute names attests to the high infant mortality rate: up to one half of all children did not live to adulthood.[44] For example, there is Nahum ("[God] has comforted"), Eliashib ("El caused [the deceased child] to return"), and Shelomit ("[female] substitute"). Albertz affirms that the latter name indicates that Israelites mourned the deaths of their daughters as well as their sons. He notes that four times as many substitute names were secular as were religious. Albertz attributes this to theological difficulties with infant mortality that could not be resolved.[45] This is supposition. The distribution might also suggest a reluctance to attach divine causality to these young deaths. Nevertheless, Albertz has provided a wide-ranging collection of textual and other evidence to survey birth and youth in Israelite family contexts.

The names of thanksgiving favoured "more concrete descriptions of God's saving acts" rather than less specific ones.[46] For Albertz, the confessional names regularly refer to personal salvation, not that of the nation, tribe, or family.[47]

A major argument to support this assumes that the connecting *yod*, between the predicate and the theophoric element, must always be a first common singular. Thus Hezekiah must mean, "Yahweh is my strength". It cannot mean, "Yahweh is strong". Yet the basis for this conclusion is never well established.[48] It seems rather to depend upon the assumption that the names must be personal. This vowel is not necessarily either an old construct form or a pronominal suffix. It can be understood otherwise. Scott Layton, while remaining sympathetic to pronominal suffix forms, nevertheless denies it for a name like Hezekiah, based on the vocalised cuneiform spelling of Hezekiah.[49] This is important

---

44 Albertz and Schmitt 2012, 294.
45 Albertz and Schmitt 2012, 296.
46 Albertz and Schmitt 2012, 304.
47 Albertz and Schmitt 2012, 311.
48 Albertz and Schmitt 2012, 332 n. 190.
49 Layton 1990, 107–54.

because it casts doubt upon blanket assumptions that assign every two-element name with a connecting *yod* as possessing a first common singular suffix. We must admit that we often do not know and cannot ascertain this by the name alone.

In his list of names denoting trust in a deity, Albertz lists five divine names in the (preexilic) Hebrew material: *'āb* (divine) father, *'am* (divine) uncle, Baal, Horus, and Mot. The first two could designate Yahweh, as in Abijah. Baal is dominant in the Samaria ostraca from the early eighth century, but much rarer elsewhere. Note also the appearance, in the personal names, of the divine names of Horus and Mot. Both of these rarely occur. In the midst of thousands of attestations of personal names, it is difficult to be certain what this says about personal Israelite beliefs outside of the Northern Kingdom during the age of Jeroboam II (and the prophets Amos and Hosea) in the early part of the eighth century.

Nevertheless, it is likely that the preponderance of personal names arises from the individual's or family's trust in Yahweh or dependence upon Yahweh. This has led to the belief that the personal relationship with Yahweh was the most certain and reliable of relationships.[50]

Albertz discusses at length different divine names in the personal names.[51] While the *'el* element could denote the divine name El (Ilu at Ugarit), it could just as likely, and perhaps more probably, denote a generic term for "God", as in Elijah. The references to kinship names, as noted above, could be ascribed to any deity and prove nothing about specific gods. Yahweh's name remains dominant as by far the most frequently named deity in personal names, 59.4% of all names and 67.6% of all instances. Albertz lists only eleven Baal names with twenty occurrences; or 2.8% of all names and 1% of all instances. Albertz's list of other divine names includes dubious examples. While Sahar and Shalem may be deities in other societies, it does not follow that these cannot be common nouns in Hebrew. The goddess Anat occurs in the name Shamgar ben Anat, from the Judges period. Yet this term, "ben Anat", is not a personal name but a title found on Iron Age I arrowheads and elsewhere, denoting perhaps a warrior guild.[52] So Albertz's calculation of non-Yahwistic deities mentioned at 9.9% of all names and 7.3% of all instances of names with other deities is overstated. It is less than this.

Further, the dominance of Yahweh, found in two-thirds of all Hebrew epigraphic names, yet rarely outside of Hebrew names, indicates a unique and special witness to a single deity in ancient Israel. The only nearby culture with a

---

50 Albertz and Schmitt 2012, 335.
51 Albertz and Schmitt 2012, 340–67.
52 Hess 2007a, 100.

lower percentage of reference to other deities than in Israel is Moab. Yet, as Albertz admits, the presence of only 37 names and 42 instances makes this small a sample statistically unreliable.[53] With respect to the Ammonite onomastica, one should not treat the 'ēl names as necessarily designating the deity "El". They could refer to a generic "god", as in Israel, and thereby not have any significance in identifying the chief deity or other deities.[54]

However, this essay must raise a much more important question in terms of method. Albertz does not make chronological distinctions between, for example, names from the early ninth century BCE kingdom of Israel and those from the late seventh and early sixth centuries in Judah. Albertz asserts that it does not matter whether a personal name came from the early ninth or late seventh century BCE because the "religion is constant".[55] This is an assumption that should be demonstrated rather than asserted.

Elsewhere I have examined four archives from Israel and Judah, each with dozens of names (or more).[56] Two of these archives were found at and date from (1) the northern kingdom of Israel in the first half of the eighth century BCE (Samaria ostraca), and (2) Jerusalem c. 587 BCE. Whereas the former included 20% of its personal names containing non-Yahwistic divine names, the bullae from the City of David (close to the time of the Babylonian destruction) include no personal names containing non-Yahwistic divine names. This change, which can be traced in other archives, is significant and does suggest an alteration in the religious beliefs reflected in the personal names. While this reviewer agrees that "polytheism as encountered by Israelite families was apparently rather limited",[57] more can be said. There is a notable change in the worship of other deities, especially Baal, between the Northern and Southern kingdoms and between the eighth and early sixth centuries BCE.

The extra biblical onomastica of preexilic Judah close to the time of Josiah, and especially the securely provenanced and dated burnt archive in the City of David, attest to hundreds of personal names but to the virtually exclusive usage of Yahweh as a theophoric element in those names. When this is compared with the onomastica of Ammon, the single other neighbouring state that is contemporary with Judah and preserved hundreds of personal names, the difference is significant. Ammon's chief deity Milkom appears in only three personal names

---

53 Albertz and Schmitt 2012, 342.
54 See Hess 2007a, 301–13, especially 304; idem forthcoming.
55 Albertz and Schmitt 2012, 18.
56 Hess 2007a.
57 Albertz and Schmitt 2012, 363.

whereas the deities *gd* and *yh/yhw*/Yahweh each appear in three names. Baal and Mot each occur in some names as do other deities.[58] In effect the state deity is not dominant in personal names. Names of other deities appear with comparable frequency. Thus, where it can be compared, the personal names of Judah in the late preexilic period attest to the virtually exclusive use of Yahweh as a theophoric element in a unique manner not found among its contemporary neighbours with large numbers of personal names from the Iron Age.

3 Conclusion

The examination of the reform text of 2Kgs 22–3, especially 23:4–16, includes the names of other deities consistent with what is known of religious beliefs in the Iron Age Levant. The absence of named deities associated with the rooftop altars and the altar of Bethel, and only with these two contexts, is significant. In the light of the larger biblical context and of West Semitic inscriptions I conclude that Yahweh was the object of worship on the rooftop and at the altar of Bethel, albeit in a manner unacceptable to the writers/ editors of the account in 2Kgs 22–3. While the absence of Yahweh in both the rooftop altars and at Bethel in 2Kgs 23 agrees with this evidence, the latter is especially significant. At Bethel the national deity would be associated with Asherah. The explicit association of Yahweh and Asherah only in eighth century BCE inscriptions in and around Judah suggests a preexilic context for the awareness of this connection and its careful and intentional omission in 2Kgs 23 by writers who at that time would have worshipped Yahweh alone. Awareness of the worship of Yahweh and Asherah as a couple is not explicitly attested after the Exile. The omission of the name of Yahweh here demonstrates an authentic preexilic recollection. A postexilic creator of the text would have inserted the names of other deities in these blank spots in 2Kgs 23. The presence of worship of Anat-Yahu and other deities at late fifth century Elephantine may reflect syncretistic elements among the Jewish, Aramaic, and Egyptian peoples there. Such outliers may exist with this group. Interestingly, there is no mention of Asherah or the other deities of 2Kgs 23. Further, Anat(-Yahu) does not appear in any of the approximately one hundred recently published texts of mid- and late sixth century Judean exiles in Babylonia.[59]

---

[58] See the summary in Hess 207c, 304–5. These counts are based on the work of scholars such as Zevit, Aufrecht, and Jackson, who are cited there. Cf. now Aufrecht 2019; Hess forthcoming.
[59] Pearce and Wunsch 2014.

Insofar as the purpose of the Judean pillar figurines has not been proven and as their clay substance and mass-produced shapes do not suggest a deity, the religious evidence regarding the material culture of this period remains inconclusive. This is compounded by the biblical tradition of not representing Yahweh with an image.

The textual evidence of the seventh and early sixth centuries BCE is consistent with the historical names and figures mentioned in 2Kgs as living at this time. Yahweh is the sole deity worshipped and appealed to for blessing, fertility, and absolution in many texts from a variety of places throughout Judah. Such witnesses of numerous texts demonstrate an exclusive emphasis upon this national deity to which neighbouring states do not attest (in terms of their own state deity or any other deity).

The etymological confessions of personal names from Judah and Israel in the Iron Age bear witness to the religious significance of their etymologies as confessions of personal and family faith (even if not exclusively limited to these social spheres). The final decades of the Judean Monarchy preserve hundreds of names whose theophoric elements identify only Yahweh and do so in a manner without comparison in contemporary states that also preserve a large number of names.

Taken together, this evidence suggests that the record of Josiah's reform toward the belief in the single deity, Yahweh, is consistent with the extra biblical textual and onomastic evidence from the period of the late seventh century BCE. Some Judeans worshipped Yahweh alone before the Exile, and they did so personally, in their families, and at times at a state or national level.

Nathan MacDonald
Did Josiah Enact a Monotheistic Reform?

1 Introduction

In the nineteenth century Old Testament scholarship faced the challenge of setting Israelite history on a firm footing. The foundation for all subsequent reconstructions of Israel's history was the identification of the book discovered in the temple during Josiah's reign with an edition of Deuteronomy, and the recognition that this book had originated within a few decades of its "discovery".[1] The dating of Deuteronomy, with its insistence on cult centralisation, allowed the rest of the Pentateuch to be dated, and the religious history of ancient Israel to be properly ordered with the prophets preceding the law.[2]

The nineteenth century advances in understanding the Old Testament were based on scepticism about the accuracy of Israel's own portrayal of its history. From the perspective of later scholarship, however, such scepticism had been rather inconsistently applied. The ability of the prophets successfully to predict the future was doubted, as was the antiquity of the law. But whilst miraculous and legendary elements were identified and expunged, the basic outline of Israelite history was accepted as accurate. The stories of the patriarchs, exodus, judges, united monarchy, divided monarchy and exile might be diminished and appear rather more sober and realistic after critical analysis, but their essential historicity survived. The working assumption was that a historical core lay at the bottom of all the stories.[3] Since the 1970s archaeological and comparative Near Eastern evidence have resulted in many scholars approaching Israel's own history with increased scepticism.[4] The Josianic reform, which was the linchpin of Old Testament history in the nineteenth century, has not escaped unscathed. Did a Josianic reform even occur?[5]

Given the centrality of Josiah's reform to the critical consensus that arose during the nineteenth century, it is no surprise that the historicity of 2Kgs

---
[1] De Wette 1805. For a translation and discussion see Harvey, Jr. and Halpern 2008, 47–85.
[2] For de Wette in his intellectual context, see Rogerson 1992.
[3] For the classic and much maligned articulation of this approach see Bright 1959.
[4] Moore and Kellee discuss the issues and provide references to most of the important literature (2011). For some of the theoretical issues that have shaped the field, see Moore 2006.
[5] For discussion of the historicity of the seventh century see BCE the different perspectives in Grabbe 2005.

22–3 has received considerable scholarly attention in recent reassessments of Israel's history. The evaluations of the issues are diverse and there is a spectrum of views on the historicity of the Josianic reformation. We may do worse than consider two scholars who represent opposite poles on that spectrum: Rainer Albertz and Herbert Niehr.[6]

Whilst Albertz accepts the basic historicity of the account of the reform in 2Kgs 22–3, he recognizes that certain elements are legendary, such as the story of the finding of the book. Nevertheless, a critical examination of the text leaves Albertz confident that the story's emphasis on cult centralisation and exclusive worship reflects the realities of Josiah's day and that Josiah's reform was based on an earlier version of the book of Deuteronomy. Albertz understands that the Josianic reformation could not have been a purely religious reform, as 2Kgs 22–3 describes, since this is unlikely to have been of interest to the king. He argues that the reform should be understood as an assertion of Judean political and religious independence in the context of the collapse of Assyrian hegemony in Palestine. The reform expunged Assyrian religious practices, but also a number of traditional, indigenous practices, which were denounced as "Canaanite". The animating religious principle was the exclusiveness of Yahweh worship. This was summarised in the opening clause of the book discovered in the temple: "Hear, Israel, Yahweh our God, Yahweh is one" (Deut 6:4). This, according to Albertz, was "the reform slogan, which was hammered home to the population time and again in public pronouncements"[7] (cf. 20:2). If the slogan excluded various forms of worship that had previously been tolerated but were now regarded as not rigorously monolatrous, it also provided a new sense of national identity. One of the strongest aspects of Albertz's historical reconstruction of the reform is his attention to the social context. In his view the radical programme of the reform could only succeed because elements of it appealed to various groups in late monarchic Judah. The reformers were an alliance of the "people of the land" (the middle-class landowners of Judah), influential court officials like Shaphan and Hilkiah, the Davidic royal family, the priesthood and some of the prophets. The different interests of these groups meant the coalition was fragile, and the rapidly changing international scene caused the movement to disintegrate quickly after Josiah's untimely end.

Niehr's understanding of Josiah's reign is very different from Albertz's. In his view the departure of Assyria from Syro-Palestine did not result in a power vacuum; rather, the Assyrians passed control over to their Egyptian allies so as to

---

[6] Albertz 1994, 1: 195–231; Albertz 2005, 27–46; Niehr 1995, 33–56.
[7] Albertz 1994, 206.

concentrate their forces in shoring up their empire against attacks from the Medes and Babylonians. Niehr also casts doubt on the idea that Assyrian religious practice had been imposed upon Judah during its vassalage. Consequently, there is little basis for believing there was a reform inspired by anti-Assyrian sentiment. Niehr attributes very little of 2Kgs 22–3 to an early source and follows Christoph Levin's literary-critical analysis. According to Levin the earliest version of Josiah's reign consisted of only 2Kgs 22:1–2; 23:8a, 25*, 28–30.[8] Josiah is remembered for his destruction of the high places in the territory of Judah and his removal of their priests. In its original scope the reform was an attempt to bring the high places under royal control. Only through a process of later scribal rewriting in the exilic and postexilic periods did this brief notice of cult reorganisation become the archetypal reform.

There are a number of points at which Albertz's and Niehr's assessments of Josiah's reign differ. First, Albertz and Niehr have different understandings of the international political context. Can Assyria's rapid decline provide the context for understanding the Josianic reform? According to Albertz, Josiah's reassertion of Judahite religious traditions is a response to Assyria's loosening grip on Palestine, whilst Niehr believes that the transfer of hegemony from Assyria to Egypt means the external political situation was virtually unchanged. Second, the discovered book plays an important role in Albertz's understanding of the reform but has no part in Niehr's. Consequently, Albertz can draw upon his reconstruction of the Josianic book of Deuteronomy for his portrayal of the reform that the book inspired. For Niehr the association of Josiah with Deuteronomy lies in the scribal expansion of 2Kgs 22–3. Third, there are different understandings of the extent of the cultic reorganisation and its underlying logic. Albertz holds that many of the measures described in 2Kgs 23, such as actions against "foreign cults", were enacted by Josiah and can be aligned with Deuteronomy's programme. According to Niehr, Josiah's actions were limited to dismantling some of the high places within Judah's borders. In the following essay I propose to look at those three different issues in turn. We shall then be in a position to address the question of my title: did Josiah enact a monotheistic reform?

2 The International Political Context

According to 2Kings, Josiah began his reign at the tender age of eight years old after his father, Amon, had died at just twenty-four years old. The year was 640

---

8 Levin 1984, 351–71.

BCE. He was to reign for thirty-one years. During his reign the face of the Near East was to be completely transformed. When Josiah ascended the throne the neo-Assyrian empire was at the height of its power under Ashurbanipal, who had finally eliminated the threats from Babylon and Elam. When he died in 609 BCE, Assyria was no more.

How did this political transformation impact the small vassal state of Judah, and was the Josianic reform a response to Assyria's retreat from Palestine? Was there an orderly transfer of power from Assyria to Egypt, or did Assyria simply withdraw from the Syro-Palestine sphere leaving a power vacuum in its wake? The different historical reconstructions proposed by Albertz and Niehr highlight the indeterminacy of our sources on this question. The possibility that Egypt was gifted Assyria's Levantine territory, though a popular opinion in biblical scholarship, is conjectural and, I think, rather improbable.[9] Psammetichus I originally enjoyed Assyrian patronage and owed his position to Assyrian support. At some stage, however, he had acted to throw off Assyrian overlordship, probably in the 650s. Much later, when Assyria was close to collapse, Psammetichus I sent support to Sin-shar-ishkun of Assyria. It is ambitious to deduce from this that Assyria would have chosen to transfer part of its empire to Egypt. In every instance we observe Egypt and Assyria pursuing a pragmatic course to suit their own interests. The question is not, "Were Egypt and Assyria such good allies in this period that Assyria could hand over some of its holdings to Egypt?", but "Did it make strategic sense for Assyria to act in this way?" I am not sure it does. The weakened and fractured states of Palestine offered no existential threat to Assyria in the way that an energetic and revivified Egyptian empire might. If Assyria abandoned its holdings in the west it might hope to recapture them after it had put down the Babylonian rebellions, but that would be so much more difficult were they in the hands of another great power. From Assyria's perspective, if Egypt wanted to take over the former Assyrian dominions, it would have to conquer them. The result would be a weaker Egypt and weaker Levantine states. So much the better for Assyria, which would not have a strong neighbour on its western borders to worry about.

If Assyria withdrew from Palestine without making any provision for its administration, it is reasonable to assume that Josiah would have acted to take best advantage of this new situation. The dating of the reforms in 2Kgs 22 accords reasonably well with the weakening of Assyria's hegemony in the Levant. The Babylonian revolts which were eventually to prove fatal to the Assyrian empire

---

9 For a detailed defence of Egypt as a "successor state" to Assyria, see Na'aman 1991b, 3–71 and 2005, 189–247.

began in 626, and it was probably sometime after this date that Assyria chose to relinquish its western holdings and concentrate its resources on the threat from Media and Babylonia.[10] Josiah's cultic reorganisation is placed in the eighteenth year of his reign, 622 BCE, and it seems reasonably likely that Josiah chose to act because of the Assyria's weakening grip on its empire.

But what evidence is there that Josiah's reforms were anti-Assyrian? The account of Josiah's reign in 2Kgs 22–3 makes no reference to the Assyrians. That in itself need not be decisive, for there is no mention of the Assyrians in the accounts of Manasseh and Amon, even though it is likely that Judah was subject to Assyria during both their reigns. In the view of the book of Kings, the Assyrians were expelled in the reign of Hezekiah and Judah was able to determine its own course from 701 BCE until the appearance of the Babylonians almost a century later. In addition, whilst careful attention must be given to the biblical text's focus on the religious basis for Josiah's actions, it does not necessarily exclude the possibility that events could have been the result of different socio-historical factors. An important contribution to the issue can be made through an analysis of the reform measures (23:4–20). Are any of them directed against specifically Assyrian cultic practices? An answer to that question will have to wait until the third section of this essay.

3 The Discovery of the Book of the Law

The account of Josiah's reign in the book of Kings divides into two main parts: the discovery of the book of the law (22:3–20) and the purification of the cult (23:4–24). The two parts are linked through the act of making a covenant (23:1–3).[11] The book that is discovered in the temple is also "the book of the covenant", and the stipulations of the covenant concern the removal of all alien cultic paraphernalia. Thus, in the present form of the narrative, the book is indispensable. But what precisely was this book, and was it discovered in the reign of Josiah? We shall address these questions in reverse order.

Whilst 2Kgs makes the book and its discovery integral to the whole course of events, this was clearly not the only way to tell the story. In its retelling of Josiah's reign, the book of Chronicles tells how Josiah, whilst still a boy, initiated a purge of illicit forms of worship. A decade later Josiah turns his attention to the

---

10 For the chronology of the period see Na'aman 1991a, 243–67.
11 Lohfink 1987, 459–75.

repair of the Jerusalem temple. It is as those repairs are being undertaken that the book of the law is discovered. Purification precedes discovery.

Chronicles opens up the possibility of a Josianic reform without a book, an idea that has proved attractive to a number of scholars.[12] One reason for entertaining this idea is that the "discovery" of an authoritative text as a blueprint for cultic reform is a familiar trope from the Near East.[13] Could it be that a later scribe embellished the account of Josiah's restructuring of the cult so as to make it a story of how an original cult was restored? On its own, the existence of a literary trope is far from decisive. It is equally possible that the priests of Josiah's day were familiar with this idea of discovering ancient blueprints and contrived for such a document to be "found" in the Jerusalem temple. Far more compelling evidence is the literary observation that the discovery of the book fits rather awkwardly in the story of temple repair. The first mention of the book disturbs the natural connection between the king's commandment about the financing of the temple repairs (22:3–7) and Shaphan's report of their fulfilment (22:9). Further, the connection between Shaphan's assignment and the discovery of the book of the law is not made clear within 2Kgs. The two matters—repair and discovery—are almost independent of each other. Their near independence is vividly indicated by the fact that after v. 10 the book of the law becomes entirely the focus of attention, and the concerns of temple financing and renovation vanish. It would appear, therefore, that the book of the law is a secondary addition to the story of repair. The main characters in the finding of the book of the law—Shaphan and Hilkiah—are introduced in the story of the repair, and this account functions quite happily without any mention of a book.

That the repair story could exist without the book is apparent from 2Kgs 12, the story of Joash's repair of the temple. The financing of the repairs is described in an almost identical manner in 2Kgs 12 and 22, and the similarities between the two passages leave no doubt that there exists a literary relationship between the two. Unfortunately, there is no agreement about the nature of the relationship: is 2Kgs 12 dependent on 2Kgs 22, or *vice versa*, or is there a common source?[14] To answer this question we should first observe that the account of the repairs in Joash's reign has been revised in light of later Pentateuchal legislation, most notably in 12:5 [Eng 12:4].

---

12 For a discussion and critique, see Spieckermann 1982, 30–41.
13 For a discussion of some Near Eastern examples, see Ambos 2013, 55–65.
14 See Spieckermann 1982, 175–84 and Levin 2003, 198–216, who argue that 2Kgs 12 is dependent on 2Kgs 22; Pietsch 2013, 66–89, argues the reverse.

If we set this Pentateuchal material to one side, we appear to have the story about temple financing that is familiar to us from 2Kgs 22 and, in addition, what appears to be another distinct account of temple repair. According to this latter account, Joash ordered that votive gifts should be used for temple repairs (12:5–6* [Eng 12:4–5*]), rather than cultic paraphernalia (12:14 [Eng 12:13]). This proves to be a rather astute decision for the transportable cultic objects were removed from the temple in order to pay off Hazael of Damascus (12:18–9 [Eng 12:17–8]). Thus, the present form of 2Kgs 12 appears to be made up of two distinguishable accounts of temple repair. One of these accounts is almost identical to what we find in 2Kgs 22:3–7, whilst the other account has no overlap with 2Kgs 22. As a result almost every aspect of the temple repairs in Josiah's reign has a parallel in Joash's reign, but the reverse is not the case.[15] The most convincing way of explaining this observation is that an earlier account of temple repair in 2Kgs 12:14, 18–9 [Eng 12:13, 17–8] was secondarily expanded under the influence of 2Kgs 22. This textual material was integrated into the account of repairs in 2Kgs 12 in order to present Joash as a proleptic anticipation of Josiah.[16] Consequently we should view the story of temple financing and repair in 2Kgs 22 as original,[17] but this story probably did not make any mention of a finding of a book.

Such an analysis indicates that Josiah was first presented as a supporter of the temple in Jerusalem who reformed its financing and ensured its effective repair. The legend of the finding of a book was only added secondarily. Yet, as we have seen, the book became essential to the overall account of Josiah's reform. What, then, was the book discovered by Hilkiah? There are two different approaches we may take: first, the way the book is identified in 2Kgs 22–3; and second, the nature of the reform that resulted from the discovery of the book. I shall discuss each of these items in turn.

The book discovered by Hilkiah is identified in a number of different ways. It is "the scroll of the law" (*sēper hattôrāh*, 22:8, 11), "the scroll of the covenant" (*sēper habbərît*, 23:2, 21), and possibly "the law of Moses" (*tôrat mōšeh*, 23:25). The first of these titles, "the scroll of the law", is one of Deuteronomy's preferred ways of speaking about itself (Deut 28:61; 29:20 [Eng 29:21]; 30:10; 31:26). It is also a title used twice in Joshua. In both cases the envisaged document is probably Deuteronomy (Josh 1:8; 8:34). The second title, "the book of the covenant", is relatively rare. Outside 2Kgs 23 and 2Chr 34 it is only used in Exod 24:7, where it

---

15 22:4||12:10 [Eng 12:9]; 22:5–6||12:12–3 [Eng 12:11–2]; 22:7||12:16 [Eng 12:15].
16 Hardmeier 2005, 123–63 esp. p. 135.
17 See Kratz 2005, 168–9.

refers to Exod 20:22–23:33, which, on the basis of Exod 24:7, scholars usually name "the Covenant Code". The Hebrew expression "the book of the covenant" would, however, be equally apt as a description of the canonical book of Deuteronomy, which describes a covenant being made between Israel and its God on the fields of Moab. The third title, "the law of Moses", is used elsewhere of any of the commandments given by Moses. Thus, in Josh 8:31 it refers to Exod 20:25, but in 2Kgs 14:6 it refers to Deut 24:16.[18]

From a literary-critical perspective, the existence of three titles for the same document could be evidence of a literary development. The logical relationship between the first two is easy to establish. Without the discovery of the book of the law in 2Kgs 22:8, 11, there is no covenant. The expression "the book of the covenant" appears to be a reappropriation of "the book of the law" in the context of the making of a covenant. Similarly, the approbation of Josiah in 2Kgs 23:25 stems from his obedience to the book that was discovered by Hilkiah (v. 24). Thus, "the law of Moses" is also a creative reformulating of "the book of the law". Whether the logical dependence of the last two titles on the first reflects different compositional layers would need further discussion beyond my present concern.

We can learn some more about the identification of the book by examining the cultic reforms that are associated with it. It is striking that the main collection of reforms in 23:4–20 makes no reference to the book, in sharp contrast to the measures described in 23:21–4, which are explicitly tied to the book's prescriptions:

> as prescribed in this book of the covenant (*kakkātûb 'al sēper habbərît hazzeh*, 2Kgs 23:21)
>
> in order to establish the words of the law that were prescribed in the book that Hilkiah the priest found in the house of Yahweh (*ləma'an hāqîm 'et-dibrê hattôrāh hakkətubîm 'al-hassēper 'ăšer māṣā' ḥilqîyāhû hakkōhēn bêt yhwh*, 2Kgs 23:24).

Positively, the people keep the Passover. The brief observation that the Passover was kept "in Jerusalem" (v. 23) is highly significant. In the book of Exodus the Passover is observed in individual homes, whilst in Deuteronomy the Passover is celebrated in the chosen sanctuary.[19] Thus, it is Deuteronomy's Passover regulations that are followed, rather than Exodus'. Negatively, Josiah expelled the mediums, spiritists, teraphim, idols and all the abominations. The condemnation of soothsayers and idolatry is characteristic of both the Holiness Code and

---

[18] For further discussion, see Lohfink 1990, 99–166, especially 123–6.
[19] For the transformation of Passover in the Deuteronomic code see Levinson 1997, 53–97.

Deuteronomy.[20] It would appear, then, that the reform measures provide further confirmation that the book described was a form of Deuteronomy.[21] These measures are, however, usually thought to be secondary, occurring after the main account of reforms in 23:4–20.[22] What evidence might the reforms in vv. 4–20 provide for the identity of the book they never mention? We have put off discussing these verses for long enough.

4 The Religious Reform

Josiah's religious reform is described in 2Kgs 23:4–20, a description that is lengthy, multifaceted and repetitious. Although most scholars agree that it is not of one piece, the quest to distinguish the original reform account from its secondary accretions has not resulted in one single proposal that commends widespread assent. There are places where the assessment of individual verses or sections commands a considerable degree of agreement. The excursion to Bethel in vv. 15–20 is widely judged to be a later addition, and the same is true of the mention of Bethel in v. 4bβ, which forms an *inclusio* with it.[23] On the other hand, there are other verses where scholars have come to contrary assessments. Barrick judges the appearance of the *weqatal* form in v. 5 to be evidence of a secondary insertion, but Uehlinger regards the unusual term *kəmārîm* to be evidence of an astral cult that did not thrive after the seventh century, and so belongs to the original reform account. For a historical assessment of the Josianic period and for understanding the development of the account of Josiah's reign these difficult problems cannot be sidestepped. Nevertheless, the limits of our knowledge about the development of 2Kgs 23 need to be recognised and literary-critical proposals treated accordingly.

There are three different tools that scholars have utilised to distinguish the original report of Josiah's reform and its literary growth. First, there are the standard tools of literary analysis, such as the identification of doublets, grammatical incongruence etc. Secondly, there is the use of archaeological and comparative sources to identify Judahite religious practices and attitudes that belong in Iron Age IIC, but not later. Thirdly, there is the redactional analysis of the

---

20 The mediums and spiritists are condemned in the Holiness Code (Lev 19–20) and in the Deuteronomic Code (Deut 18). The teraphim are not censured in any of the biblical codes, but idols and abominations are both condemned in Deut 29:17.
21 For careful consideration of the implications of this hypothesis, see Lohfink 1990.
22 Note the *Wiederaufnahme*, "and he commanded", in vv. 4 and 21.
23 For v. 4bβ as an addition, see Barrick 2002, 73–6.

Deuteronomistic History, which can assist in identifying patterns of expansion. Although some scholars have preferred one form of analysis over another, they each have value and can be mutually informing.

The description of Josiah's actions suggests a religious reform directed against a multitude of illicit religious practices. The impression is given that the composers of 2Kgs 23 wanted to credit Josiah with the purging of every cultic infraction that had sullied Judah's worship over the centuries that the monarchy had existed. It is his devotion to a purified cult that will bring the approbation of the Deuteronomists: "Before him there was no king like him, who turned to the LORD with all his heart, with all his soul and with all his might, according to all the law of Moses; nor did any like him arise after him" (v. 25). Whilst this impression is not incorrect, it is also the case that the illicit practices can be brought under three heads. First, Josiah takes concerted action against the high places. He defiles the sites (vv. 5, 8–9, 10, 13–4, 15–20) and deposes their officiating priests (vv. 5, 8–9). Secondly, Josiah acts against the cult of Asherah (vv. 4, 6–7, 14). Thirdly, he acts against the cultic adoration of heavenly beings (vv. 4, 5, 11). In its final form the description of the reform weaves around these three topics, often blending them together. In our analysis we shall consider each of these topics in turn.

4.1 The High Places in Josiah's Reform

The issue that is most prominent in Josiah's reform is his action against the high places (vv. 5, 8–9, 10, 13–4, 15–20). The verb repeatedly used is "defiled" (*ṭmʾ*, 23:8, 10, 13, 16). The word occurs nowhere else in Joshua–2Kings and is otherwise a favourite of the priestly literature.[24]

It is the use of *ṭmʾ* in v. 10 that makes it clear that Tophet was also considered a high place (cf. Jer 7:31). The only instance where it is absent is v. 5, which speaks of the deposing of the officiating priests, rather than the defiling of the high place.

Beginning with v. 5, there are some grounds for thinking that this verse is an insertion into its literary context. First, the *weqatal* interrupts the typical Hebrew narrative style with *wayyiqtol* and *qatal* forms found in vv. 4* and 6.[25] Second,

---

24 Cf. Eynikel 1996, 233.
25 V. 4bβ should be regarded as an addition to v. 4. First, it presumes and provides an *inclusio* with Josiah's actions in vv. 15–20, which there are also good reasons to regard as secondary. Secondly, it is written with a *weqatal* form. Thirdly, the bearing away of the ash seems unnecessary

the actions against the *kəmārîm* break the connection between the bringing out (*ləhôṣî'*) of the vessels for Baal, Asherah and the host of heaven (v. 4), and the bringing out (*wayyōṣē'*) of the asherah (v. 6). Finally, the deposing of the *kəmārîm* in v. 5 appears to duplicate v. 8, which speaks of the removal of the *kōhănîm*.

Whilst a number of scholars have addressed the problem of duplication by arguing that v. 5 concerns a pagan priesthood and v. 8 a Yahwistic priesthood, the attempt to distinguish two different priesthoods is artificial. The overlap in the description of both groups is striking: both the *kəmārîm* and the *kōhănîm* served at the high places in the cities of Judah and both burned incense. They are the same group of cultic functionaries. What the attempt to distinguish between a pagan and a Yahwistic priesthood rightly recognises is that the priests in v. 8 are not portrayed negatively. They are not associated with other deities; it is only the high places that are condemned. Their absence from the altar at Jerusalem, together with their access to the priestly perquisites (v. 9), suggests that they are treated in the same manner as a priest with a blemish (cf. Lev 21).

The most compelling way of understanding the relationship between v. 5 and v. 8 is that a scribal writer has dramatically reassessed the priests of the high places. They are not simply blemished, but guilty of worshipping other gods. By prefixing vv. 8–9 with v. 5, the scribal writer has ensured that future readers understand the priests of v. 8 as idolatrous. Quite possibly v. 5 is an example of innerbiblical *Fortschreibung* added under the influence of Zeph 1:4–5.[26] To a scribal writer the mention of Baal and the host of heavens in 2Kgs 23:4 would have brought to mind the prophecy in Zeph 1:4–5. Here, Zephaniah, a contemporary of Josiah, prophesies the end of the *kəmārîm* and the worshippers of Baal and the host of heavens. The scribal writer presented Zephaniah's prophecy as realised in the reform of Josiah by combining the prophet's words with 2Kgs 23:4 and 8.

The condemnation of the high places in vv. 8–9 is not due to their association with other deities, but because they contradict the primacy of the Jerusalem temple. The treatment is consistent with many other parts of the Deuteronomistic History that criticise successive monarchs, with the honourable exception of Hezekiah, for their failure to remove the high places. The passage 2Kgs 23:8a, 9 is unusual, however, for its concern with the priesthood and its language of defilement. It marks a development beyond that of the original Deuteronomistic

---

after the burning of the objects. There is, writes Richard D. Nelson, "no conceivable reason why Josiah would have done this" (1981, 81).

26 Most scholarship on these verses appears to assume that the similarities in both texts can be explained as a common religious practice from the seventh century.

History.[27] There are some grounds for thinking, then, that the original reference to the high places was the very specific action against the high place in Jerusalem: "he broke down the high place of the gates that were at the entrance of the gate of Joshua the governor of the city, which were on the left of the gate of the city" (23:8b). There are no good reasons to question the originality of v. 8b.[28] At an early stage it was repurposed so as to address the status of the priesthood that had officiated at the high places. One of the results of this scribal activity was the orphaning of the reference to "the city" (*hāʿîr*) in v. 8b.

The inclusion of Tophet in 2Kgs 23 is due to its identification as a high place (cf. Jer 7:31). Like the other high places mentioned in 2Kgs 23 it is to be defiled (*ṭmʾ*; 23:8, 10, 13, 16). The use of the *weqatal* form provides an argument for its identification as secondary. Tophet is only otherwise mentioned in Jeremiah (7:30–1; 19:6, 11–4),[29] and it is likely that the destruction of Tophet was a scribal addition in 2Kgs 23 inspired by the developing prophetic corpus.[30] This is not the only similarity 2Kgs 23:10 shares with the mention of the *kəmārîm* in v. 5. Both verses condemn the high places for their association with other deities, and not for their challenge to centralisation. It is possible that they come from the same scribal hand.

The changing perception of the high places means that it is also possible to identify vv. 13–4 as secondary. These verses associate the high places with the worship of deities from the surrounding nations: Astarte, Chemosh and Milcom. Clearly Josiah is also being portrayed as the king who undid the cultic infractions that had endured since the reign of Solomon (1Kgs 11:7), and we have here an instance of a cultic action that reflects later editing of the Deuteronomistic History. Finally, we have the extensive story of the high places at Bethel and in Samaria (2Kgs 23:15–20). Its secondary nature is indicated by its position at the end of the reform account, by the loose connective *wəgam* "and also", and the geographical extension of Josiah's activities outside Judah. The priests at these sites are not simply made redundant as occurred in vv. 8–9, they are also slaughtered on the altars (v. 20).

---

[27] Provan 1988, 82–8.
[28] Levin objects that the verse is a late attempt to add historical colour: "Die genaue Ortsangabe ist, wie ebenso in v. 11aβγ. 12aα, 13aα, späte historisierende Zutat" (1984, 360).
[29] Mention should also be made of Isa 30:33 which speaks of the "burning place" (*topteh*) that has been prepared. A geographical reading of *topteh* is precluded in this verse. The context speaks of a pyre being prepared for Assyria.
[30] The mention of Tophet in Jeremiah occurs in contexts that are themselves secondary (for discussion, see McKane 1986, 449–57). The mention of Tophet in 2Kgs 23:10 does not make these additions to Jeremiah Deuteronomistic.

4.2 The Asherah in Josiah's Reform

The first mention of Asherah in Josiah's reform is found in v. 4. The vessels for Baal, Asherah and the host of heaven are removed from the temple and destroyed. There is a measure of duplication with v. 6: objects are removed (*yṣ'*) from the temple to outside Jerusalem (*miḥûṣ lîrûšālayim*) where they are burned (*śrp*). Despite the similarities there are a number of points at which v. 4 and v. 6 differ. First, in v. 6, as elsewhere in the reform account, the actions are attributed to Josiah, but in v. 4 the high priest, the second-order priests and the threshold guards are commanded to act. Secondly, in v. 6, and elsewhere in the reform account, the temple in Jerusalem is called the "house" (*bayit*), but in v. 4 it is called the "temple" (*hêkāl*). Finally, in v. 6 the asherah is an object that is removed from the temple, but in v. 4 Asherah is a deity alongside Baal and the host of heavens, whose vessels are removed from the temple.

These novel elements can be taken as evidence that v. 4 is a secondary text. Just as v. 5 duplicated elements of v. 8, so also v. 4 duplicates parts of v. 6, and v. 4, like v. 5, has been prefixed to the earlier reform account so as to reshape it. The earlier account in v. 6 described Josiah's removal and destruction of the asherah, a cultic object in the Jerusalem Temple. The new material in v. 4 is more than simply a duplicate; it heaps further opprobrium on the cultic practices that Josiah rejected. The worship in the temple did not simply involve deficient cultic practices but was directed towards other gods. Here, as in other parts of the Deuteronomistic History, the asherah was originally an object used in cultic worship that only later received greater censure by being equated with a female deity and by association with Baal.[31]

In verse 7 the weaving of "houses" for Asherah is linked with *haqqədēšîm*, a term usually understood to refer to prostitution. Although the Masoretes understood asherah in v. 7 as an object, pointing it with a definite article, it is possible that *lā'ăšērāh* relates to a female deity, as it does in v. 4. The association of Asherah with *haqqədēšîm* is not made elsewhere and is a clear example of defamation. It is possible, then, that v. 7 is a later addition to v. 6, but there is no evidence of literary problems. As Pakkala rightly observes, "literary-critical methods are rather toothless on these verses".[32] A degree of agnosticism about this verse is appropriate. In v. 14 we encounter *'ăšērîm* from the high places to the east of Jerusalem. We have already seen that there is reason to believe that the reference to the high places in v. 13 is later, and this is true of the closely related v. 14. It is

---

[31] For discussion see Hadley 2000 and Olyan 1988.
[32] Pakkala 1999, 174.

noticeable that the high places and the asherah, which were originally separate, have been combined here. The same is also true of the occurrence in v. 15.

4.3 The Worship of Heavenly Bodies in Josiah's Reform

The adoration of the heavenly bodies is mentioned in vv. 4, 5 and 11. We have already seen that there are good grounds for thinking that vv. 4 and 5 were not part of the original account of Josiah's reform. It is interesting to observe that the worship of the heavenly bodies is associated with Asherah in v. 4 and is located on the high places that Josiah destroys in v. 5. These associations do not occur in what I have argued are the earliest references to the asherah and the high places.

The only other explicit reference to the worship of heavenly bodies is found in v. 11: Josiah removed the horses dedicated to the sun and burned the chariots of the sun. The following verse does refer to altars on the roof, but the recipients of this sacrificial worship are not identified (v. 12a). The location of the altars, together with the mention of roof-top altars in Jer 19:13 and Zeph 1:5, suggests that we should understand them to have been used to worship astral deities. The altars that Manasseh made (v. 12b) likewise lack an indication of the recipient of the sacrifices. These altars are also mentioned in 2Kgs 21:5, which describes them as "for all the host of heaven".[33]

The horses and chariots of the sun are often thought to be one of the strongest candidates for a seventh-century religious practice that Josiah outlawed. There is a lack of Deuteronomistic vocabulary in the verse,[34] and the imagery of Shamash driving a chariot is known in Assyria.[35] In addition, it is interesting to observe that the horses and chariots are not dedicated to any specific deity. It is possible that the solar deity who was honoured by such paraphernalia was Yahweh. In verse 12 "the altars ... that the kings of Judah made" and "the altars ... that Manasseh made" appear unduly repetitious, and it is possible that the reference to Manasseh in 12aβ, γ was added at a later stage in order to produce a literary cross-reference to Judah's most heinous king. As was the case in v. 11, none of the altars is explicitly associated in 2Kgs 23 with the worship of other deities.

---

[33] For the impact of astral imagery in the Assyrian period, see Keel and Uehlinger 1998, 283–372.
[34] Spieckermann 1982, 107.
[35] Uehlinger 2005, 279–316.

4.4 Josiah's Reform in 2 Kings 23

Whilst my proposed reconstruction of the textual history of 2Kgs 23 should be used with caution, it has some heuristic value in helping us think about the text, its internal relationships and connections to other biblical texts. I have suggested that the original report of the reform may have described the king's removal of the asherah from the temple and burning it in the Kidron valley (v. 6a*), the breaking down of the high places at the Joshua gate (v. 8b), the removal of the horses and burning of the chariots of the sun, and the breaking of the rooftop altars (vv. 11–12aα*). Josiah's actions are entirely focused on Jerusalem and involved the removal and destruction of cultic paraphernalia relating to three distinct areas of religious practice: the asherah, the high places, and the solar (and astral) cult. There is no indication that the rejected practices are associated with other deities, and it is possible that they were part of the Yahweh cult in Jerusalem.

Scribal alterations to the text resulted in a number of significant developments affecting how the reform was portrayed. First, the reform account saw a gradual geographical extension. Activities that took place only in Jerusalem were extended to elsewhere in Judah (vv. 8a, 9), and eventually to Bethel and Samaria (15–20). The earliest account of the reform already had a degree of movement to it with the king's actions of purging the temple taking him into and out of the city. The movement of the king in the final forms of the reform account are far more complex: oscillating between the capital and the surrounding country. Secondly, the aim of the reform goes through various shifts. It begins as a purge of Jerusalem and its temple, quite possibly a cleansing of the Yahweh cult. At an early stage it was repurposed as a vehicle for cult centralisation with Josiah portrayed as opposing the high places in Judah's territory (vv. 9–10). Still later, however, Josiah's reform is portrayed as opposed to any worship of other deities, particularly the deities of surrounding nations. Thirdly, the practices brought to an end by Josiah are identified as those that previous kings had initiated. This idea may already have been present in the earliest composition with earlier kings identified as the founders of the solar and astral cult. Further additions portrayed Josiah as the king who opposed the apostate actions of Manasseh and Jeroboam, but also even king Solomon. Some of these practices are identified with those of the surrounding nations (v. 13), but 2Kgs 23 avoids classifying them as "Canaanite" or "Assyrian". Thus, the book of Kings insists upon judging the reform according to its own concern with kingship, rather than the scholarly question of whether these practices are Assyrian or indigenous. Fourthly, the biases of Kings do not mean we are completely unable to discern what were probably the original motives. The original purge of the Jerusalem cult may well have been directed against religious practices that were associated with the Assyrians, or with kings that had sought an accommodation with Assyria. It is only with its repurposing for cult centralisation that we can identify a Deuteronomic or Deuteronomistic character to the reform. Fifthly, the three distinct areas that Josiah tackles in the original reform account are increasingly brought together. Thus, the high places are the locations where both Asherah and the host of heavens are worshipped (cf. v. 4).

5 Josiah's Reform and the Question of Monotheism

Our examination of Josiah's reign as recorded in 2Kgs 22–3 has not been exhaustive, but it does provide a sufficient basis to tackle the question that is posed in the title of my essay: did Josiah enact a monotheistic reform? Although I shall argue that the answer to this question is "no", the nature of the "no" differs as the story about Josiah develops over time. An examination of these changes can tell us about the changing perception of Josiah's reform and of monotheism.

First, we can address the question by asking about what I have reconstructed as the earliest account of Josiah's reform. Josiah's actions were entirely restricted to Jerusalem and involved a reform of the temple finances and its worship. Josiah commits to the physical structure of the building and the removal of certain paraphernalia. Unfortunately, the reconstructed text of 2Kgs 22–3 itself provides no clear indication of the logic for Josiah's reform. The concurrence of reforms in Josiah's eighteenth year and the period when Assyria probably retreated from the Levant seem more than serendipitous. The withdrawal of Assyrian overlordship would have allowed the king to reassert his own fiscal control over the temple and reinstate cultic practices that were indigenous or were perceived to be. Such assertions of Judahite sovereignty seem likely to have been anti-Assyrian, rather than specifically monotheistic.

Secondly, I suggested that secondary expansions of the account of Josiah's reign included the story of the finding of the book of the law and the actions against high places outside Jerusalem. It is well known that the key emphasis of the earliest version of Deuteronomy was that worship only be conducted at the divinely chosen sanctuary. Thus, it is possible that these secondary expansions in 2Kgs 22–3 were added by the same scribal hand.

Was cult centralisation justified on the grounds of monotheism? It has been common to assert that monolatry, frequently seen as the precursor to monotheism, justified Deuteronomy's policy of cult centralisation. Albertz, as we have seen, associates Deut 6:4, "Hear O Israel. Yahweh our God, Yahweh is one", with the Josianic reform and cult centralisation. Yet, despite Albertz's claims that this was a slogan of the reform, the relationship between the two is more problematic. There is not only the fact that the original account of Josiah's reign did not include any mention of a book, or that the original reform does not appear to have been inspired by Deuteronomy. It is also that the connection between Deut 6:4 and cult centralisation is less than certain. Despite the appeal of the idea of "one God, one temple", the Hebrew word for "one", 'eḥād, is simply not used to justify cult centralisation in Deut 12–8.[36] Such theological uses of "one" are not found until the Greco-Roman period,[37] and may reflect apologetic strategies that appealed to a Hellenistic audience.[38] In addition, Deut 6:4 makes very little impact on subsequent biblical literature; an observation that casts doubt on Deut 6:4 having functioned as a popular slogan.[39]

Thirdly, we have seen that the account of Josiah's reign continued to develop until the reform became a comprehensive elimination of the cult of all other deities that had been promoted by previous kings of Israel and Judah. The cult of these deities is portrayed as a serious threat to the cult of Yahweh. There is nothing in these verses to suggest that the gods are thought to be non-existent. In other words, these verses are consistent with many other parts of the developed Deuteronomistic History, which Pakkala has described as "intolerant monolatry".

In some places in the Deuteronomistic History, however, this intolerant monolatry is expressed in an elevated form of rhetoric that denies the existence of other gods. Although this has often been portrayed as a new stage in religious thinking—"the breakthrough of monotheism"—there is much to be said for Mark Smith's suggestion that we see this instead as a new stage in religious

---

36 A relationship is often claimed between 'eḥād in Deut 6:4 and 'eḥād in Deut 12:14 (Römer 2004, 170). This is far from convincing. The use of 'eḥād in Deut 12:14 is not in a rhetorically prominent position, nor is the expression "one of your tribes" found anywhere else in Deuteronomy. Deuteronomy insists not that people and sanctuary are "one", but that they are "chosen" (bḥr).
37 Philo writes that "as God is one, his temple also should be one" (*Spec* 1.7) and Josephus claims that there should be "one temple of the one God" (*Ag. Ap.* 2.193).
38 Guerra writes that the discussion of oneness provided "a bridge between their religion and the growing theological consensus of the contemporary educated gentile of the Hellenistic period" (1995, 94).
39 See MacDonald 2014, 103–23.

rhetoric.⁴⁰ Indeed, this religious rhetoric flourishes for a relatively short period of time in the postexilic period and is characteristic of Deutero-Isaiah and some of the latest additions to the Deuteronomistic History.

Given that this monotheistic rhetoric does appear in the Deuteronomistic History, it is interesting to wonder why it was not employed in 2Kgs 22–3, not least because it is used at many of the other critical moments of Israel and Judah's history. It occurs at the climax of Moses' first speech (Deut 4:35, 39; cf. 7:9), in David's prayer at the founding of his dynasty (2Sam 7:22), at the climax of Solomon's prayer at the dedication of the temple (1Kgs 8:60), in Elijah's conflict with the prophets of Baal (1Kgs 18:21, 24, 39), and in Hezekiah's prayer (2Kgs 19:15, 19).⁴¹ It should be observed that in each case the monotheistic affirmation occurs as part of the Deuteronomistic History recording the speech of major heroes in its narrative: Moses, David, Solomon, Elijah and Hezekiah. In some cases the affirmation is part of a speech seeking to persuade other Israelites of the uniqueness of Israel's God (Deut 4; 1Kgs 18:21, 24), and the remaining cases occur within prayers that emphasise the total commitment of the speaker to Yahweh (2Sam 7; 1Kgs 8, 18:39; 2Kgs 19).

It is evident, then, that as a simple matter of genre we should not expect monotheistic rhetoric in the reform account of 2Kgs 23:4–20. For its absence elsewhere, it may simply be that the developing account of Josiah's reform offered no obvious opportunities for the scribal composer(s) of the monotheistic portions of the Deuteronomistic History to add another example of their distinctive rhetoric. The only extended speech in 2Kgs 22–3 is that of Huldah the prophetess (2Kgs 22:15–20), which is a prophecy of destruction followed by a prophecy of assurance.⁴² The language is thoroughly Deuteronomistic, but this is neither prayer nor persuasion. Josiah, for all his piety, is not portrayed praying. Nor does he need to persuade the people, as do Moses and Elijah. He is the king, and not a prophet. He simply calls the people to hear the book of the law and concludes a covenant with Yahweh on their behalf. Thus, the reform of Josiah is not monotheistic, but with prayer and prophetic exhortation it could have been!

---

40 Smith 2000, 193. See also Christopher R. Seitz who writes that similar expressions in Deutero-Isaiah expresses "not a sublime monotheism capable of differentiation from a more concrete henotheism—rather it is henotheism of a particularly potent stripe" (1998, 225).
41 Pakkala 2007, 159–78).
42 For the two parts of Huldah's prayer, see O'Long 1991, 263–4.

Part II: **Continuing the Dialogue on Monotheism**

Nathan MacDonald
Response to Richard S. Hess

In his essay Richard Hess sets outs to do two things. First, he argues that 2Kgs 22–3 is "an authentic record"[1] of a seventh century Josianic reform in which the worship of just one deity, Yahweh, was promoted. Second, Hess claims that Josiah's reform was consistent with the belief of a substantial part of the population of the kingdom of Judah.

In the first section, Hess concentrates on the reform account in 23:4–15. Within this account Hess distinguishes two kinds of condemned practice that Josiah reforms. The first kind of condemned practice is the worship of deities other than Yahweh. All of these deities "are known in the preexilic period. They are not attested in the postexilic period in Yehud".[2] Since these preexilic religious realities were unknown to writers in the postexilic period, the account of these reforms must have been composed in the preexilic period. The second kind of condemned practice is worship of a recipient who is unnamed. Giving special attention to the altars on the roof (v. 12), Hess makes the suggestive argument that no deity is identified because the worship was syncretistic.[3] The writer of 2Kgs 23 discretely avoided the idea that Yahweh could have been worshipped alongside other deities. Hess argues that such syncretism would have been alien to postexilic writers. If they had invented the use of roof-top altars we would have expected them to identify the recipients of the worship as other deities. In the second section, Hess produces archaeological evidence that around the turn of the sixth century BCE most of the population of Judah and Jerusalem worshipped just one deity, Yahweh. He reviews the clay figurines, inscriptional evidence, and onomastic evidence. Hess concludes, "this evidence suggests that the record of Josiah's reform toward the belief in the single deity, Yahweh, is consistent with the extra biblical textual and onomastic evidence from the period of the late seventh century BCE".[4]

In terms of his positive arguments, much of what Hess says is plausible, and often convincing. He makes a good case that Yahweh was one of the recipients of the roof-top worship alongside other deities.[5] In my own essay I argued that the

---

[1] Above, p. 135.
[2] Above, p. 137.
[3] Above, pp. 137–40.
[4] Above, p. 150.
[5] I am not persuaded that this took place at the royal palace. Hess's association of the altars with the palace depends on the words "the upper chamber of Ahaz", *'ălîyat 'āḥāz*, which

worship on the roof was directed towards the "host of heaven". In light of the evidence for Yahweh's association with the sun and his title "the Lord of hosts" (*yhwh ṣəbā'ôt*), it seems more than likely that Yahweh and his host were worshipped together. It is worth noting that Josiah pulled down a plurality of altars (*hammizbəḥôt*). Hess's argument that the recipient of worship is suppressed in order to avoid associating Yahweh with other deities is, ultimately, one from silence. Nevertheless, Hess has drawn our attention to an interesting moment of reticence in the text, and his interpretation is certainly plausible and worth serious consideration. One question I still have about this reading is whether it is sufficient to justify seeing the Josianic reformation as monolatrous. Might it be that the text avoids the opprobrium of associating Yahweh with the deities honoured by the Assyrians? I wonder whether Hess is deducing from the text's silence more than is justified. In the second part of the essay Hess makes a number of observations that struck me as important and apposite. I agree that the terracotta female figurines are not sufficient evidence of goddess worship,[6] and the epigraphic and onomastic evidence suggests that many Judahites were monolatrous.

My difficulties with Hess's essay lie not so much with his treatment of ancient evidence, but his account of contemporary scholarship. First, I am not convinced that Hess understands well the concerns and arguments of those with whom he disagrees. Second, Hess simplifies the positions on the historicity of 2Kgs 22–3 in a way that serves the rhetoric of his argument but occludes more compelling alternatives.

First, Hess criticises Ahlström, Stavrakopoulou and Niehr for denying to 2Kgs 22–3 a "historical kernel as describing a religious reform in the time of Josiah that recognised only Yahweh [sic] and rejected other deities".[7] Elsewhere he identifies them as "those who understand this account as a later and postexilic ideological construct of the religious reform".[8] It seems to me that this is an apt

---

many scholars regard as a gloss. The words are suspicious for two reasons. First, they are grammatically awkward: the words *'ălîyat 'āḥāz* are simply juxtaposed to the preceding word "the roof", *haggāg*. Most modern English translations that seek to make sense of the text either ignore the definite article and render "roof" as if it were a construct form, "the roof of the upper chamber of Ahaz" (so NRSV), or introduce a preposition, "on the roof near the upper room of Ahaz" (so NIV). Both solutions illustrate the difficulties with the Hebrew text. Second, the reference to the palace interrupts a focus on the temple that is found in v. 11 and continues in v. 12aγ. These two difficulties are removed if we assume that *'ălîyat 'āḥāz* was added as a gloss under the influence of 2Kgs 20:11.

6 See now Erin Darby's study (2014).
7 Above, p. 136.
8 Above, p. 137.

characterisation of Niehr's view, since he insists that it is only in the postexilic period that we have a demoting of the members of the divine council to mere messengers. Niehr follows Levin's redactional reconstruction, which identified the centralisation of the cult and its officials to Jerusalem (23:9a) as the kernel of the reform account. This reform is not undertaken for religious reasons, but primarily as an administrative measure.[9] In the case of Ahlström and Stavrakopoulou, I think Hess reads rather more into their statements than is warranted.

Ahlström's concern is, as Hess rightly notes,[10] with "pure" religion as a postexilic creation. It is important, however, to understand what Ahlström means by this and to avoid too quickly relating it to Hess's own concern that Josiah's reform be recognised as monolatrous. Ahlström's point appears to be to contrast the religious and cultic concerns of the postexilic temple community with the social, political, economic and (even!) religious interests of the late Iron Age kingdom of Judah.[11] Thus, Ahlström does not deny a religious aspect to Josiah's reform, but he does think it needs to be understood primarily in terms of the political context of the late seventh century BCE.

Thus, Ahlström is far from seeing 2Kgs 22–3 as a postexilic construct. He argues that the description of syncretistic religion in 2Kgs 23 provides "good information about what the preexilic Judahite cult was all about".[12] There was a reform by Josiah, which Ahlström views as just one instance of numerous "cultic reorganisations" that occurred during Judah's history.[13] The reform should probably be viewed as a response to the changing political situation with Assyria's decline and Egypt's ascendancy. According to Ahlström these "may have inspired him [Josiah] to make sweeping administrative changes that affected the cultic system too".[14] Did this reform deploy monolatrous rhetoric and an appeal to native Judahite traditions about Yahweh as a means to further the reform agenda? Ahlström does not enlighten us about his views on these matters. Where he is clear is in his assessment that there is a disparity between what happened in Josiah's reform and the book of Deuteronomy or the Torah that was apparently found in the temple. As a result Ahlström opines that "the story about

---

9 Niehr 2010, Niehr 1995.
10 Above, p. 136.
11 We might well wonder about Ahlström's categories. Did the postexilic community not also have social, political and economic concerns? Ahlström is not unaware of some of these difficulties. In a footnote he observes, "it could be asked whether there has ever existed a pure religion in history" (1993, 770 n. 1).
12 Ahlström 1993, 771.
13 Ahlström 1993, 777.
14 Ahlström 1993, 778.

the 'law scroll' may be fictional".[15] It would appear that the postexilic historiographer has "anchored" a law code from his own period into the preexilic period.[16]

I am even more puzzled by Hess's inclusion of Stavrakopoulou amongst those he criticises. Her statements about 2Kgs 22–3 mostly concern the finding of the book of the law, rather than the reform account in 23:4–20. Stavrakopoulou agrees with Ahlström that the finding of a book is a postexilic creation,[17] and elsewhere suggests that the account of Bethel's desecration in 23:15–20 stems "more plausibly" from the "early Persian period".[18] Her judgment about Bethel is expressed in a suitably cautious manner, and I think it likely that she would exercise similar reticence about the rest of the reform in 23:4–14. Indeed, she notes its "seemingly complex compositional history", which rather suggests that she would be unlikely to date all of it simply to the Persian period.[19] Quite what she thinks inspired any reform in Josiah's reign is difficult to say; it is clear only that it was not a book. But the account of the book-finding is a matter that Hess assiduously avoids discussing in his essay.

Secondly, I would like to observe the way that Hess frames his essay as a contrast between "a substantial historicity to the account" of 2Kgs 22–3[20] and "those who understand this account as a later and postexilic ideological construct of the religious reform".[21] There is, as we have seen, one place that Ahlström and Stavrakopolou agree in discerning postexilic construction without any preexilic core and that is the account of the finding of the book. But in the crucial account of the reform in 2Kgs 23:4–20, they agree that we have an account with a complex history, some of which may go back to the last decades of the Judahite monarchy.

Framing the discussion in terms of preexilic authenticity versus postexilic construction serves Hess's arguments in favour of understanding 2Kgs 22–3 as a genuine reflection of Josiah's reform. He provides the briefest of justifications for accepting all of 23:4–15 as historical: "In 2Kgs 23:4–15 the authors or editors have made use of many names of gods and goddesses, all of whom are known in

---

15 Ahlström 1993, 772.
16 Ahlström 1993, 777.
17 Stavrakopoulou 2010b, 37–58.
18 Stavrakopoulou 2010a, 89.
19 Stavrakopoulou 2010a, 84.
20 Above, p. 136.
21 Above, p. 137.

the preexilic period. They are not attested in the postexilic period in Yehud".[22] Hess's argument seems compelling until we subject it to closer scrutiny.

First, as we have seen, the choice is not simply between preexilic and postexilic. If there was at least some core of material that originated during the reign of Josiah or soon thereafter and described an anti-Assyrian cultic reorganisation, the expansion of this text through scribal *Fortschreibung* could have occurred at any point thereafter as the text was copied and transmitted. This could have been during the dying years of the Judahite monarchy or the neo-Babylonian period (the period of the "exile"). Indeed, most theories of a Deuteronomistic History (or, if you wish, simply the book of Kings) posit a significant occasion of composition and editing sometime between the release of Jehoiachin in 562 BCE, the last event described in the book of Kings (2Kgs 25:27–30), and the conquest of Babylon by Cyrus in 539 BCE. Had Judahite scribes simply forgotten about the various deities worshipped by their ancestors a mere generation or so earlier?

Second, whilst Hess's contrast of the "preexilic period" with the "postexilic period in Yehud" is not substantiated in any detail, it is not clear that he is comparing like with like. For the preexilic evidence Hess merely refers the reader in a footnote to Tadmor and Cogan's *Anchor Bible* commentary on 2Kgs.[23] But the evidence they appeal to includes not only the Iron Age, but also the Late Bronze Age. It includes the considerably larger territory of the Iron Age kingdoms of Israel and Judah, as well as perhaps their neighbours. In contrast, Persian Yehud was an extremely circumscribed territory, and the excavated material remains are, as often noted by interpreters, rather meagre as are the textual material that Hess would be willing to attribute to that period. In addition, the relevant time-frame is less than two hundred years from the initial moves towards the restoration of the Temple in 520 BCE to the triumph of Alexander the Great in 333 BCE. The paucity of evidence for the postexilic period is such that we must take great care to venture conclusions rather cautiously, and much more so than Hess does. To recall the old dictum, absence of evidence is not evidence of absence. A chastening example is the goddess Anat who is known from Ugarit and appears in a few names preserved in the biblical text. Yet, she reappears centuries later amongst the Jewish community in Elephantine in the deity name Anat-Yahu. We know far too little about scribal knowledge and traditions to insist that significant portions of 2Kgs 23 *cannot* have been written in the postexilic period.

---

22 Above, p. 137.
23 Above, p. 137 n. 7.

Richard S. Hess
Response to Nathan MacDonald

Nathan MacDonald's study provides a useful review of the critical literature that discusses the nature of 2Kgs 22–3 and the reforms described there. As I read MacDonald, his conclusion is that the reforms of Josiah were not monotheistic as described in 2Kings. This is because his reconstruction of the original form of the text does not explicitly remove the possible presence of other recognised deities. However, MacDonald does believe that there were reforms. Insofar as this is his conclusion, we are in substantial agreement.

I originally agreed to contribute an essay to this project wherein I would argue (1) that there was a belief in a single deity in the time of Josiah in preexilic Jerusalem and (2) that the text of 2Kgs 22–3 represented that belief. From this perspective, I did not intend to argue for the denial of any belief in the existence of other deities at this time and in this text. When the original respondent, who did not hold this view, did not provide a contribution, Nathan MacDonald kindly stepped in with his essay. While he might emphasise the extent to which other deities were recognised by Josiah, whereas I might emphasise the extent to which Josiah affirmed belief in the single deity, Yahweh, our views overlap considerably and do not provide for substantial disagreement, beyond some nuancing.

Providing a greater measure of distinction is the method by which we come to our conclusions and whence we draw the evidence used to establish the argument. My work focuses on the extent to which the biblical claims can be measured extra-biblically with evidence from the Iron Age and later. This includes awareness that many of the deities mentioned in 2Kgs 22–3 are absent in the worship of the Jews in the Persian period (whether within or without the Yehud province) and that a form of Yahweh worship that accepts Asherah as consort is implicitly rejected. MacDonald's work emphasises a literary and redaction critical approach that distinguishes earlier text pieces dating to the time of Josiah from those sections added later. The remainder of this essay will consider his method and evidence.

MacDonald moves forward with an examination of the international political context, the question of whether a book of the law was involved in Josiah's historic reform, and the nature of any related acts undertaken by the king. The first point actually distils into the issue as to whether or not Assyria turned over control of Judah to Egypt in its declining years (the two decades before 609 BCE). The putative archaeological and textual evidence for this position is well documented and critiqued elsewhere.¹ While MacDonald's argument that the creation of an Egyptian empire would not be in Assyria's interest is helpful, the ideology of the late Neo-Assyrian empire relegated even cultic matters to a position subservient to the pragmatic concerns of imperial control and expansion.² Such ideology would not tolerate alliances that involved the ceding of Assyrian territory and control to other countries. Egypt's assistance comes late and serves its own continuing interests (already well attested in the Levant), when the Assyrian army is no longer in a position to dictate terms.

The second area that MacDonald addresses has to do with the discovery of the Book of the Law. He argues that the account of the finding of the Book of the Law was added secondarily and that the original text consisted only of 2Kgs 22:3–7, 9. 2Kgs 22:8, 10–20 describe the finding of the book of the law and should be understood as later additions to a text about repairing the temple. The following arguments are made to support this. First, the account of Josiah's life in 2Chr "opens up the possibility of a Josianic reform without a book".³ Second, the high priest's discovery of the book of the Law (v. 8) "disturbs the natural connection" between Josiah's instructions to Shaphan about the financing of the temple repairs (vv. 3–7) and Shaphan's report as to how this was done (v. 9).⁴ Third, the temple repairs and the book's discovery are never connected and are "almost independent of each other".⁵ Fourth, the parallel with part of Joash's temple repair in 2Kgs 12 demonstrates that "[t]he legend of the finding of a book was only added secondarily".⁶ Fifth, Josiah's reforms of 23:4–20 make no reference to the book, which is identified by at least two different terms, "book of the law" (22:8, 11) and "book of the covenant" (23:2, 21). This "could be evidence of a literary development".⁷

Regarding the use of these points to establish distinct literary strata within the text, the following observations should be made. First, 2Chr 34:3–7 describes an early reform undertaken by the twelfth year of Josiah's reign. Verses 8–33 describe the purification of the temple and the finding of the Book of the Law in the eighteenth year of Josiah's reign. However this account may be related in its details to the one in 2Kgs, it is clear that 2Chr in no sense envisions much of Josiah's life and ministry "without a book". While this early reform does not

---

1 Kelle 2014, 377.
2 Holloway, 2002.
3 Above, p. 156.
4 Above, p. 156.
5 Above, p. 156.
6 Above, p. 157.
7 Above, p. 158.

mention the use of a book, 2Chronicles does connect the reform of Josiah's eighteenth year, with the finding of the Book of the Law. The vocabulary and syntax of 2Chr 34:9 and 34:14 suggest that the events that follow in each of these sections are presented as occurring at the same time. The tasks are undertaken with the general purpose of purifying the lands, as well as repairing the temple, according to v. 8. It is possible that 2Kgs 23, where the details of purification of the land are discussed, may have begun before the eighteenth year of Josiah's reign (22:3). 2Chronicles 34:3–7 begins with an explicit statement that these reforms were begun in Josiah's 12th year; not that they were completed. 2Kings explicitly connects the discovery of the Book of the Law with the purification of the land. 2Chronicles does not deny this but does suggest something of the reform began a few years earlier.

Second, the literary form of 2Kgs 22:3–20 finds both chronological and stylistic support without the need to assume a disturbance in the force of the narrative. Chronologically, vv. 1–7 must occur first as they constitute the royal command to begin the project. Verse 8 describes an unforeseen event that occurs after the project has begun. Verse 9 follows vv. 1–7 with Shaphan's report concerning the project. Verse 9 also comes subsequent to v. 8 because v. 9 is tied with v. 10 where Shaphan presents the book to Josiah. Verses 9 and 10 both take place during Shaphan's audience with the king. Stylistically, this narrative is structured as A (vv. 1–7)—B (v. 8)—A″ (v. 9)—B″ (vv. 10–20). Such semantic parallelism is known in West Semitic rhetorical prose. If one excludes examples from the Hebrew Bible because they are liable to accusations of later editing, the style nevertheless can be found, for example, in the Jerusalem Amarna texts.[8]

The third and fourth points find illumination in the study of comparative temple reform texts found in the Neo-Assyrian writings, especially King Esarhaddon's mid-seventh century BC rebuilding of the Assur Temple, Esharra. Following the reconstruction of the temple and its dedication, "foreign seed" is removed and there follows a celebration by the king, his nobles, and the people of the land.[9] The term, "foreign seed" (NUMUN *a-ḫu-ú*), is translated in *CAD* as "foreigners". However, it could refer to anything or anyone who might defile the temple. The point is that contemporary reform accounts, where there is no speculation regarding multiple layers of text, make the shift from temple reform activities to the purging of the anything that might defile the presence of the god, to a festival. This parallels what we find in 2Kgs 22–3. The temple rebuilding and

---

[8] Hess 2003, 221–44.
[9] On the overall structure, see Hurowitz 1992, 76–8. For the text, see Leichty 2011, 4: 119–29, text #57.

reform under king Josiah (22:3–9) is followed by the identification and purgation of everything in the temple and land to which Yahweh would object (22:10–23:20) and then by the king and all the people celebrating the Passover festival (23:21–3). That this parallel in rebuilding, reform, and celebration exists between two texts that reflect events separated by only a few decades invites consideration that we do not have the juxtaposition of several editorial layers in 2Kgs 22–3. Rather, we find a literary form that demonstrates a cultural continuity over the remnants of the Neo-Assyrian empire, albeit with profound differences in the nature of the religions under consideration.

As for the fifth point, references to the book of the covenant at the beginning and end of the details of the reforms in 2Kgs 23:4–20 provide an inclusio for this section and demonstrate the overall influence of this text as operational in the removal of non-Yahwistic deities and influence. The change of terms from "book of the Law" when it is found in the temple in 2Kgs 22, to "book of the covenant" when it is publicly read and obeyed in 2Kgs 23, is an intentional shift from its initial identification as a legal text to its use in renewing Yahweh's covenant with his people (as in Exod 24:1–11; the one other occurrence of the term outside of Josiah's narratives).

When we turn to the third section, regarding the specifics of Josiah's reforms in 2Kgs 23:4–20, we see MacDonald separating out those discussions that deal with high places, asherah, and astral figures. At this point I find it difficult to distinguish the actual sequence of phrases and texts that MacDonald feels were added by editors. Until I can understand more clearly that sequence as well as when and by whom these additions were made, I am unable to comment on them. I would only wish to make a few general comments.

First, the occurrence of *weqatal* forms do not guarantee later editorial insertions. While the use of the preterite (*waw* consecutive) may diminish from biblical Hebrew to Qumran Hebrew, the same sort of generalisation cannot be made regarding the *weqatal* form.[10] As noted elsewhere, such forms can be used to link more closely two points of discourse. So 2Kgs 23:4 may connect the act of burning the cultic items with the act of transporting the ashes to Bethel.[11]

Second, it is overly simplistic to assume that Asherah in earlier biblical Hebrew texts should be understood exclusively as a cultic object, and only as a deity in later texts. Not only does this require redactional arguments to exclude the deity from generally recognised earlier texts such as 1Kgs 18:19, it creates issues as to why the Deuteronomists and others would write the existence of an-

---

10 Naudé 2012, 61–81.
11 Waltke and O'Connor 1990, 541.

other deity back into the biblical texts, when they were championing the worship of Yahweh alone. It presumes that the extra-biblical mention of Asherah at Iron Age II Khirbet el-Qom and Kuntillet Ajrud must be a cult object, rather than the deity; an increasingly unlikely picture given the parallelism with Yahweh in the blessing formulas. Finally, the deity Asherah is attested in the earlier (pre-Israelite) period but not in the postexilic period. It therefore remains conjecture to argue for a reappearance of Asherah as a deity late in Israel's history.[12]

Third, I am unwilling to accept that Josiah's reforms were confined to Jerusalem.[13] Now, MacDonald does not specify when the later editorial insertions were made in the text of 2Kgs 23. I suppose it is possible that he believes this was done during Josiah's lifetime. Be that as it may, my survey of the late Iron Age evidence in the southern Levant conforms to the picture of a widespread public emphasis on the worship of Yahweh alone in Judah, in an exclusive manner unlike any of the neighbouring states and their national deities.[14] This picture is consistent with that described in the reforms of Josiah in 2Kgs 23:4–20.

Thus I return to my original statement in this conclusion. Taken together, this evidence suggests that the record of Josiah's reform toward the belief in the single deity, Yahweh, is consistent with the extra biblical textual and onomastic evidence from the period of the late seventh century BCE. Some Judeans worshipped Yahweh alone before the Exile, and they did so personally, in their families, and at times at a state or national level.

---

12 Hess 2007b, 66–79, 98–9, 151–2, 283–9, 308–11.
13 Dever 2017, 612.
14 Hess 2007b, 247–335; Hess 2007a; Kelle 2014, 370–1.

Part III: **Final Reflections**

Richard S. Hess
Some Observations on Nathan MacDonald's Response

I very much appreciate MacDonald's opening response. He illuminates the positions of other scholars. Yet none of the references that MacDonald culls from the writers cited overturn my contention that they do not accept a monolatrous Josiah. My point is not that they deny any kernel of history or religion to a preexilic king named Josiah. Rather, whatever may or may not be recognised about this ruler's era, the consistent claim is that there was no official worship of a single deity to the exclusion of others. In that context, (1) Ahlström's view that "cultic reorganisations" took place[1] but 2Kgs 23 provides "good information about what the preexilic Judahite cult was all about" in terms of its polytheistic nature;[2] (2) Stavrakopoulou's possible willingness to recognise some events, such as Bethel's desecration, as preexilic; and (3) Niehr's openness to seeing some evidence of a preexilic reform, though driven by administrative purposes—all this does not overturn my contention that these scholars do "argue against" the view of "a religious reform in the time of Josiah that recognised only Yahweh and rejected other deities".[3] The attribution of cultic reforms to the time of Josiah, however motivated, is not something I denied to any of those cited. I suspect that we will remain in disagreement, except for Niehr's position where I believe we have some common ground of understanding. For Ahlström and for Stavrakopoulou, our differences are due in part to the absence of clearer statements regarding the nature of Josiah's religious reforms.

The discovery of the book of the law and its redaction is recognised but not addressed in this essay because the purpose of the essay is not about this discovery but about the portrayal of the larger nature of Josiah's religion and reforms. My statement about the knowledge of the names of gods and goddesses in 2Kgs 23:4–15 should be understood in the context of the rest of the paper. I am not trying to argue that such a document would not have been transmitted through the Persian period. Of course it would have been. Rather, in the context of the unusual omission of the names of specific deities associated with rooftop worship and especially with the altar at Bethel I conclude that this implies an authentic preexilic text.

---

[1] Ahlström 1993, 777; quoted by Macdonald on p. 173 above.
[2] Ahlström 1993, 771; quoted by Macdonald on p. 173 above.
[3] Above, p. 136.

MacDonald wishes to focus the redaction of this text in the exilic period when people would still have remembered the names of these deities. I would respond that the reconstruction of the detailed sites and the specific deities associated with each one would not have been readily accessible after the destruction of Jerusalem. Further, the nature of worship at a northern site such as Bethel would not have been so well known by anyone among the Jewish community in exilic Babylon. Nor do the facts that postexilic Yehud was smaller and that Elephantine preserves syncretistic divine names deny my case. In my view, if one can assert a variety of redactional and compositional activity in the exilic and postexilic periods for the Bible, then one can also use the archaeological evidence that does exist to argue the converse. The heterodoxy of the Elephantine community is well established with the appearance of Egyptian and various West Semitic influences and ethnicities. Contrast the archive from the (even earlier) late sixth and early fifth century Judean community in Babylonia where Anat and names of non-Yahwistic deities of biblical Israel and Judah do not appear, even as theophoric elements of Jewish names.[4]

As regards the question of the literary form and redaction of 2Kgs 23, my point is that whatever changes may have occurred to the text, they do not affect a presentation of Josiah's reforms as oriented toward the worship of a single deity. Thus a dichotomy between the contextualised study of Josianic religion and a "literary-theological" method is one I reject. Nor is the concern whether some or all of the text could have been written after the time of Josiah. The question is rather whether the text substantially describes what Josiah attempted to do and why he did it.

Grammatically, two *weqatal* forms appear in 2Kgs 23:4b and 5a, in a verbal sequence following a preterite form. The use of the *weqatal* in such a sequence diminishes in Qumran Hebrew. Instead, the *waw* (if it appears) is not attached to the main verb in the clause. The three examples of Qumran Hebrew that Naudé provides have no *weqatal* forms in a sequence following the initial verb.[5] In the example from 1QM 14:5 the perfect verb following the initial preterite form is separated from the *waw* that begins the sequential clause. Thus the sequential *weqatal* forms in 2Kgs 23:4b and 5a do not indicate later linguistic developments.

My concern in the essay was with the religious practice of Josiah and his reforms and with the manner in which the text may be used as a testimony to those reforms (so my title). I have not denied that the scholars cited in the discussion accept historicity in some elements of the biblical text, but I do not see in their

---

4 Pearce and Wunsch 2014, esp. 306–11.
5 Naudé 2012, 61–81 (here 76–7).

writings (not to mention some of the public presentations that have been made in popular media) acceptance of the view that Josiah worshipped only one deity.

Early parallels from the Iron Age do not support a late invention of 2Kgs 22–3.[6] Rather, they suggest sources that reflect a contemporary and authentic reading of the king's reform. Josiah was not made into an archetypal reform figure by later editors. Josiah was the archetypal reform figure.

---

6 Cf. Dever 2017, 612.

Nathan MacDonald
Some Observations on Richard S. Hess's Response

I am grateful to Hess for his detailed rejoinder. His arguments merit a longer response than there is space for here. Instead, I offer two reflections on broader issues: the significance of the book-finding episode for assessing Josiah's reform, and our different understandings of the nature of the biblical text.

First, recent scholarship's assessments of the reform are closely tied to scepticism about the book-finding. On this matter, Ählstrom, Niehr and Stavrakopoulou agree! For them, the bookish reform is a projection of postexilic religiosity onto the monarchic period. Without a book, Josiah's reform is best seen as a pragmatic assertion of sovereignty in a changing political environment.

Since the assessment of the reform and the book-finding episode are so interconnected, it is helpful that Hess's response expresses his belief in the basic historicity of the book finding episode. Unfortunately, his arguments are not compelling. First, Hess insists that 2Kgs 22:3–20 has a literary structure that is found in other West Semitic prose. The examples from Amarna that Hess references are short and balanced, unlike 2Kgs 22. Secondly, Hess argues that the account of Esharra's rebuilding rebuts my observations about the lack of connections between temple repairs and the book discovery. I am unclear what Hess thinks he is rebutting. At Esharra there is a temple reconstruction followed by a purge of foreign elements and a festival, just as I envisage Josiah having a temple repair and removing certain foreign features. The Esharra parallel presents me with no difficulties and lacks a book-finding episode.

Secondly, I wish to highlight our different understandings of the biblical text. Hess insists that 2Kgs 22–3 accurately reflects the events it purports to portray, and he resists any suggestion that the text may have been altered later. Although Hess appeals to Near Eastern parallels to defend the text's integrity, these are not convincing. Recent scholarship has been impressed by a different kind of external evidence: the growing evidence of Hebrew scribalism seen in the Dead Sea Scrolls, the Septuagint and other works from the Second Temple period. These provide conclusive evidence that scribes edited texts to a significant degree during transmission. Any attempt to reconstruct the history of the text is hypothetical and should be ventured with appropriate caution. Nevertheless, redactional theories highlight important features in the text and provide compelling explanations. By contrast Hess's approach often obscures textual difficulties.

Hess brushes aside difficulties with the conjunctive *weqatal*. He is rather confusing on this matter, appearing to suggest that I entertain the idea that there is a diminishment in the use of the *weqatal* from biblical to Qumran Hebrew. I do not know anyone who would argue that. Hess is perhaps denying that we can generalise about a changing frequency of usage of the *weqatal* form. But we can! Naudé, whom Hess cites, writes: "The consecutive verbal forms at Qumran have become dramatically less frequent than the conjunctive *waw* with finite verb and, in fact, the conjunctive forms are statistically more frequent in Qumran Hebrew than in Biblical Hebrew".[1] Thus, in 2Kgs 23 where the conjunctive *weqatal* disrupts the *waw* consecutive, these can be seen as the work of later scribes more accustomed to the conjunctive *weqatal*.

Hess also conflates different uses of *'ăšērāh*. On many occasions in DtrH verbs of destruction imply an object is in view. Whether this object represents the female deity Asherah is a matter of some debate, though I am cautious about Hess's equation. The reason that such an equation might be made is that there are places in DtrH where *'ăšērāh* may refer to a deity, including in 2Kgs 23. There are good redaction-critical reasons for judging all of these references to be late Deuteronomistic. Hess cannot understand why Deuteronomists would write other deities back into the biblical texts. I would argue that late Deuteronomists wanted to paint earlier practices in the darkest hues and asherah poles, already rejected in the earlier DtrH, were explicitly identified with the worship of a goddess.

Ultimately, Hess and I have different assessments of the text. Hess misappraises the nature of the references to other deities in 2Kgs 23 by understanding them as religio-historical issues, rather than as literary-theological ones. Assuming that there is a direct correspondence between 2Kgs 23 and religious practice in particular historical periods, he offers a choice between Josiah's reign and the postexilic period. But we should first take 2Kgs 23 seriously as a text and assess the references to cultic practices on a literary level before proceeding to a historical assessment. If we do so, it becomes apparent that there is a close correspondence between the report of Josiah's reform and acts of idolatry earlier in Israel's history. Through these allusions Josiah's cultic reorganisation is made into the archetypal reform according to Deuteronomistic principles.

---

[1] Naudé 2012, 76–7.

Richard S. Hess and Nathan MacDonald
Some Joint Concluding Reflections on Monotheism

In the foregoing essays, in our responses to each other's essay and now in our final reflections, we have sought to answer the questions of what happened during Josiah's reform and whether the reform was monotheistic. In his response Hess has rightly pointed out the existence of methodological differences, and how these relate to evidence. Though Hess focuses primarily on extra-biblical evidence and MacDonald on the biblical text, they agree that both forms of evidence need to be considered. Where they differ is how precisely they coordinate them. For Hess the extra-biblical evidence provides a useful external measure by which to confirm the biblical portrayal of Josiah's reform. For MacDonald the text of 2Kgs 22–3 needs to be assessed redaction-critically and only then related to relevant Near Eastern evidence.

Despite our different methodological starting points, we agree that some form of cultic reorganisation or reform occurred during Josiah's reign. Where we disagree is about its character. Hess accepts the basic portrayal in 2Kgs 23:4–20 and sees the reform as a wide-ranging purge of many forms of non-Yahwistic practice. It took place not only in Jerusalem but further afield in the territory ruled by Josiah, including at Bethel. MacDonald sees Josiah's actions as a limited cult reorganisation aimed principally at removing distinctive Assyrian cultic practices. Only in later retellings did it become the archetypal cultic reform against all forms of false religion in Jerusalem and beyond.

Both would agree that the issues at stake are important, both for the understanding of a historical Josianic reform and for the understanding of the biblical text. If positions are stated sharply, it is because the issues matter. Nonetheless, as the foregoing conversation testifies, difficulties in seeking a consensus on these questions operate at a fundamental level, in particular hinging on the problem of attaining agreement even about the relative value of different forms of evidence or the most appropriate methods with which to address our core question of the historicity and extent of Josiah's reform.

Bibliography

Aharoni, Yohanan. 1981. *Arad Inscriptions*. JDS. Jerusalem: Israel Exploration Society.
Ahlström, Gösta W. 1993. *The History of Ancient Palestine from the Palaeolithic Period to Alexander's Conquest*. JSOTSup 146. Sheffield: JSOT.
Aḥituv, Shmuel. 2008. *Echoes from the Past: Hebrew and Cognate Inscriptions from the Biblical Period*. Translated and edited by Anson F. Rainey. Jerusalem: Carta.
Aḥituv, Shmuel, Esther Eshel and Ze'ev Meshel. 2012. "Chapter 5: The Inscriptions". In *Kuntillet 'Ajrud (Ḥorvat Teman): An Iron Age II Religious Site on the Judah-Sinai Border*, by Ze'ev Meshel et al., edited by Liora Freud, 73–142. Jerusalem: Israel Exploration Society.
Albertz, Rainer. 1994. *A History of Israelite Religion in the Old Testament Period*. 2 vols. OTL. Louisville, KY: Westminster/John Knox Press.
Albertz, Rainer. 2005. "Why a Reform Like Josiah's Must Have Happened". In *Good Kings and Bad Kings: The Kingdom of Judah in the Seventh Century BCE*, edited by Lester L. Grabbe, 27–46. LHBOTS 393. London: T. & T. Clark.
Albertz, Rainer, and Rüdiger Schmitt. 2012. *Family and Household Religion in Ancient Israel and the Levant*. Winona Lake, IN: Eisenbrauns.
Ambos, Claus. 2013. "Überlegungen zu den Voraussetzungen für göttliche Präsenz im Alten Orient und zu den Gefahren ihrer Beeinträchtigung". In *Divine Presence and Absence in Exilic and Post-Exilic Judaism*, edited by Nathan MacDonald and Izaak J. de Hulster, 55–65. FAT 2/61. Tübingen: Mohr Siebeck.
Aufrecht Walter E. 1989. *A Corpus of Ammonite Inscriptions*. Ancient Near Eastern Texts and Studies 4. Lewiston: Edwin Mellon.
Aufrecht, Walter E. 2019. *A Corpus of Ammonite Inscriptions*. Second edition. University Park: Eisenbrauns.
Barkay, Gabriel, Andrew G. Vaughn, Marilyn J. Lundberg and Bruce Zuckerman. 2004. "The Amulets from Ketef Hinnom: A New Edition and Evaluation". *BASOR* 334: 41–71.
Barrick, W. Boyd. 2002. *The Kings and the Cemeteries: Toward a New Understanding of Josiah's Reform*. VTSup 88. Leiden: Brill.
Bright, John. 1959. *A History of Israel*. Philadelphia, PA: Westminster.
Brueggemann, Walter. 2000. *1 & 2 Kings*. Smyth & Helwys Bible Commentary. Macon, GA: Smyth & Helwys.
Cogan, Mordechai, and Hayim Tadmor. 1988. *II Kings: A New Translation with Introduction and Commentary*. AB 11. New Haven: Yale.
Davies, Graham I. 1991. *Ancient Hebrew Inscriptions: Corpus and Concordance*. Cambridge: CUP.
Davies, Graham I. 2004. *Ancient Hebrew Inscriptions*. Vol. 2, *Corpus and Concordance*. Cambridge: CUP.
Dearman, J. Andrew. 1990. "My Servants the Scribes: Composition and Context in Jeremiah 36". *JBL* 109: 403–21.
Darby, Erin. 2014. *Interpreting Judean Pillar Figurines: Gender and Empire in Judean Apotropaic Ritual*. FAT 2/69. Tübingen: Mohr Siebeck.
Deutsch, Robert. 1999. *Messages from the Past: Hebrew Bullae from the Time of Isaiah through the Destruction of the First Temple*. Tel Aviv: Archaeological Centre.

Deutsch, Robert. 2003a. *Biblical Period Hebrew Bullae: The Josef Chaim Kaufman Collection*. Tel Aviv: Archaeological Centre.

Deutsch, Robert. 2003b. "A Hoard of Fifty Hebrew Clay Bullae from the Time of Hezekiah". In *Shlomo: Studies in Epigraphy, Iconography, History and Archaeology in Honor of Shlomo Moussaieff*, edited by Robert Deutsch, 45–98. Tel Aviv: Archaeological Centre.

Deutsch, Robert, and André Lemaire. 2000. *Biblical Period Personal Seals in the Shlomo Moussaieff Collection*. Tel Aviv: Archaeological Centre.

Dever, William G. 2005. *Did God Have a Wife? Archaeology and Folk Religion in Ancient Israel*. Grand Rapids, MI: Eerdmans.

Dever, William G. 2017. *Beyond the Texts: An Archaeological Portrait of Ancient Israel and Judah*. Atlanta, GA: SBL.

de Wette, W. M. L. 1805. "Dissertatio critico-exegetica qua Deuteronomium a prioribus Pentateuchi Libris diversum, alius cuiusdam recentioris auctoris opus esse monstratur". PhD diss., University of Jena.

Dobbs-Allsopp, F. W., J. J. M. Roberts, C. L. Seow and R. E. Whitaker. 2005. *Hebrew Inscriptions: Texts from the Biblical Period of the Monarchy with Concordance*. New Haven, CT: Yale University Press.

Eynikel, Erik. 1996. *The Reform of King Josiah and the Composition of the Deuteronomistic History*. OTS 33. Leiden: Brill.

Eph'al, Israel. 1978. "The Western Minorities in Babylonia in the 6th–5th Centuries B.C.: Maintenance and Cohesion". *Orientalia* n.s. 47: 84–7.

Gitin, Seymour, Trude Dothan and Joseph Naveh. 1997. "A Royal Dedicatory Inscription from Ekron". *IEJ* 47: 1–16.

Gitin, Seymour, and Mordechai Cogan. 1999. "A New Type of Dedicatory Inscription from Ekron". *IEJ* 49: 193–202.

Grabbe, Lester L., ed. 2005. *Good Kings and Bad Kings: The Kingdom of Judah in the Seventh Century BCE*. LHBOTS 393. London: T. & T. Clark.

Guerra, Anthony J. 1995. *Romans and the Apologetic Tradition: The Purpose, Genre and Audience of Paul's Letter*. SNTSMS 81. Cambridge: CUP.

Hadley, Judith M. 2000. *The Cult of Asherah in Ancient Israel and Judah: Evidence for a Hebrew Goddess*. UCOP 57. Cambridge: CUP.

Halpern, Baruch. 2009. "Brisker Pipes than Poetry". In *From Gods to God*, edited by Baruch Halpern, 13–56. FAT 63. Tübingen: Mohr Siebeck.

Harvey, P. B., Jr., and Baruch Halpern. 2008. "W. M. L. de Wette's 'Dissertatio critico-exegetica qua Deuteronomium a prioribus Pentateuchi Libris diversum, alius cuiusdam recentioris auctoris opus esse monstratur': Context and Translation". *ZABR* 14: 47–85.

Heltzer, Michael, and Robert Deutsch. 1994. *Forty New Ancient West Semitic Inscriptions*. Tel Aviv: Archaeological Centre.

Heltzer, Michael, and Robert Deutsch. 1995. *New Epigraphic Evidence from the Biblical Period*. Tel Aviv: Archaeological Centre.

Heltzer, Michael, and Robert Deutsch. 1997. *Windows to the Past*. Tel Aviv: Archaeological Centre.

Heltzer, Michael, and Robert Deutsch. 1999. *West Semitic Epigraphic News of the 1st Millennium BCE*. Tel Aviv: Archaeological Centre.

Hess, Richard S. 1993. "Yahweh and His Asherah? Religious Pluralism in the Old Testament World". In *One God, One Lord. Christianity in a World of Religious Pluralism*, edited by Andrew D. Clarke and Bruce W. Winter, 13–42. 2nd edition. Grand Rapids, MI: Baker Academic.

Hess, Richard S. 2003. "Rhetorical Forms in the Amarna Correspondence from Jerusalem". *Maarav* 10: 221–44.

Hess, Richard S. 2007a. "Aspects of Israelite Personal Names and Pre-Exilic Israelite Religion". In *New Seals and Inscriptions, Hebrew, Idumean and Cuneiform*, edited by Meir Lubetski, 301–13. HBM 8. Sheffield: Sheffield Phoenix.

Hess, Richard S. 2007b. *Israelite Religions: An Archaeological and Biblical Survey*. Grand Rapids, MI: Baker Academic.

Hess, Richard S. Forthcoming. "Deities in the Ammonite Personal Names". In a Festschrift.

Hobbs, T. R. 1985. *2 Kings*. WBC 13. Waco, TX: Word.

Holloway, Steven W. 2002. *Aššur is King! Aššur is King! Religion in the Exercise of Power in the Neo-Assyrian Empire*. CHANE 10. Leiden: Brill.

Hurowitz, Victor (Avigdor). 1992. *I Have Built You an Exalted House: Temple Building in the Bible in Light of Mesopotamian and Northwest Semitic Writings*. JSOTSup 115; JSOT/ASOR Monograph Series 5. Sheffield: Sheffield Academic Press.

Jones, Gwilym H. 1984. *1 and 2 Kings*. Vol. 2, *1 Kings 17:1–2 Kings 25:30*. NCB. Grand Rapids, MI: Eerdmans; London: Marshall, Morgan & Scott.

Jursa, Michael. 2008. "Nabû-šarrūssu-ukīn, *rab ša rēši*, und 'Nebusarsekim' (Jer. 39:3)". *NABU* 2008/1: 9–10.

Keel, Othmar, and Christoph Uehlinger. 1998. *Gods, Goddesses, and Images of God in Ancient Israel*. Translated by Thomas H. Trapp. Minneapolis, MN: Fortress.

Kelle, Brad E. 2014. "Judah in the Seventh Century: From the Aftermath of Sennacherib's Invasion to the Beginning of Jehoiakim's Rebellion". In *Ancient Israel's History: An Introduction to Issues and Sources*, edited by Bill T. Arnold and Richard S. Hess, 350–82. Grand Rapids, MI: Baker.

Kratz. Reinhard G. 2005. *The Composition of the Narrative Books of the Old Testament*. London: SCM Press.

Lambert, Wilfred G. 2004. "Mesopotamian Sources and Pre-Exilic Israel". In *In Search of Pre-Exilic Israel*, edited by John Day, 352–65. JSOTSup 406. London: T. & T. Clark.

Layton, Scott. 1990. *Archaic Features of Canaanite Personal Names in the Hebrew Bible*. HSM 47. Atlanta, GA: Scholars Press.

Leichty, Erle. 2011. *The Royal Inscriptions of Esarhaddon, King of Assyria (68–669 BC)*. Vol 4, *The Royal Inscriptions of the Neo-Assyrian Period*. Winona Lake, IN: Eisenbrauns.

Lemaire, André. 2001. *Nouvelles tablettes araméenes*. Haute études orientales 34. Geneva: Droz.

Lemaire, André. 2004. "Hebrew and West Semitic Inscriptions and Pre-Exilic Israel". In *In Search of Pre-Exilic Israel*, edited by John Day, 366–85. JSOTSup 406. London: T. & T. Clark.

Lemaire André. 2006. "Khirbet el-Qôm and Hebrew and Aramaic Inscriptions". In *Confronting the Past: Archaeological and Historical Essays on Ancient Israel in Honor of William G. Dever*, edited by Seymour Gitin, J. Edward Wright, and J. P. Dessel. Winona Lake, IN: Eisenbrauns.

Lemaire, André, and Ada Yardeni. 2006. "New Hebrew Ostraca from the Shephelah". In *Biblical Hebrew in Its Northwest Semitic Setting: Typological and Historical Perspectives*, edited by Steven E. Fassberg and Avi Hurvitz, 197–223. Publications of the Institute for Advanced Studies 1; Jerusalem: Magnes; Winona Lake, IN: Eisenbrauns.

Levin, Christoph. 1984. "Joschija im Deuteronomistischen Geschichtswerk". *ZAW* 96: 351.

Levin, Christoph. 2003. "Die Instandsetzung des Tempels unter Joas ben Ahasja". In Christoph Levin, *Fortschreibungen: Gesammelte Studien zum Alten Testament*, 351–71. BZAW, 316. Berlin: de Gruyter.

Levinson, Bernard M. 1997. *Deuteronomy and the Hermeneutics of Legal Innovation*. New York: OUP.

Lohfink, Norbert. 1987. "The Cult Reform of Josiah of Judah: 2 Kings 22–3 as a Source for the History of Israelite Religion". In *Ancient Israelite Religion: Essays in Honor of Frank Moore Cross*, edited by Patrick D. Miller, Paul D. Hanson, and S. Dean McBride, 459–75. Philadelphia, PA: Fortress Press.

Lohfink, Norbert. 1990. "Die Bundesurkunde des Königs Josias (Eine Frage an die Deuteronomiumsforschung)". In *Studien zum Deuteronomium und zur Deuteronomistischen Literatur*. Vol. 1, edited by Norbert Lohfink, 99–166. SBAB 8. Stuttgart: Katholisches Bibelwerk.

MacDonald, Nathan. 2014. "The Beginnings of One-ness Theology in Late Israelite Prophetic Literature". In *Monotheism in Late Prophetic and Early Apocalyptic Literature: Studies of the Sofja Kovalevskaja Research Group on Early Jewish Monotheism*. Vol. 3, edited by Nathan MacDonald and Ken Brown, 103–23. FAT 2/72. Tübingen: Mohr Siebeck.

McKane, William. 1986. *Jeremiah*. 2 vols. ICC. Edinburgh: T. & T. Clark.

Moberly, R. W. L. 2013. *Old Testament Theology: Reading the Hebrew Bible as Christian Scripture*. Grand Rapids, MI: Baker Academic.

Moore, Megan Bishop. 2006. *Philosophy and Practice in Writing a History of Ancient Israel*. LHBOTS 435. London: T. & T. Clark.

Moore, Megan Bishop, and Brad E. Kellee. 2011. *Biblical History and Israel's Past: The Changing Study of the Bible and History*. Grand Rapids, MI: Eerdmans.

Na'aman, Nadav. 1991a. "The Kingdom of Judah under Josiah". *Tel Aviv* 18: 3–71.

Na'aman, Nadav. 1991b. "Chronology and History in the Late Assyrian Empire (631–619 B.C.)". *ZA* 81: 243–67.

Na'aman, Nadav. 2005. "Josiah and the Kingdom of Judah". In *Good Kings and Bad Kings: The Kingdom of Judah in the Seventh Century BCE*, edited by Lester L. Grabbe, 189–247. ESHM 5; LHBOTS 393; London: T. & T. Clark.

Na'aman, Nadav. 2013. "A New Outlook at Kuntillet 'Ajrud and Its Inscriptions'". *Maarav* 20: 39–51.

Naudé, Jacobus A. 2012. "Diachrony and a Theory of Language Change and Diffusion". In *Diachrony in Biblical Hebrew*, edited by Cynthia Miller-Naudé and Ziony Zevit, 61–81. LSAWS 8. Winona Lake, IN: Eisenbrauns.

Nelson, Richard D. 1981. *The Double Redaction of the Deuteronomistic History*. JSOTSup 18. Sheffield: JSOT.

Niehr, Herbert. 1995. "Die Reform des Joschija: Methodische, historische und religionsgeschichtliche Aspekte", In *Jeremia und die 'Deuteronomistische Bewegung'*, edited by Walter Gross, 33–55. BBB 98. Athenäum: Beltz.

Niehr, Herbert. 2010. "'Israelite' Religion' and 'Canaanite' Religion". In *Religious Diversity in Ancient Israel and Judah*, edited by. Francesca Stavrakopoulou and John Barton, 23–36. New York: T. & T. Clark.
Noth, Martin. 1928. *Die israelitischen Personennamen im Rahmen der gemeinsemitischen Namengebung*. BWANT 46. Leipzig: Hinrichs.
O'Long, Burke. 1991. *2 Kings*. FOTL. Grand Rapids, MI: Eerdmans.
Olyan, Saul M. 1988. *Asherah and the Cult of Yahweh in Israel*. SBLMS 34. Atlanta, GA: Scholars Press.
Pakkala, Juha. 1999. *Intolerant Monolatry in the Deuteronomistic History*. Publications of the Finnish Exegetical Society 76; Helsinki: Finnish Exegetical Society.
Pakkala, Juha. 2007. "The Monotheism of the Deuteronomistic History". *SJOT* 21/2: 159–78.
Pardee, Dennis G. 1988. "An Evaluation of the Proper Names from Ebla from a West Semitic Perspective: Pantheon Distribution according to Genre". In *Eblaite Personal Names and Semitic Name Giving: Papers of a Symposium Held in Rome, July 15–17, 1985*, edited by Alfonso Archi, 119–51. Archiv reali di Ebla 1. Missione Archaeologica Italiana in Siria. Rome: Universita degli Studi di Roma—"La Sapienza".
Pardee, Dennis G. 2002. *Ritual and Cult at Ugarit*. SBLWAW 10. Atlanta, GA: SBL.
Pearce, Laurie E., and Cornelia Wunsch. 2014. *Documents of Judean Exiles and West Semites in Babylonia in the Collection of David Sofer*. CUSAS 28; Bethesda: CDL Press.
Pietsch, Michael. 2013. *Die Kultreform Josias: Studien zur Religionsgeschichte Israels in der späten Königszeit*. FAT 86. Tübingen: Mohr Siebeck.
Provan, Iain W. 1984. *1 and 2 Kings*. NIBCOT. Peabody, MA: Hendrickson.
Provan, Iain W. 1988. *Hezekiah and the Books of Kings: A Contribution to the Debate about the Composition of the Deuteronomistic History*. BZAW 172. Berlin: de Gruyter.
Renz, Johannes. 1995. *Die Althebräischen Inschriften*. 3 vols. Darmstadt: Wissenschaftliche Buchgesellschaft.
Rogerson, John W. 1992. *W.M.L. de Wette. Founder of Modern Biblical Criticism: An Intellectual Biography*. JSOTSup, 126. Sheffield: Sheffield Academic Press.
Römer, Thomas C. 2004. "Cult Centralization in Deuteronomy 12: Between Deuteronomistic History and Pentateuch". In *Das Deuteronomium zwischen Pentateuch und Deuteronomistischen Geschichtswerk*, edited by Eckart Otto and Reinhard Achenbach. FRLANT 206; Göttingen: Vandenhoeck & Ruprecht.
Seitz, Christopher R. 1998. *Word Without End: The Old Testament as Abiding Theological Witness*. Grand Rapids, MI: Eerdmans.
Smith, Mark S. 2001. *The Origins of Biblical Monotheism: Israel's Polytheistic Background and the Ugaritic Texts*. Oxford: OUP.
Spieckermann, Hermann. 1982. *Juda unter Assur in der Sargonidenzeit*. FRLANT 129. Göttingen: Vandenhoeck & Ruprecht.
Stavrakopoulou, Francesca. 2010a. *Land of Our Fathers: The Roles of Ancestor Veneration in Biblical Land Claims*. LHBOTS 473. London: T. & T. Clark.
Stavrakopoulou, Francesca. 2010b. "'Popular' Religion and 'Official' Religion: Practice, Perception, Portrayal". In *Religious Diversity in Ancient Israel and Judah*, edited by Francesca Stavrakopoulou and John Barton, 37–58. New York: T. & T. Clark.
Sweeney, Marvin, A. 2007. *I & II Kings: A Commentary*. OTL. Louisville, KY: Westminster John Knox.

Van der Veen, Peter G.. 2005. "The Final Phase of Iron Age IIC and the Babylonian Conquest: A Reassessment with Special Emphasis on Names and Bureaucratic Titles on Provenanced Seals and Bullae from Israel and Judah". PhD diss., University of Bristol.

Volkmar, Fritz. 2003. *1 & 2 Kings: A Continental Commentary*. Translated by Anselm Hagedorn. CC. Minneapolis, MN: Fortress.

Waltke, Bruce K., and M. O'Connor. 1990. *An Introduction to Biblical Hebrew Syntax*. Winona Lake, IN: Eisenbrauns.

Wiseman, Donald J. 1993. *1 and 2 Kings: An Introduction and Commentary*. TOTC. Leicester: IVP.

**Third Conversation
Creation and Chaos in Biblical Thought**

Part I: **Engagement**

The question of creation in the Bible, its means and materials, and its antecedents, if any, remains a topic of lively dispute and discussion among scholars. Was there *"creatio ex nihilo"*? Was there an antecedent "chaos"? How far did biblical thought go beyond other ancient Near Eastern thinking? Was it *sui generis* or part of a general search? If the latter, did it lead to similar answers? Is it meaningful to describe the biblical view as "demythologised"? Furthermore, to what degree should we regard the biblical tradition as a wholly new departure in ancient Near Eastern literature, and how far should it be seen within the broader context of tradition? These are the issues which will be discussed from different perspectives by David Tsumura and Nicolas Wyatt. We shall focus on Genesis 1 and Psalm 74 as providing the most accessible entrée to the discussion.

Nicolas Wyatt and David T. Tsumura

Nicolas Wyatt
Distinguishing Wood and Trees in the Waters: Creation in Biblical Thought

> I never could accept the first step of the Genesis story: "In the beginning the earth was without form and void". That primary *tabula rasa* would have set a formidable problem in thermodynamics for the next billion years.
>
> Gregory *Bateson*. 1979. *Mind and Nature: A Necessary Unity*. New York: E. P. Dutton, p. 5.

1 Introduction: Creation in Ancient Near Eastern Thought

It is probably fair to say that in every cultural tradition, which implicitly contains a religious dimension, there is some kind of "belief" that the gods, or one of the gods, or God, created the world. I have put the term "belief" in inverted commas because I do not wish to give the impression that there were necessarily formal "doctrines" on the matter. In any event, they would be relatively esoteric doctrines, reserved for a professional priesthood. Speculations, ritual practices, explanations of these, and any number of other scenarios may be imagined.

The surviving written evidence from the ancient Near East gives us the first possibility of dealing seriously with such beliefs, since for the first time we have the evidence of language to go on, thus enabling us to engage however hesitantly with people's actual thoughts, and to trace developments in their beliefs and practices; and this has left us with a considerable amount of material, offering a variety of narratives.[1] And it is on narratives that we rely. They tell a story (which I think is to be classified as myth[2]) and leave it to readers and hearers to understand as they will.[3] The narratives fall into four main types, which we

---

[1] See Brandon 1963; Westermann 1984, 18–47; Clifford 1994; Wyatt 2001a, 95–120; Batto 2013a, 7–53.
[2] For my assessment of the problem of myth, particularly as it relates to biblical thought and modern biblical studies, see Wyatt 2001b and 2008a.
[3] The process of assessing authorial motives and appropriate reader responses grows ever more complicated. See now Lowery (2013). It is worth bearing in mind that neither authors nor readers in the ancient word were necessarily as sophisticated, or perhaps as devious, as modern academics like to think! This is not to deny them considerable literary skill, and an imagination not necessarily trammelled in doctrinal straitjackets.

may classify as follows, with some examples.[4] The order is interesting from a developmental point of view, though perhaps the relative positions of §§2 and 3 are reversible.[5] That is, the idioms used probably developed in this chronological order, though we cannot be certain of this in absolute terms. At any rate, there is a rough development in sophistication and abstraction:

1 A sexual process. The Egyptian Shabako stone, narrating the so-called "Memphite theology", combines this motif, in an androgynous idiom, with speech (below), possibly declaring itself superior to the older Heliopolitan Ra^c and Theban Amun theologies, both sexual, in the process. There are elements of this motif in the Old Testament, in its several versions of the theogonic tradition exemplified in Ugarit in text *KTU* 1.23, the so-called "Gracious Gods" poem, which appears to be a Late Bronze version of the motif reappearing in various biblical passages.[6]

2 A military process. This is the so-called "*Chaoskampf*" tradition, relating the construction of the world by the victorious storm-god from the corpse of a vanquished divine dragon.[7] The only example of this widespread tradition which, from a purist perspective actually narrates a cosmogonic process, is the story of Marduk overcoming Tiamat, in Babylonian tradition, and building the world out of her body-parts, and whether even this formally constitutes a *Chaoskampf* is disputed.[8] However, many scholars use the term in a wider sense, and arguably with some justification, in that the trope deals broadly with the construction of the world as we know it, as the outcome of a mythical battle between a deity and his draconian opponent.

3 A technical process. The story describes the construction of the world by means of a "making". We have a biblical example of this in Gen 1, a complex narrative, which uses a number of terms to denote the process involved. Some verses describe how God "makes" the world (Hebrew *'āśāh*)—Genesis 1:7, 16, 25, 26, 31; 2:2. The means of making is not specified. But in the second narrative beginning at 2:4b (which also uses the same verb), the interesting technical term *yāṣar*, "to make (a pot)" is used of the making of the first man (2:7), which has a clear Egyp-

---

[4] For convenience, with further examples, see Wyatt 2001a, 53–75, 95–120. Some of the materials given there are extensions of the theme of cosmogony (world creation), covering theogony and anthropogony, the creation of gods and humans respectively.
[5] As in my brief treatment in Wyatt 2001a, 53–4.
[6] See Wyatt 1994, 1995, 1996, 240–59, and previous literature cited.
[7] In general, see Forsyth 1987; Lewis 1996; Wyatt 1998.
[8] Interestingly, in his Translator's Preface to Gunkel [1895, 1921²] 2006, K. W. Whitney noted that Gunkel himself had not used the term *Chaoskampf*, though his interpreters did (Gunkel 2006, xxvii and 287 n. 26).

tian analogue in Khnum's production of the king and his ka. A sub-set of "making" in Gen 1 is dividing (*hibdîl*), occurring in 1:4, 7, 14, 18. The first account (Gen 1–2:4a) also uses the verb *bārā'* (1:1, 21, 27; 2:3), usually translated "create", and supposedly one of the key terms in our discussion.

4 A verbal process. The Shabako stone inscription also tells how Ptah (whose name has been construed as "the Potter") created all things by divine *fiat*. This is also a means of creation in Genesis 1. There are three elements in the Genesis narrative, using different formulations of the process of speech: firstly, "and God said" (*'āmar*) followed by a jussive ("let there be"): 1:3, 6, 9, 11, 14, 20, 24, 26, 29; secondly, "and God called (that is, named)" (*qārā'*): 1:5, 8, 10;[9] and thirdly, "and God blessed" (*bārak*): 1:20, 22, 28; 2:3, a (verbal) affirmation of the value of the thing made. 1:26–7 uses all three forms, *'āmar*, *'āśāh* and the contentious term *bārā'* (× 3!). Like the Shabako stone inscription, which mixes sexual and speech imagery, Genesis 1 also mixes its language, since it has the idioms of creating, dividing, making and saying as its modes of creation.

It is no accident that all of these methods of creating, including the verbal, implicitly involve processes of differentiation, distinction and separation. They are in effect all metaphorical (which is not to say that they are sub-mythical) ways of coming to terms with one's own distinction and alienation from the world (as with the post-coital Enkidu), on an individual and societal level.

2 Judahite Religious Thought in Context

The purpose of these preliminary remarks has been to set biblical ideas about creation in the broader cultural context. Biblical ideas did not develop in a vacuum: Israel's (and perhaps more pertinently, Judah's) historical experience was firmly embedded within ancient Near Eastern history, as was its language, its technology, its political and religious experience, institutions and traditions. While all scholars will agree on the first three of these sub-categories of culture, and happily acknowledge the debt to the wider world, on the last matter, religion, many wish to see an entirely new departure, "Israelite (read Judahite or Judean) religion" being considered from a theological perspective as *sui generis*, because, unlike other ancient systems, it is the product of a historical divine revelation.

---

9 The naming of the animals by the man in Eden (Gen 2:19–20) is to be understood as incorporating the man in the creative process, an aspect of his potential divinity.

There is a great deal of evidence that even if Judah did not consciously, as a matter of policy on the part of ruler or priesthood, borrow religious ideas from its neighbours, it certainly absorbed some, and was heir to a common fund of religious beliefs and practices current throughout the ancient Near East. Its inheritance of the traditions found embodied in the Ugaritic evidence is perhaps the most substantial, though Egyptian and Babylonian influences have been detected by many scholars. Time and again, the Ugaritic texts contain material which is closely related to biblical thought, in its language, its theological conceptions and its political ideology. The fundamental issue underlying this discussion is the degree to which biblical thought is heir to the cultural substrate, and that to which it is to be understood to be offering a new departure, perhaps still with an organic connection with the past, but in the final analysis a radically different approach to its subject matter.

3 The Problem of Myth in Relation to Genesis 1

Closely linked to this issue is the other fundamental question, often playing the role of the elephant in the room: how far is it legitimate to think of biblical material of the kind with which we are here engaged as myth? Many commentators are at pains to regard the narrative of Gen 1, for example, as demythologised.[10]

While many are happy to refer to myth in relation to Gen 1, others are strongly opposed to such a position, and many would like it simply to go away, as having no relevance to the interpretation of biblical texts. I take the opposite view. I think that it is an essential conceptual tool, and that without taking it into account, religious thought is inexplicable.

So why should some see myth as a problem, with regard to the narrative in Gen 1? Since opposite positions *can* be taken by different commentators, starting with the same data, and using genre as a category for understanding, it is worth considering whether it really is a literary genre at all, or does not rather transcend genre. Myth is so polymorphous that the usual classifications of a form-critical kind simply do not cover the range of material. Defining it, as do many biblical scholars, as stories about the gods, is merely a circular argument and a pretext, unconscious or otherwise, the definition being thus formulated

---

10 See Wyatt 2001b, 4–5 n. 4, in which I cited such writers as H. and H. A. Frankfort (1946, 1949); Irwin (1946); Murray (1992, 11); and Otzen (1980, 28–39), and discussed Otzen's view in detail. Cf. McKenzie 1950, 281: "The creation accounts of the Bible were studiously composed to exclude mythological elements" (cited in Waltke 1975, 35); Day 1985, 49 (and my reaction, Wyatt 1985); Becking and Korpel 2010, 18–9.

precisely to exclude the monotheistic Bible. In no other cultural context is it so defined. As Mark Smith asked, "why should the form of divinity serve as the criterion for the genre of myth?"[11] I think it is better explained as a mental disposition, which is undoubtedly a very archaic survival, but like religion itself, has persisted precisely because it has survival value. It is really only within Judaism and above all Christianity that it has even become problematic.[12] The latter's increasing reliance down the centuries on precision and orthodoxy in doctrinal matters has made it peculiarly self-conscious and even obsessively hyperlogical, as though religion were essentially an intellectual exercise. Because the crucial element of the incarnation (a mythical category if ever there was one!) is its supposed historicity, an increasingly historical consciousness has also insisted on the essential historicity, however much it may be qualified in detail, of the biblical narratives, of both Old and New Testaments. It is as though the only kind of truth to be taken seriously is historical truth. This remains a sharp bone of contention in biblical studies, as any consideration of the minimalist and maximalist positions readily shows.[13] In my view the historical reality of Christian belief, in so far as it remains uncontentious (leaving aside such minor problematic elements as the virgin birth, miracles and resurrection), in no way disqualifies it from also being mythical, as for instance in the categories just noted, and for purposes of the present discussion, in the way that the stilling of the storm and walking on the sea episodes in the gospels are to be read in the context of the *Chaoskampf* trope.

---

11 Smith 2010, 141. His whole discussion (139–59) is useful. See also Aaron's analysis (2001, 32 and n. 11). He rightly questioned the assumption that a prose narrative is implicitly demythologised.
12 The position owes much to a very self-conscious historical consciousness, at times manifesting as historicism, which is the hallmark of Western intellectual thinking. We can however detect the development of such an attitude, undoubtedly owing something to Western intellectual influence, in modern Hindu nationalism, where the ancient Vedic myths are presented as substantially historical (and at the same time transcendent). See van der Veer 1994, 138–64. On the other hand, van der Veer rightly deplored Western misconceptions of the Indian world-view: "On the face of it the whole notion that Indians lack a sense of history seems ridiculous. Nevertheless, it is repeated again and again, especially by Indological experts on the Hindu civilization", citing Pollock 1989 as a good survey of such ideas. We may compare the ahistorical claims made by the Frankforts and their co-authors (Frankfort [1946] 1949) about the cultures of the ancient Near East, trying to credit Israel alone with a historical sense. The corrective was Albrektson 1967. See also Wyatt 1996, 382–98. Recent examples of a serious historical evaluation of the Genesis narratives are Collins 2006 and Lowery 2013. See Kazmi 2000 for Islamic ideas on history.
13 A classic (and lively!) instance is the clash of views represented by Provan 1995, Davies 1995 and Thompson 1995.

4 The problem of the Doctrine of *Creatio ex Nihilo*

It is often supposed that the narrative in Gen 1 not only supports, but is actually intended to articulate, a doctrine of *creatio ex nihilo*;[14] and although the problem is strictly independent of the question of translation, this is understood most readily on the basis of the common translation of 1:1, when understood to be a complete sentence. The Hebrew text reads as follows:

> bərē'šît bārā' 'ĕlōhîm 'ēt haššāmayîm wə'ēt hā'āreṣ

and this is translated similarly according to a number of versions:

> *En archē epoiēsen ho theos tov ouranon kai tēn gēn (LXX),*
> *In principio creavit Deus cælum et terram (Vulgate),*
> In the beginning God created the heavens and the earth (Aquila, Theodotion, Symmachus, Targum Onkelos, AV [= KJV], RSV, ASV, CJB, JB, NJB, NIV, etc.)[15]

---

14 For all the clever footwork of linguists and those interested primarily in the history of human thought, some of which is noted here, this issue remains for many a specifically *theological* problem (that is, not a matter of historical interest, but an existential matter). This is well illustrated by Waltke's extraordinary observation (1975, 25):

> "In place of God they find a cloud of gas, and in place of a well-organized universe they find a blob of mud. Instead of beginning with the Spirit of God, the new story begins with inanimate matter which, through some blind force inherent in the material substance, brought the world to its present state during the course of billions of years. This substitution of matter for spirit accounts for the death of Western civilization as known about a century ago."

This seems a rather harsh, even ludicrous, judgment on the long history of human scientific thought. More to the point, it appears that with the theological agenda in the driving seat, the search is in danger of compromise, as with von Rad's perspective cited below, p. 227 n. 70. Waltke (1975, 137) also candidly noted that "how we understand the syntax of Genesis 1:1–3 has a significant effect on our theology": this is not a purely intellectual debate. This is even clearer if we reverse the proposition: "how we understand the theology ... has a significant effect on how we understand the syntax". If grammatical insight and theological claim are in collision, which should prevail? Linguistic precision should surely have priority here. Holmstedt nicely observed (2008, 65) that "the problem [in interpreting Gen 1:1–3] lies in target language issues and theological objection". On the whole sensitive issue of the interface of theology and (secular) scholarship, see Simkins 2011 and its useful bibliography.

15 So also, for example, C. J. Collins (2006, 44–5).

There is a literary splendour about this as a theological statement. It contains within it the seeds of all that is to follow. But for many commentators there is unfortunately a problem with this interpretation of the text as it stands. Some modern versions read significantly differently, taking it as a subordinate temporal clause within a longer sentence:

> When God began to create heaven and earth (JPS),
> When God began to create the heavens and the earth (RSV footnote, NRSV, CEB),
> In the beginning, when God created the universe (GNB),

and similarly several other versions (e.g. NAB, NEB). For either construal,[16] the pointing of the text appears to require adjustment. That is, we cannot simply say that one of these sets of translation is wrong. It is the text that is problematic. To justify the first set of translations given here, the text would have to be pointed thus:

> bārē'šît bārā' 'ĕlōhîm 'ēt haššāmayîm wə'ēt hā'āreṣ.

To justify the second set, it would have to be pointed thus:

> bərē'šît bərō' 'ĕlōhîm 'ēt haššāmayîm wə'ēt hā'āreṣ

So, starting from the same consonantal skeleton, both lines of interpretation have already made a compromise, the first with the very first word (!), and the second with the second.[17] The consonantal text allows either approach.[18] The

---

[16] There seems to be a third, in addition to the two options adopted by scholars and discussed here. This is to see verses 1 and 2 as one sentence, with the main clause in v. 2. However for present purposes—the recognition that v. 1 is a subordinate clause—this third possibility may be taken along with the alternative (second version) pursued here. But the second version is preferable, if the stylistic feature of moving to a climax in v. 3, as in the Akkadian passages cited here, is to be seen as literary finesse, that is, working to a climax in one sentence rather than merely having a new sentence.

[17] Working from Holmstedt's (2008) analysis, van Wolde (2009, 7–8) defended the finite form of the verb in a relative clause.

[18] Westermann (1984, 94–5) argued that both approaches are technically feasible. For an excellent analysis of the pointed text and its grammatical implications, see Holmstedt 2008. He observed that Gen 1:1 is "an unmarked, restrictive relative clause". Van Wolde (2009, 7–8) was critical not so much of his methods as of the *style* of his translation ("rather artificial and ... only marginally interpretable"!). The pointing of the Masoretic text is of course fairly late, though it should be seen as reflecting the hermeneutic (perhaps one among many) of its day. See also Beauchamp [1969] 2005, 149–60; Kerr 2013.

Masoretes appear to have hedged their bets. The question of deciding between them, of determining what the original author meant,[19] can be answered only in the wider context of 1:1–3, to be seen either as separate sentences (the first approach), or as one extended sentence (the second approach, held by Rashi[20]). If the second version is preferable, which is increasingly the view of scholars,[21] and which I am inclined to share, we have to look elsewhere for the main clause of the sentence. Let us see the greater whole:

In the beginning of God's creating of heaven and the underworld,[22]

---

[19] With modern literary criticism, the question of approach to a text is obviously immeasurably more complex than this (see Lowery 2013 for a thorough survey of the field), but the original authorial intention is not to be simply brushed aside. It is still a question worth asking. Reader-response and reception criticism can be in danger of validating any nonsense in interpretation.

[20] Cited in Waltke 1975, 222.

[21] Those who adopt the second approach include Jacob (1934, 21–2; followed by Noort 2005, 14); Speiser (1964, 3, 12); Zornberg (1995, 2–3; citing Rashi with approval); Alter (1996, 3); Holmstedt (2008); van Wolde (2009); Smith (2010, 43–6); Blenkinsopp (2011, 30); Fisher (2011, 37); and Zevit (2013, 50–1). Those who reject this approach include Cassuto (1961, 19–20, claiming that the syntax of v. 2 requires it to be a new sentence), Waltke (1975, 224) and von Rad (1962, 1:142; 1963, 46–7). Waltke shot himself in the foot by insisting on just such a structure in Gen 2:4b–7, though he tried to get off the hook (to mix the metaphor) by not dividing v. 4 between sources. Westermann (1984, 94) took the first verse as a heading to the whole narrative. The brilliant analysis of Gen 1:1–3 in Baasten 2007, championing Rashi over against Qimḥi, and generally consistent with my findings, came to my notice nearly a year after completion of this study. It seems to have remained unnoticed by most of the scholars mentioned here but should be part of any future discussion.

[22] My translation of the first colon is provisional, to be reviewed below. I agree with Waltke (1975, 218) that the expression *haššāmayîm wə ... hā'āreṣ* is a merism, so that the two terms denote "everything". However, the fact that the constructed aspects of the two extremes are made only in v. 6 (firmament) and v. 9 (dry land) respectively means that neither *haššāmayîm* nor *hā'āreṣ* are seriously to be equated with either of them. Rather, they constitute the furthest extremities of the inchoate reservoir whose as yet unorganised contents are to be organised in the following, hence "underworld" rather than "earth" for *hā'āreṣ*. The term has both senses, to be construed according to context. Cf. the similarly ambiguous, or rather bivalent, Ugaritic term *arṣ* and Akkadian *irṣitu*.

Graeme Auld has taken issue with me on this translation (email, 1 November 2014):

> You rightly scored one point on me, when you observed that readers bring their wider experience to the reading of a text: not everything has to be explicitly stated within the body of the text. And of course I agree that a reader could have brought *'ereṣ* = underworld to the reading of Gen 1:1, when first heard.

> the underworld was chaotic and empty,
> and darkness was over the face of (the) deep,
> and the spirit of God was hovering over the face of (the) waters;
> then²³ God said, "Let there be light!"
> And there was light.²⁴

I have set this out as verse here, as the style suggests, rather than prose, though its supposedly prose form has been used as an argument in the discussion of syntax.²⁵ Here the point is its progression, through a number of stages, towards the climactic, magisterial statement of the main clause ("then God said"). The long sentence begins with no less than four circumstantial clauses, only at the

---

> BUT, I continue to maintain that the reading of the whole chapter should have persuaded such a reader that a mistake had thereby been made. Of the two terms introduced and counterposed in v. 1, one has been defined by the end of day 2 (heaven) and the other by the end of day 3 (earth). *Yabbāšāh* is mentioned in only one context (9–10), to help define *'ereṣ*—and preclude (mis-)understanding *'ereṣ* as underworld. In the remainder of the account, it is *'ereṣ* that puts up greenery and on which animals and humans move, never *yabbāšāh*. (I wonder, in fact, whether a Hebrew reader might not think of what is dry putting up greenery as a contradiction in terms.)

I concede the force of the argument here but insist on what we may call the pregnant sense of *'ereṣ*, involving the "earth" in three-dimensional terms, and including its substrate (precisely the "underworld") obtaining particularly in v. 1, in view of its merismic nature. Noegel 2017 entirely endorsed the approach I have taken here, with copious additional Hebrew, Ugaritic, Akkadian and Sumerian evidence. See further pp. 232–3 n. 86 below.

23 The particle is still *wə*; the nuance is required for the breaking of the series: "... and, and, and, *then* ...".

24 Wyatt 1996, 195–6, with change in punctuation.

25 Von Rad 1961, 46 [= 1963, 45; 1962–5 in bibliography], cited by Waltke (1975, 137). Cf. Westermann 1984, 90: "Gen 1 contains a fusion of poetry and prose that is unique in the Old Testament". Polak (2002) noted the extensive poetic usages in vocabulary, syntax and style. In particular (p. 11), he made this observation:

> In Gunkel's opinion the poetic overtones are limited to the description of chaos in the first stanza. These strophes, however, are not to be viewed in isolation. In modern poetics the opening pericope is considered formative for the rhetorical attitude of the reader and/or listener. A constellation in which almost the entire first stanza consists of poetry evokes the poetic code, entailing a rhythmic, balanced reading, rather than a prosaic stance that centres on the action sequence ... almost the entire opening of the creation account can be read as poetry, maybe apart from the divine praise of the light (v. 4). Thus the poetic code imposes itself upon the reader.

On pp. 23–5 he set out the entire passage as a poetic composition. Holmstedt (2008, 58), stated that "Genesis i is prose (its 'poetic' features notwithstanding)". Becking and Korpel (2010, 2), described the narrative as a "hymnic text".

end coming to the main clause, which relieves the growing tension. This long preamble with its abrupt climax is then sharply counterpointed by the two-word sequel (in Hebrew: *wayəhî 'ôr*), describing the upshot of God's command in one short sentence, "And there was light". On this reading the passage makes no reference to *creatio ex nihilo*, but rather presupposes the existence of raw material, already present in v. 2, before the cosmogonic process begins.

Some scholars have drawn attention to the similar structure of the opening lines of the Babylonian creation narrative, *Enuma Elish* (i 1–9). This is Lambert's 2013 translation:

> When the heavens above did not exist,
> And earth (*ammatum*) beneath had not come into being—
> There was Apsû, the first in order, their begetter;
> And demiurge Tiāmat, who gave birth to them all;
> They had mingled their waters together
> Before meadow-land had coalesced and reed-bed was to be found—
> When not one of the gods had been formed
> Or had come into being, when no destinies had been decreed,
> The gods were created within them;
> Laḥmu and Laḥamu were formed and came into being.[26]

The double main clause of this extended sentence occurs in the final two lines. All that precedes them is the framework within which this first divine act takes place, in a series of circumstantial clauses. The two narratives, Akkadian and Hebrew, use the same stylistic structure to highlight the divine act.[27] But while the

---

[26] Lambert (2013a, 51, ll. 1–10). The first two lines are translated rather freely. More literally: "When above, the heaven(s) had not been named || below, the earth/underworld had not been given a name". In l. 1, *ammatum* can hardly mean "earth" in distinction from "underworld" here, since this was only formed later, as with Gen 1. See Horowitz (1998, 268): "Most [Sumerian and Akkadian] names for earth are also names for the earth's surface and underworld". In terms of its punctuation, which it broadly shares with the translations of Heidel ([1942] 1963, 18), Speiser, ([1950] 1969, 61), Jacobsen (1976, 168) and Dalley (1991, 233), the translation is more satisfactory than that of Foster (1997, 391). The appearance of a main clause in l. 5 is deceptive. Cf. the translation of ll. 3–5 by Jacobsen:
  (when) but primeval Apsû, their begetter,
  and the matrix, Ti'āmat—she who gave birth to them all—
  were mingling their waters in one
[27] Westermann (1984, 94) argued that Gen 1:1 does not fit the circumstantial style of the opening phrase in other ancient Near Eastern creation stories (including the narrative beginning at Gen 2:4b); the true parallel to these other accounts is 1:2.

narrative of *Enuma Elish* is filled with competing deities and relentless violence (the classic *Chaoskampf* context, whether or not this is strictly the way to characterise it), that of Genesis 1 breathes tranquillity and confident, unchallenged power. Heidel drew attention to a number of features of the two creation traditions.[28] These were his points: both stories presuppose a watery chaos; both have "an etymological equivalence in the names (*sic*) denoting this chaos" (a debated issue[29]); both refer to light before the sun and moon are created; they agree as to the order "in which the points of contact follow upon one another; and the number seven is significant in both". In spite of this he then set about rejecting any meaningful theological significance in the comparison, writing against the background of pan-Babylonian scholarship, which had been perceived as trying to make everything in the Bible derivative from Babylonian antecedents. While this reassessment was of value, he rather overstated his case, because in trying to show that the biblical account was not derivative he concluded that it was not cognate with it, in which case the parallels he alleged became rather problematic.

A more sophisticated discussion of the relationship of Genesis (and for our purposes, chapter 1 in particular) and Babylonian literature and *Enuma Elish* was that by Sparks, who argued that the sociological principle of "elite emulation" would have governed exilic Jewish engagement with Babylonian cultural influence.[30]

---

28 Heidel 1963, 82 (see further 82–139); discussed by Speiser (1964, 9–11): "It is clear that the biblical approach to creation as reflected in *P* is closely related to traditional Mesopotamian beliefs" (1964, 10). Cf. Clifford 1994, 138–41.
29 See further below, pp. 232–4 nn. 86–9.
30 Sparks 2007. This assessment may now be developed considerably further in the light of the discussion in Flynn 2014. Flynn offered a useful comparison of the theology of Marduk and Yahweh as universal creator kings among the gods, arguing that both cults developed in this direction by reaction to Assyrian theology in the wake of Assyrian imperial expansion, using the anthropological concept of "cultural translation" as an analytical tool. In their evolution high gods (most notably Yahweh) developed beyond the early warrior-king conception to a universal world-ruler and upholder of law. But this does not mean that the warrior element was suppressed or entirely superseded, as is clear from the narrative of *Enuma Elish* and the echoes of conflict that can be discerned in Genesis 1. Flynn's chart (2014, 29–31) candidly admitted the faint survivals in the *Yahweh mālak* psalms, though he *wanted* it to have been superseded (2014, 137, where he wrote of "the lack of a warrior tradition ... a warrior element of YHWH could no longer be sustained for the new political and religious context" in relation to Ps 93, 95–9). On p. 138, he wrote of "the more dominant expression", adding that "[t]here are a few exceptions where the warrior tradition is present Clearly the warrior tradition is in the purview of the scribes". The qualification says it all! Similar concessions are made on 139–40. The very survival of older traditions, which might easily have been destroyed, shows that old and new

Another analogue to Gen 1:1–3 as construed above is provided by a further Akkadian text from Assur. Not only does it work systematically through seven lines of poetry to its main clause at the end—the seven is surely significant in a cosmological setting, as it is in Genesis[31]—but it offers a close parallel to the idea that *'ēt haššāmayîm wə'ēt hā'āreṣ* of Gen 1:1 are references to heaven and the underworld, over against heaven and "earth", a sense which is possibly also implicit in *Enuma Elish* above, but more unambiguously so in this text:

> When Anu, Enlil and Ea, the great gods,
> Created heaven and underworld (*erṣeta*^{ta}), distinguished them,
> Established stations, founded positions (for the stars),
> Appointed the gods of the night, divided the courses,
> Drew the constellations, the patterns of the stars,
> Divided night from daylight, [measured] the month and formed the year,
> For Moon and Sun ... [...] they measured the decrees for heaven and underworld (*erṣetim*^{tim}).[32]

It seems clear from the above passages that there is a steady progress towards a climactic main clause concluding the first sentence, similar to the construction put upon Gen 1:1–3 by many recent assessments of the text and accepted here.

None of this material disproves the presence of a doctrine of *creatio ex nihilo* in Genesis, but it at least casts doubt on it as the likely sense, and I think we can make a stronger case against it upon other grounds by further reflection. But let us first acknowledge that it is not a matter of logic as to whether or not such a doctrine was conceivable in the Hebrew Bible, for the concept was already half-present in the early first millennium in *Enuma Elish* iv 19–28:

> [The gods] set a constellation in the middle
> And addressed Marduk, their son,
> "Your destiny, Bēl, is superior to that of all the gods,
> Command and bring about annihilation and recreation.
> Let the constellation disappear at your utterance,

---

could be held comfortably in balance. It is important to stress this point in view of the prevalent view that Genesis 1 constitutes an entirely new departure in theology. It retains evidence of its roots in the past.

31 See most recently Day 2013, 1–2.
32 K 5981 and K 11867, VAT 9805 + 9808 14ff., Lambert 2013a, 177 (the two dimensions governed respectively by the Igigi and the Anunnaki). Lambert noted that this is the closest in structure to *Enuma Elish* of the seven accounts he cited in 173–7, this being the last. See also the same seven-line sentence-structure in VAT 9307, K 4175, A 17643 (Lambert 2013a, 352–5). Note the use of the pregnant *erṣeta*^{ta}, *erṣetim*^{tim} here, compared with the neutral *ammatum* of *Enuma Elish* i 2. See Horowitz 1998, 268 (cited above p. 212 n. 26), and general treatment in 268–317.

With a second command let the constellation reappear".
He gave command and the constellation disappeared,
With a second command the constellation came into being again.
When the gods, his fathers, saw (the effect of) his utterance,
They rejoiced and offered congratulation: "Marduk is the king!"³³

I write "half-present", because though this passage clearly demonstrates the presence of the idea as a logical possibility, it does not occur in an absolute context (it is not how Marduk actually created the world), but in one conditioned by the prior presence not only of the speaking gods (these are the primaeval gods), but also of the constellation which already exists, and is recreated after its destruction. It is a celestial conjuring trick, by which Marduk shows that he has more wit than the opposition, rather like Moses in his dealings with Pharaoh's magicians. So it does not constitute a serious precedent to the alleged presence of the doctrine in Genesis 1.

Other biblical passages, in Deutero-Isaiah, *do* however appear to express the idea of *creatio ex nihilo*.³⁴ Isa 45:7 reads:

---

33 Lambert 2013a, 87.
34 Given the clarity of the formulation here, it is the more surprising to read Blenkinsopp's assessment of the language of Deutero-Isaiah: "The call to Yhwh to take up arms once again against the forces of evil represented as malevolent monsters, denizens of the Abyss (Rahab, Tannin, Yamm [Isa 51:9–10]), adopts the Canaanite combat myth but without any necessary connection with creation" (Blenkinsopp 2011b, 493 n. 2.) It seems to me that Isa 51:9–10 should be evaluated precisely in the context of the passages cited above. Blenkinsopp sees in the cosmogonic ("cosmological", "protological") language of Isa 40–8 the likely influence not so much of Zoroastrian thought, as supposed by some, as propaganda against the soteriological claims of Marduk (506–10). On the problem of the Zoroastrian factor, see also Nilson 2013. Perhaps even more significantly, the point made by Lindström (1983, 298; cited by Lee 1993, 201) is worth reiterating:

> the action ascribed to YHWH in Isa 45, 7 refers solely to the imminent liberation of Israel from her Babylonian captivity. The *positive* phrases "who forms light" and "who makes weal" have to do with YHWH's saving intervention on behalf of his people, while the negative phrases "who creates darkness" and "who creates woe" refer to YHWH's destruction of the Babylonian empire.

As Lee noted (*loc. cit.*) in citing this, "the metaphysical origin of evil does not come into consideration if the verb *bārā'* carries the meaning of control and not that of *creatio ex nihilo*". (It is in any event a gratuitous introduction into the argument.) Therefore to read the verse as an absolute account of creation of the world is a misrepresentation of Deutero-Isaiah's message, hence my observing that this "appear[s] to express the idea ..." Another aspect to which Lee's analysis relates is the equivalence between creation and redemption discerned by von Rad (1962–5, 1: 136–9, 2: 240–1) and Stuhlmueller (1970) (both noted in Wyatt 1996, 24). On the question of pri-

yôṣēr 'ôr ûbôrē' ḥōšek	The fashioner of light and the creator* of darkness,
'ōśeh šālôm ûbôrē' rā'	the maker of well-being and the creator* of woe,
'ănî yhwh 'ōśeh kol-'ēlleh	I am Yahweh, the maker of all these things!

Isa 43:1, 15 speak in similar language of the creation of man:

kōh-'āmar yhwh	Thus says Yahweh,
bôra'ăkā ya'ăqōb	your creator*, Jacob,
wəyōṣerkā yiśrā'ēl	and your fashioner, Israel
...	
'ănî yhwh qədôšəkem	I am Yahweh, your Holy one,
bôrē' yiśrā'ēl malkəkem	the creator* of Israel, your king.

These passages, more or less contemporary with Genesis 1, use the same key cosmogonic terms, *bārā'*, *yāṣar*, and *'āśāh* and evidently belong to the same intellectual milieu as Genesis 1. But do they presuppose the doctrine? (Understanding *bōrē'* as "creator*" in each case is contentious.) The first of these passages, Isa 45:7, is the key one, but it cannot formally be said to do so, since it remains silent on the question of whether light and darkness are made out of nothing, or whether they are simply distinguished. As far as Gen 1:4 is concerned, which clearly has a bearing on this verse, they are explicitly *separated*. This suggests that we should discern the same nuance here. Here we may examine the etymology of the verb *bārā'*, noting incidentally that it is roughly synonymous[35] with the other terms, the *b* word to the *a* words *yāṣar* and *'āśāh*. The three terms are used throughout the narrative of Gen 1:1–2:4a, along with one other key term, *hibdîl*, "divide". The other three words here (besides *bārā'*) all presuppose the prior existence of something to be manufactured, transformed, or divided, or named (*qārā'*): the clay implicit with *yāṣar* (as in Gen 2:7), the division or distinguishing of the light and dark, or upper and lower waters (*hibdîl*), and so forth. The term *bārā'* on the other hand has always been placed on a theological pedestal in biblical scholarship; its use only with the deity as subject is noted, and it is supposed to have an absolute sense of "create", often, so the argument goes, *ex nihilo*. *HALOT* remarks, for example: "in the OT I [*br'*] is a specifically theolog-

---

mordial evil see also Kister 2007, 236 and n. 33. It is perhaps significant that Gen 1:4 articulates the thought that I am arguing underlies Isa 45:7.

35 I mean this no more specifically than that they are terms used in synonymous and synthetic parallelism. In fact, as van Wolde and Rezetko (2011; discussed below) demonstrated, the apparently similar terms are in fact to be differentiated. They are not simple synonyms (if such a thing were even possible), but further develop the thought being expressed. They belong to the same semantic field.

ical term, the subject of which is invariably God".³⁶ But it also gives a number of cognates: "Arb. *bara'a* to create (God), OSArb. *br'* to build, Soq. to give birth ...". BDB gives: "shape, create (cf. Ar. *[baray], form, fashion by cutting, shape out, pare a reed for writing, a stick for an arrow*, but also *[bara'a], create*; Phoen. *[hbr']* ... *incisor, a trade involving cutting*; As. [= Akk.] *barû, make, create ...* [Heb] *shape, fashion, create*, always of divine activity ..." BDB cites a piel usage in Josh 17:15, 18, Ezek 21:24, 23:47, "cut down".³⁷ So the insistence on the exclusive sense "create" may be a mirage, a reality drawing on later convictions, if it is understood that it is obliged to carry this nuance in the present context as originally understood by the tradition. For philology should have a voice at least equal to tradition.³⁸

The radical sense of the term appears to involve separation, so that it implies, in the process of separation, the pre-existence of that thing or those things that are separated. A good equivalent may be "cosmicise", with its nuance that the organisation of the world will involve the (re-)organisation of that which precedes it. Claus Westermann, tending to a "separatist" understanding, made a useful observation:

> If this is correct [the tracing of a radical sense of separation in *bārā'*]—and there is no other convincing attempt to trace the derivation of ברא—then the Priestly ברא is based on a concrete idea, something like יצר. We do not know if the word was used of creation by God in this sense before the Deutero-Isaiah and P. One must be cautious about attributing too much to the word as if it could of itself say something about the uniqueness of the creative act of God. It is clear that it was P's intention to use a special theological word for creation

---

36 On the idea of severance, splitting, cutting, etc., see van der Ploeg 1946, Dantinne 1961. On the peculiarly strong sense that is commonly given to it, that it implies *creatio ex nihilo*, we should note that if the counter-argument is right, that the narrative does not imply this, then it follows that *bārā'* does not have this sense.

37 There is a useful summary of the history of scholarship on *bārā'* as separation in Becking and Korpel 2010, 3–5, complemented by references in van der Wolde and Rezetko 2011, 9 nn. 21–3, discussed further below. Note also the useful citation from van der Ploeg in n. 36 above. He did in fact accept the view that the verb indicated *creatio ex nihilo*, as did Dantinne (1961, 448); see also the discussion in Wolde and Rezetko 2011, 10. The presence of the doctrine was denied by López-Ruiz (2012, 35–6): "Creation of the world is nothing but transformation, expansion, and differentiation, not much different from what literary creation is". Beauchamp [1969] 2005 is disappointing, in spite of its title, because the nuances of *bārā'* are ignored, despite the emphasis on separation. Polak, (2002, 10) noted that "[t]he verb ברא ... belongs to the lexical register of poetry, rather than to the creation theme as such".

38 While Barr's strictures about the "root fallacy" (1961, 100; and see also Osborne 1991, 84–91) still ring in our ears, perhaps it is time to concede that philology has a legitimate place and may inform the present discussion.

by God. But it is not correct to regard this word as the only one and to neglect such words as עשׂה and יצר. Nor is it correct to read *creatio ex nihilo* out of the word as such ...[39]

We may state this more boldly. If it is wrong to read the sense *creatio ex nihilo* into or out of the word *bārā'*, then the verb cannot mean "create" in the absolute sense the theologians have foisted upon it. We are thus left with a sense more organically linked to its etymology. We may also suppose that the choice of the word in Gen 1:1 was determined in part by its assonantal relationship to the preceding *bərē'šît*. It is even possible that it was also chosen here because of another important exilic theme being developed in the contemporaneous patriarchal narratives, that of covenant (*bərît*). In other words, poetic and broader literary rather than purely philological considerations are to be invoked to explain its presence here.

To this set of three mutually evocative words, *bārā'*, *bərē'šît*, *bərît*, we should perhaps add a fourth, *bərešet*, "in a net", according to Margaret Barker, who discussed this issue with me, remarking that "the Lady (aka Wisdom) becomes the Holy Spirit in the NT ... the Orthodox liturgy sings of the Lady's web for all creation":

> Blessed art thou O Christ our God, who hast revealed fishers most wise, sending down upon them thy Holy Spirit, and thereby catching the universe in a net.
>
> Orthodox Antiphon for Pentecost

Recognition of this possible, unspoken allusion considerably enriches our understanding of the development of the cosmogonic tradition as it moved towards its present form. The reasons for supposing this possible allusion to be already intended in the pre-Christian era are as follows: in Ben Sira 6:29, the Greek text, speaking of Wisdom (see the whole of vv. 18–33) reads:

> *Kai esontai soi hai pedai eis skepēn ischuos*
> *kai hoi kloioi autēs eis stolēn doxēs*
> And her fetters will be for you a strong shelter,
> and her collars a glorious robe.

For *pedai*, the Hebrew text, however, reads *ršth*:

> whyth lk ršth mkwn 'z
> wḥblth bgdy ktm

---

[39] Westermann 1984, 99–100. Or indeed "into the word"! See also Scurlock 2013, 51.

And her *nets* will be for you a stronghold,
and her snares* a glorious robe.   *or: weavings

(The image has arguably changed from one of imprisonment to a piscatorial one. The Greek has moved in the opposite direction, reshaping the whole passage.) The phrasing of 6:24 LXX is similar, also containing the term *pedai*, but no Hebrew text survives. LXX reads:

Kai eisenegkon tous podas sou eis tas pedas autēs
Kai eis tov kloion autēs ton trachēlon sou.
And put your feet into her *fetters*,
and into her collar your neck.

The term *ršt*, "net", in its Ugaritic form *rṯt*, occurs in *KTU* 1.4 ii 32, a broken text, but in a context in which Aṯiratu (the equivalent of *'Ašerah*) is found, together with her maritime assistant *dgy*, "Fisherman", which helps to specify the sense of *rṯt*. The consort of El in Ugaritian, and of Yahweh in Israelite and Judahite religion, she survived the exile by transformation into the literary figure (and divine hypostasis?) of Wisdom, who is intimately involved with God in creation in Proverbs 8:22–31, Ben Sira 1:1–10 (as she had been in Ugarit in the important *royal* theogonic text *KTU* 1.23[40]), and later in the Targum Neofiti: "In the beginning with wisdom (*bhkm'*) the *Memra* of the Lord created ...".[41] The Targum Onqelos avoids the term *bərē'šît*, instead using the neutral *bqdmyn*,[42] as does the Targum Pseudo-Jonathan, replacing it with *mn 'wwl'*.[43] In either the Hebrew or Ugaritic, or even in both, there may be a further paronomasia between the divine names and the term for "net", since they share three letters in common, with a simple metathesis. If this is the case, then we have no fewer than five key words, two appearing in Genesis 1, and the other three evoked in the mind of the thoughtful reader: *bārā'*, *bərē'šît*, *bərît*, *rešet*, *'ăšērāh*. And while we are at it, why not also include *bārak*, occurring four times in the narrative, making altogether six words in play?[44] Beginning to feel like Abraham arguing with God, I add, why not include *bāraq*, too, since it is an attribute of the storm god, with

---

[40] See Wyatt 1994, 1995b.
[41] McNamara 1992, 52. See also the Jerusalem Targum: "In wisdom *(be-hukema)* the Lord created". Cited thus, http://targum.info/pj/pjgen1-6.htm.
[42] Grossfeld 1988, 42; Knudsen 1981, 19.
[43] Maher 1992, 16 and n. 1.
[44] See *Sefer Bahir* 1:3 below.

whom Yahweh-Elohim is often associated, since while not mentioned, it may be hovering, even crackling, over the waters? That gives seven evocations!

On Wisdom's role in creation, see also Proverbs 3:19, 8:22, Wisdom 9:9 and Psalm 104:24. With regard to Proverbs 8:23, Margaret Barker suggested to me that *nissaktî* may mean, not "hidden away", but "I was weaving". This intuition is supported by the following cognates: √*saq*, "weave, plait"; West Chadic *saq*, "plait"; Central Chadic *sasaka, saka'*, "plait, twist".[45] The late text Hekhalot Rabbati, giving the teaching of Rabbi Nehunya ben Hakkanah, contains classic references to the weaving motif:

> Years very many, generations without end have passed
> Since thou didst drive the peg for the weaving of the web
> On which the perfection of the world and the excellence thereof do stand.

Hekhalot Rabbati 3:97.[46]

> Said Rabbi Ishmael: When my ears heard this warning my strength grew feeble. I said to Rabbi Nehunya ben Hakkanah my master, "If so, there is no end to the matter. For you will find no man whose soul is yet in his body who is clean and guiltless of these eight matters". He said to me, "Scion of nobles, and if not—? Arise and bring before me all the great ones of the company and all the mighty ones of the academy, and I shall declare before them the hidden, the concealed secrets, wonders of the ascent, and the weaving of the web upon which the perfection of the world and the excellence thereof doth stand, and the beauty of heaven and earth (wherein all the ends of the earth and the world and the ends of the firmaments of the height are bound, sewed and joined, hung and standing) and the path."

Hekhalot Rabbati 14:201.[47]

Why should a net feature in a cosmogonic context? One clear possibility is that Marduk uses a net in overcoming Tiamat in *Enuma Elish* iv 95. This may thus be a further echo of the *Chaoskampf* element we discern lurking in the shadows of Genesis 1. The Ugaritic passage cited here (KTU 1.4 ii 32) culminates in the construction of Baal's temple, which I think has a cosmogonic sense in that temples are microcosms,[48] but whether the passage mentioning Athirat and her assistant can in turn be closely linked to the later narrative remains uncertain, if probable. A first century CE passage which reflects the thinking behind the present wordplays is the Kabbalistic *Sefer Bahir* 1:3, which reads:

---

45 Orel-Stolbova 1994, 460, §2178. My thanks to Wilfred Watson for this reference.
46 Smith 2013, 6.
47 Smith 2013, 25.
48 See the discussion below.

> Why does the Torah begin with the letter Bet? In order that it begin with a blessing (ברכה). How do we know that the Torah is called a blessing? Because it is written (Deuteronomy 33:23), "The filling is God's blessing possessing the Sea and the South". The Sea is nothing other than the Torah, as it is written (Job 11:9), "It is wider than the sea". What is the meaning of the verse, "The filling is God's blessing?" This means that wherever we find the letter Bet it indicates a blessing. It is thus written (Genesis 1:1), "In the beginning (בראשית) [God created the heaven and the earth". בראשית is ראשית בית.] The word "beginning" (ראשית) is nothing other than Wisdom. It is thus written (Psalm 111:10), "The beginning is wisdom, the fear of God".[49]

The same author, incidentally, also rejected the doctrine of *creatio ex nihilo* in *Sefer Bahir* 1:2:

> It is written, "The earth was Chaos (*Tohu*) and Desolation (*Bohu*). What is the meaning of the word "was" in this verse? This indicates that the Chaos existed previously [and already was].[50]

It is this kind of playfulness which is too often dismissed by biblical scholars as having nothing to offer in the solution to a particular exegetical knot. An observation of John Collins may be useful here:

> Biblical scholarship in general has suffered from a preoccupation with the referential aspects of language and with the factual information that can be extracted from a text. Such an attitude is especially detrimental to the study of poetic and mythological material, which is expressive language, articulating feelings and attitudes rather than describing reality in an objective way.[51]

Also very apposite in the present context is the observation of Peters:[52]

> Despite the many benefits that have come about because of a rigorous language-internal approach to word meaning, this approach has also come under serious scrutiny within mainstream linguistics. How could language possibly be studied only by looking at the language system without studying the mind and world of its users?

He then proceeded to address the issues involved, in this case the writing of apocalyptic literature, but his insights are equally applicable to our present material.

---

49 Kaplan 1979, 1–2.
50 Kaplan 1979, 1.
51 J. J. Collins 1998, 17.
52 Peters 2014, 64.

There has been some important recent discussion on *bārā'*.[53] Ellen van Wolde argued that in Gen 1 it means not "to create", but "to separate", in accordance with the points made above. Interestingly, in her analysis of the precise wording of each phase of the creation process (2009, 5), she argued that there was no direct statement in vv. 20–1 (the fifth day) of the making of the "sea-monsters" (dragons: *tannînîm*) as of the birds and fishes, by a divine word and a jussive, as in all the previous acts. Rather the verb *bārā'* here qualifies the work of the day, indicating, she argued, the differentiation (sc. separation) of all the distinct species, marine and aerial. She also noted that (the supposedly key) term *bārā'* is not used of the creation of light, the firmament, the heavenly bodies, earth, plants, nor those things for which *hibdîl* is used: day and night, separated waters, or distinction of times.[54] Her implication is that *bārā'* is not the key term in the narrative, eclipsing all others.

Even if for the sake of argument we ignore the previous discussion, and conclude that the first interpretation, to take 1:1 as a complete sentence, is the better option, as Waltke expressed it, an "introductory summary statement",[55] the translation of the verb *bārā'* as "separate" is still the best choice. Van Wolde's analysis perhaps implies that the idea behind *bārā'* is to be seen fairly specifically within the preoccupation of the author of Genesis 1 with the different species (*mîn*) of animals, a distinction concerned primarily with the principles of *kašrût*.[56] This also applies to the complementary yet differentiated human sexes, with their distinct roles in life, distinguished in vv. 26–7. The firm separa-

---

[53] See van Wolde 2009; her article drew the response of Becking and Korpel (2010) leading on in turn to van Wolde and Rezetko 2011. See also the further contribution of Wardlaw (2014) also discussed below, and cf. the earlier observation of Otzen in Otzen *et al.* (1980, 27–8).

[54] Van Wolde 2009, 6.

[55] Waltke (1975, 227), an option also allowed by van Wolde (2009, 8). Her further discussion of the duality of v. 1, together with the additional deep that follows, as the constituents of a tripartite cosmology (2009, 8 and n. 9) is of interest for the unfolding process. On the general features of the cosmology see Wyatt 1996, 20–6. This point illustrates the process: heaven and underworld (originally mingling, as in v. 2), are drawn apart to allow the habitable world to be constructed between the outer parts. With the flood, the intervening space is filled up again as the waters rush back in (Gen 7:11, 8:2). It should be noted that the firmament in the flood narrative lies below the upper waters, an indication that its placing there was part of the differentiating, organisational process. Cf. van Wolde 2009, 9 n. 10. On pp. 10–2 she noted a number of further Sumerian and Akkadian analogues (the relative terms for separation, Sumerian *bad* and Akkadian *parāsu*, being used).

[56] The world as created is thus ruled not only by the sabbatical structure of time, but by the regulations of *kašrût*. See also Beauchamp [1969] 2005, 240–7 and Neville 2011. Westermann (1984, 125) rejected the link suggested here.

tion of the sexes here is perhaps in intentional contrast to the hint at an androgynous primal man in 2:21–2, where the man mothers the woman.

The critique of van Wolde's argument by Bob Becking and Marjo Korpel noted that no prepositions were used with *bārā'*, indicating, they considered, that whatever the etymology, there was no sense of separation, of this from that, in the biblical usage. Furthermore, they pointed out that contrary to her argument that it is not found, the participial term *bōrē'* appears a number of times in a substantival sense in Deutero-Isaiah, where its obvious meaning, they argued, is "creator" rather than "separator" or the like.[57] In their discussion Becking and Korpel, however, immediately ruled out a doctrine of *creatio ex nihilo*, pointing out that it is the choice of verbs in the Greek and Latin versions which "have given rise to the misconception that in Genesis the idea of a *creatio ex nihilo* is spelled out".[58] This proved slightly problematic when it came to assessing the distinctive nature of the term *bārā'*. They noted that its use was restricted to fairly late texts, while *qānāh* was used in earlier ones.[59] The former term, they suggested, "would have been exchanged then for ברא—a verb for building that had become obsolete in everyday Hebrew and therefore was a suitable choice if one wanted to avoid an anthropomorphism". (Is not God's *speaking* an anthropomorphism?) But in declaring that *bārā'* was a neologism to express the new, more sophisticated conception of creation which the exilic authors envisaged, Becking and Korpel unjustifiably implied that the term would have completely shed its semantic prehistory. If this was not the case (and why use a "new" word which had a dubious prehistory and was to be evacuated of its radical sense?), then perhaps the biblical writers used the term precisely *because* of its echoes of separation, even if they no longer saw it as having this primary range of meaning. It looks as if Becking and Korpel were wanting it both ways.

The main fault of the Becking and Korpel analysis lies in its insistence on univocal meanings for words, as though no influences, nuances, or overtones are possible. An educated writer in the sixth or fifth century BCE using *bārā'* qal in a literary composition would presumably hardly be unaware that its intensive use (*br'* piel) had the sense of "cut". It might indeed be no more than an echo, but that is precisely what literary usage depends upon, with its powers of evocation and suggestion. A similar argument should be applied with regard to the relationship of *təhôm* and *ti'āmat*, to be discussed below.

---

57 Becking and Korpel 2010, 12, citing Isa 40:26, 28; 42:5; 43:1, 15 (noted above, p. 222 n. 53), and in Trito-Isa, 57:18–9, 65:17 and 66:22.
58 Becking and Korpel 2010, 2.
59 Becking and Korpel 2010, 15.

The critique of van Wolde's article by Becking and Korpel in turn drew a response from van Wolde and Robert Rezetko.[60] In a wide-ranging discussion of the points at issue, they drew attention among other matters to the piel usage of *br'*, "to cut", in Josh 17:15, 18 and Ezek 21:24.[61] So the semantic field certainly had not been forgotten. And while God is indeed the only subject of the verb *br'* in the Bible, this is true only of the qal form.[62] The verb *'śh* and *br'* are each used seven times in Gen 1, they stated,[63] and the two terms clearly have broadly the same sense, though of course each is making its individual point. But the sense of "creation" was overstated for *bārā'*.[64] If it were so precise in its reference to creation, why was it not used in Gen 14:19, 22 and in Exod 20:11? If the term is so distinctive for Gen 1:1, yet vv. 6–10, which describe the creation in progress, use *'śh* and *hbdyl*, "the verb ברא in v. 1 should signify at least both 'to create' and 'to divide'".[65]

A point which van Wolde and Rezetko reiterated was that God did not *create* the Sea Monsters in v. 21 (where the verb *br'* is used), because they were already in existence (as indicated in Isa 51:9–10, Pss 74:13–4 and 148:7). They posed the question, "if the sea monsters were already present, how then could the verb ברא in v. 21 indicate that God creates these animals?"[66] Arguably a clear case of *br'*

---

60 Van Wolde and Rezetko 2011. In his brief treatment of the three articles in this discussion, Day (2013, 5–6) dismissed the final position of van Wolde and Rezetko as having "gained little support". This was in my view a premature judgment.

61 Van Wolde and Rezetko 2011, 2.

62 Van Wolde and Rezetko 2011, 4.

63 The incidences are: *'āsāh*, 1:7, 16, 25, 26, 31; 2:2, 2, 3 (1:12 × 2 have different subject); *bārā'*, 1:1, 21, 27 × 3; 2:3, respectively. Other terms also occur with a liturgical regularity (*'āmar* [× 10], *bārak* [× 4], *hibdîl* [× 4], *qārā'* [× 14], *ṭôb* [× 7!]), in addition to the seven numbered days. Garr (2004, 90) noted the significance for *bārā'*: "six times—one short of seven, a number suggesting completeness … It also demonstrates God's triumphant force that controls and quiets restive rivals". This is in fact ambiguous: is it six or seven which represents completeness here? If the latter, the six times reflects a continuing dynamism … Note also Garr's radical understanding of *bārā'*, n. 66 below.

64 Van Wolde and Rezetko argued in 2011, 4 (where the wrong computation is found) that "Lee has shown convincingly in his survey of the 48 occurrences in the Hebrew Bible that the concept of novelty has been wrongly connected with this verb" (with reference to Lee, 1993, 211).

65 Van Wolde and Rezetko (2011, 5). Cf. Smith (2010, 51).

66 Van Wolde and Rezetko 2011, 5. Garr's treatment of this issue, (2004, 86 and 90) is very interesting. He pointed out (86, 88) that these monsters:

> have a mythological prehistory. They appear in "precreation battle traditions … where they are turbulent, restive and antagonistic creatures *that must be quelled by the Creator's might* [my italics]" [citing Fishbane 1979, 15]. There, at least, they represent active opponents of God. Here, they symbolise "all the menacing creatures, all the elements of life that make

being best understood as "separate" is in the earthquake narrative of Numbers 16:30 (wəʾim-bərîʾāh yibrāʾ yhwh). It is at least ambiguous, and not in any case a statement about creation. Furthermore, in the context of Isa 45:6–7, the sense of "create" for brʾ would make the verses state that God had created darkness, in clear contradiction to Gen 1:2, unless one subscribes to the *ex nihilo* doctrine (in which case, darkness may be supposed to be incorporated in the "heavens and the earth/underworld" of v. 1). This is all the clearer in view of the close relationship between the two passages (Isaiah and Genesis), which on the Becking and Korpel argument would be in contradiction.[67] In view of this discussion, it seems to me that a perfectly correct translation of Gen 1:1, following van Wolde's and Rezetko's analysis and effective rebuttal of the arguments of Becking and Korpel, and my argument about the precise nuance of *hāʾāreṣ* in v. 1, is:

> In the beginning of God's separating of the heavens and the underworld.

> life precarious and uncertain." In both cases, they are antithetical to God and "hostile to God" [citing Skinner 1910, 28]. But in the cosmogony, they are also powerless. Without ceremony, they are "created"; they are incorporated into a wider, unpernicious zoological category …

> He quiets the turbulent land. He takes control of the sea monsters. And he ousts his divine colleagues. ברא is an interventionist activity through which God demonstrates that he is "Omnipotent and without rival".

God has, as it were, overcome his opponents on a *divide* and rule principle. Perhaps in view of the radical sense of *bārāʾ*, we could translate v. 21 as "God cut the sea monsters down to size".

Garr went further. Citing his 2003 volume (203–4) in support, he offered a sharp understanding of vv. 26–7, the making of man:

> נעשה is the key. For between the proposal to make a human race and its execution, two parts of this verb form are replaced. Its grammatically plural subject, which includes God and his divine council, is replaced by an unambiguous singular (cf. Job 38:4–7). Conjointly, the egalitarian verb "make", which appropriately includes God and his council in the scope of this divine plan, is replaced by God's exclusive "create". This bipartite replacement, though, does not happen only once. It happens repeatedly, three times, in the three overlapping sentences of v. 27. Its significance seems unmistakable: God's power thoroughly replaces that of his council and, in so doing, completely precludes any involvement of theirs whatsoever in humankind. God's last act of creation vaporizes his divine peers.

He did therefore clearly subscribe to the "creative" interpretation of *bārāʾ*, though with interesting nuances. But his further comments above modify its force.

67 Van Wolde and Rezetko 2011, 6. They explained the relation as Deutero-Isaiah being dependent on Gen 1. It seems to me that the reverse is even more likely, though certainty either way is impossible.

This discussion was taken up yet again by Terrance Wardlaw. He criticised the three treatments noted above. His own position may be summarised as follows. The key to the argument is the issue of syntax. Concerning the creation of *'ādām*, he observed that:

> "When God created man, he made him in the likeness of God" (ESV), serves well as a prototypical example. First, one observes from this context that there is only one direct object אָדָם in valence with the verb ברא (n. 17). Therefore, this evidence suggests that the meaning is not separation since there are not two objects identified as being separated (ditransitivity).[68]

(His n. 17 here reads: "This indicates that the occurrence of "male and female" in v. 2 is coreferential rather than ditransitive. Ditransitivity would be present in the case of separation of one thing from another".) The issue of the absence of two objects had been noted by Becking and Korpel, but was now expressed more elegantly and concisely. He also noted Susan Niditch's observation[69] on the formulaic nature of the early chapters of Genesis, and the fact that within this verse *'śh* "to make, create", occurs in parallel with *br'*, which would have much the same force, since, he observed,

> [a]lthough this parallelism does not necessitate that these two words be full synonyms, the identical object and the same subject matter of creation suggests that they are near-synonyms with semantic convergence.

As for two other key passages, he noted with regard to Jeremiah 31:22 that there is again only one object, and that "This suggests that ברא within Israel's traditions indicates a novel act of God in bringing something forth", and similarly with Numbers 16:30, Jeremiah 31:20; Isa 65:17; and Psalm 104:30.

The "ditransivity" element shows a weakness in Wardlaw's argument, because the Man is not "created" and then "divided", as his logic requires, but presumably created and divided together in one overall creative and differentiating act. Furthermore, the criticism made above with regard to Becking and Korpel also applies to him, in my estimation, regarding univocality. While his syntactical analysis certainly appears to weaken the case for the strict sense of "separate" for *bārā'* in the passages under discussion, he did not make adequate allowance for the richness implicit in language, and certainly in a context as suggestive as Genesis 1. The fact remains that in its radical sense, preserved in the piel form, *bārā' does* have the sense of separation.

---

68 Wardlaw 2014, 506.
69 Niditch 1996.

Finally, the bottom line of any discussion of the term *bārā'* should always be that the historical evidence for the qal form of the verb, so central to arguments on all sides, is no older than the earliest pointed Masoretic text (9th – 10th century AD/CE). So the very insistence that *bārā'* is a key theological term in Genesis appeals to Mediaeval tradition, and cannot claim direct access to the original authorial mind.

As for the *ex nihilo* interpretation, which has been so important for some commentators, it is notable that when Gerhard von Rad asserted that the Genesis passage *had* to be interpreted this way,[70] he was making essentially an anachronistic appeal, quite apart from the question of dogmatism. This is analogous to his misuse of evidence in the broader context of Old Testament theology, as argued by Robert Murray:

> If an interpretative scheme is chosen depending on philosophical concepts which are not of purely biblical origin (as G. von Rad employs history), there will be the danger of imposing alien categories on the Bible.[71]

It is ironic that Murray should have argued thus (though I entirely agree with him here), since on the matter of *creatio ex nihilo*, he himself took the same line as von Rad.

One approach to this problem is to look at Genesis 1 in the broader context of other biblical passages on creation. There is no other account or reference which presupposes the doctrine. This should give us pause, if its only justification is an

---

70 Von Rad 1963, 46: discussing the options for translating v. 1, he observed, "syntactically perhaps both translations are possible, *but not theologically*" (my emphasis). When theology is in the driving seat, it seems that linguistic evaluation is compromised. Cf. p. 208 n. 14 above, and Beauchamp [1969] 2005, 153, who observed, on the idea of chaos, that one way of explaining the first three verses "aboutirait à faire coiffer par *berê'šît* principalement l'idée de chaos et, de manière adventice, celle de création, *ce qui est peu acceptable*" (my emphasis). This kind of theologically motivated analysis was shrewdly criticised by Aaron (2001, 44):

> when a scholar moves through the text interpreting phrases as figurative speech *on the basis of a theological or literary imperative* not blatantly disclosed by the text, we only rarely seek a comprehensive justification for the approach offered. (My emphasis)

In case some readers think that I gratuitously use the term "theologians" in a disparaging manner in this paper, it is not so intended, but serves as shorthand for the kind of disposition and priority in interpretation as is exemplified here and in n. 72 below, in contrast to the neutral viewpoint enunciated by Jowett (see n. 71).

71 Murray (1992, xix) cited and discussed further in Wyatt 1996, 374–9. See also Jowett (1860, 343): "It is better to close the book than to read it under conditions imposed from without".

import from outside the tradition, as with von Rad, and some Church fathers.[72] So we are thrown back on the matter of exegesis, and what may be legitimately inferred from the text itself. We may bear the position of van Wolde and Rezetko in mind, with Wardlaw's attempt at a corrective, while recalling Lee's insistence on the element of power contained in the term *br'*, and suggest that while, as I wrote above, there is no hint of conflict in the creation narrative of Genesis 1—in the sense that God is presently combatting any foe—there is nevertheless a very probable allusion to the theme of conflict, and indeed a deliberate echo of the primordial battle in the use of *br'*, whose radical sense of separation is not in dispute.[73] This "contest" is a walkover, but it remains a contest.

5 The Question of Chaos

In his 2005a volume addressing the issues of this paper, in his discussion of *təhôm*, David Tsumura cited some words uttered by Mot in the *Baal* narrative

---

[72] John O'Neill noted the presence of the idea in 2 Maccabees 7:28 (O'Neill 2002). Day (2013, 6–8) cited this as the likely first statement of the doctrine: "this was probably a philosophical question that P was not concerned with". Scurlock (2013, 49) made the same point, noting Romans 4:17 and Hebrews 11:3 as New Testament accounts. Note also the important study of Kister (2007), who drew attention to Jubilees 2:2–3 (second century BCE) and 1 Enoch 18:11–6 and 21 (third and second century BCE: in this compilation, *thw* and *bhw* have become distinct locations), and traced Philonic, rabbinic and patristic developments of the idea. See also Young 1991, May 1994 and the essays in Burrell et al. 2010. Keller (2003, 4,6) observed:

> the [doctrine of] *creatio ex nihilo* has reigned largely uncontested in the language of the church since the third century ACE. This doctrinal hegemony might not surprise us, but for the untoward fact that the Bible does not support it ... The Bible knows only of the divine formation of the world out of a chaotic something: not *creatio ex nihilo*, but *ex nihilo nihil fit* ('from nothing comes nothing'), the common sense of the ancient world ... It is not the flimsy biblical case for the *ex nihilo* doctrine but a hermeneutical desire for a deeply resonant alternative that ... provokes the deconstructive movement of the present writing.

Another important recent discussion is Bockmuehl 2012; he also noted such additional passages as John 1:3, Colossians 1:16 and Hebrews 11:3, observing that "[w]hile we may all agree that such statements are compatible with God's sovereign creation out of nothing, what they actually affirm seems to be rather less than this" (258). He went on, however, to argue that the germ of the *ex nihilo* doctrine was already taking shape, though without explicit formulation, within the second temple period, in early rabbinic and Qumran materials (see references cited by Kister above).

[73] Cf. Wyatt 1996, 194–207, though my argument here goes rather further.

from Ugarit.⁷⁴ The passage contains the Ugaritic term *thw*, relating to the *tōhû* of Genesis 1:2. I give my own translation:

p.npš.lbim ₁₅ *thw.*   My appetite is the appetite of the lion in the wasteland,
hm.brlt.anḫr ₁₆ *bym.*   as the desire of the shark is in the sea …
KTU 1.5 i 14–6⁷⁵

(I have translated *anḫr* here in l. 15 freely as "shark" because of its resonances.⁷⁶) The term *thw* (of which the Hebrew equivalent occurs as half of the binomial formula *tōhû wā bōhû*) I translate here as "wasteland". In a footnote to Wyatt 2002,⁷⁷ I offered an alternative reading and sense for the bicolon, as follows:

---

74 Tsumura 2005a, 10–2. His translation of the bicolon reads:
And my appetite is an appetite of the lion(s) in/of the desert(s)
or a desire of the dolphin(?) in the sea.
75 Wyatt 2002, 116.
76 Wyatt 2002, 117 n. 14. Ugaritic *anḫr*, "dolphin", "whale", *DUL*³. Akkadian *nāḫiru: CAD. CDA* explained this as "snorter" (cf. *naḫīru[m]*, "nostril", and similar forms).
77 Wyatt 2002, 116 n. 11. The note, cited here in full as germane to the present discussion, argues in support of this view:

> It is possible, however, that we should reconstruct the colon as follows, *lbim thw hm* > **lbim th(w)m*, to yield … [as above]. This would give a maritime bicolon, followed by a wilderness bicolon ("wild bulls … hind …") in ll. 16–7. Such an arrangement is arguably a better prosody in terms of the internal construction of each bicolon than that given above. The term *lbu*, while normally construed as 'lion', appears as a designation of Tiamat in monstrous form in CT 13.33–4 obv. 17, 24, rev. 4, 7, 9 (Lewis [1996, 32–4], translated "dragon", and explained by reference to Wiggerman [1989, 118]). Spronk (1999, 684) wonders whether this Akk. term and Heb. *rahab* (a designation of the raging sea) are not perhaps cognate. See already Gunkel [1895, 1921²] 2006, 20, 295 n. 58 (view attributed to H. Zimmern). We may ask whether a link may not also exist between *labbû* and *ltn/lwytn*. Watson (1994, 280) has also drawn attention to Ahiqar §34 (viii 117: Eng. trans. of Charlesworth [1983–5, 2: 502 and see n. i]):
>
>> There is no lion in the sea;
>> therefore the sea-snake is called *labbu*.
>
> For further comments see also Lindberger (1983, 105–7). Cf. also Ahiqar §28 (vii 110), and now Jones (2011 *passim*, but especially 668–70 and 669 n. 47). While *thw* means "wilderness" (Heb *tōhû*), *thm* (Heb *təhôm* [*thwm*]) means "deep", as in "cosmic ocean" (*KTU* 1.23.30, 1.100.1). Its written form *thwm* is not otherwise attested in Ugaritic, and the error may be scribal. Either the "o" vowel has been written inadvertently, or, a better explanation, the *w.h* sequence is an erroneous insertion, anticipating the *hm* of the following colon. This conjecture cannot however be squared with the reading of *KTU* 1.133.2–5—which is why it is relegated to a footnote—though the latter is not necessarily to be preferred, especially since it is a scribal exercise (*KTU* ³ *ad loc.*). See Pardee (1988, pp. 158–61) for comments on the

> *p.npš.lbim* ₁₅ **thm.*   My appetite is (the appetite) of the monster of the deep,
> {*hm.}brlt.anḫr* ₁₆ *bym.*   the desire of the shark in the sea …

On this reading, the particle *hm* of the second colon is argued to belong to the first, the reading *thw.hm* understood to be a corruption of a possible reading **thwm* (corresponding to the biblical consonantal form *thwm*) or even **thm*. The reading *thwt* proposed by Dietrich, Loretz and Sanmartín, and followed by Tsumura,[78] does not in any case correspond to what is written on the tablet.[79]

However, let us remain with the conventional reading and Tsumura's engagement with it. His detailed analysis concluded that the basic sense of the term is "desert".[80] I think that the alternative he cited (Pardee's "wasteland") may be more helpful here, or even better the more neutral "waste"—in view of the interesting Talmudic passage cited below—because we must surely take into account the poetic nuances of the language. The "waste", be it wet (ocean) or dry (desert), is surely something "uncosmicised", since the process of organisation into a cosmos, that is, a habitable world, is the subject of the following narrative. Regarding the two words *tōhû* and *təhôm*, we may usefully recall the view of Arent J. Wensinck, who acknowledged that they were distinct

---

two passages. Another possible parallel is 1QH 5:9–10, where *kəpîrîm* appears in parallel with *tannînîm*. Because it is usually translated "young lions … vipers" or similarly, the possible maritime origin of the image has been missed. While *kəpîrîm* occurs here, *ləbî'îm* occurs in ll. 7, 13 (ref. to the lions' den), and *'ariyôt* in l. 19. A wide range of chthonian images appear in this hymn, and it seems to me that ll. 9–10 may have been intended as an allusion to the sea-monster (a putative **labbû* ‖ *tannîn*, both terms subsequently pluralised).

The three passages (1.5 original and my suggestion, and 1.133) compare as follows:

KTU 1.5 i 14–6		*p.npš.*	*lbim*	*thw. hm.*	*brlt.*	*anḫr bym.*
KTU 1.5 i 14–6 corr.	*p.npš.*	*lbim*	**thm.*	*brlt.*	*anḫr bym.*
KTU 1.133.2–5		*npšm npš.*	*lbim*	*thw.*		*wnpš anḫr bym.*

The last of these is a true variant of 1.5 and cannot be used as a corrective against my proposal. Tsumura reads this bicolon as paralleling a desert creature with a marine one: on my translation, it is two marine creatures, followed by two land-creatures in the following bicolon.

Other passages of interest for comparison are Deut 33:22, Ps 91:13 and Luke 10:19, discussed in Wyatt 2003a, 232–3. See also Wyatt 2003a, 213–5. Rebecca Watson drew my attention (personal communication) to Ezek 32:2, omitted from the above-cited note (Wyatt 2002, 116 n. 11), which is surely a further example. Egypt is even called Rahab here (< *labbû*, see above), and *tannîn* (read *tannîn*, with *BHS*, and not the *tannîm* of MT, which means "jackals"!). On Egypt as representing "a chaotic force" see Strine and Crouch 2013, 891–6.

78 Tsumura 1975, 537; 2005a, 11. In *KTU*², 22 (= *KTU*³, 25) the Münster team changed their mind, reading *thw*.
79 Pardee 1988, 154–5.
80 Tsumura 2005a, 12, adding (n. 18) "or 'wasteland' (Pardee in 1997, 265)".

roots, yet recognised a poetic association between them, citing *T. Hagiga* 12a: "*Tohu* is the green cord that surrounds the whole earth and from which darkness springs". He observed, "*thw* [*sic*] is the technical term for chaos and the ocean as chaos. *thw* is also a designation of the desert and the desert as chaos".[81] The "green cord" can only be the cosmic ocean.

Whatever precise etymology we accept, the whole point of the usage is the deliberate echo of *tōhû* in the following *təhôm* in v. 2. The writer invents and evokes a link between them. They share a common quality. The *tōhû* and its associated *bōhû* are nevertheless distinct from the *təhôm*, since they are a quality of *hā'āreṣ*, though it should be noted that there is no temporal sequence here, the *'ereṣ*, the waste (here "chaotic and empty", rephrasing "waste and emptiness"), the darkness and the deep all coexisting in a "pre-existential" way:

hā'āreṣ hāyətāh tōhû wābōhû	The *'ereṣ* was chaotic and empty,
wəḥōšek 'al-pənê təhôm	and there was darkness over the deep,
wərûaḥ 'ĕlōhîm məraḥepet 'al-pənê hammayîm	and a divine spirit was hovering over the waters ...

It is important not to read any kind of theological or moral opposition into these verses. The opposition is ontological.

Paradoxically, since the idea of divine spirituality and activity is generally associated with light, darkness is here the medium for the inchoate divine activity: if the production of light is the first creative act, this verse describes the moment before, in which divine preparations are afoot. The Great Event is about to happen. The darkness is often presented as inherently evil.[82] While the idea has many associations, including evil and despair, there is no warrant for such an interpretation in Genesis 1. Rather is it here the medium of the primordial and future theophany.[83] The crucial element in the whole verse is that the precosmic material is suffused with divine spirit. That is surely the point of the divine spirit hovering over the waters. Any battle hinted at in the *bārā'* of v. 1 is already over.

This is very different, however, from Noort's view as outlined in this observation:

---

81 Wensinck 1918, 41, 49–50, 53. The passage was also noted by Kister (2007, 234). Was Beauchamp ([1969] 2005, 161–3) on the cusp of the same point? Note his citation of Isa 34:11.
82 Cf. Noort (2005, 16–20) appealing to the usage of Isa 45:7 as a basis.
83 See Wyatt 1993 and such passages as Deut 4:11, 5:23, Ps 18:12 [Eng 11] // 2Sam 22:12 (*ḥōšek*); Exod 19:16, 18, 20:21, Deut 4:11, 5:22, 1Kgs 8:12 // 2Chr 6:1, Job 38:9, Joel 2:2, Zeph 1:15 (*'ărāpēl*). Cf. Lambert 2013b, 45.

> Two extremes should be avoided for the function of v. 2. Neither the description of the earth as תהו ובהו, the תהום, or the ורוח אלהים מרחפת על-פני-המים are material with which or out of which creation occurred, nor is it the monstrous chaos which was conquered by the battle powers of the creator god. תהום is silent here. It has only the etymology in common with the battle monster from *Enuma elish*, nothing more.[84]

It seems to me that there is no warrant for a judgment of this kind, and certainly not on a linguistic basis. It has all the quality of a theological pronouncement along the lines of von Rad's insistence noted above. Something is pre-existent here, not pre-existing God, of course, but pre-existing the initial divine act in v. 3. The *thwm* is obviously real enough, and since *thw* in Ugaritic usage (*thw*) denotes a real place—the wasteland, which is the haunt of lions (*KTU* 1.5 i 14 cited above, accepting the usual reading) or the sea waste, haunt of marine monsters (my suggested reading)—there is no reason to deny this of the present use. And as we saw immediately above, darkness as the salient quality of this inchoate material is the medium of the primordial theophany.

What is the precise significance here of the term *hā'āreṣ* in v. 1? Since dry land (*hayyabbāšāh*), which corresponds to the everyday usage of *hā'āreṣ* as "land", "earth", "ground", appears only at v. 9 in the narrative, following the formation of the firmament (*rāqîaʿ*) in v. 6, the initial use of *hā'āreṣ* cannot have this sense.[85] It precedes the formation of the earth by three stages (light, day and night, and firmament). So it must mean something different. While it is perhaps beyond proof, an elegant solution is suggested by the *Enuma Elish* account of Marduk's creation of the world by cutting Tiamat in two:

> He split her into two, like a dried fish:
> One half of her he set up and stretched out as the heavens.
> He stretched the skin and appointed a watch
> With the instruction not to let her waters escape ...
>
> ...
>
> [(Thus) the half of her] he stretched out and made it firm as the earth (*er-ṣe-ti*).
> *Enuma Elish* iv 137–40, v 62[86]

---

84 Noort 2005, 14–5.
85 Cf. the sophisticated treatment of the problem with reference to both *Enuma Elish* and Gen 1:2 by López-Ruiz 2012, 34–5. Cf. my conversation with Auld in pp. 210–11 n. 22 above.
86 Lambert 2013a, 95, 101. For the end of v 62 cf. Foster 1997, 399: "netherworld". Notice the difference from *Enuma Elish* i 2 above (*ammatum*) and see pp. 210–11 n. 22 above. On the nuance see Hutter 1985 and Noegel 2017, 14–44, particularly n. 78. Note also the image of the stretching out of tent fabric. This image is strong in the Bible: Habel 1972; Wyatt 1996, 213–8; 2001a, 173–6. It may even follow on logically from the weaving language discussed on p. 220 above. On the

Here the two halves of Tiamat become the upper and lower oceans respectively, her severed skin forming the boundaries keeping the upper one above (corresponding to the biblical *rāqîaʿ* with its windows to contain the upper ocean— cf. Genesis 7:11, 2Kgs 7:19) and the lower one below the created world. The nuance of "earth" here is "netherworld", as in Foster's translation.[87]

The problem which faces us at this stage in the discussion is whether there is an equivalence or even identity, in some manner, of the primordial chaos and those living creatures, not mentioned here, but implicit in the explication of van Wolde and Rezetko, that inhabit it before creation. Is Tiamat to be identified with the precosmic waters, or is she to be differentiated from them? And are they, the monsters, to be seen as representing chaos? Is the sea-god Yam in Ugaritic cosmology in some way to be linked or identified with the deeps amidst which El is enthroned? Is the material described in Genesis 1:2 to be associated or identified with the sea-monster or sea-monsters which appear to dwell in it? The passage we have just cited is a useful starting point. Tiamat's two halves are separated (note the theme!) into the outer structural limits of the world about to be made. The dimension in which she and all the other primaeval deities and even Marduk the creator already have their being is precosmic, not yet organised. In some sense, at least, it is chaotic.[88] As part of this argument, there is the vexed question of the relation between Hebrew *těhôm* in Genesis 1:2 and *Ti'āmat* appearing in *Enuma Elish*. Some scholars insist on there being essentially no con-

---

idea of liquid becoming solid, and thus a fabric, as with the skin of Tiamat (and so susceptible of conversion into the cosmic tent), see Kloos 1986, 136–7.
87 See above, n. 86.
88 Sonik (2013, 16) was initially of the opposite view:

> There is as yet no trace of cosmogonic or precosmic chaos here except in its most generic sense as primeval matter, no hint of disorder or disarray in the placidly mingling waters ...

The qualification ("except") says it all. And the chaos need not be at war, nor morally polarised, to be chaotic. It needs only to be not yet differentiated and organised in the way in which the creator god wills. Sonik (2013, 16) went on to describe the developing conflict between Tiamat and her children. She later (2013, 17) noted that this "comes at last to resemble something of chaos". These remarks also qualified the earlier observation; her comparison of this material with Ovid's *Metamorphoses* seems strained; and she finally contradicted herself entirely on pp. 19–20 (and see p. 49 cited below), conceding that kings played their part in "the cosmic struggle" in hunting and warfare scenes. The Mari text A 1968, discussed below, is relevant here.
Lambert (2013b, 44) described Gunkel's whole approach as "now completely discredited", continuing, "I know of no single occurrence of the word or concept *chaos* in any Sumerian or Babylonian creation material". This judgment was perhaps premature, since Scurlock (2013, 49) could write that in *Enuma Elish*, "Marduk will have created the world by consecutive acts of separation using what might, with justice, be described as primordial Chaos as raw material".

nection, while others insist that there is.[89] My view may be summarised fairly briefly: as with the discussion of *bārā'* above, so with *təhôm:* it is simply inconceivable that the author of Genesis 1, if he was writing in a Babylonian context, and in some sense offering a counter to Babylonian cosmology and the claims for Marduk made in *Enuma Elish*, would not have fully intended that his presentation of *təhôm*, which we shall for the sake of argument consider to be imper-

---

[89] Tsumura 1994a, 33; 1994b, *passim*; 2005a, 36–57, addressing the problem of chaos on pp. 12–3. *A propos* the technical difficulties addressed by Tsumura on the precise relationship between the Hebrew, Ugaritic and Akkadian forms, we may point to Hebrew *rə'ēm* and *rēm* (aurochs)—cf. *bərē'šît*, *bərešet*, on pp. 218–21 above—clearly cognates in spite of the disappearance of the medial aleph from one form by *sandhi*. See now Tsumura 2014. As for his interesting discussion of the problematic term from Ugarit, *tu-a-bi*[*ù*(?)] (2005b, 16–22), it is all very inconclusive, especially since he would be the first to object to others using comparative data in this manner. After the completion of this paper I received a notification on Academia of Tsumura 2015b, a review of Walton 2011 which is critical of its attempt to contextualise Gen 1 in the broader ancient Near Eastern cultural framework.

Jacobsen (1968, 108) proposed a West Semitic (Amorite) form *tihāmatum*, which travelled with the Amorites who moved east to found the first dynasty of Babylon and would adequately account for both the West Semitic and Akkadian forms. For two recent discussions which give a very different account from Tsumura, see Sparks 2007 and Pardee 2012. The former appositely remarks (p. 630 n. 14):

> That Tiamat and תהום are cognate terms designating the "sea" (in this case, the primeval sea) has been carefully argued in Wayne Horowitz, *Mesopotamian Cosmic Geography* (Mesoptamian Civilizations 8; Winona Lake, IN: Eisenbrauns, 1998), 301–6. Not long ago, David T. Tsumura made a similar observation about תהום and Tiamat but drew from this an errant conclusion. According to Tsumura, because תהום is a native Hebrew word rather than an Akkadian loanword, it is unlikely that the תהום of Gen 1 represents the demythologized Tiamat. This argument does not hold. There is nothing whatsoever to preclude a Hebrew author using his own term, תהום, in a polemic against the obviously related cognate term Tiamat. For Tsumura's otherwise useful discussion, see *The Earth and the Waters in Genesis 1 and 2: A Linguistic Investigation* (JSOTSup 83; Sheffield: Sheffield Academic Press, 1989),, 45–83, 15–59.

Compare also Pardee 2012, 27 and n. 55:

> (text): ... *Têmtum*, an evolved form of *Ti'amtum/Ti'āmat* ... cognate with Ugaritic *Tahāmu* and Hebrew *Tᵉhōm* ...
> (note): The syllabically attested forms are derived by regular phonological processes in Amorite and Akkadian from a base form /tihām-/ (qitāl). The Ugaritic form with /a/ in the first syllable is the result of vowel harmonization (J. Huehnergard, *Ugaritic Vocabulary in Syllabic Transcription* [Harvard Semitic Studies 32; Atlanta: Scholars Press, 1987/2008], 184–5), the Hebrew form the result of regular phonological developments in Canaanite and Biblical Hebrew, that is, the earlier 'Canaanite shift' (/ā/ > /ō/) and the later pretonic reduction of /i/.

sonal (though it carries no article, and so may well be a proper noun), was a deliberate counterpart to *Ti'āmat*. The precise philological relationship of the various terms cited in discussion (Hebrew *təhôm*, Ugaritic *thm*, *thmt*, Akkadian *Ti'āmat*, *tâmtum*, *têmtum*) is quite immaterial here. Ultimately, they are of course cognate (*thm), and in practice they clearly had different precise significations in their various usages, though covering similar themes. But what is driving the literary function of the words in their contexts is assonance and association. And this is not to be reduced to or judged on the basis of etymological arguments, however seriously they are to be taken. The question of the relationship of these materials to the idea of chaos is our concern now.

As part of her strategy for showing that the term *Chaoskampf* was misused, Rebecca Watson firmly rejected the idea that the beginning of Genesis involves chaos.[90] She began her discussion by pointing out that "the word 'chaos' derives from Greek cosmology", that the Hebrew Bible lacks any "overarching designation" of the concept, and that different attempts at definition, ancient and modern, remain at variance.[91] She appears to have demanded coherence in what

---

[90] She finally conceded that the word may be used with caution (Watson 2005, 379–80). I hope we use all our words with caution. The entry in the *Online Etymological Dictionary* (https://www.etymonline.com/search?q=chaos; accessed 3 December 2021) reads as follows:

> late 14c., "gaping void; empty, immeasurable space," from Old French *chaos* (14c.) or directly from Latin *chaos*, from Greek *khaos* "abyss, that which gapes wide open, that which is vast and empty," from *khnwos*, from PIE root *ghieh- "to yawn, gape, be wide open."
>
> Meaning "utter confusion" (c. 1600) is an extended sense from theological use of *chaos* in the Vulgate version of "Genesis" (1530s in English) for "the void at the beginning of creation, the confused, formless, elementary state of the universe." The Greek for "disorder" was *tarakhe*, but the use of *chaos* here was rooted in Hesiod ("*Theogony*"), who describes *khaos* as the primeval emptiness of the Universe, and in Ovid ("*Metamorphoses*"), who opposes *Khaos* to *Kosmos*, "the ordered Universe."
>
> Meaning "orderless confusion" in human affairs is from c. 1600. *Chaos theory* in the modern mathematical sense is attested from c. 1977.

Liddell, Scott and Jones online (http://stephanus.tlg.uci.edu/lsj/#eid=116323&context=lsj&action=from-search, accessed 28 March 2014) gives the following meanings: "1, *chaos*, the first state of the universe; 2, *space, the expanse of air*; 3, *the nether abyss, infinite darkness*; 4, *any vast gulf* or *chasm*; 5, Pythag. name for *one*". This last denotes the undifferentiated substance of the primordial world.

*For *tōhû wā bōhû* in Gen 1:2, the Vulgate reads "*inanis et vacua*", which indicates that it was taken to mean "chaos". Further reading on chaos is listed in Sonik 2013, 5 n. 13. See also Niditch 1985, 12–22.

[91] Watson (2005, 13–4). For critiques see Wyatt 2008b, Ortlund 2010, 72–9, and Batto 2013b, 219–27. For a more positive response see Sonik 2013. Her observation (2013, 6) that in Hesiod

were essentially attempts to describe incoherence. And while the term "chaos" is of course Greek, it is wrong to suppose that the underlying concept is uniquely represented in Greek cosmology.[92] It has an ancient Asian pedigree[93] and is indeed at home in every culture and religion.[94]

Chaos has two primary characteristics. It is, as we have noted, "inchoate", containing the seeds of future development, but being undeveloped, it has no clear form, is undifferentiated and fluid. If it is a void, then it is a void full of potential, waiting to be filled, the void created by the separation of the primordial halves by Marduk or Elohim. When it is represented mythologically,[95] it may be independent of or identical with the chaos monsters, and they are chimaeric, hybrid, neither one thing nor another, but a disturbing blend, as with some of Hesiod's splendid inventions. They can be tamed, and cherubs (= sphinxes) and griffins, which blend avian and mammalian qualities, thus inhabiting air and land, serve as ambivalent agents of the divine, not least in Genesis 3:24 (their power residing precisely in their ambivalence: their sharing in two natures marks them as liminal figures, who have the guardianship of boundaries, and are placed there to maintain them). Even Leviathan survives (in spite of multiple killings!) to be a plaything of God (Psalm 104:26). He is monstrous because he has seven heads, a serious birth defect—we would call a child born with

---

... "Chaos serves as the starting point for cosmic differentiation, originating without antecedent and functioning as an apparent abyss or chasm", seems to me a good point of departure for a discussion of *tōhû wā bōhû*.

92 The source of most of our knowledge of early Greek cosmology, Hesiod's *Theogony*, is in any event nowadays recognised by all scholars as the heir to a rich oriental tradition. It is precisely the Hurro-Hittite, Akkadian and West Semitic traditions of divine generations and their internecine warfare (theomachy) that informs its violence and process. And while Hesiod is late (seventh century), his material was not recently imported into the Greek sphere, since the influences can be traced back to the second millennium, and point to Mycenaean relations with Anatolia and Syria (already attested at Ugarit, the Troad and in Homer), and he was himself the son of an immigrant from Aeolia in Asia Minor (*Works and Days* 636), and settled in Boeotia, which had a strong ancient oriental tradition (Kadmos, Europa, Ogygos = Og!). For discussion see Burkert 1992, Penglase 1994, West 1997, Noegel 1998, Wyatt 2007a, Lopez Ruiz 2010, 2012 etc.

93 The conflict of Ouranos and Kronos (*Theogony*, 165–92) owes much to Kumarbi.

94 For a wide-ranging and profound treatment of monsters see the superb study of Beal (2002; reviewed in Wyatt 2003b). Beal carries our understanding of these products of human imagination to a level beyond the ken of most biblical scholars.

95 It is wrong to suppose, as many scholars do, that simply to treat the raw material as impersonal, or non-divine, is to assert a demythologisation. All language of this kind is by definition mythological. It is certainly not "proto-science"! For a critique of the compulsion among biblical scholars to see demythologisation constantly at work see Aaron 2001, and with regard to prose, especially 44–6.

seven heads a "monster"—and in some iconographic representations breathes fire; and his representation in Job 41 perfectly demonstrates his protean form. The term *tōhû wābōhû* seems to be the most succinct Hebrew way of expressing these ideas. The combination is probably to be understood as more than the sum of its parts. Indeed, we may well suppose that the writer of Genesis 1 took as his model the grim depiction of anarchy, social, economic and environmental breakdown and destruction expressed by the visionary in Jeremiah 4:23–8:

rā'îtî 'et-hā'āreṣ wəhinnēh-tōhû wābōhû	I looked at the earth,[96] and lo! it was chaotic and empty,
wə'el-haššāmayim wə'ên 'ôrām	and up to the heavens, and they had no light.
rā'îtî hehārîm wəhinnēh rō'ăšîm wəkol-haggəbā'ôt hitqalqālû	I looked at the mountains, and lo! they were quaking, and all the hills were in commotion.
rā'îtî wəhinnēh 'ên 'ādām wəkol-'ôp haššāmayim nādādû	I looked, and lo! there was no man, and all the birds of the sky had disappeared.
rā'îtî wəhinnēh hakkarmel hammidbār	I looked, and lo! the farmland was a wilderness,
wəkol-'ārāw nittəṣû	and all its cities were in ruins,
mippənê yhwh mippənê ḥărôn 'appô	before Yahweh, before the heat of his anger.

The *mippənê yhwh* is the opposite of his presence in the cult: *lippənê* [normally *lipnê*] *yhwh*). Here Yahweh has turned his face away. All the subsequent cola in this passage qualify the first, so that the expression *tōhû wābōhû* is characterised by all that follows. It is the absence of the fixed and stable qualities of "cosmos", of an environment where civilised life can be conducted. "Chaos" seems the perfect English word for it.[97] The prophet's vision here corresponds closely to the Priestly account of the flood story (Genesis 7:11) where it is the reversal of the creative, differentiating process which is implied in this description:

... *nibqə'û kol-ma'yənôt təhôm rabbāh wa'ărubbôt haššāmayim niptāḥû*
... all the springs of the great deep broke through, and the windows of the sky were opened.

---

[96] The term *hā'āreṣ* is obviously richly nuanced. It is appropriate to translate it here as "earth": this is what the prophet saw in his vision. In Gen 1:1 it cannot have this precise sense, as discussed above (pp. 210–11, 212 n. 26, 214, 225, 231). It may even be better left untranslated.
[97] Note the title of van Ruiten's 2005 paper on Jer 4:23–8: "Back to Chaos ...". See also Childs (1959) and Fishbane (1971; discussing this passage with Job 3). Childs noted the linking of the use of the verb *rā'aš* and the return to chaos (Childs 1959, 187–90) but why he regarded it as an eschatological usage here (1959, 189) is unclear. In my view, too many futuristic passages are misidentified by biblical scholars as eschatological.

The flood story culminates in a recreation of the world following its dissolution, with the dry land emerging from the waters as before. The only substantial difference between the accounts is that a shipload of creatures has survived the cataclysm, rendering their recreation unnecessary.

5.1 The Relevance of Psalm 74 to Discussion about Creation

Many writers have noted the great frequency with which the combat myth is described or alluded to in the Hebrew Bible.[98] While it would be wrong to claim that the biblical narratives derive immediately from the Ugaritic one, it is unquestionable that they are joint heirs to one West Semitic strand of the tradition. Both end up with the victor claiming a patrimony described as his "inheritance"[99] and they share many significant items of vocabulary, as detailed in Table 2 below.[100] The real significance of these terms is not just their usage across the divide between Ugaritic and Hebrew literature, suggesting a cognate relationship (which spreads more widely across diverse recensions of the tradition), but also their capacity, as key poetic terms, to evoke the trope even when they are used in isolation, as in some cases instanced here.[101] These points of contact are too numerous to claim that any similarity is superficial and inconsequential. They are evidently organically linked.

---

98 See for example Day 1985, *passim*. Day identified forty-four allusions to or recitations of the scene. I added eight more (Wyatt 1996, 122 n. 4).
99 See further below, pp. 249 for discussion of Exod 15:17 and *KTU* 1.3 iii 28–30 // 1.3 iv 19–20.
100 In some instances the Hebrew uses a different term (translating, e.g. ḥrb along with ybṭ, ybš). The whole point here is the evocative, "triggering" nature of the term or idea: one word or even idea evokes a whole mythic nexus.
101 Further examples of the transfer of vocabulary between the traditions is also evident in the material adduced immediately below.

Table 2: Relevant Combat Myth Vocabulary Shared with Ugaritic

Term(s) used	Ugaritic	Hebrew
a. gʻr, "rebuke":	KTU 1.2 i 24 (gʻr), iv 28 (gʻr)[102]	Psalm 104:6–7 (gʻr), 106:9 (gʻr), Nahum 1:4 (gʻr), Isa 50:2 (gʻr)
b. ybṯ, ybš, ḥrb, "dry up":[103]	KTU 1.2 iv 29 (ybṯ), 31 (ybṯ)	Isa 50:2 (ḥrb), Jer 51:36 (ḥrb), Nah 1:4 (ybš), Josh 2:10 (ybš) etc., Ps 74:15 (ybš), Isa 42:15 (ybš), 44:27 (ḥrb, ybš), Zech 10:11 (ybš), Exod 14:21 (ḥrb), Isa 44:27 (ḥrb).
c. mḫṣ, mḫš, nkh, hrg, "smite":[104]	KTU 1.2 iv 9 (mḫṣ)	Exod 7:20, 7:25, 17:5 (all nkh); Isa 27:1 (hrg)
d. ṣmt, "destroy":	KTU 1.2 iv 9 (ṣmt)	Ps 88:17 (ṣmt)[105]
e. šty, "drink", "dry up":[106]	KTU 1.2 iv 27 (šty)	cf. b above
f. bqʻ, brʼ, prr, "divide", "split":	KTU 1.6 ii 32 (bqʻ)[107]	Gen 1:1 etc. (brʼ), Ps 74:13 (prr)

The biblical versions have diversified in form and purpose, and many allusions are merely the choice of key words or phrases to evoke the tradition without expanding it. Of particular significance for our present discussion is the passage in the middle of Psalm 74, vv. 13–14a, 15b:

---

102 In *KTU* 1.2 i 24, Baal rebukes the gods who cower before Yam's ambassadors; in 1.2 iv 28, ʻAṯtart appears to rebuke Baal for not being sufficiently harsh. On the latter passage, see Smith 1994, 356: "Athtart's rebuke of Baal regarding Yamm may represent an ironic play on a traditional notion of the storm-god rebuking Yamm", citing the above biblical passages as analogues. He did not comment on the earlier instance.
103 *bwṯ/ybṯ, ybwš*: see Wyatt 2002, 68 n. 150 for "dry up" as preferable to "shame" for Ugaritic *bṯ*.
104 *mḫš* is the by-form of *mḫṣ* found in Anat's account of her battles, *KTU* 1.3 iii 38–45 (× 4). In Ex 7:20, 25, 17:5 the reference is to Moses' actions, and the language is allusive. As a royal figure he mythically enacts the *Chaoskampf* or analogous roles (e.g. splitting the sea, splitting the rock).
105 Re *ṣmt* in Ps 88:17, note the reference to water in the following verse, suggesting an allusion to the conflict motif.
106 Cf. a) immediately above. On the translation options for the term, see Wyatt 2002, 67–8 n. 148.
107 This Ugaritic passage occurs in Anat's treatment of Mot (to be restored in 1.6 v 12–3: Wyatt 2007a, 763–4). The goddess's combat with Mot is to be linked intimately with Baal's struggle, just as her earlier list of victories paralleled Baal's victory over Yam. Cf. Marduk's action, *Enuma Elish* iv 137, cited above.

'attāh pôrartā bəʻozzəkā yām	You split Sea by your power;
šibbartā rāʼšê tannînîm ʻal-hāmmayim	you shattered the heads of *Dragon;
'attāh riṣṣaṣtā rāʼšê liwyātān	you crushed the heads of Leviathan
...	...
'attāh bāqaʻtā maʻyān wānāḥal	You have cleft spring and torrent.
'attāh hôbaštā nahărôt 'êtān	you dried up perennial *River.

It is arguable that Psalm 74:14b–15a is intrusive, because it breaks the poetic structure cited here, and introduces an extraneous theme, which transforms the meaning of the passage.[108] The section omitted reads as follows:

tittənennû maʻăkāl ləʻām ləṣiyyîm	You have given him as food for the people, for the wild beasts.

This is perhaps the first part of the transformation of the myth into the larger body of the psalm. The text we isolated before could be almost a translation of a digest of the Ugaritic tradition. Now, by the insertion of this bicolon, it is transformed into a larger unit, anticipating a victory feast after the enemy is vanquished anew.

The five cola in the original unit say essentially the same thing in five different ways. There is no reason for thinking that this is a catalogue of separate combats, as with the enemies of Ninurta or Anat. Even in those cases there is a "collectivity" of the foes, very clear in the case of some of Anat's, their plurality being a metaphor for their overwhelming power, like the many heads of the Hydra or Leviathan, thus emphasising the greater power of the divine victor. The various foes identified in the present instance are really one and the same figure, distributed among the cola as successive extensions, highlighting the prowess of their conqueror. We may even suspect that given that four of the identiates in these cola may serve specifically as names of the one adversary, one colon is already an addition, namely the fourth of five, "you have cleft spring and torrent". It is probably the incorporation of this line into an earlier tetracolon which has attracted an originally singular *nahar* into the plural. The same thing probably happened with *tannînîm* from an original singular *tannîn*, where the original *rāʼšê* referred, like those in the following colon, to the *seven* heads of the *one* dragon.[109] Following this intuition, we find that four names appear, in a chiastic pattern, the first and the fourth matching, Sea || River, and the second and third matching, Dragon || Leviathan.[110] The sea graphically *envelops* the dragon. The

---

108 Wyatt 1996, 163–8.
109 One dragon: see also Smith and Pitard 2009, 249.
110 Cf. Wyatt 1996, 90–1, 164.

closeness of the relationship with Ugaritic tradition is shown by the fact that all four names appear there too, in *KTU* 1.3 iii 38–46 (40). The first four named here are again evidently to be identified, as with the psalm passage:

lmḫšt.mdd il ym.	Surely I smote the Beloved of El, Yam?
lklt.nhr.il.rbm	Surely I exterminated Nahar, the mighty god?
lištbm.tnn.	Surely I bound Dragon:
ištmdh	I overpowered him!
mḫšt.bṯn.ʿqltn	I smote writhing Serpent,
šlyṭ.d.šbʿt.rašm	Encircler-with-seven-heads!

Here the cola identify the same enemy in five different terms: Yam, Nahar, Dragon, Serpent, Encircler. We may usefully compare this with another pair of closely associated texts, *KTU* 1.5 i 1–3 and Isa 27:1. The first reads:

ktmḫṣ.ltn.bṯn.brḥ	Though you smote Litanu (the) wriggling serpent,
tkly.bṯn.ʿqltn	finished off (the) writhing Serpent,
šlyṭ.d.šbʿt.rašm	Encircler-with-seven-heads …

the second as follows:

bayyôm hahû' yipqôd yhwh	On that day Yahweh will chastise
…	…
ʿal liwyātān nāḥāš bāriaḥ	Leviathan (the) wriggling Serpent,
wəʿal liwyātān nāḥāš ʿăqallātôn	Leviathan (the) writhing Serpent,
wəhārag 'et-hattannîn 'ăšer bayyām	and he will slay the Dragon which is in the sea.

In the Ugaritic passage Litanu, the serpent and Encircler are clearly one and the same, while in the Hebrew passage Leviathan, the serpent and the dragon are to be identified. These various designations of the same monster are evidently interchangeable across the tradition.[111]

5.2 The Historical Context of Gen 1 and Ps 74

The choice of two such different texts as Gen 1 and Ps 74 for discussion is not as quixotic as may first appear. Their significance in a discussion of this kind depends on the historical circumstances of their composition. They are to be understood as two specifically religious or theological responses to the cataclysm of

---

[111] See also Job 26:12–3 for Sea, Rahab, Sea and Serpent in parallel: Tur-Sinai 1967, 382–4; Pope 1973, 185–6; Wyatt 1996, 170–1; Batto 2013b, 224–6.

the destruction of the old kingdom of Judah. These events would have left two fractured communities: the more or less headless state that survived, though no doubt with various factions filling the political vacuum in so far as they were tolerated by the Babylonian hegemony, and the deported aristocracy, priesthood and civil service, settled in a suburb of Babylon (Tel Aviv) and probably other cities. It is possible that each of our two texts comes from a different geographical source.[112]

Genesis 1 surely betrays close familiarity with Babylonian theology, and even more specifically with *Enuma Elish*. Marduk was after all the chief deity in Babylon. His victory over his rivals and establishment of a great earthly empire would be seen as mocking the pretensions of Judahite theology, in which Yahweh was the universal deity.[113] Indeed, many would argue that the zenith of monotheistic speculation, in the poetry of Deutero-Isaiah, was composed precisely as a theological counterpart to the rival Babylonian claims. It is a reasonable hypothesis that Genesis 1 was written in Babylon.

Psalm 74 on the other hand perhaps betrays first-hand acquaintance with the destruction of the Jerusalem temple in 587–6 BCE and its ruined condition. If this scenario is cogent, we have two complementary perspectives on the exile, reflected in our two texts. Sparks' observation on "elite emulation", noted above,[114] has an explanatory function, showing how exiles in Babylon could even consider responding to the triumphant enemy's tradition. A "borrowing" of a motif which is now generally regarded as incontrovertible is the flood story, found in *Atraḫasis* and *Gilgamesh*.[115] The so-called *Chaoskampf* tradition, of the existence of which Tsumura is rather sceptical, but which I am happy to endorse with appropriate qualifications, is less clear-cut. However, it seems to

---

112 Zadok 1984; Pearce and Wunsch 2014.
113 See the perceptive observation of Smith (2001, 165): "As Judah's situation on the mundane level deteriorated in history, the cosmic status of its deity soared in its literature".
114 See the reference on p. 213 n. 30.
115 See George 2003, 70–1. Whether this was adopted during the exile, or at an earlier time, is uncertain. The presence of fragments of *Atraḫasis* (RS 22.421) and *Gilgamesh* (RS 94.2066, 94.2082, 94.2083, 94.2191) in Ugarit (Arnaud 2007, 128–38; George 2007, 237); Emar and Megiddo (George 2007, 237; Goren *et al.*, 2009) shows that the narrative was already known in the West in the second millennium: "These finds demonstrate that copying the poem of Gilgameš was a part of the curriculum of scribal learning in the West throughout the Late Bronze Age". Various Amarna letters, copies of missives sent to or from Levantine cities (e. g. Gezer, EA 270, 271, 273; Hazor, EA 227; Jerusalem, EA 285–290), and the Akkadian fragment discovered in Jerusalem (Mazar *et al.*, 2010), and *varia* from Beth Shean, Hazor, Hebron, Lachish, Shechem, Taanach and other places (Horowitz *et al.* 2006, van Soldt 2013) indicate the presence of scribal schools in Palestine (in addition to evidence from cities from Tyre northwards) in the second millennium.

me not unreasonable to see Genesis 1 as belonging to the same body of tradition as *Enuma Elish*, but subverting it to Judahite theological ends in the authorial process. That is, it is not strictly within the continuum of material descending from the West Semitic tradition within the Levant but is a direct response to the Babylonian composition.

However, it is not so simple as this. Is the *Chaoskampf* tradition a Babylonian or West Semitic trope? Gunkel's problem was that he wrote over thirty years before the discovery of Ugarit. The only serious candidate in his day as a source for biblical material of this kind was Mesopotamia, with *Enuma Elish* as the chief exemplar.[116] Since the Ugaritic *Baal* cycle was discovered, there has been a growing tendency to see the whole tradition as West Semitic in origin, with *Enuma Elish* as one of its derivative forms.[117] The generality of biblical allusions to the tradition seems most closely associated with the Ugaritic material—that is, directly within the West Semitic tradition, without the Babylonian influence as mediatory—as most graphically shown above by the evident close relationship between *KTU* 1.5 i 1–3 and Isa 27:1. And yet Genesis 1, as I have just argued, is more directly linked to *Enuma Elish*. But it is his long familiarity with the West Semitic tradition, deeply embedded in his own culture, that has enabled the exilic writer to deal so confidently with the Babylonian opposition by what amounts almost to a satire on *their* sacred story.

5.3 Uses and misuses of the term "*Chaoskampf*"

A case can be made for preferring the term "combat myth" to that of "*Chaoskampf*". It allows a broader coverage than the conventional German term, which involves the specific opposition of cosmos and chaos. But as we have seen above, the rejection by some scholars of the very concept of chaos from the Genesis 1 narrative is perhaps premature, and so long as we work in accordance with an agreed definition, there should be no problem, except perhaps in the minds of the strictest purists. Many scholars begin a study by defining their terms, and individual definitions are bound to differ, be it ever so slightly. It is on this basis that I have in the past used the term *Chaoskampf* in a broader sense than its strictly etymological basis justifies, as have other writers. Here I shall offer a defence for my position, having first given a definition:

---

116 Gunkel [1895] 2006, *passim*.
117 Jacobsen 1968, 104–8; Day 1985, 11. Cf. the discussion in Smith 1994, 110–4.

> The *Chaoskampf* myth is a category of divine combat narratives with cosmogonic overtones, though at times turned secondarily to other purposes, in which the hero god vanquishes a power or powers opposed to him, which generally dwell in, or are identified with, the sea, and are presented as chaotic, dissolutory forces.

This is, I think, broad enough to be useful, narrow enough to satisfy those suspicious of the term, and sufficiently focused on the genre of stories in question.[118]

Let us begin with the more general trope, the combat myth. We shall see that the element of *Chaoskampf* is frequently implicit in its use or reference. It is reasonable to take the mythic form to be the archetype (sc. the pattern) on which human combats are modelled. In reality, of course, the mythic expression derives from the human cultural form. The myth with which we are concerned here, in spite of variations according to local influences, maintains its basic structure with remarkable fidelity throughout the ancient Near East over millennia. The term "combat myth" is just as dangerous a term if used indiscriminately and has the disadvantage of inviting an unconscious linking of all combat myths as not just generic in literary terms, but as cognate in historical terms. They are also just too broad a genre to be useful in any comparative study. With my use of *Chaoskampf* as the preferred term, albeit to be used with cautions and qualifications all the way, I am actually proposing a cognate element: a significant number of the versions we encounter in ancient Near Eastern literature can be argued to be either cognate, parts of a genealogy, or at any rate, where of distinct origin, infected by contact with other versions.[119]

A number of scholars have noted the importance of the text published by Jean-Marie Durand.[120] It is in the form of an oracle delivered to Zimri-Lim of Mari, referred to in a letter from Nur-Sin, and reads thus:

> Thus speaks Adad:
>
> I have brought you back to the throne of your father, and have given you the arms with which I fought against Tiamat (*Temtum*). I have anointed you with the oil of my victory, and no one has withstood you. (ARMT A 1968)

---

118 See Forsyth 1987, Mills 2002, Beal 2002. The term *Chaoskampf*, appropriately used, is alive and well: see the recent studies of Crouch (2009, 29–32, 65–79; 2011) and Strine and Crouch (2013).
119 See Wyatt (1998, 2001a, 95–120 for several versions in translation, and 2003a, 254–9 = 2005a, 221–5): flood stories often belong back-to-back with creation stories, as is clear in the overall structure of Gen 1–9.
120 Durand 1993. See Smith 1994, 108–10, 360–1; Wyatt 1998, 841–4 = 2005b, 158–60. On sacred weapons see also del Olmo Lete 1992, Watson and Wyatt 1997, Wyatt 1998, 868–70 = 2005b, 182–4, Vidal 2011a, 2011b.

This short text really transforms our entire enquiry. The speaker quotes the words of the storm god, who here presents sacred weapons to the king for use in his battles. They are the very weapons, says the god, with which he fought the primordial sea, enabling him to construct the world. This element does not require to be stated: it is implicit in the deity's words. Why else would he fight the sea? It implies in turn that the king's battles are to be fought in terms of a process of world construction. It may be reconstruction, of course, with the pushing forward of frontiers, the seizure of territory and control of raw materials. The distinction is immaterial: the presentation (in today's terms, the "spin") is all. A classical expression of the achievement of victory is the washing of weapons in the sea which bounds the ideal empire.[121] This may be extravagant and cynical, but it is the way kings speak. Every new king must found his kingdom anew. We have an allusion to the myth in Psalm 2:1–3, where at the accession of a new king his vassals plot uprisings and rebellions. Like Baal, Marduk or Yahweh, he must overcome his foes in order to rule. Without his victory, the kingdom will relapse into chaos. As Louis XV is supposed to have remarked, "Après moi, le déluge!".[122]

The following table represents selected instances of typical versions of the narrative around the central paradigmatic core, dealt with below as numbered in accordance with their particular adaptations. The core itself is an abstraction, an attempt to represent the essence of the narrative form. The derivative forms may or may not be classifiable as examples of the *Chaoskampf*. If their relation to a core of tradition is conceded, I would argue that they can be seen precisely as congeners. The table necessarily oversimplifies matters and is intended to illustrate a possible historical sequence of events. But all history necessarily simplifies complex data to get to the heart of an issue, so the present table needs no apology, unless it is to be regarded as perverse for too conveniently finding seven heads, like those of Leviathan.

---

121 The king washes his weapons in the sea as a symbol of victory over his enemies and the forces of chaos: Wyatt 1998, 844–6 (= 2005b, 160–2).
122 And Churchill wrote of Wellington's first government (1827): "The political views of the Government were simple—defence of existing institutions, conviction that they alone stood between order and chaos" (Churchill 1958, 4: 28).

Table 3: Selected Instances of Typical Versions of the *Chaoskampf* Narrative

1	*Chaoskampf* / **Combat Myth**		
2	Chaos *versus* Cosmos Cosmogony		*Enuma Elish*; Genesis 1, 9 Psalm 74
3	Succession and Inheritance (divine)	Yam, Baal, Mot	Baal cycle
4	Succession and Inheritance (divine-human)		Exodus 15, Egypt as Rahab
5	Succession and Inheritance (human)		Mari oracle A 1968; Psalm 2
6	Chaos *versus* Cosmos Dissolution > Recreation	Flood Stories *Atraḫasis* and congeners	Tišpak-Labbu; Genesis 6–8
7	Eschatology (> "Recosmogony")	(late development)	Revelation 12, 20

1. This represents the fundamental conceptual form, the "Ur-Mythus", a basic meme[123] generated in remote antiquity, in which a problem ("chaos": a confusion of desires and fears leading to stress) is resolved by the killing ("cosmos": rivals removed, food provided, etc.). JoAnn Scurlock was surely too harsh in accusing Gunkel of manufacturing his own myth, through inadequate knowledge of his sources.[124] The logic of this view is that no one will ever have a real insight into an ancient tradition because the surviving record is never complete, and the constructive mind of the bolder scholar is always imposing an intuited pattern on the partially-known—a propensity to which even the conservative scholar is not immune. Witness the way in which our current knowledge of Ugaritic material transformed the present discussion (and it has taken eighty years to refine our understanding, through a whole gamut of misperceptions such as the notorious seasonal interpretation, to the present one,[125] which will doubtless be modified in turn by future studies). But there will be future textual discoveries. This is the finitude of all scholarship. As to Scurlock's suggestion that "Gunkel required all myths of the ancient Near East to be telling essentially the same story", this does him an injustice, and fails to allow for the adaptation of a basic plot, or even at a more elemental level, a symbol, to changing situations. The present diagram is an attempt to show how the process works.

---

[123] On the importance of the meme, a coinage of Richard Dawkins (*The Selfish Gene*), see Blackmore 1999.
[124] Scurlock in Scurlock and Beal (2013, ix–x). Some of her more waspish observations on subsequent scholarship (xii) are however to be applauded!
[125] See Wyatt 2017.

2. This already appears to be an extension of the basic core narrative. But of course the core itself is a mere abstraction. I place the present form first in the developing sequence because it is the nearest thing to a root meaning in all the more developed contexts. In a sense all the following examples (3–7) and any imaginable number of further developments are essentially extensions and transformations of the main theme, which is (re)newal and (re)construction: either a making of a reality or a remaking of an idealised former reality. In a sense, every king's reign begins with "year zero", and he has to remake the pattern which either his predecessors or those who took advantage of the power vacuum at his predecessor's death have failed to maintain, or actively attempted to destroy. There is an inherent polarity, a necessary opposition between two alternative realities. This is why the natural opposite to cosmos is chaos, even if it has only conceptual reality. But even as a mere concept, it tends always to be reified in the mind in terms of a contrary power to be reckoned with—since you cannot tell a story about a concept—and what better symbolic image than that universal *Mischwesen*, the dragon? Its chief characteristic is not simply its mixed nature, itself representing a non-fixity which is dangerous (almost a Darwinian threat to the mental *status quo!*), but also its fluidity and its ever-changing nature, epitomised in Proteus and his wily ways. It lacks classifiability, and thus in the language of Genesis 1 (and Leviticus 11) fails to conform to the boundaries of a *mîn* (which in turn serves as boundary for the rules of *kašrût*). This marks it out as a dangerous threat to stability. *Enuma Elish* is our primary example of the *Chaoskampf*, however qualified our use of the term with reference to it. Genesis 1 should be seen in conjunction with Genesis 9—they are surely by the same hand—with the intervening flood story, as one coherent narrative. In the light of our discussion of the verb *bārā'*, I am happy to see it as a deliberate echo of the *Chaoskampf*, though the conflictual element has been eclipsed in the present form of the narrative.

3. Though I have argued for a creation element in the Baal-Yam conflict,[126] so that it should be classified as another example of the *Chaoskampf*, I am happy to concede that it has taken on a different role in its present setting. It has a connection with history, in that we may reasonably seek a historical context (such as temple construction) for its composition. But the myth is in any event still linked to the

---

[126] Wyatt 1985; likewise Fisher 1965, Day 1985. Against this view see the nuanced account by Tugendhaft (2012a, 2012b). I think the perspective outlined here answers some of Tugendhaft's objections, which I find compelling. It is a matter of balancing realism and idealism. In recent and forthcoming studies, I am further exploring the connections between the Baal cycle and the historical world of Ugarit: see Wyatt 2017, 2018, 2019.

theme of creation. The climax to the *Baal* cycle is really the establishment and inauguration of Baal's palace-temple in *KTU* 1.4 vi 24–35. The Baal-Mot conflict is in essence a replay of the Baal-Yam conflict, a last desperate assault by the enemy. And the enemy, in either guise, is real enough, representing the dissolution of all that Baal represents. The construction of his dwelling takes seven days. The parallel with the seven days of creation in Genesis is unmistakable, and also the seven years of the construction of Yahweh's temple in Jerusalem (1Kgs 6:38). In each case it is six days or years of labour, followed by the seventh of rest and inaugural rites. Mark Smith and Wayne Pitard argued that not too much should be made of the parallel,[127] but it *is* a parallel, hardly to be dismissed as merely a coincidence. The ancients never used numbers carelessly! Behind the myth, which is probably to be interpreted as that of the founding of or current repairs to the Baal temple at Ugarit,[128] lies a rich tradition of kings repairing temples and representing their work as refoundation, construction from new. Temples were regarded as microcosms, as models of the universe (cf. Solomon's words in 1Kings 8:27). An important feature in the royal accounts of such works[129] is their presentation of the process as implicitly cosmogonic. Douglas Green hinted at the point nicely with reference to Assyrian royal construction projects:

> Kings create order and this order has a "structural" or "architectural" dimension as well as an agricultural dimension … Kings create this "structural order" in two ways. On one hand they reverse disorder by rebuilding existing ruined or dilapidated structures, but they also create a "heightened order" through new construction projects …[130]

It is at the same time an adaptation of the larger mythic grouping, concerned with succession in the rule of the gods (and this surely reflects the political realia of royal successions, as with the Zimri-Lim text), comparable to, and probably cognate with or at least affected by, the traditions underlying *Kumarbi* and Hesiod's *Theogony*. Zeus, Poseidon and Hades are perfect counterparts to Baal (Hadad), Yam and Mot. In establishing his house, Baal constructs his own cos-

---

[127] Smith and Pitard (2009, 615–6), criticising the view of Fisher (1963, 40–1). We may also ask whether the theme of the reconstruction of the Jerusalem temple lay in part behind the composition of Gen 1.
[128] See Wyatt 2017 for my latest assessment.
[129] See Luckenbill, 1926–7, *passim*.
[130] Green 2010, 64. See also van Leeuwen 2010. Holloway (1991) argued that Noah's ark was modelled on temple-construction theory, the floating ark corresponding rather well to the earth (of which it, like a temple, was a microcosm) founded *upon* the waters. See also Hendel 1995, and Holloway's response (1998).

mos. If the Amorite origin of the trope is maintained, then the Ugaritic myths, from the thirteenth century in Ilimilku's version, may have a more ancient pedigree than *Enuma Elish*, which cannot be pushed back in its present form beyond the ninth century[131] though both undoubtedly have a long prehistory.

4. Here we move to the cusp of historical (perhaps rather historiographical) narratives and allusions. Lying behind Exodus 15 is the classic myth, but now the enemy is the king of Egypt and his troops. Here perhaps lies the origin of the later identification of Egypt as *Rahab*.[132] The sea in Exodus 15 is almost an ally of Yahweh, conspiring in the destruction of the enemy. But the genetic link with the Baal myth may be seen by comparing the theme of inheritance of the sacred mountain in both passages. In *KTU* 1.3 iii 28–30 // 1.3 iv 19–20 (formula truncated) we read:

atm.wank ibǵyh.btk.ǵry.il.ṣpn	Come, and I shall reveal it in the midst of my divine mountain, Saphon,
bqdš.bǵr.nḥlty	in the sanctuary, on the mountain of my inheritance,
bnʻm.bgbʻ.tliyt	in Paradise, on the hill of victory ...

while Exod 15:17 reads:

təbîʼēmô wətiṭṭāʻēmô bəhar naḥălātəkā	You brought them and planted them on the mountain of your inheritance,
mākôn ləšibtəkā pāʻaltā yhwh	the foundation (which) you made for your dwelling, Yahweh,
miqdāš ʼădōnāy kônənû yādêkā	the sanctuary, my lord, which your hands established.

If the Ugaritic formula is any guide, we should interpret the latter passage as belonging to the foundation myth of the Jerusalem temple, and so the same quasi-cosmogonic element, now twisted into "historical" victory, is to be discerned. The Mari text (next item) also comes to mind: the ancient divine victory (read now as victory over Egypt) leads to the establishment of a secure reign and territory, represented symbolically in Exodus 15 by the housing of the national god, another parallel with Ugarit.

---

131 Lambert 2013a, 4.
132 See p. 229 n. 77 above.

5. The Mari text A 1968 is used as the mythic underpinning of the establishment of a new reign (in this case Zimri-Lim's regaining of his throne). Psalm 2 is the obvious biblical exemplar of this ideological formulation.

6. The Tišpak combat with Labbu is strictly speaking the reversal of a flood (a dragon fifty miles long looks like an inundated river flood plain), and is again not strictly cosmogonic, except in the sense that it renews a habitable world, as does Genesis 9.[133]

7. This is the eschatological projection of the myth, as represented by Revelation 12 and 20. The outcome is a new heaven and a new earth (thus a "recosmogony").[134]

To conclude this survey, a discussion which I think *does* involve a usage altogether too broad to justify the use of *Chaoskampf* (or even "combat myth") is that of Richard Averbeck, when he applied it to the narrative in Genesis 3.[135] Given my defence above of a broader usage for the term, my reaction here may be surprising. But in the context of Genesis 3 the matter of the meaning of the narrative is thoroughly contentious,[136] and it seems to me that Averbeck's contribution to its evaluation is problematic. It is worth citing an extended passage to see the thrust of his approach:

> Genesis 1, of course, does not include a theogony, and this is part of the underlying polemic against the ancient Near eastern environment of the Israelites. This polemic ... also includes a reaction to the notion that God created the world by defeating the evil forces of chaos, although even *Enuma eliš* does not begin with *Chaoskampf*, so "polemic" might not be the right word here. In any case, the lack of *Chaoskampf* in Genesis 1 is not the end of the story. The fact of the matter is that there is a cosmic battle in the early chapters of Genesis, but it has been transformed in accordance with the nature and concerns of Yahweh. The battle really begins in Genesis 3, and it is here that the correspondences to *Chaoskampf* in the early chapters of Genesis appear, but in a thoroughly transformed way ...[137]

He went on to argue that:

---

133 For a discussion, with texts and references to other treatments, see Lewis 1996 and Wyatt 1998.
134 Gunkel [1895, 1921²] 2006, 115–250.
135 Averbeck 2013, 252–5.
136 See in particular Zevit 2013 and Wyatt 2014a. The serpent serves the important purpose of forcing Eve to examine God's words. The sequel, that "their eyes were opened", shows that the serpent spoke truly!
137 Averbeck 2013, 252–3.

the chaos of the *Chaoskampf* in Genesis 3 is the corruption of the world, beginning with human beings. The battle is a battle of redemption—redemption, not creation—but it began during the time of creation. The writer of Genesis 3 and the ancient Israelites overall would have seen this in the account and viewed it as the core of the cosmic battle ..."[138]

Apart from there being a wide range of estimates of Genesis 3, it is only a post-biblical (post-Hebrew Bible) reading which implicitly or explicitly identifies the serpent with Satan, thus being an embodiment of evil, and capable of justifying as radical a reassessment of the narrative as this. There is no hint of the snake's evil nature in the narrative itself.[139] This tendentious attribution is similar to that of some "cosmic evil" sense for the *tōhû wā bōhû* of Genesis 1:2, as proposed by Averbeck in his expression "the evil forces of chaos". But nor is there by any stretch of eisegesis a cosmic battle going on in the Eden story, and even if there were, which I do not concede, we would have to accept that such a transformation of the original theme has taken place that it has become unrecognisable. There is no victor in this "battle"! It is an interesting take on von Rad's problem above, but with a nice reversal: it may be great theology, as an exercise of the imagination, but it is stretching the narrative beyond breaking point.

---

138 Averbeck 2013, 255.
139 The contrary position has recently been reasserted in Korpel and de Moor 2014.

David Toshio Tsumura
Chaos and *Chaoskampf* in the Bible: Is "Chaos" a Suitable Term to Describe Creation or Conflict in the Bible?

1 Introduction

Since the time of Gunkel the existence of the so-called *Chaoskampf* myth has been assumed in the background of the Biblical creation accounts, especially in the background of Genesis 1:2 and other poetic texts such as Psalm 74. According to this view, Genesis 1:2 describes the chaotic state of the earth in the pre-creation stage. Hence, it is often argued, creation in the Bible is not *creatio ex nihilo* but is rather God's bringing "order out of chaos".[1]

However, the term "chaos" has been variously understood and there is no clearly established definition. As Eric M. Vail recently notes, after a detailed survey of the various usages of the word, "one of the greatest difficulties with the use of the term 'chaos', especially in biblical and ancient Near Eastern studies, is its lack of clear definition and consistent application".[2]

2 Definitions

2.1 "Chaos"

In modern English, "chaos" means "complete disorder and confusion" (OED). However, the term originally meant "emptiness", as its Greek etymology *chaos*, "chasm" or "yawning space" suggests,[3] and it referred to the pre-created state of the "cosmos" as being of indistinguishable material as in the Greek and Chinese myths.

Hence, "chaos" is often understood as cosmically "uncreation". Ortlund takes the chaos as "uncreation" and furthermore identifies it with "evil" and

---

[1] For example, *HALOT* explains *təhôm* as "one of the prominent elements in creation (no *creatio ex nihilo*)". On this issue, see Tsumura 2012, 3–21.
[2] Vail 2012, 16.
[3] See van der Horst 1999, 185–6; Tsumura 1989, 20 n. 18.

says, "Chaos transgresses the order of creation and that of moral laws".[4] Waltke uses the term "chaos" not only for moral evil but also for physical or "surd evil",[5] that is, natural disasters such as tsunami.

Thus, the term "chaos" has experienced a semantic change from "emptiness" to "undistinguishedness", then to "disorder" or "confusion". Then, finally, among some recent theologians the term has acquired the meaning "evil".

Table 4: Semantic Developments in the Interpretation of "Chaos"

				Heavens & earth		
"chaos"	"emptiness"	"undistinguishedness"	"disorder"	"confusion"	"uncreation"	"evil"

However, since we already have the word "evil", there is no reason to call evil "chaos".

Gunkel in his now classical book, *Schöpfung und Chaos in Urzeit und Endzeit: Eine religionsgeschichtliche Untersuchung über Gen 1 und Ap. Jon 12*, 1895,[6] made a thorough investigation of the "theme of chaos" behind Gen 1:2 and other various biblical passages[7] and claimed that fundamentally Genesis 1 goes back to the Babylonian chaos myth.[8] Gunkel's view has been highly influential not only on Old Testament scholars such as von Rad but also on theologians like K. Barth, whose concept of "das Nichtige" is based on Gunkel's view of "chaos".

Eric M. Vail recently, following Irenaeus, suggested that "the imagery of Genesis 1:2 be viewed as *infancy* instead of within notions of chaos"[9] and holds that "Within the infant creation in Genesis 1:2 God is seen as relating positively with it in continuing to offer himself in gift".[10] On the other hand, the scientist-theologian S. L. Bonting advocates "chaos theology" instead of "creation theology" in the Bible.[11] Catherine Keller[12] sees a positive side of *təhôm* and advocates "Tehom theology", that is, a theology of becoming in a pantheistic framework.

---

4 Ortlund 2010, 16.
5 Waltke 2001, 68–697 on "surd evil"; cf. Walton 2009, 2011, etc.
6 Gunkel [1895, 1921²] 2006. I quote from this translation. For the most recent evaluation of Gunkel's view of *Chaoskampf*, see Scurlock and Beal 2013.
7 Gunkel [1895, 1921²] 2006, 6–8.
8 Gunkel [1895, 1921²] 2006, 79.
9 Vail 2012, 205. See also Vail 2015, 55–67.
10 Vail 2012, 206.
11 Bonting 2005. Also note his previous book (2002).
12 Keller 2003.

Without entering theological arguments, I would like to clarify some terminologies.

2.2 *Chaoskampf*

The term *Chaoskampf* literally means "the battle against chaos". It was first used of the combination of the conflict motif with the creation theme, as in *Enuma Elish*, where the "creation" of heavens and earth was brought about by the destruction of the "chaotic" dragon Tiamat. Here, "creation" was interpreted as bringing "order out of chaos". However, scholars have actually used the term *Chaoskampf* not only of *Enuma Elish* but also of any divine warfare, for example, the conflicts between Yahweh and his enemies as well as the battle between the storm god Baal and the "chaotic" sea god Yam in Canaanite myth, even though there is no creation motif involved there.

One should note, however, that the term "chaos" is not suitable even for *Enuma Elish*, as the so-called "chaos" dragon Tiamat was not *chaotic* in the real beginning. *Enuma Elish* depicts a harmonious mingling of Apsu and Tiamat at the beginning of the story and there is nothing "chaotic" or "in confusion" until Marduk fights with Tiamat. As W. G. Lambert recently wrote, "there is no chaos here: everything is peaceful and purposeful".[13] The meaning of the term, it seems, first became negatively understood when applied to the "Kampf" with reference to the divine conflict between Marduk and Tiamat in *Enuma Elish*.[14]

In my opinion we should stop using the term "chaos" when dealing with the biblical concept of "creation", i. e. cosmic origin, because neither *təhôm* nor *tōhû wābōhû* in Gen 1:2 has anything to do with chaos.[15] Especially, Gen 1:2 is concerned with "the earth", which is distinct from "the heavens", so one would be forced to say that only the earth was "chaotic" while in *Enuma Elish*, both heavens and earth were "created" by splitting the dead corpse of the "chaotic" sea dragon Tiamat. In other words, it is not consistent to use the term "chaos" sometimes for the undistinguished state of universe, as in the case of Greek and Chinese myths as well as in *Enuma Elish*, and sometimes only for an initial (or "inchoate") state of the earth, as in the case of Gen 1:2.

---

13 Lambert 2013b, 46.
14 See Gunkel [1895, 1921²] 2006, 76–7. K. W. Whitney, the translator of Gunkel's *Schöpfung und Chaos*, notes that Gunkel himself did not use the term *Chaoskampf* in his original edition.
15 Tsumura 1989, 2005. See Watson 2005. Smith (2010, 234) now agrees that the translation "chaos" should be avoided.

One would also be wise not to expand the meaning of the term *Chaoskampf* when discussing the Ugaritic dragon myths, which have nothing to do with cosmic origins.

2.3 Theomachy

The phrase *Chaoskampf* nowadays seems even to be used to refer to a dualistic battle between two gods. When Ortlund, like his teacher N.W., talks about "extended mythic discourse", he seems to assume that there was originally a myth about Yahweh fighting a dragon that was transformed into the biblical passages. But do the passages he mentions really require such an assumption? I think not (see below, for example, on Ps 74). Some of them do not refer to a battle against a divine being and others are not related to a battle at all.[16]

I would like to propose to use the term *theomachy* for a combat between two gods, and I believe we should reserve the term *Chaoskampf* for battles with a creation theme such as that in *Enuma Elish*.

In the case of the Ugaritic polytheistic myths, the phrase *theomachy* is probably the most suitable since the conflict motif there is not related to that of creation, i.e. origination. In fact, Baal in Ugaritic myths is not a creator god; he did not originate anything. Though he inaugurated his palace-temple in *KTU* 1.4 vi 24–35, I do not see how one can say that Baal myths are somehow related to the theme of creation, the act of origination, as N.W. holds.[17] The fact that Baal fights against a raging sea god Yam or his dragons does not give us a reason to call them the powers of "chaos".[18]

2.4 Divine battle

On the other hand, when Yahweh is depicted as fighting from heaven on behalf of Israel, as M. Klingbeil puts it, "He is not engaged in a struggle against the

---

16 See below, for example, p. 271.
17 One should note different semantic usages even of the English term "creation". It is well known that the term can mean either the *act* of origination of the world or the *result* of this act, i.e. creatures (e.g. *ktisis* "creation" in Rom. 8:19–22, 39). So, when one uses the phrase "theology of creation", it may refer either to a theology of God as creator or to a theology of the cosmos, namely the created world. Similarly, the term "destruction" can mean either the act of destroying or the result of an act of destruction (see below p. 270).
18 Tsumura 2007a, 478 n. 14.

chaos or the enemy, but his victory is an anticipated fact and his dominion over the chaotic forces a *fait accompli*".[19] We might call this as a *divine battle*, instead of *theomachy*, because God is not fighting against his divine enemy dualistically as in the Canaanite traditions.

2.5 Summary

The distinction between these three categories may be summarised as in Table 5:

Table 5: The Differences between *Chaoskampf*, Theomachy and Divine Battle

Chaoskampf	Battle between Creator god and Chaos	*Enuma Elish*
Theomachy	Battle between two deities	Baal myths
Divine battle	Battle between a god and his people's enemy	Yahweh, Assur, Kemosh, etc.

One should note that Gen 1:2 does not belong to any of these categories since it has no theme of conflict or battle against any entity, either divine or non-divine.

In the following section we examine several biblical passages exegetically.

3 Examples

3.1 Genesis 1:1–3

3.1.1 Verse 1—"In the Beginning God Created the Heavens and the Earth"

Regardless of whether one takes this verse as an independent sentence or a temporal clause,[20] the merismatic word pair "the heaven and the earth" refers to the entire cosmos.[21] Hence, the verse is certainly intended to be a summary state-

---

[19] Klingbeil 1999, 306. Klingbeil discusses the metaphors of Yahweh as God-of-heaven and as warrior in eight psalms, i.e. Pss 18, 21, 29, 46, 65, 68, 83 and 144.
[20] For various attempts, see Wenham 1987, 11–3; Westermann [1974] 1984, 93–7; Winther-Nielsen 1992, 67–80; Day 2013, 6–7. See also the recent attempt by Holmstedt (2008, 56–67) to see in v. 1 a "restrictive relative clause" and his translation "In the initial period that/in which God created the heavens and the earth …"
[21] I have noted elsewhere that there are two ways of describing the cosmos in the Old Testament: 1) bi-partite "heaven and earth"; 2) tri-partite "heaven, earth and waters". In the tri-partite case, the third element "water(s)" is always referred to as "the sea" or the like, never as the

ment for the subsequent narrative. In other words, the author does not intend to suggest that the "heaven and earth" in v. 1 is something different from the "heaven" (v. 8) and the "earth" (v. 10) in the following narrative. In fact, all of the story of the creation of the universe is narrated only from the perspective of human beings, who are standing on the "earth", using ordinary observational language. As for the events which they did not observe, the only way they can be described is from a negative experiential point of view, that is, as a description of the events as "not yet",[22] like Gen 2:5a, "When no bush of the field was yet in the land and no small plant of the field had yet sprung up—" (ESV) and the beginning of *Enuma Elish*, "When the heavens above did not exist, and earth beneath had not come into being –" (*Enuma Elish* i 1–2).[23] Hence, one would not expect that the initial verses of Genesis 1 describe the events positively like they would report things which they had observed or knew by experience.

The Hebrew term *bārā'*, which is usually understood as "created", has been recently explained by E. van Wolde and her followers as "to separate",[24] and N.W. holds that this sense "implies, in the process of separation, the pre-existence of that thing or those things that are separated".[25] Walton's "functional" theory, which denies the origin of substance in the Genesis story, depends on the meaning of *bārā'* as "to separate".[26] However, the use of this term with other synonymous terms such as *'śh* "to make" and *yṣr* "to form" in such texts as Amos 4:13, Isa 43:1, 45:18, etc. hardly supports their semantic argument. Their etymological argument has also gained little support among scholars.[27] I do not think that van Wolde and others' new proposal is necessary.

---

tehom-water which normally means "underground fresh water". Hence, it is reasonable to assume that Gen 1:1 describes the cosmos as a bi-partite entity. (See Tsumura 1989, 72–4; 2005a, 63–9).

22 Tsumura 1989, 168; Westermann 1984, 197.

23 Lambert 2013, 51.

24 Ellen van Wolde (2009): "to separate" vs. Becking and Korpel's (2010, 1–21) suggestion "to construct". In the following year (2011), a response by Wolde and Rezetko followed. Walton (2011, 127–33) has a detailed analysis of the verb *bārā'*.

25 Above, p. 217.

26 Walton 2011, 133. He interprets Gen 1:1 as "In the initial period, God brought cosmic functions into existence".

27 Wardlaw, Jr. in his most recent article (2014, 502–13) presents a detailed study of the Hebrew root *BR'* and concludes that the qal and niphal of *BR'* mean "to create, do (something new)" while piel means "to cut, hew". Day (2013, 5–6) also supports the traditional view "to create".

Whatever its etymology may be,[28] it is the usage of a word that finally determines its meaning. One should note that verbs are distinct in having different kind of objects, depending on their basic meanings. For examples, the verbs "eat" and "give" do something to existing objects as "a loaf of bread" or "a book". On the other hand, the verbs such as "to build" (also Akkadian *banû*) and "to dig" result in their objects such as a house or a hole. The verb "to create" is better taken as belonging to the latter group, which results in "the cosmos", while on the other hand the verb "to divide" is better taken as belonging to the former group with an existent object.

3.1.2 Verse 2

3.1.2.1 "And The Earth Was ..."
With the initial word, "the earth", preceded by a simple conjunction *waw*, the narrator here focuses the subject matter on the "earth", putting the "heaven" aside.[29] Thus, the narrator narrows down the topic by focusing only on the earthly matter. Considering the hyponymous relationship[30] between the "earth" and the "*tehom*-water" in the Biblical usages, the *tehom*-water in this verse is a part of the earth, which refers to everything other than the heaven, i.e. all under the heaven. In other words, from the Biblical narrator's point of view, the *tehom*-water is also "created" by God. No hint can be seen of any "conflict" between the creator God and the *tehom*-water.

Gunkel held that the Biblical author borrowed the Akkadian *Tiamat* and transferred it to Hebrew cosmology. However, the "Canaanite" languages such as Ugaritic and Hebrew clearly distinguish between *yam* "sea" and *thm* "deep water",[31] while on the other hand the East Semitic Akkadian cosmology clearly distinguished between Tiamat and Apsu, the sea water and the fresh water respectively. Not only is a transformation of Tiamat into *təhôm* through borrowing

---

[28] While an etymological investigation is meaningful in some cases, as in my study of *tōhû* in the Bible (1989, 17–20), one cannot argue productively for or against the doctrine of *creatio ex nihilo* just based on the meaning of *bārā'*.

[29] "Sometimes it is still suggested that Gen 1:1 is a later addition (by P) to the older source which begins with v. 2. However, if this were the case, it would be strange that a Hebrew creation narrative should begin with the present word order of v. 2, i.e. *waw*+NP VP, without any temporal description" (Tsumura 1989, 78 n. 41).

[30] Tsumura 1988, 258–69; 2005, 58–63. In the context of Gen 1:1–2, what the term *'rṣ* refers to is everything which is other than the "heavens" (see v. 1), while on the other hand the Hebrew term *thm* normally refers to the underground water which is a part of the "earth" (*'rṣ*).

[31] Pardee 2012, 27 and n. 55.

linguistically impossible,[32] but no Hebrew author would make the mistake of taking Tiamat as parallel to the Canaanite *thm*, for it is *ym* which corresponds to Tiamat cosmologically. But, in the Genesis story, the term for "seas", *yammîm*, appears for the first time in v. 10.

Since the motif of the storm-sea conflict seems to be West Semitic in origin as Jacobson and others hold,[33] any Hebrew author who tried to seek "a polemic"[34] against Tiamat by responding directly to the Babylonian composition would have made Marduk correspond to the storm god Baal and Tiamat to the sea god Yam, not to the *tehom*-water. Moreover, one should be aware that among the ancient Near Eastern mythologies the conflict motif is associated with the creation motif only in *Enuma Elish* (thus as a *Chaoskampf*),[35] while on the other hand these two motifs are not directly related in the Canaanite Baal myth (*theomachy*), for the god Baal was never a creator god in Ugaritic mythology.[36]

Table 6: Summary of Commonalities and Differences Between the Baal Myths, *Enuma Elish* and Gen 1:2

	Conflict	"storm"	"sea"	"fresh-water"	Creation
Baal myths	✓	Baal	Yam	thm	x
Enuma Elish	✓	Marduk	Tiamat	Apsu	✓
Gen 1:2	x	(Yahweh)		təhôm	✓

3.1.2.2 The Earth Was *tōhû wābōhû*—"Desolate and Empty"

This phase[37] has been taken as referring to the state of "chaos". N.W. thinks the phrase is "the most succinct Hebrew way of expressing" the "inchoate" chaos,[38] "the absence of the fixed and stable qualities of 'cosmos'".[39] He also holds that "darkness is here the medium for the inchoate divine activity: if the production of light is the first creative act, this is the moment before, in which divine prep-

---

32 A simple borrowing of the Akkadian term *ti'amat* or *tâmtu* into Hebrew cannot result in Hebrew *təhôm*. For a detailed discussion, see Tsumura 1989, 45–53.
33 Tsumura 2005a, 38–41.
34 Above, p. 234 n. 89; Hasel 1974, 81–102; also Enns 2012, 41.
35 Tsumura 2007a, 499.
36 Tsumura 2005a, 55–6.
37 Tsumura 1989, 17–43; 2005a, 9–35.
38 Above, p. 236–7.
39 Above, p. 237.

arations are afoot".⁴⁰ Similarly, John Day holds that "the heavens and earth were created first (in some inchoate form)", and "the fullness of creation emerged from them ... Indeed, in v. 2 the earth already exists in inchoate state".⁴¹ J. Day, while accepting my view that *tōhû wābōhû* has "sometimes been wrongly understood as chaos", still holds that the term "chaos" can be used for "the raging waters that God has to do battle with ... at the time of creation (e.g. Ps 104.6–9), and which ultimately lies behind the waters of the deep in Gen 1.2".⁴² N.W. also admits the chaos theme in v. 2. Note that both Day and N.W. make no distinction among the motifs, i.e. *Chaoskampf, theomachy* and *divine battle*.

To summarise my view, which has been expressed elsewhere,

Table 7: Summary of the Meaning of *tōhû* According to its Sphere of Reference

tōhû	Basic meaning: "desert"	Metaphor: "desert-like"	State of "desert-like-ness"
REF	Desert, wilderness	Earth, land, city, etc.	Abstract concept
MEAN	"desert", "wasteland"⁴³	"desolate", "waste"⁴⁴	"vain", "nothingness"⁴⁵

tōhû in Gen 1:2 has a metaphorical meaning, and it explains that the earth was a "desert-like" state, that is, a "desolate" (i.e. "uninhabitable" Isa 45:18) place. The other term *bōhû* most likely means "empty".

With this explanation, the narrator prepares the audience by informing that the earth was not yet normal as we know it with no plants, no animals and no human beings. In this sense, the earth was "desert-like", i.e. "desolate". The reference to "darkness" informs the audience that "light" did not yet exist. (The creation of invisible "spiritual" matter is not mentioned in the Genesis story.) The purpose of the narrator is not to say positively that the earth was in a certain unknown state (e.g. N.W.'s "uncosmicised" state) and the darkness existed. Rather, even though the expressions are positive grammatically, the author's intention was to explain to the audience negatively, that the earth was "not yet" in a normal condition.

---

40 Above, p. 231.
41 Day 2013, 7.
42 Day 2013, 9.
43 Deut 32:10; Job 6:18, 12:24; Ps 107:40.
44 Gen 1:2; Isa 24:10, 34:11, 45:18, 19; Jer 4:23; Job 26:7.
45 1Sam 12:21 (× 2); Isa 29:21, 40:17, 23, 41:29, 44:9, 49:4, 59:4.

3.1.2.3 The Spirit (*rûaḥ*) of God Was

As for the sentence "The spirit (*rûaḥ*) of God was moving", it denotes the condition that "God's spirit" was positively involved in the waters, "hovering" (*rḥp)[46] being ready for the first EVENT ("to speak") in v. 3. Here "God's spirit", which has often been considered to be a divine or mighty wind,[47] refers to his breath, which is about to utter his first creative word in v. 3. Ps 33:6 probably refers indirectly to this fact: "By the word of the LORD the heavens were made, and by the breath (*rûaḥ*) of his mouth all their host" (ESV). Also, Heb 11:3 supports this interpretation: "the universe was created by the word of God (*rhēmati theou*)".[48] It is noteworthy that such an "anthropomorphism" is adopted here in describing a personal deity who created the cosmos, though no goddess is involved in creating or producing the existing world. Gen 1 is unique in this regard among the ancient Near Eastern creation narratives.

3.1.3 Verse 3—"And God Said"

The verbal sequence of *qtl* (*bārā'*)—*qtl* (*hāyətāh*)—*ptc* (*mərahepet*)—*wayqtl* (*wayyō'mer*) in vv. 1–3 indicates that the first three verbal forms in vv. 1–2 denote the SETTING for the following EVENT (v. 3):[49]

Table 8: The Division of Genesis 1:1–3 into Setting and Event

vv. 1–2	SETTING:
	Title: Summary Statement: creation of the cosmos
	State of the earth and its water, with darkness & God's spirit
v. 3	EVENT: creation of light by God's fiat

---

46 See most recently JoAnn Scurlock 2013, 52–61. After the long discussion of the term *rḥp*, she speculatively translates *mərahepet* (Gen 1:2) as "surveying" on the basis of Akk. *ḫiāṭu*. Note that Vail (2012, 206), based on the view that it means "brooding (and fertilizing)" (BDB, 934), holds: "As a mother hen broods over her chicks, the Spirit broods over the waters". He further explains: "The divine Parent holds a young, at-this-time barren and empty creation ... God is the perfect Possibility to the extreme youthfulness of his creation. It is not that God makes a chaos, a *dis*-order, and *anti*-order" (2012, 206). Vail thus rejects the idea of "chaos" for Gen 1:2 but, based on an older etymology, accepts a kind of "world-egg" theory (see Gunkel [1895, 1921²] 2016, 7) for explaining a positive relation of God's spirit with the not-yet-productive creation (i.e. creature).
47 See, for example, Day 2013, 9–10.
48 Tsumura 2012, 20; also 1998, 21–30 [in Japanese with an English summary].
49 Tsumura 2012, 20.

Based on the discourse grammatical view of the verbal sequence in vv. 1–3, we see that the Hebrew narrator presents God's fiat ("Let there be light!") in v. 3 as the first EVENT in this narrative, since it is introduced by the first *wayqtl* verb (i.e. "and he said"), a form that is used to express the "narrative tense".[50]

The "in the beginning" (v. 1) seems to correspond chronologically either to the first three days, the period of the creation of "heavens" and "earth", or to the first six days when God completed the creation of the entire cosmos, namely "the heavens and the earth".

As for verse 2, as part of the SETTING, it provides the audience beforehand with information about the earth, necessary for them to understand the subsequent narrative where it is mentioned that God's fiat caused "the earth" to become inhabitable by human beings. The information given in the SETTING is that God is the One who originated everything (v. 1), including the earth, where human beings will soon live, though it is not yet suitable (v. 2). By God's "breath" the entire cosmos, not simply the first "light" in v. 3, came to exist, as the following narrative explains (see vv. 3, 6, 9, 11, 14–5, 20, 24, 26).

Hence, v. 3 does not simply follow vv. 1–2 chronologically. Since vv. 1–2 is a SETTING while v. 3 is an EVENT, the narrator's concern was that God by his fiat created the "light" as his first creature. The subsequent verses describe how God completed the work of creation by fiat, by causing the earth to bring forth plants on the third day and animals on the sixth day to prepare the environment for human beings. Finally, God himself created human beings as his representatives ("God's images" in vv. 26–7) on the earth which he had prepared.

Thus, the purpose of Genesis 1 is not to say positively that there was a pre-existing "inchoate state"[51] or "preworld"[52] before God began creating cosmos, but rather to describe how God, the creator of the cosmos, prepared an inhabitable place for human beings by transforming the "not yet" normal earth by his fiat.

---

50 For the basic structure of narrative discourse, see Tsumura 2007b, 49–52.
51 Day (2013, 7, 9); also N.W. explains that "chaos" is "'inchoate', containing the seeds of future development, but being undeveloped, it has no clear form, is undifferentiated and fluid. If it is a void, then it is a void full of potential, waiting to be filled, the void created by the separation of the primordial halves by Marduk or Elohim" (above, p. 236).
52 Smith 2010, 51.

3.2 Genesis 3

In the prose text of Gen 3, some scholars associate the serpent with the chaos dragon and interpret the story itself as a *Chaoskampf*. R. Averbeck, who accepts the existence of "the evil forces of chaos" in the Bible, thinks that the "explicit" challenge raised by the serpent to God in Gen 3 is "the battle between God and the serpent".[53] He further holds that the "crushing" of the serpent's head in Gen 3:15 should be compared with the "crushing" of the "heads of Leviathan" in Ps 74:14.

In response I should like to note that it is no longer accepted that the term *šwp* in Gen 3:15 means "to crush", since it is used not only for the head but also for the heel in that verse.

> "He shall *šwp* you on the head,
> and you shall *šwp* him on the heel".

There is no strong reason why we should read here two different etymologies for *šwp*^{I} and *šwp*^{II} as once advocated (e.g. KB) and translate accordingly. For example,

> "he will crush your head,
> and you will strike his heel". (NIV)

However, LXX translates both in the same way and the recent lexicon *HALOT* no longer posits two different roots; it now suggests "to grip someone hard", not "to crush".

Moreover, there is no "explicit" battle between God and the serpent in Gen 3. As even Gunkel himself noted, "comparison of the Paradise serpent with the Babylonian Tiamat (so also Zimmern, KAT³, 529) is inadequate. Indeed both are evil, but Tiamat is a frightfully powerful, world-ruling monster, whereas the serpent is cunning. They are (apparently) entirely separate figures".[54] In other words, while Tiamat and Marduk fight each other dualistically, the serpent in Gen 3 is certainly not a worthy opponent of Yahweh. It is no adversary of Yahweh but the adversary of mankind. A challenge and a battle are certainly not same. Therefore, to call this a battle in any sense comparable to *Chaoskampf* or *theomachy* is very unhelpful.

---

[53] Averbeck 2004, 354; also Averbeck 2013, 237–56.
[54] Gunkel [1910] 1997, 16.

3.3 Psalm 74:12–14

Because of the phrases "salvation in the earth" (v. 12) and "You divided the sea" (v. 13a), Psalm 74:12–14[55] has traditionally been taken as referring to the deliverance of the Israelites at the time of the Exodus (see Exod 14:21). However, since the time of Gunkel it has frequently been asserted that the "dividing or splitting" of the sea in association with the sea dragons and Leviathan (vv. 13–14) refers to the defeat of the chaos monster at the time of creation.[56]

To decide the meaning of the passage, we have to determine what the verb *prr in the phrase "you *prr* the sea" means.

3.3.1 Proposed Meanings of *PRR

1) "to divide or split"

Both the Exodus and Chaoskampf interpretations take the verbal root *prr* in v. 13a as meaning "to divide"[57] or, more specifically, "to split open" (so NIV) or "to cleave in two".[58] REB goes as far as to insert the dragon motif into the text itself (v. 13a), translating *yām* as "the sea monster":

> by your power you cleft the sea monster in two
> and broke the sea serpent's heads in the waters;[59]

However, there is no strong etymological support for the translation "to divide" for the verb, even though the verbal roots such as *prs, *prd, and *prṣ do have a meaning of "separation". *HALOT* does not list "to divide" and suggests "to stir, rouse".[60] Neither *NIDOTTE*[61] nor *TWOT* holds that the term means "to divide".

Ancient versions do not help much in the etymological argument. The LXX gives the translation *su ekrataiōsas* ("to prevail [over]"), while the Targum's "you

---

55 For a detailed study of the passage, see Tsumura 2015a.
56 Gunkel [1895, 1921²] 2006, 28. This view is followed by such scholars as Kraus 1978, 681; Day 1985, 21–2 and 39; Day 1992; Bratcher and Reyburn 1991, 653; Tate 2002, 251; Hossfeld and Zenger 2005, 248 and 286; Smith 2010, 50 and 68; Day 2013, 20; Batto 2013a, 137 and 150; 2013b.
57 So RSV, NRSV, ESV.
58 REB; cf. NEB.
59 REB; cf. NEB.
60 Also see "to stir up" (Jenni-Westermann).
61 Williams 1996: "the parallelism of *prr* and *šbr*, break, in Ps 74:13 commends a translation like *break apart*, or *put down*".

cut the water of the sea with your strength" (*'nt gzrth b'wšnk mwy dym'*) is influenced by the Exodus tradition.

But as there is no support for the meaning "divide", Gunkel's starting point has no foundation.

2) "to make flee"

As for recent suggestions regarding its meaning, Greenfield understood *prr as denoting "to make ... flee", in the light of the Ugaritic *tpr* "to flee" in the Aqhat epic, and translated:[62]

> It was You who made the sea flee by Your might,
>   who smashed the heads of the dragon in the waters;
> it was you who crushed the heads of Leviathan.

Certainly this interpretation makes better sense than translating the verb *prr as "to divide". In this context, while the sea is forced to flee or is driven back,[63] the sea dragons and their representative, Leviathan, are smashed/crushed (*šbr // *rṣṣ) on the heads *over the waters* (*'l-hmym*).

However, again, the interpretation "flee" is etymologically weak. Greenfield based his argument on the Ugaritic text *KTU* 1.19 iii 14, 28, a passage which describes an eagle's fleeing and flying away. However, as reflected in the recent Ugaritic dictionary, it is now generally agreed that the word *pr* here is not from the root *prr, but from *npr.[64]

3) "to shake"

It has been suggested that the idea of "shaking back and forth" is present in Ps 74:13–4, and therefore the translation "to stir, rouse the sea"[65] has been proposed for the poel stem of *prr II in this passage. But, as Tate notes,[66] this does not fit in with crushing the heads of the sea monsters in the parallel line. Certainly, God would not stir up the sea so that he might calm it down again.

4) "to break (up)"

Etymologically the most natural meaning of *prr is "to break". This meaning is well attested in Biblical Hebrew[67] as well as in Ugaritic.[68] Moreover, the Ugaritic verb *prr* "to break" and *ṯbr* "to crush" appear in parallel just as *prr and *šbr

---

62 Greenfield 1994, 119.
63 See JPS.
64 Del Olmo Lete and Sanmartín, 2003, 635.
65 HALOT.
66 Tate 2002, 243.
67 HALOT, TWOT, NIDOTTE.
68 DULAT.

do in Ps 74:13b–14a.[69] Also, in Akkadian, *parāru* means "to break up, shatter, etc".[70] It can means "to shatter, rupture the body or a part of the body".[71] This use of the verb fits the context of the Psalm, where God first "broke up" (*prr) the sea and then "smashed" (*šbr) and "crushed" (*rṣṣ) the heads of the sea-dragon. Here the "heads" of the sea-dragon probably are a poetic description of the waves of the raging sea.

It should be noted that in *Enuma Elish* the "splitting" of Tiamat occurs after she was killed by Marduk and her hosts were dispersed (*prr).

Enuma Elish iv 103–4:[72]

ik-mi-ši-ma nap-šá-tuš ú-bal-li   He bound her and extinguished her life,
šá-lam-taš id-da-a elī-šá i-zi-za   He threw down her corpse and stood on it.

The "extinguishing" refers to killing Tiamat. But Marduk does *not* split her corpse here.

Line 105 of *Enuma Elish* repeats that Marduk had *killed* Tiamat, and it is in the line *after* that, i.e. line 106, where the verb *prr* appears, where Marduk dispersed (*parāru*) her assembly:[73]

ul-tu ti-amat a-lik pa-ni i-na-ru   After he had killed Tiāmat, the leader,
ki-iṣ-ri-šá up-tar-ri-ra pu-ḫur-šá is-sap-ḫa   Her assembly dispersed (*prr), her host scattered.

As for the line 106, B. R. Foster translates: "He shattered her forces, he dispersed her host".[74] While Lambert takes the line as a synonymous "internal parallelism"[75] (*kiṣriša uptarrira // puḫurša issapḫa*), Foster takes it as a sequential event, i.e. "shattered and dispersed". Etymologically, Foster's proposal seems better, since the basic meaning of Akkadian *parāru* is "to break up, shatter", as noted above. Again, there is no reference here to "splitting" Tiamat's corpse in two. That act of dividing (*ḫepû*) does not occur until much later, in lines 137–8:

---

69 M. Dahood 1972, 316.
70 *CAD*.
71 *CAD*.
72 The translation and the text are by Lambert 2013, 92–3.
73 See Kämmerer and Metzler 2012, 219.
74 Foster 1991, 398.
75 See Watson's terminology (1994).

iḫ-pi-ši-ma ki-ma nu-un maš-ṭe-e a-na ši-ni-šu   He split her into two like a dried fish:

mi-iš-lu-uš-ša iš-ku-nam-ma šá-ma-mi uṣ-ṣal-lil   One half of her he set up and stretched out as the heavens.

Thus, in *Enuma Elish* first the leader Tiamat herself was "killed" (103–5), and then her assembly or hosts "shattered" (*prr) and "dispersed, scattered". Marduk "bound them and broke their weapons" and they "lay enmeshed, sitting in a snare" (111–2). It is only after all these actions, when the battle was completely over, that Marduk "split" (*ḫp') Tiamat in two (IV 137). Hence, the Akkadian verb *parāru* has nothing to do with the idea of "splitting" or "dividing".

3.3.2 Divine Battle and Metaphor

One must admit that the description of Yahweh's destroying his enemies and Marduk's destroying Tiamat and her hosts in *Enuma Elish* have a similar pattern and share *the common motif of the destruction of enemies*. However, this is due to common linguistic expressions based on a common literary description of *warfare*.

Both pieces of literature, *Enuma Elish* and Ps 74, reflect the two stages of actual battle. In the psalm, first a warrior king destroys (lit. "breaks up" *prr) the enemy leader, and then after that, the enemy hosts are scattered, with their heads smashed (*šbr*) or crushed (*rṣṣ*). On the actual battlefield, heads were usually crushed with "maces",[76] as is depicted in a number of the Assyrian and Egyptian reliefs.[77]

Table 9: Warfare Motifs in *Enuma Elish* and Ps 74

Destruction of Enemies	Leader	Its hosts	Warrior	Battle
Enuma Elish	Tiamat (sea)	Her hosts	Marduk	Chaoskampf
Ps 74	Yam (sea)	*tnynym, lwytn*	Yahweh	Divine battle
Actual warfare	General	His hosts	King	Actual battle

---

76 CAD.
77 For example, see the reliefs depicting Asshurbanipal's war against Elam in 646 BCE at the Ulai River. There Teumman king of Susa is seen "crumpling under the shattering blows of an Assyrian's mace"; see Frankfort 1954, 186.

The battle is described metaphorically in terms of natural phenomena,[78] that is, two stages of the calming down of the raging sea. First, the body of the raging sea is broken (*prr); then, the high waves, represented by the "heads" of the associates of the sea,[79] are smashed/crushed (*šbr// rṣṣ);[80] thus, the enemy represented by the raging sea is destroyed completely.

The sea-dragons and Leviathan in the psalm are to be compared with the seven-headed serpent or dragon in the ancient Near Eastern mythology such as that seen in the Ugaritic Baal myth *KTU* 1.5 i 1–3:

> When you smite Lotan, the fleeing serpent,
> finish off the twisting serpent,
> the close-coiling one with seven heads ....[81]

It is probable that in Israel this multi-headed dragon was used as an idiom for strong enemies in general. Thus for the author of Ps 74 "to crush the heads of dragons or Leviathan" meant "to destroy the enemy completely". Therefore, in this psalm, highly metaphorical expressions with literary clichés are used to present a battle which ends in Yahweh's complete victory.

This interpretation certainly fits the context, which describes Yahweh's "working salvation in the midst of the earth" (v. 12). Yahweh is here acting as a warrior who fights against his enemies, both historical and spiritual. His salvation (yšw'wt) is a result of his victory as king in the battle against his and his people's enemies in the present world. There is no reason to connect it with his creation of the cosmos in the primordial time.

3.3.3 Conflict Without Creation

One should note carefully that there is no creation motif[82] in the description of conflict in Ps 74.[83] The destruction of the dragon here does not lead to the cre-

---

78 Tsumura 2005a, 184–7.
79 See Unger 1938, 231–5; Collon 1987, 179 (No. 839–40); also Dietrich and Loretz 1999, 75. Note that on one mace-head a seven-headed dragon is depicted; see Frankfort 1970, 68.
80 Perhaps by a "seven-headed mace"? See the phrases "my mace with the seven heads" (Angim III 40) in *CAD*, and "(Ninurta's seven-headed mace) which has seven heads like a serpent, wreaking carnage" (Angim III 38 [= 138]) in *CAD*.
81 Pardee in *COS*, 1, 265.
82 In a recent monograph, Ballentine (2015; 123, 186–9) following Tsumura (2005a), analyses the conflict myths as having no connection with the creation motif. Like me, she avoids using the terms "chaos" and *Chaoskampf* throughout the book.

ation of the cosmos as in *Enuma Elish*, but to "salvations". Verses 15–7 are simply a description of the created order brought about by Yahweh, similar to Ps 104:10, rather than of his creative action (i.e. origination) itself.

Table 10: Comparison of Psalm 74:13, 15 with Creation in Gen 1:1 and *Enuma Elish*

CREATION	Action	Patient	Result
Marduk	split	Tiamat	heavens and earth
Yahweh in Gen 1:1	create		the cosmos
Yahweh in Ps 74:13	break up	the sea	
Yahweh in Pa. 74:15	split open		springs and brooks

"You split open (*bqʽ) springs and brooks" in v. 15a expresses the idea of creation by the *resultative*, i.e. the outcome of a creative action, like the "house" in the phrase "to build a house" as noted above, and it means that God causes springs and brooks to exist as the outcome of his creative action. Verses 16 and 17 describe the organisation of the earth with springs and brooks rather than the origination of the earth itself. On the other hand, in *Enuma Elish* iv 137–8, Marduk "split" Tiamat into two, one half of her stretching out "as the heavens", while in v 62, he stretched out the half of her and "made it firm as the earth".[84]

Thus, the psalmist simply is explaining the saving act of Yahweh, who is the lord of creation, i.e. not only the originator of the world but also the controller of the created world. He controls his created world in various ways, such as by making waters flow in springs and brooks or by making waters cease to flow in everflowing streams (v. 15). In this psalm, the conflict motif has no more relation to the idea of creation, i.e. the origination of the world, than it does in the Ugaritic Baal cycle, in which the conflict has nothing to do with creation, and furthermore Baal is not a creator god. In fact, of all the cosmological myths of the ancient Near East, only in *Enuma Elish* do the conflict motif and the creation motif co-exist.[85]

---

83 See Tsumura 2005a, 55–6; 2015a, 547–55. Pitard 2002, 262–3.
84 Lambert 2013a, 95, 101.
85 Tsumura 2007a, 473–99.

3.3.4 Not Creation but Destruction

Thus, Ps 74:12–4[86] has a *destruction* motif rather than a *creation* motif. Yahweh is represented as the one who brings salvation to his people by destroying his and their enemies. The motif of conquering the raging sea is thus used to describe a *divine battle* in which God's enemies are completely destroyed by him, whether they are the historical enemies of Israel as in Exod 15:8–10 or the spiritual enemies as in Isa 27. It is possible that one of these victories the psalmist had in mind was the Exodus, though there is no etymological support for *prr "to divide".

Table 11: Comparison of Creation and Destruction Motifs in the Baal Myths, *Enuma Elish*, Gen 1:2 and Ps 74:12–4

	Conflict	"storm"	"sea"	"fresh-water"	Creation
Baal myths	✓	Baal	Yam	*thm*	x
Enuma Elish	✓	Marduk	Tiamat	Apsu	✓
Gen 1:2	x			*təhôm*	✓
Ps 74:12–4	✓	(Yahweh)	*yām* & dragons	Springs and brooks	x

References to storms, floods or seas in poetic texts of the Bible have no relationship with the *creation* theme. Rather, they refer to the destructive features of storm and war; hence, in the following Biblical texts the motif is *destruction*, not creation.

3.4 Psalm 46:1–4

Ever since Gunkel's work, many scholars have taken the first part of Ps 46 as having a "creation" motif. Since vv. 2–3 speak of a "chaotic" sea, they automatically assume that its waters are those which existed before "creation".[87]

However, the statements that "the nations are in an uproar, the kingdoms totter" (v. 6) and "he breaks the bow, and shatters the spear" (v. 9) show that the raging seas are a figurative description of the "nations" that are the enemies of Yahweh's people. The theme of the psalm is the overcoming of destructive enemies, not creation. Verse 8 says: "Come, behold the works of the LORD; see

---

86 Tsumura 2015a, 547–55.
87 For example, Mowinckel (1962, 1: 87); Weiser ([1959] 1962, 368). Cf. Neve 1975, 243–6.

what desolations he has brought on the earth" (NRSV). This "desolation" was certainly brought about by Yahweh's victory, but this victory is not evidence for the existence of the *Chaoskampf* motif in this psalm as Ortlund claims.[88] For one thing, the flooding water was threatening Yahweh's people, not Yahweh himself.

3.5 Habakkuk 3:8

Habakkuk 3 is also a passage that has often been suggested as having links with the *Chaoskampf* myth. Verse 8 has been taken as the Hebrew counterpart of the Canaanite *Chaoskampf* motif in the Ugaritic Baal-Yam myth, because of the parallel pair (*nəhārîm* //*yām*):

> Was your wrath against the rivers, O LORD?
>   Or your anger against the rivers,
>   or your rage against the sea,
> when you drove your horses,
>   your chariots to victory? (NRSV)

However, if Hab 3:8 were based on a Ugaritic conflict myth, one would expect the pair *yām* // *nāhār*.[89] Yet Habakkuk does not use this word pair, but rather the unusual pair *nəhārîm* //*yām*. The corresponding word pair *nhrm* // *ym* does appear in Ugaritic, but in a non-conflict, non-creation passage where they are simply rivers and the sea. So there is no warrant for claiming the rivers and the sea are mythological beings. Habakkuk simply used this word pair metaphorically for describing the "enemy" of Yahweh and his people.

Thus, the appearance of the semi-traditional word pair "rivers" and "sea" in v. 8 does not automatically justify presupposing that the background is the Canaanite *conflict* motif of the Ugaritic Baal-Yam myth. The "chariots" (v. 8) and the "bow" and "mace" (v. 9) are to be compared with the ancient Near Eastern depictions of a victorious human king riding in a chariot with a bow and a mace in his hands.[90]

Hab 3:13b "you crushed the head of the wicked ..." also seems to be imagery reflecting a human battle situation rather than a particular Canaanite myth.[91]

---

88 Ortlund 2010, 71.
89 Note the Akkadian equivalent of this pair, *ti-a-am-ta* "sea" // *na-ra-am* "river" (*Atraḫasis* III: iv:5–6) in Lambert and Millard 1969, 96–7.
90 Tsumura 1996a, 357–65.
91 Tsumura 2005a, 164–82.

Also, the description is not so much that of a battle between divine beings who fight back (i.e. *theomachy*) as that of Yahweh's destroying his enemy (i.e. *divine battle*) "the wicked one", which is symbolised by the destructive "sea" and "rivers".

Table 12: Comparison of Creation and Destruction Motifs in the Baal Myths, *Enuma Elish*, Gen 1:2, Pss 74:12–4, 46:1–4 and Hab 3

	Conflict	Victor	Enemy	Destruction	Creation
Baal myths	Theomachy	Baal	Yam	✓	x
Enuma Elish	Chaoskampf	Marduk	Tiamat	✓	✓
Gen 1:2	x			x	✓
Ps 74:12–4	Divine battle	Yahweh	"sea & dragons"	✓	x
Ps 46:1–4	Divine battle	Yahweh	"sea"	✓	x
Hab 3	Divine battle	Yahweh	"sea"-"rivers"	✓	x

The idea of the sea as an enemy, however, goes for back in ancient Near Eastern literature. In Sumerian, for example, the most frequent attribute of the sea is "frightening" or "terrifying". For example, in TCL 16, 77:4–7, Nergal is described thus:

> Nergal, terrifying sea *(aba-ḫu-luḫ)*, invested with awesome terror, no one knows how to confront him.[92]
> (The god) is terrifying like a flood-wave, furious like the wind, furious like the sea ...[93]

These expressions describe the awesomeness and terribleness of gods.

In Habakkuk 3 the "sea" and the "mighty waters" of vv. 8 and 15 stand for Yahweh's enemies who are destined to be destroyed. In other words, Yahweh is described as warrior king[94] fighting with enemies who are symbolised by destructive waters such as the "sea" and "mighty waters" (Hab 3:15). These enemies of God are treated as those who are to be destroyed by the God Yahweh.

---

[92] Sjöberg, ZA 63, 2, no. 1:14.
[93] See *SD*, A/II: 135.
[94] Tsumura 2005a, Ch. 10.

3.6 Theomachy in Psalm 29?

A passage where *theomachy* often is even read into a context where there is no hint of battle is Ps 29. In v. 3, God's voice thunders over the waters, and in v. 10 he sits enthroned upon the flood, hence the reasoning is, "Baal, the storm god thunders and also conquered the sea, so this psalm has a similar *theomachy* as a background". However, this idea will not hold up.

In the Ugaritic mythological text *KTU* 1. 4 vii 27–31, the storm god Baal is depicted as opening a rift in the clouds and thundering.

> (So) he opens up a window in the house,
> a latticed window in the palace.
> Ba'lu (himself) opens up the rift in the clouds,
> Ba'lu emits his holy voice,
> Ba'lu makes the thunder roll over and over again.[95]

Such a description is what one would expect for a storm god. However, there is no battle or conflict between Baal and his enemy in this context. The imagery of the storm-god's voice, i.e. thunder, appears in poetical texts such as Ps 29 for describing the theophanic activities of Yahweh in nature without any reference to battle or conflict.

On the other hand, it should be noted that when Baal actually engages in battle, his weapons are not thunder, lighting and wind as one would expect, but two maces[96] that attack Baal's enemy Yam like an eagle and drive him from his throne. Thus the imagery is not that of natural phenomena, but that of human combat with human weapons. Thus to claim that reference to thunder and waves as in this psalm or in contexts such as Ps 18 must be related to the Canaanite/Ugaritic battle between Baal and Yam is certainly stretching the evidence.

Consider v. 10 of this psalm:[97]

> The LORD sits enthroned over the flood (*lammabbûl*);
> the LORD sits enthroned as king forever. (NRSV)

It has been claimed that the phrase *lammabbûl*, "over the flood", symbolises the subjugation of chaotic forces, and "the Canaanite tradition may be seen in the

---

95 Pardee, 1997, 262.
96 *KTU* 1.2 iv.
97 See Loretz 1987, 415–21; 1984, 49–51.

depiction of the enthronement of Baal over the conquered 'flood' (Ugaritic *mdb*; see RS. 24.245 [*KTU* 1.101]. 1–2)".[98]

However, there is no evidence in Ugaritic mythology that Baal established his residence on his conquered enemy. Even Marduk, the Akkadian counterpart of Baal, never sat enthroned over the sea-dragon Tiamat. Moreover, the Ugaritic term *mdb* "flood, flow of the sea" is never used for describing Yam/Nahar, the enemy of Baal.

The Hebrew *mabbûl* in Ps 29 is the word used in reference to the great Deluge. It was not Yahweh's enemy: it was his agent, by which he brought about total destruction. Similarly, the Akkadian word for Deluge, *abūbu*, is not Marduk's enemy, but the divine weapon, "the Deluge-weapon"[99] by which Marduk attacked his enemy Tiamat (*Enuma Elish* iv 49; cf. vi 125).

It is thus difficult to claim that *mabbûl* in the Bible or *mdb* in Ugaritic refers to some kind of dragon, the enemy of a god in a so-called *Chaoskampf*. The Canaanite influence in Ps 29 has been rather overstated.[100] The fact that in earlier verses the glory of Yahweh is described using storm terminology does not automatically associate it with the Baal-Yam fight. There is no mention of a battle in the psalm, nor is there in *KTU* 1. 4 vii 27–31, where the thundering of the storm god Baal is depicted. The psalm should be appreciated as a Hebrew hymn of praise to Yahweh, using "storm" language in metaphorical expressions. Here again, the psalmist describes Yahweh as the only one who is worthy of praise and to whom "glory and strength" is to be ascribed.

Rebecca Watson, who also disagrees with using the term "chaos" for the conflict psalms, approaches the topic similarly. She holds that "any received Canaanite traditions utilised here [Ps 29] have been reformulated anew as a vehicle for claiming Yahweh's absolute supremacy. Unlike Baal, his kingship is unchallenged".[101]

3.7 Imagery of Storm, Flood, and War

There are passages where we find references to storms and the raging of the sea and battles, but that hardly means they refer to a fight between Yahweh as the storm god and the primeval *təhôm*.

---

98 Craigie 1983, 248–9.
99 Edzard 1993, 3.
100 Malamat would see in Ps 29 an Amorite, or an early Mesopotamian, background; see Malamat 1988, 156–60.
101 Watson 2005, 64.

Storms and floods and battles have in common the fact that they are destructive, and in many ancient Near Eastern texts they are used as imagery for each other. For example, in the flood stories from Mesopotamia, a literal flood and storm are described using war imagery.[102]

a) *Atraḥasis* III iii 12; AH, U rev. 19 (also see III viii 12)[103]

[The flood (*abūbu*)'s] might came upon the peoples [like an assault].
([kīma qabl]i eli nišī ibā' kašūšu)

b) *Gilgamesh* XI 129 – 31

When the seventh day arrived, the windstorm (*meḫû*) and deluge (*abūbu*) left off their assault (*qabla*),
Which they had launched, like a fight to the death (*kīma ḫayālti*).
The sea grew calm, the tempest grew still, the deluge (*abūbu*) ceased.[104]

On the other hand, military action and its result are described using "storm" imagery in many Mesopotamian literatures, especially in the royal inscriptions. For example, an Old Babylonian inscription states that Ibbi-Sin "roared like a storm against Susa".[105] In the Annals of Neo-Assyrian kings, the expression *kīma tīb meḫê* ("like the onset of a storm") appears in contexts describing the destruction of enemies.

Also in the "Lamentation over the Destruction of Sumer and Ur", the enemy attack which resulted in the destruction of the city is depicted as a "storm":[106]

On that day, when that storm (Sumerian u_4) had pounded again and again,
When in the presence of the lady her city was destroyed .... (lines 137–8)

It should be noted that flood imagery often appears in the context of destruction in the ancient Near Eastern literature, as illustrated by a well-known Akkadian literary cliché *kīma til abūbi* ("like ruin hills of the Deluge"):

The entire land of the Qutu [I made (look) like] ruin hills (created by) the Deluge (*kīma til abūbi*) (and) I surrounded their army with a circle of sandstorms.

(Tukulti-Ninurta 1 ii 14 – 20)

---

102 On war imagery, see also Klingbeil 1999, 360.
103 Lambert and Millard 1969, 94, 104, 124. Foster, *COS* 1: 452; *CAD*.
104 Foster 1997, 459.
105 Frayne, *COS* 2: 391.
106 Klein comments: "It is assumed that 'storm' is here a poetic-theological metaphor for the onslaught of the enemy and the destruction of the city" (*COS* 1: 536 n. 16).

and the metaphorical expression "like the Deluge" (*abūbāniš, abūbiš*),¹⁰⁷ which often appears in the context of the military activities of the Assyrian kings.¹⁰⁸

In the Bible the Hebrew term *šeṭep*, "a flood",¹⁰⁹ is also used metaphorically in Nah 1:8 for the mighty power by which Yahweh brings about the *kālāh* "complete destruction" of Nineveh.

> But with an overflowing flood
>   he will completely destroy its place/ his foes¹¹⁰
>   and will pursue his enemies into darkness.

Thus, in many literary contexts the storm imagery or war imagery has nothing to do with the *theomachy* or the *Chaoskampf* theme. It is simply a metaphor describing an actual war or storm. A reference to storms or floods, whether in the ancient Near East or the Bible, is often a metaphor and cannot be assumed to be "an extended mythic discourse" as Ortlund suggests.¹¹¹

3.8 Fossilisation and Metaphorisation

In the Mesopotamian traditions the sea was personified and deified as the goddess *Tiamat*. In the Biblical traditions, the sea and many waters are often used as symbols of evil, *personified* as Rahab (Ps 89:10, Isa 51:9, Job 9:13, 26:12), Leviathan (Ps 74:14, Isa 27:1), dragons (Ps 74:13), etc.¹¹²

In Ps 89:9–10, the two verses express God's mighty rule over his enemies, symbolised by the sea and Rahab. The expression "the raging of the sea" (*gēʾût hayyām*) in the first line of v. 9 is balanced by "when its waves rise" (*bǝśôʾ gallâw*) in the second line. In v. 10, it is clear from the parallelistic structure that Yahweh's "enemies" are personified as Rahab.

The expression, "you crushed Rahab (**dkʾ + Rahab*)" is restated as "you scattered your enemies" (**pzr + ʾôyǝbêkā*) in the second line of parallelism. Similar parallel expressions "to cut Rahab in pieces (**ḥṣb + rahab*)" // "to pierce the

---

107 *CAD.* Such similes are not limited to military contexts; they are also attested in Ugaritic literature in describing the strength of El's sexual power (lit. "hand"): "El's hand is strong" *k ym* "like a sea" // *k mdb* "like a flood" (*KTU* 1.23 [UT 52]:33–5), or the power of Baal's glorious mountain: *kmdb* "like a flood" in *KTU* 1.101:2.
108 See Tsumura 2005a, 187–8.
109 *Šeṭep mayim rabbîm*, "flood of mighty waters" (Ps 32:6); *HALOT*.
110 See Tsumura 1983a, 109–11.
111 Ortlund 2010, 18.
112 For this section, see Tsumura 2005a, 182–195.

dragon (*ḫll + *tannîn*)" and "to still the Sea (*rg' + *hayyām*)" // "to strike down Rahab (*mḫṣ + *rahab*)" appear in Isa 51:9 and in Job 26:12 respectively.

These destructive actions of Yahweh are understood as having happened in the ancient times, as Isa 51:9 says:

> Awake, awake, put on strength,
>   O arm of the LORD!
>
> Awake, as in days of old,
>   the generations of long ago!
>
> Was it not you who cut Rahab in pieces (*ḫṣb + *rahab*),
>   who pierced the dragon (*ḫll + *tannîn*)? (NRSV)

These Biblical texts might possibly refer indirectly to a mythological scene where a dragon was destroyed, similar to the Ugaritic mythological texts *KTU* 1.3 iii 37– iv 3 (I.A.3.b) and 1.5 I 1–3 (I.A.3.c), which mention Anat's or Baal's defeat of his enemy Yam and his associates, such as the dragon *Tnn* and the serpent *Ltn*. However, although these events, like those in Isa 51:9, are taken as already having happened in very ancient times, they have nothing to do with cosmic origins.

Similarly, in these Biblical passages there is no allusion to the "creation" of the heaven and the earth as in the case of *Enuma Elish*. The name *Rahab*, still unattested in any extra-biblical text,[113] is another indication of the diversity of the dragon myths in Canaan. The Biblical authors of the Iron Age could use these then already antiquated or "fossilised" expressions ("fossilisation") to describe metaphorically Yahweh's destructive actions toward his enemies ("metaphorisation").[114] This is not the so-called "historicisation"[115] of myth, or "demythologisation"[116] for there is nothing here of a transfer of mythological theme or concept into a historical reality.

Furthermore, these metaphorical expressions seem to have already become idiomatic or nearly idiomatic when the authors used them, as Isa 30:7 seems to suggest:

> For Egypt's help is worthless and empty,
>   therefore I have called her,
>   "Rahab who sits still (*rahab hēm šābet*)". (NRSV)

---

[113] The phrase *brḫbn* (*KTU* 9.432:18) has nothing to do with "Rahab" (*rahab*), since the consonant involved is /ḫ/, not /h/.
[114] The terms "fossilisation" and "metaphorisation" are discussed in Gibson 1981, 123–4, etc.
[115] Day 1985, 88–140.
[116] Day 2013, 20.

3.8.1 Canaanite Literary Traditions

As noted by D. Pardee, the Ugaritians also used metaphors such as a window of Baal's palace to describe a rift in the clouds, and yet they clearly distinguished the window and the rift in *KTU* 1.4 vii 25–31 (II.A.2.b).[117] The Hebrews were no exception among ancient people in the use of metaphorical language to describe the physical realm. It is no wonder that we find many similarities with the Canaanite or Ugaritic mythological expressions in the poetic texts of the Bible, for the Biblical poets used those then already widely-known expressions, including the common word pairs, literary cliché, and metaphor, to give vividness to their expressions.

For example, Isa 27:1 is in the same literary tradition as the Canaanite mythopoetic literature, though the author uses the similar expressions as a metaphor for the destruction of evil in an eschatological context:

> On that day the LORD with his cruel and great and strong sword will punish Leviathan the fleeing serpent, Leviathan the twisting serpent, and he will kill the dragon that is in the sea. (NRSV)

While the extra-Biblical evidence for such dragon stories is no longer available in southern Canaan due to the perishable nature of the writing materials (e.g. papyrus), northern Syrian and Anatolia provide evidence of them. The evidence that the Canaanite divine conflict myths were known in Anatolia is available from two mythological fragments which may belong to the Baal Cycle. One text, KUB 33, 108, even alludes to the victory of the Storm-god over the Sea.[118] These are certainly indications that the divine conflict traditions (*theomachy*) were widespread *before* the Late Bronze age in East Mediterranean. Myths were presumably well-known orally before they were written down, i.e. during the pre-historic era.[119]

Therefore, it is reasonable to assume that many people in ancient Israel knew about the divine conflict myths, understood what the expressions "to smash the heads of the dragons" and "to crush the heads of Leviathan" meant and to what they referred, and used them as a metaphor to describe the defeat of their enemies, even if they knew only fragments of myths or had different, often contradictory, versions.[120]

---

[117] See Pardee 1997, 262 n. 184.
[118] See Beckman 1997, 569.
[119] See Wyatt 2005a, 219–21.
[120] On the wide variations of the *conflict* myth, see Wyatt 2015b, 151–89.

Moreover, just as the Ugaritic Baal Cycle had nothing to do with the *creation*, the Hebrew poets had no intention of bringing the creation theme into their poems. The idea here is Yahweh's complete destruction of his enemies, both historical and spiritual, symbolised by the "sea" and the "waters". By such destructive action against his enemies, Yahweh accomplished his salvation; hence, passages such as Ps 74:13–4 have nothing to do with the creation-and-chaos (uncreation) motif.[121]

However, the issue we are facing is not simply terminological. As Wyatt and his pupil Ortlund have argued, the real problem is not simply the matter of metaphor. What kind of reality, that is, what they call a mythopoetic reality, should be detected behind the metaphors is certainly significant for interpreting these conflict themes. But there is little evidence that a complete myth of the *Chaoskampf* was available in ancient Israel as "an extended mythic discourse", as Ortlund holds.

3.9 Chaos Unfitting

R. S. Watson[122] in her recent study deals thoroughly with the poetic texts relating to the "chaos" motif, such as Pss 18, 24, 29, 68, 74, 77, 89, 114, etc. and some passages in Isa (51:9) and Job (26:12).[123] She convincingly argues that there is no intrinsic connection between *"Chaoskampf"* and creation in the extant Israelite texts. She concludes that "the term 'chaos' should be abandoned in respect of the Old Testament, since this literary collection does not seem to possess a clear expression of the idea that Yahweh engaged in combat with the sea or a sea monster in primordial times".[124] Mark S. Smith in his most recent book,[125] tends to agree with Watson and me that the translation "chaos" does not fit Gen 1:1–2.

If the idea of "chaos" is unfitting to the Biblical creation texts, both prose and poetry, Ortlund's dealing with both "uncreation" and "evil" under the designation "chaos" is best avoided. As we have already suggested, the passages that are identified as having the so-called *Chaoskampf* motif are, for the most cases, to be explained as describing a *divine battle* between Yahweh and the en-

---

[121] Day 1985, 39; 1994, 43.
[122] Watson 2005.
[123] In the same year, in the Part 2 of 2005a, 143–95, I dealt with the *Chaoskampf* motif in some poetic texts of the Old Testament.
[124] Watson 2005, 397
[125] Smith 2010, 234 n. 149.

emies of his people in the Biblical context. J. Day, while accepting my view that *tōhû wābōhû* should not be understood as "chaos", still thinks that the term "chaos" is to be used of "the raging waters that God has to do battle with in some parts of the Old Testament at the time of creation (e.g. Ps 104.6–9), and which ultimately lies behind the waters of the deep in Gen 1.2".[126] I would insist again that there is no evidence that the creation theme and the conflict theme coexisted in ancient Canaan.

4 Conclusion

It is neither adequate nor correct to use the term "chaos" and hence to see a *Chaoskampf* motif in texts such as Gen 1:2 and the so-called "chaos dragon" passages such as Ps 74:12–4. It is significant that the translator(s) of LXX did not use the term *chaos* for the Hebrew *tōhû*. In fact, LXX uses the term *chaos* only twice in the Old Testament, i.e. Mic 1:6, Zech 14:4, with the sense of "gaping abyss, chasm", corresponding to "valley" (*gayʼ*, *gēʼ*).[127]

The Ugaritic mythological texts which deal with the "conflict" motif should not be treated as the examples of the *Chaoskampf* either. They are depicting *theomachy* between two or more deities. But in the case of Yahweh's battles against the power of evil, those struggles might be described as *divine battle* rather than *theomachy*, because his enemies are nothing like a deity who can cope with Yahweh but simply creatures destined to be destroyed by Yahweh. They have nothing to do with the motif of creation, i.e. the idea of cosmic origin, and there is no cosmic dualism in the whole Bible. Hence, the term *Chaoskampf* is unsuitable for the designation of the Biblical passages, including Gen 1:2.

---

[126] Day 2013, 9.
[127] For a detailed discussion of this, see Tsumura 2012, 18 n. 49.

Part II: Continuing the Dialogue on Creation and Chaos

David Toshio Tsumura
Response to Nicolas Wyatt

1 General

N. Wyatt's interest in the intertextuality of the biblical and the ancient Near Eastern texts is illustrated by his concern with how various texts sound in relation to each other, with resonance and association. For example, he takes note of four "mutually evocative words", *bārā'*, *bərē'šît*, *bərît*, and *bərešet*, "in a net".[1] As for *tōhû* and *təhôm*, he holds that "whatever precise etymology we accept, the whole point of the usage is the deliberate echo of *tōhû* in the following *təhôm* in v. 2". The author, he thinks, evokes a link between them[2] with "a poetic association". Wyatt is therefore more interested in the usage of terms in their context than in etymology; his use of such phrases as "pregnant sense"[3] in association with other terms illustrates that a major concern in his hermeneutical effort to interpret ancient texts such as the Hebrew Bible and Ugaritic mythological texts is sound association.

Certainly, etymology cannot be the final word in deciding the meaning of any word, and the use of a word in a specific context, both linguistic and extra-linguistic, is the most important point for grasping its precise meaning. And well controlled intertextuality in ancient texts is essential to their literary quality and cannot be ignored in the biblical studies. But I think each text should first be interpreted in its own immediate context, with a rigorous philological, literary and rhetorical understanding, taking note of all the linguistic aspects, before widening one's perspective and digging deeper into the literary and theological implications. Such a priority is especially necessary for the study of the ancient religious texts, which reflect religious practices unfamiliar to modern or postmodern readers.

---

1 Above, p. 218.
2 Above, p. 231.
3 Above, p. 211 n. 22.

2 Specific

2.1 Methodological Differences

Wyatt is absolutely right when he says, "If grammatical insight and theological claim are in collision, ... linguistic precision should surely have priority here".[4] Also, I agree with him and Albrektson[5] in their reluctant attitude toward von Rad's "demythologisation" approach. However, Wyatt seems to have overreacted. It seems to me that the point at issue is not so much a "history-versus-myth" approach as the linguistic phenomenon of "metaphorisation".[6] (Here I use the term "linguistic" rather broadly, to include phonetic spellings,[7] stylistics[8] and poetics[9] as well as supra-sentential "discourse grammar"[10] and pragmatics.)

Literary historically, Wyatt follows the contemporary view on Pentateuchal studies, which places the origin of Genesis during the Persian era. Hence, he sees "Genesis 1 as belonging to the same body of tradition as *Enuma Elish*, but subverting it to Judahite theological ends in the authorial process. That is, it is not strictly within the continuum of material descending from the West Semitic tradition within the Levant, but is a direct response to the Babylonian composition".[11]

However, the real situation is not so simple as this, as Wyatt himself acknowledges.[12] Wyatt holds that Gen 1:2 was the Israelite postexilic reaction toward the idea of the *Chaoskampf* myth which they first, according to him, confronted in the form of *Enuma Elish*. But such a view means we have to assume that the Israelites were ignorant of the story of *Enuma Elish* until the time of the Babylonian exile. However, just like the *Gilgamesh* epic, a fragment of which has been found in Megiddo,[13] the Babylonian story of creation, either in the form of *Enuma Elish* or in a similar version, must have been known among the West Semites in Syria-Palestine, at least from Amarna Age onward.

---

4 Above, p. 208 n. 14.
5 Albrektson 1967.
6 See Tsumura 2005a; and in press (a).
7 Tsumura 1997, 1999, 2005a, 2014.
8 Tsumura 1983b, 1988, 1996a, 1996b.
9 Tsumura 1983a, 2004, 2008, 2009, 2014, 2017, 2018a, 2019.
10 See Tsumura 2010; 2016.
11 Above, p. 243.
12 Above, p. 243.
13 See George 2003, 24–5.

Recent discoveries of cuneiform tablets from Hazor[14] as well as a fragment of an Amarna-like tablet from pre-Israelite Jerusalem[15] suggest indirectly the possibility of the existence of Mesopotamian literary traditions in the Levant at least from the early Iron Age. Here, Wyatt and I disagree with each other sharply.

Another point is that Wyatt's view of the *Chaoskampf* motif is much wider than mine. I have suggested that three types of battle in ancient Near Eastern religious writings should be distinguished: 1) the *Chaoskampf* myth of creation as the result of conflict, 2) *theomachy*, that is, battle between gods, and 3) divine battle, a god fighting the enemies of his people. Since among the ancient Near Eastern mythologies only *Enuma Elish* has both *creation* and *conflict* motifs, the term "*Chaoskampf*", which has been used in the context of the Gunkelian hypothesis, should be reserved only for *Enuma Elish*, not for the Genesis 1 story, where no conflict motif exists. Wyatt also claims that the *Chaoskampf* motif appears in Ps 74, but since the psalm has no creation motif, as I argued in detail elsewhere,[16] the battle should be categorised not as a *Chaoskampf* but as a divine battle.

Since Wyatt takes both Gen 1 and Ps 74 as the Hebrew versions of an original *Chaoskampf* myth, he has to ask himself: "Is the Chaoskampf tradition a Babylonian or West Semitic trope?"[17] But the question is not adequate for our discussion. It is certainly proper to ask whether Genesis 1 is a *Chaoskampf* like *Enuma Elish* since Genesis 1 also deals with the creation motif. By contrast, there exists no reason why we should compare Ps 74 with *Enuma Elish*, since the former has no creation motif. Conversely, whether the sea dragon motif is a "West Semitic trope" or not is relevant for Ps 74, not for Gen 1.

2.2 Terminology and Distinct Notions

2.2.1 Cosmogony

Both Wyatt and I agree that the *Chaoskampf* myth is concerned with "the construction of the world by the victorious storm-god from the corpse of a vanquished divine dragon".[18] But he expands its meaning thus: "The *Chaoskampf* myth is a category of divine combat narratives with cosmogonic overtones, though at

---

14 Horowitz and Oshima 2006.
15 Mazar *et al.* 2010.
16 Tsumura 2015a.
17 Above, p. 243.
18 Above, p. 204.

times turned *secondarily* [my italics] to other purposes, in which the hero god vanquishes a power or powers opposed to him, which generally dwell in, or are identified with, the sea, and are presented as chaotic, dissolutory forces".[19]

Hence, Wyatt includes both Gen 1 and Ps 74 in "Chaos *versus* Cosmos" Cosmogony[20] and even thinks that "the stilling of the storm and walking on the sea episodes in the gospels are to be read in the context of the *Chaoskampf* trope".[21] But one should note that there is no creation motif or, more strictly, theme of the construction (or "origination") of the world in either Ps 74 or the gospel accounts! Not every storm motif is related to the creation motif, though many have a conflict motif.[22] One gets the impression that Wyatt broadens his definition of this myth too widely.

2.2.2 Creation ex Nihilo

As both Wyatt and I agree, a doctrine can be neither proved nor disproved simply on an etymological basis. The doctrine of *creatio ex nihilo*, however, now appears to be denied by some on the basis of the etymology of the term *bārā'*. In the Hebrew Bible, the subject of this verb is always "God", and the traditional view is that it means "to create". However, there is a recent view that it means "to divide, separate".[23] As I discussed in my essay above,[24] I agree with the traditional view that it means "to create".

At the same time, it is true that an etymological issue should be examined before going into a theological debate, such as whether Gen 1–2 refers to a preexistent material "chaos" or not. However, etymology is not the only issue in the linguistic approach. Before going into a theological discussion, one should carefully read the text from a linguistic perspective, for good theological reasoning based on a wrong understanding of the text will not be useful in the long run.

Let us look at several words in Gen 1:1–3. Wyatt translates it as follows:

> In the beginning of God's creating of heaven and the underworld,
> the underworld was chaotic and empty,
> and darkness was over the face of (the) deep,

---

[19] Above, p. 244.
[20] Above, p. 246.
[21] Above, p. 207. On Genesis 1 as cosmogony, see Walton 2011.
[22] Tsumura 2005a. Note that the comment in the gospels is, "Even the wind and sea obey him" (Mark 4:41), which does not even suggest conflict. See further Ballentine 2015.
[23] See Wyatt's argument above, pp. 222–8.
[24] P. 258.

and the spirit of God was hovering over the face of (the) waters;
then God said, "Let there be light!"
And there was light.[25]

2.2.2.1 'ereṣ

While there are a few passages where it is possible to translate 'ereṣ as "underworld", here it seems that "heaven and earth" constitute a merismatic pair, referring to the entire cosmos. And in v. 2, as I discussed in my article,[26] a narrowing down or a focusing on the "earth", as opposed to the "heavens", is intended, for it is the "earth" where human beings will be placed eventually.

Wyatt holds that, "On this reading the passage makes no reference to *creatio ex nihilo*, but rather presupposes the existence of raw material, already present in v. 2, before the cosmogonic process begins".[27] However, one should note that Gen 1 is written from a human standpoint, i.e. an "earth-oriented" viewpoint. The language used here is that of humans who have experienced nothing except a cosmos in which materials exist. The point is how a human being can describe the situation as it was before anything ever existed. The description of the very initial state of the earth can be made *only negatively* as "*not yet* normal as we know". Grammatically, however, the expression *tōhû wābōhû* is "positive" in Gen 1:2, as contrasted with the "negative" formulation in Gen 2:5–6.

2.2.2.2 tōhû

On the meaning of Ugaritic *thw* in *KTU* 1.5 i 14–6,[28] Wyatt takes an issue with me about my translation as "desert", preferring "wasteland" (Pardee) or "waste",[29] but there is no great difference between those translations, for all these terms refer to the earth's "desolate" situation without vegetation, animals, or human beings. Hence, the phrase *tōhû wābōhû* functions not so much a positive description (i.e. "abnormal") as a negative description (i.e. "not yet normal").

Wyatt holds: "The 'waste', be it wet (ocean) or dry (desert), is surely something 'uncosmicised', since the process of organisation into a cosmos, that is, a habitable world, is the subject of the following narrative".[30] The basic difference

---

25 Above, pp. 210–11 and Wyatt 1996, 195–6.
26 Above, p. 259.
27 Above, p. 212.
28 See pp. 228–30 above.
29 Above, pp. 230–1.
30 Above, p. 230.

between Wyatt's view and mine should be clarified: while he thinks the concern of the text is basically ontological, I think it is cognitive and epistemological as well. In other words, while he takes the earth (v. 1) as "uncosmicised", hence not organised yet into a cosmos, I take the earth and its hyponymous *tehom*-water, normally[31] the subterranean water, as parts of the created cosmos, i.e. "heaven and earth" (v. 1). (Note that the Genesis creation story is mainly concerned with material origin and its function[32] rather than with the invisible immaterial world.[33])

Wyatt holds that v. 2 refers to the pre-existing "uncosmicised" state of pre-cosmic material and concludes that "Something is pre-existent here, not pre-existing God, of course, but pre-existing the initial divine act in v. 3".[34] On the other hand, I hold that v. 2 explains the initial state of the creation of the earth, a part of the cosmos, in terms of human experiential language. The first creative action by God is his speech act, "Let there be light!" (v. 3). Verse 2 is simply a SETTING for the following EVENT.

2.2.2.3 ḥōšek

For Wyatt, "darkness is here the medium for the inchoate divine activity";[35] for me, the term "darkness" simply explains that no light existed yet. For Wyatt, "if the production of light is the first creative act, this verse describes the moment before, in which divine preparations are afoot";[36] thus, he presupposes a progression of time between v. 2 and v. 3. For me, on the other hand, v. 2 is simply preparing the audience for the God's initial fiat of creation in v. 3. Temporally, nothing happened in v. 2. Only God's breath ("spirit") was ready, supra-temporally so to speak, to be articulated in v. 3 as a "voice" in time, where the first nar-

---

[31] In this particular context, in v. 2, the *tehom*-water which was later subterranean was overflowing and totally covered what was later the "earth"; the situation was a flooded, hence not yet normal, "earth". The author's intention was to let the audience know, not in abstract-scientific language but in observational-descriptive language, that in the initial situation, the earth was "not yet" the "normal" earth the audience knew by experience.

[32] Note that Walton's "functional" view (2009, 2011) denies the material origin. (See Tsumura 2015a, 356–7). It seems that Walton overreacts against the so-called concordists who try to harmonise the biblical description and the scientific "fact".

[33] Gen 1:1–3 does not deal with the creation of any spiritual beings, even though it mentions the role of God's breath, i.e. "spirit".

[34] Above, p. 232.

[35] Above, p. 231.

[36] Above, p. 231.

rative tense *wayqtl* form is used. And thus, time begins with the creation of light.³⁷

Certainly, "it is important not to read any kind of theological or moral opposition into these verses", as Wyatt holds.³⁸ Wyatt assumes that "the idea of divine spirituality and activity is generally associated with light."³⁹ However, in the Old Testament, God is associated not only with light but also with darkness, as in the Solomonic prayer in 1Kgs 8:12 ("Then Solomon said, 'The LORD has said that he would dwell in thick darkness'" [ESV]). Amos 4:13 even states that God is the creator of darkness:

> For behold, he who forms the mountains and creates the wind,
>   who makes the morning darkness,
> and declares to man what is his thought,
>   and treads on the heights of the earth—
>   the LORD, the God of hosts, is his name! (ESV)

Wyatt, it seems to me, reads an ontological opposition, darkness vs. light as well as chaos vs. cosmos, into the text, Gen 1:2–3, whereas the author makes an epistemological and cognitive distinction between "darkness" and "light" and between the "not yet normal earth" and "the normal earth".

2.2.2.4 Relationship Between təhôm and Tiamat

Wyatt thinks that my arguments have been adequately rebutted by those of Sparks and Pardee.⁴⁰ However, Wyatt seems to misunderstand both Pardee's view and mine. Let us first note Pardee's comment:⁴¹

> (text): ... *Têmtum*, an evolved form of *Ti'amtum/Ti'āmat* ... cognate [yes!] with Ugaritic *Tahāmu* and Hebrew *Tᵉhōm* ... (note): The syllabically attested forms are derived by regular phonological processes in Amorite and Akkadian from a base form /tihām-/ (qitāl). The Ugaritic form with /a/ in the first syllable is the result of vowel harmonization (J. Huehnergard, *Ugaritic Vocabulary in Syllabic Transcription* [Harvard Semitic Studies 32; Atlanta: Scholars Press, 1987/2008], 184–5), the Hebrew form the result of regular phonological developments in Canaanite and Biblical Hebrew, that is, the earlier 'Canaanite shift' (/ā/ > /ō/) and the later pretonic reduction of /i/.

---

37 Tsumura 2010; 2019.
38 Above, p. 231.
39 Above, p. 231.
40 Above, p. 234 n. 89.
41 Pardee 2012, 27 and n. 55.

Pardee simply holds that the Hebrew form *təhôm* resulted from the proto-Semitic or "base" form *tihām- with the Canaanite shift. He neither asserts that the Hebrew is a borrowing from Akkadian nor holds that the use of *təhôm* in Gen 1 is a polemic against the Mesopotamian view.

Since the motif of the storm-sea conflict seems to be West Semitic in origin, as Jacobson and others hold,[42] any Hebrew author seeking to write "a polemic"[43] against Tiamat by responding directly to the Babylonian composition, would have made Marduk correspond to the storm god Baal and Tiamat to the sea god Yam, not to the *təhôm*-water.

Here, I disagree sharply with N. Wyatt, who takes Gen 1 as "more directly linked to *Enuma Elish*".[44] Wyatt assumes that *Enuma Elish* and Gen 1 share the common *Chaoskampf* tradition and that the latter is "a direct response to the Babylonian composition",[45] written during the Exilic period, when the Israelites, according to his view, were confronted for the first time with *Enuma Elish*, which is "not strictly within the continuum of material descending from the West Semitic tradition within the Levant".[46] See Tsumura 2015a on my view that any similarities between *Enuma Elish* and biblical texts are due to common linguistic expressions about the actual warfare.

As for Sparks:[47]

> David T. Tsumura made a similar observation about תהום and Tiamat but drew from this an errant conclusion. According to Tsumura, because תהום is a native Hebrew word rather than an Akkadian loanword, it is unlikely that the תהום of Genesis 1 represents the demythologized Tiamat. This argument does not hold. There is nothing whatsoever to preclude a Hebrew author using his own term, תהום, in a polemic against the obviously related cognate term Tiamat.

For one thing, Sparks misunderstands not only my view but the basic principles of comparative linguistics. What I am concerned here is not so much that *təhôm* is a native Hebrew word, but that it was used broadly in Semitic languages, like Ugaritic *thm*, going back to the proto-Semitic *tihām-. Sparks claims that I did not prove that it was not polemic. But I was not arguing about it there, so saying that I did not prove it there misses the point! I was not discussing the possibility that the Hebrew term was a "polemic" against "the obviously related cognate

---

42 See Tsumura 2005a, 38–41.
43 Hasel 1974; Enns 2012, 41
44 Above, p. 243.
45 Above, p. 243.
46 Above, p. 243.
47 Sparks 2007, 630 n. 14.

term Tiamat". But here I will say that the Hebrew author had no need to polemicise against *Enuma Elish* in particular, when the Israelites were confronted with many once-mythological phraseologies in ordinary life. Through the long oral history of mythological traditions in ancient Canaan, going back perhaps to the Neolithic era, the Israelites were the latecomers in the literary and poetic history of Canaanite traditions. It was quite natural for them not only to adopt then-already idiomatised expressions, but also to metaphorise mythological expressions for poetic use.

Wyatt similarly holds the polemic view.

> It is simply inconceivable that the author of Genesis 1, *if* [my italics] he was writing in a Babylonian context, and in some sense offering a counter to Babylonian cosmology and the claims for Marduk made in Enuma Elish, would not have fully intended that his presentation of *təhôm*, which we shall for the sake of argument consider to be impersonal (though it carries no article, and so may well be a proper noun), was a deliberate counterpart to *Ti'āmat*. The precise philological relationship of the various terms cited in discussion (Hebrew *təhôm*, Ugaritic *thm, thmt*, Akkadian *Ti'āmat, tâmtum, têmtum*) is quite immaterial here. Ultimately they are of course cognate (*thm), and in practice they clearly had different precise significations in their various usages, though covering similar themes. But what is driving the literary function of the words in their contexts is assonance and association. And this is not to be reduced to or judged on the basis of etymological arguments, however seriously they are to be taken.[48]

Wyatt's great "if" refers to two major speculations: that the author is writing in a Babylonian context, and that he intends it as a counter to Babylonian cosmology.

One must wonder if a Hebrew author would ever use *thm*, the "Canaanite" (e.g. Hebrew and Ugaritic) native term for the subterranean "fresh" water,[49] to correspond to *Ti'amatum*, the Akkadian term for the sea (cf. Apsû for the fresh water; the Hebrew cognate term *'aps* became an idiom as *'apsê 'āreṣ*). Surely not! For a Hebrew native, the term that corresponded with a god-defying sea was *yām*, the sea or salt water. Moreover, phonologically, Wyatt's argument seems to miss the point. The demythologisation of *Ti'amat* in terms of *təhôm* would have nothing to do with "the disappearance of the medial aleph".[50] Furthermore, if one wants to bring Ps 74 into the picture, no one can deny that the motif in Ps 74 is "Canaanite", not "Mesopotamian", since the passage is con-

---

48 Above, pp. 234–5.
49 See Tsumura 1988; 1989, 67–74.
50 Above, p. 234 n. 89.

cerned with the destruction of *yām, tannînîm* and *Leviathan*, all of which are the Hebrew cognates of Ugaritic *ym, tnnm,* and *ltn*.

Similarly, some biblical scholars without a proper linguistic, or more specifically, comparative linguistic, training have completely misunderstood my view. For example, P. K.-K. Cho[51] in his Harvard dissertation holds that "Tsumura ... denies any linguistic relationship between the Babylonian *ti'āmat* and the Hebrew תהום". I have never denied that there is a "linguistic" relationship between the Akkadian (or Babylonian) *ti'amat* and Hebrew *təhôm*. Of course there is! As I explained, the Hebrew term is not a loanword from the Akkadian Tiamat: both terms go back to the common Semitic word **tihām-*.[52] However, the etymological similarities do not assure a "conceptual" relationship in our case, since the Akkadian *tiamatu* "sea" and the Canaanite, or NW Semitic, *thm* "fresh water" refer to distinct bodies of water. Note Akkadian *šarru* "king" corresponds to Hebrew *śar* "prince", while Akkadian *malku* "prince" corresponds to Hebrew *melek* "king".

Moreover, I cannot understand Wyatt's following comment:

> *A propos* the technical difficulties addressed by Tsumura on the precise relationship between the Hebrew, Ugaritic and Akkadian forms, we may point to Hebrew *rĕ'ēm* and *rēm* (aurochs)—cf. *bĕrē'šît, bĕrešet*, on pp. 218–21 above—clearly cognates in spite of the disappearance of the medial aleph from one form by *sandhi*.[53]

I have never discussed the problem of the disappearance of the medial aleph and the subsequent *fusion* of the two vowels by *sandhi*[54] in our discussion of the relationship between *təhôm* and *Tiamat*. Of course, *Ti'amat* has variant forms *tâmtum* and *têmtum*[55] in Akkadian, and all these forms are cognates of Hebrew *təhôm*, and all these forms go back to the proto-Semitic or "base" form **tihām-*. Such a fact does not explain the loss of /h/ from the Akkadian form, but in fact there is no /h/. If Akk. Tiamat were borrowed into Hebrew, the form would have been *ti'ama*, which would have been realised as *tēma* or *tāma*, but never as *təhôm*. If the Hebrew author were writing a polemic against Tiamat, one would expect that he would either use the proper noun *Ti'ama(t)*, *Tēma(t)* or *Tāma(t)* directly or perhaps use Yam, the west Semitic "Sea", the enemy of the storm god Baal, who is the West Semitic counterpart of the Mesopotamian Mar-

---

51 P. K.-K. Cho 2014, 132.
52 See Tsumura 2005a, 42–3.
53 Above, p. 234 n. 89.
54 Tsumura 1997.
55 Mari document; see Tsumura 2007.

duk, but not that he would use the meaning-wise unrelated *təhôm*. Note that the Canaanite *thm* would referentially correspond to Apsû, the male counterpart of Tiamat in *Enuma Elish*, for both *thm* and Apsû refer to the fresh water.

In Mesopotamian cosmology, it is the god Ea who established the earth over Apsû. The "harmonious" (regardless of their possible conflict in their previous stages) relationship between a creator god and the water, it should be noted,[56] can be seen in the relation between El and *thmtm* in the Ugaritic myths, between Ea and Apsû water in *Enuma Elish*, and between Elohim and *təhôm* in Gen 1. In all three accounts the deity certainly rules over the water. Gen 1:2 also refers to Elohim's positive involvement toward the *təhôm* water through his spirit.

2.2.2.5 prr "To Divide"?

Wyatt takes both *prr* in Ps 74:13 and *brʾ* in Gen 1:1 as meaning "divide" or "split" like Ug. *bqʿ*,[57] but his etymological argument for these two roots is without a solid linguistic foundation, as discussed in the main article. As I discussed elsewhere,[58] the similar root formation, *prr, *prd, *prs, *prṣ, *pry, etc. with two radicals P and R, does not necessarily indicate a similar meaning, as once advocated by some linguists. The same is true with two similar roots, *brʾ* and *prr*, the former with the voiced counterpart (*b*) of the latter *p*. Of course, it is true that the etymology is not decisive, and the poet may have used two etymologically unrelated terms side by side for a literary effect such as a word play or sound symbolism like assonance and alliteration. However, it is a sheer speculation to read the theme of creation in psalms like Ps 74 by assuming the theme of "splitting a chaos dragon" behind the text. For a detailed discussion, see my article above.[59]

2.2.2.6 The Concept of "Chaos"

According to Wyatt, "chaos" has the following two primary characteristics:
1) "inchoate": it contains "the seeds of future development" but is "undeveloped"; "it has no clear form, is undifferentiated and fluid".[60]

---

[56] See Tsumura 1989, 141–53; 2005a, 128–39.
[57] Above, p. 239.
[58] Tsumura 2015, 549.
[59] Pp. 265–8.
[60] Above, p. 236.

2) "If it is a void, then it is a void full of potential, waiting to be filled, the void created by the separation of the primordial halves by Marduk or Elohim".[61]

Wyatt is certainly right to avoid reading any form of cosmic dualism in Gen 1 and to take the "chaos" in v. 2 as having a potential nature with an expectation to a "future development". He explains the concept of "chaos" variously:
1. "not yet differentiated"[62]
2. "uncosmicised"[63]
3. "inchoate"[64]
4. "not yet organised"[65]
5. "precosmic"[66]
6. "It is the absence of the fixed and stable qualities of 'cosmos', of an environment where civilised life can be conducted".[67]

Thus, the "chaos" in Wyatt's understanding is not so much a confusion or disorder, as often advocated by modern scholars, as an undifferentiated "void"[68] as in the ancient Greek and Chinese mythologies.

However, as I discussed in my article,[69] the term "chaos" in modern English has changed meaning greatly due to its semantic development, from "emptiness" to "disorder" or "confusion", and even to "evil" for some scholars. Along with this diachronic change in meaning, what the term "chaos" refers to has also changed, i.e. from the entire cosmos (rather, in Wyatt's term, the "uncosmicised" cosmos) to the earth itself (Gen 1:2). Hence, in modern Bible translations, an earth which was "chaos" or "chaotic" would mean nothing but a confused earth.

It is obvious that LXX's *aoratos kai akataskeuastos*, "invisible and unformed" is greatly influenced by the Platonic myth *Timaeus* in its choice of Greek terms for *tōhû wābōhû*.[70] Yet, it is noteworthy, LXX did not adopt the

---

61 Above, p. 236.
62 Above, p. 233 n. 88.
63 Above, p. 230.
64 Above, p. 236.
65 Above, p. 233.
66 Above, p. 233.
67 Above, p. 237.
68 Above, p. 236.
69 Above, pp. 253–4.
70 LXX's, hence Plato's, influence on Augustine has been detected in his writings. See Tsumura 2012.

term *chaos*, "chaos", in translating *tōhû wābōhû*.[71] Therefore, it might be wise not to use the term "chaos" not only for Gen 1:2 but also for the theme of creation during Biblical times. In fact, recently Mark Smith[72] expressed his willingness to follow the Tsumura-Watson line and holds, with Bruce Zuckerman, that the term "chaos" is "unsuitable" for pre-Hellenistic Near Eastern texts.

As for Jer 4:23–8, Wyatt holds that "The prophet's vision here corresponds closely to the Priestly account of the flood story (Genesis 7:11) where it is the reversal of the creative, differentiating process".[73] But it should be noted that in Jer 4:23 *tōhû wābōhû* refers only to the earth, not an "uncosmicised" substance, while the then existing "heavens" did not have "their" light, namely, the luminaries in the heavens. As I discussed elsewhere, the only clear similarity between Gen 1 and Jer 4 is the pairing of the expression *tōhû wābōhû* with "darkness" (Gen 1:2) / "no light" (Jer 4:23). Other than these two phrases, clearly different items are mentioned in the two texts, e.g. Jer 4 has no water, while in Gen 1, there are no "mountains", "hills", "fruitful land", or "cities" (Jer 4:24–6).[74] Jeremiah's message is summarised in v. 27:

> For thus says the Lord, "The whole land shall be a desolation; yet I will not make a full end."

Hence, however attractive theologically, one cannot say that the theme of Jeremiah 4 is either "creation" or "uncreation". It is simply conveying the prophetic message of "destruction".[75]

3 Final Reflection

To summarise our debate, the disagreement between Nick Wyatt and me is mainly methodological. Being one of the experts of comparative mythology, particularly of Ugaritic myths, Nick Wyatt has a wide knowledge of mythological thinking as well as a postmodern sensitivity in the method of interpretation of ancient texts. The combination of such characteristics is exhibited in his analysis of the theme of *Chaoskampf* in the Old Testament and other ancient Near Eastern literatures. In particular, his use of the method of intertextuality, noting textual and

---

71 Tsumura 2012. Note that Modern German dictionaries explain *tōhû wābōhû* as "Chaos".
72 Smith 2010, 234.
73 Above, p. 237.
74 See Tsumura 1989, 2005a.
75 For double meanings of "creation" and "destruction" in English, see above, p. 256 n. 17.

thematic "resonance" and "association" among Semitic mythological texts, is notable.

On the other hand, as I have been trained in traditional Semitic philology in Hebrew and Ugaritic as well as in comparative Semitic studies, my approach is narrower in perspective than his, dealing with the specific ancient texts themselves, and paying attention to the etymology of individual words as well as their use in their immediate contexts. At the same time, I am interested in recent synchronic linguistic approaches such as discourse grammatical analysis[76] as well as the vertical grammatical analysis of poetic parallelism.[77] I tried to analyse the primary source as much as possible before entering the wider perspective of these ancient texts.

Methodologically, however, I am convinced that word semantics should remain the primary concern in understanding texts, and the meaning of a word within a single thought unit, i.e. a sentence, is the most crucial concern in conveying the message of any text. Wyatt's definition of "chaos" and the *Chaoskampf* seems to be too wide to be adequate for a proper interpretation of creation matter.

While Wyatt's concern is seemingly ontological, asking *what* kind of reality Gen 1:2 can refer to, my concern is more epistemological, asking *how* Gen 1:2 describes the reality which human beings had not experienced. While Wyatt's answer to his question is the pre-existence of "uncosmicised" chaos, my answer to my question is the "metaphorical" information that the cosmos was "not yet" the normal cosmos human beings knew by experience. In my understanding, the creation of the entire cosmos, i.e., "heavens and earth", that is material origin, is asserted in Gen 1:1, while Gen 1:2–31 are simply developing the theme by describing *how* God created the earth, on which human beings will be placed eventually. The biblical author is of course concerned with the function of each created substance, but material origin is not ignored. Thus, our point of separation is the questions we ask concerning Gen 1:1–3.[78]

---

[76] Tsumura 2016, 2021.
[77] Tsumura 2009, 2017, 2019, in press (b).
[78] See now Tsumura 2018, 2021.

Nicolas Wyatt
Response to David Tsumura

1 Generalities

I have a feeling of inevitability about the paper submitted by David Tsumura. I suspect that he has the same feeling with regard to mine. I also have a suspicion that the polarity of which I am writing will typify most of the opposed pairings of contributions to this book—and perhaps the readership—particularly since it is intended precisely to juxtapose conflicting assessments of a selection of problems. The feeling I have is that a scholar, he or I, or any other, shapes his or her arguments precisely to end up in a predetermined position. He—David—is determined to maintain two positions: the reality (the truth) of the doctrine of *creatio ex nihilo*, and the inappropriateness of seeing in Genesis 1 even a hint of the idea of chaos. I am equally determined, it would appear, to maintain the opposite position on both points. Can this *impasse* be resolved, or should we shake hands and agree to differ?[1]

So far as I am concerned, I must make a plea in my own defence. This is that, when I begin to write on a given topic, I often have no idea where my nose will lead me. At times I surprise myself and end up a long way from where I expected to be. The same is true in the present instance. In my earlier work I have admittedly argued along the familiar lines, as those who know my work will agree. But as I remarked to Rebecca Watson as I began to read Tsumura 2005a as a starting point for my discussion above, it seemed that he and I agreed rather more than I expected. But when I put finger to keyboard, things loosened up considerably. As opponents of my views might argue, my old prejudices kicked in.

My main problem is the precision, that is, the over-precision, of some of David's arguments. He argues that a, but not b, can be the case: that is, a and b (representing any two alternatives) are mutually exclusive. At the most elementary level, it is a question of the precise meaning, and even etymology, of words. Who can disagree with this in principle? You cannot seriously build an argument

---

[1] One dimension in which this discussion could progress is the theological. I understand David's starting point to be that of evangelical Christianity. Mine is a non-theistic, humanistic stance, but reasonably tolerant of alternative religious assessments, and indeed benignly disposed towards religion. Theology is often at the root of academic disagreements, and often unacknowledged. We saw in my paper above that some "academic" arguments were actually based on theological premises, as with von Rad and Waltke.

on a false etymology. But many biblical writers are poets (and when *they* try etymology, are invariably wrong!), and they, and also good prose-writers, play with words, deliberately choose words that are ambiguous, or echo other ideas or words of similar sound or form.² So even if Hebrew *təhôm* is not to be derived from *Ti'āmat*, then it seems very likely that the author of Genesis 1 deliberately echoed the usage of *Enuma Elish*, by using his choice of Hebrew term for the deep with a view to its allusive quality. Biblical writers were apparently incapable, to read his line of argument, of giving the same ideological or symbolic content to a trope which may have a previous Near Eastern (pre)history of centuries, if not millennia. Myths have been reduced to metaphors; metaphors have died and become mere idioms. I cannot accept these reductive, to say nothing of reductionist, assessments. Each argument is stated as though it were self-evident. On the contrary, we should suppose the same broad mentality to persist among the people of ancient Judah as we perceive in contemporary Babylonia, Phoenicia and Egypt. To assert that their (the Judahites') world view has been radically changed requires clear demonstration, and I find no such demonstration. If we insist that the Judahite mind or the "biblical mind" was radically different from that of their ancient neighbours, then any comparative discussion is in any case ruled out as entirely irrelevant. Indeed, it would be hard to imagine how we, with yet another distinctive mind-set, could ever seriously enter their thought-world.³

If we accept that the scribes who composed and relayed the biblical books began life in scribal schools, as did their antecedents and indeed contemporaries in other cultures, then they would have been using the same kinds of materials as teaching aids (something which would not have stopped dead with the shift to a linear alphabetic script: for a half-way house, see Ugaritian practice⁴). In the Late Bronze, for example, we have clear evidence of the presence of *Gilgamesh* and *Atraḫasis* as teaching aids in the Levant. This is how the flood tradition reached the west, centuries before the rise of Israel and Judah. Are we to assert that the composers of the biblical account of the flood had an entirely different motive in relaying the tradition, which by their time must have been thoroughly appropriated into West Semitic (Levantine) culture, further down the line?⁵ Of

---

2 See the word-plays discussed above in my paper, pp. 218–20.
3 See my remarks on this issue in Wyatt 2001b, 27 = 2005a, 163.
4 See Wyatt 2015 and references. On scribal practice in Israel-Judah, see also van der Toorn 2007; Davies and Römer 2013.
5 In Greece, and probably more widely throughout the eastern Mediterranean region, literacy probably broke down in the smaller societies most impacted by the political, social and environmental breakdown of the early twelfth century, when palace administrations ceased to function.

course there are fine tunings and adjustments to local conditions to be acknowledged, and constantly reassessed, but the story, and the message, is essentially the same one. They (any generation handing down the tradition) no doubt regarded it as sober history, since the gods acted in history.[6] Most of us today think of it as myth, apart from the diehards among the guild who can stomach only a thoroughgoing demythologisation, or those who still tramp stoically up Mount Ararat. I am even happy to think of a possible historical memory[7] in the flood story,[8] but that does not prevent it from also being myth. As for stories about creation, I do not see how they can be anything other than myth. Certainly nobody was there to observe the historical unfolding of the event. And whatever else God is or was, he or she was *not* a reliable historian! The demythologisation movement is thoroughly reductionist in the pejorative sense of the term.[9] It not only does a disservice to ancient sacred traditions, but it entirely distorts for the modern reader who believes such an agenda to be the real meaning of the text before him (or her, but women generally do not have the extreme male brain of which this kind of compartmentalised thinking is the hallmark).

The situation has an iconographical analogue. We can actually *see* Tiamat and her analogues if we look at cylinder-seals and reliefs, and the gods themselves gaze out on us from the stony eyes of ancient statues.[10] The experience of these as divine presences was as real for the Israelites as for their neighbours. Hence the prophetic backlash: it was precisely the power of such imagery, such physical representations of the divine, that the iconoclasts feared. The crucial thing is that the scholar must try, however haltingly, to enter into the mind-set of his subjects, involving a suspension of his or her own perspective (*epoche*). He (for as we noted, it is primarily the male scholar!) need not have a theological

---

See Rollston (2006; 2010). Israel (and some way behind as an Iron Age reality, Judah) was only becoming established as a political entity during this period. But the later scribal schools were probably influenced by conditions in places which did not endure the breakdown, such as Egypt and Mesopotamia. The continuity between the Middle and Late Bronze Linear Canaanite script, of which Ugaritic alphabetic cuneiform was a by-form, and the Phoenician and Palaeo-Hebrew scripts of the first millennium also demonstrates that the degree of breakdown in the Levant should not be overstated.

6 Albrektson 1967.
7 Connerton 1989.
8 See Wyatt 2003a.
9 In its extreme form it leads to such sterile creationist and "young earth" discussions as pepper the pages of Charles 2013, though there are heartening signs of minds straining to be open. See the review by Clifford (2014) and cf. also p. 207 n. 12 in my paper above. The certainties expressed in the book break the law of the half-life of facts, on which see Arbesman 2012.
10 And originally met our gaze! See the interesting analysis of Jaynes [1976] 1982, 165–75.

stance to be relatively successful in this endeavour—some theological stances would be entirely out of sympathy with such a procedure and would therefore impede the achievement of *epoche*—and such a position would hardly be expected of the Assyriologist, the Egyptologist or the Ugaritologist, in their professional contexts. The scholar must also try to avoid supposing that the ancients, or at least the Israelites (and Judahites), also have a post-Reformation mind-set.

To reduce the language of myth to mere literary frill and embellishment, which is the only outcome possible on the reductionist approach, is seriously to underestimate the power of the text to actualise the religious experience. Often pursued for theological purposes, it is a self-defeating strategy. This is not the place to develop this line of discussion, which I have already done in any case in previous papers, but it seems to me that it also represents *in nuce* the deep division between the "high" and "low" church conceptions of religious symbolism, liturgy and biblical interpretation, as well as having uncomfortable implications for the opposition often held to obtain between religious and secular approaches, as here. The secular commentator is commonly thought by his or her opponents to be constitutionally incapable of appreciating the religious essence of a matter under discussion. We might counter that the religious commentator, in the Christian intellectual tradition, is often incapable of appreciating the mythological dimension. The clue here may be the relative stances of such "opponents" on comparative matters, and the study of other religions. Here, it seems to me, the secularist may be at some advantage for not having the believer's prejudices. But perhaps it is ultimately down to different psychological types? I readily concede that some people in each of these camps have the psychological and emotional disposition of the other camp.

So how far is it legitimate to see the later doctrine of *creatio ex nihilo* as present in Genesis 1? As a later reflexion on the text? There is no problem. It is an undoubted fact of the history of reception. It is equally beyond dispute a Christian dogma ("maker of heaven and earth, and of all things, visible and invisible"), even though to judge from the commentaries it may nowadays be more honoured in the breach than the observance. As an insistence that this is what the Hebrew text actually meant, as deposited by the pen of its author, prospectively? This is seriously problematic, for all the reasons given above. The issue was raised a long time ago in Jowett's famous 1860 essay.[11]

---

[11] Jowett 1860, especially 336–8 (the famous statement "His object is to read Scripture like any other book" occurs on p. 338). See also Barr 1982. This is really only an issue if one accepts the premise that the text is canonical, and therefore in some way *sui generis*. All religions which have sacred texts maintain the same or similar claims.

There is in fact a way out of the evident *impasse*. This is for the reader approaching the text from a confessional perspective to accept seriously the doctrine of (progressive) revelation, that is, seeing the Bible as a series of texts composed over a historical period, and reflecting the different priorities and beliefs of the different stages in its history. This is not so far removed from an overall neutral reception history of the text, which is how the non-believer or neutral historian of religion will view it, recognising a natural process of historical development. But he or she (the believing reader) may want to superimpose these two perceptions on each other, and this is the point at which the secular historian will probably demur, insisting that these are two distinct phases in the history of the text, which are not to be confused.

It is increasingly recognised from studies in the cognition of ancient peoples that the human mind is disposed not only to discern in, but also to impose on, the external world patterns of meaning.[12] The meanings are invented, that is, products of the human mind (though some theological minds may demur at this point and think of it as recognition of an eternal quality), and their structures and details will have evolved naturally in the context of general human mental and social evolution, though always with the need for biological survival as their fundamental *raison d'être*. We have an irreducible *need* to make sense of our world. This is as true for secular as for religious minds. The latter probably also understand meaning to imply purpose, which is where theological narratives shape and interpret experience. If we can accept that all our minds are busily at work fulfilling at least the first aspect of this universal agenda, and that all our thinking on such matters is necessarily symbolic, metaphorical, and mythical (I see here a progressive heightening and intensification of the process, each successive stage embracing and developing the earlier stages[13]), then we can share some common ground.

A further general point should perhaps be emphasised. This is that in the field of the humanities, into which the discipline of Biblical Studies commonly falls nowadays—though at times it has a separate life in Schools or Faculties of Divinity and seminaries. In these latter institutions, a certain amount of research is naturally devoted to demonstrating that a and not b is the case, by

---

[12] E.g. Guthrie 1993; Boyer 1993, 2001; Hoffmeyer 1996, Mithen 1996; Deacon 1997; Pollack 2000; Atran 2002; Newberg *et al.* 2002; Lewis-Williams 2002, 2010; Pyysiäinen 2003; Lewis-Williams and Pearce 2005; Clark 2006; Teske 2006, 2010; McCauley and Cohen 2010; Wiebe 2009; Robinson and Southgate 2010; Barrett 2012 and Davis and Peters 2012. On broader issues of belief and the problem of conflicting views, see Headland, Pike and Harris 1990; McCutcheon 1999; and Peterson 1999.

[13] See Munz 1973, and critiques in Berndt 1975 and Wyatt 1996, 399–404.

way of claiming to be "scientific", especially in institutions with an ethos geared to "religious truth". In the environment of literary criticism and analysis, the emphasis is more often on complementary ways of viewing a text, so that our understanding is enriched by the broader perspective of a plurality of viewpoints. The analogy of vision is useful here. The two eyes (even better, four eyes between David and me!) of binocular vision perceive a three-dimensional, and therefore a more rounded, image of a problem to be addressed than monoculism, which corresponds to the "either … or" position. Odysseus, with his two eyes and wily mind, easily outclassed as well as outwitted the one-eyed Polyphemus. There is in our discipline, therefore, not just a historical dialectic, moving on from one perspective to the next as each phase is successively discredited (as tends to be the case in the sciences, where an old position is of merely historical interest), but rather an increasing enrichment in the total appreciation of the text. This is why we can still turn to patristic and mediaeval commentaries, for all their inherent quaintness, and be enriched ourselves. The heartening feature of this complex and ever-developing picture is that the shrillness of one phase of reaction from one quarter to the insights of the opposite one is subsumed within a gradual convergence, as each—perhaps reluctantly and even unconsciously—accepts and acknowledges the perspective and contribution to discussion of the other. Perhaps Reception Criticism has contributed to this, as it shows that, like the Wheel of Fortune, the same ideas periodically reemerge.

In my initial discussion, I protested against the "obsessively hyperlogical" stance which as a matter of history has characterised Christian theological thinking. This is in part a contributory factor in the increasing alienation between biblical studies and theology which many scholars have recently been lamenting. A common feature of this stance has been the univocal meaning acknowledged in biblical texts, which has been inimical to the literary appreciation of the texts, and even to an adequate religious appreciation (to be distinguished from a theological one, inasmuch as this is an academic pursuit).[14] This brings us to our specific engagement with David.

2 Specifics

Since to a considerable extent our papers overlap in their details, I shall raise issues in the order in which they appear in his paper. In so far as I have already

---

14 See Noegel 2014 for a useful discussion of polysemy (a useful antidote to univocality!) in *Kirta*. See also Lewis 1989, 143–58, and Wyatt 2012, 280–1 on the polysemy in Isa 57:5–9.

addressed the points raised, I shall try to add complementary observations rather than simply repeat myself. The first is the question of myth. David writes:[15]

> Is it meaningful to describe the biblical view as "demythologised"? Furthermore, to what degree should we regard the biblical tradition as a wholly new departure ...?

Although there are two questions here, they obviously look at the same problem from different angles. The implication is that the Babylonian tradition is mythological, and that in so far as the Genesis 1 account of creation combats its teaching, it also rejects its genre. I dealt with this fairly thoroughly above, since I think the besetting sin of biblical scholarship within this area is its fear of the word "myth" and its derivative forms. In some instances I think this amounts to disingenuity, as a culpable self-delusion on the part of scholars who look at the same material in, say, the Ugaritic and Hebrew contexts, and without a hint of irony tell us that it is myth or legend in the one instance, and sober, demythologised, history on the other. What is their criterion, beyond wishful thinking? What I find deficient is the uncritical assumption by scholars at large that the narrative material has, like some disgusting disease, crossed the genre boundary, from myth to epic (as in the title of F. M. Cross's 1973 study, *Canaanite Myth and Hebrew Epic*), and accordingly been transformed into a kind of history ("historicised myth": but with an unwritten agenda in some quarters that this means sober history). But epic (even "history"!) is as mythological as any true myth. Be it the Iliad, the Odyssey or the "epics" of the Old Testament, when gods take part as *dramatis personae* in the narrative, speaking, acting, reacting, and so forth, we are in the realm of myth.

The next topic raised by David is the question of evil, and the tendency by some scholars (he cites Bonting, Ortlund, Waltke) to equate chaos with evil. It seems that by and large we are of one mind here, though it is a pity that we do *not* see eye to eye on the matter of chaos (next paragraph). But I stressed above my view that "chaos" is simply uncosmicised material, entirely neutral from a moral point of view, but in a narrative account of its transformation into cosmos it is naturally presented as in opposition to the victorious power, and with our propensity to see victory as vindication and indicative of moral superiority, we can easily fall into the trap of equating the vanquished with evil. Nowadays it is called blaming the victims.

---

[15] Above, p. 201 (in part of the joint 'Engagement' statement authored by him).

This leads on to David's treatment of Chaos. I dealt with this extensively above with reference to his earlier work. His definition of chaos is not unlike mine,[16] though he emphasises different aspects of it. He writes:[17]

> *Enuma Elish* depicts a harmonious mingling of Apsu and Tiamat at the beginning of the story and there is nothing "chaotic" or "in confusion" …

I have just a slight problem with this. It sounds as though all is peace and inertia, almost paradisal. But in that there is no differentiation ("harmonious mingling") there is implicit fusion, for which "confusion" is merely a stronger term. In a dynamic world, it must yield to its opposite: chaos must become cosmos. Indeed, the laws of *kašrût*, which I suggested should be discerned behind Genesis 1, demand the separation of unlike principles. As for the semantic development of the idea of chaos which David deplores, this is surely already implicit in all its poetic uses, as with *tōhû wā bōhû*, though David denies any link between the two ideas. This is particularly clear in the quotation from Jeremiah 4:23–8,[18] in which precisely the *confusion* of all the normal differentiations of the real world is described in the reversion to chaos.

In discussing chaos, David rightly rejects the argument of some that it is inherently evil (although I think he swithers a little!), as though we were faced with a Zoroastrian opposition. In criticising scholars' use of the term *Chaoskampf*, he prefers the more neutral term "theomachy". I am happy with this, but would make two comments. Firstly, though I agree that the German word has been overused, I see no reason to banish a powerful term altogether, especially since a case can be made for its continued use in the right circumstances. I have offered a reasonable defence of such a qualified use in my paper. Secondly, the latter term theomachy has its own baggage (we think specifically of Olympians and Titans, a conflict also called the Titanomachy, which is not itself a *Chaoskampf*). The real objection against *Chaoskampf* is of course David's supposition that there is no "chaos", sc. precosmic state of affairs, in Genesis 1. But that is ultimately a theological judgment, not a philological one. David writes that the use in our present context is wrong, "because neither *təhôm* nor *tōhûwābōhû* in Gen 1:2 has anything to do with chaos".[19] I think I have also made a case for concluding that this Hebrew expression is *precisely* a description of chaos. It does not help that the etymology of both parts of the expression is obscure,

---

16 Tsumura 2005a, 12, noted above, p. 230 n. 80.
17 Above, p. 255.
18 Above, p. 237.
19 Above, p. 255.

but the thrust of the idiom is clear enough. David acknowledges that words shift their meanings; I suggest that there is no need to think of a *shift* in this case so much as recognition of our fuller understanding of the words, both Greek and Hebrew, with rich overtones and mythical nuances, beyond the philological raw material. Here Hesiod has more to say to us than Liddell and Scott or Genesis than Köhler—Baumgartner. And we saw how Rebecca Watson initially dismissed the Greek term as inappropriate, because Hebrew had no counterpart, but ended up with a little concession in that direction.[20] At best, opinion is divided between the two camps. I think it likely that those who reject its presence are overwhelmingly the theologians, while those who defend it are the philologists (at any rate those who are not immune to poetic nuance) and historians of religion. This looks likely to remain an *impasse*. So far as Ugaritic material is concerned (where the theologians hold their counsel), I am happy with David's characterisation of the Baal and Yam conflict as theomachy, but noted above the cosmogonic nuances of the construction of the former's temple.[21] The battle is not to be separated from its outcome, which is the construction of the temple. So *this* theomachy is ultimately an example of the *Chaoskampf.*

When addressing non-cosmogonic examples of the battle between Yahweh and his divine opponents, David cites Klingbeil's assertion "He is not engaged in a struggle against the chaos or the enemy, but his victory is an anticipated fact and his dominion over the chaotic forces a *fait accompli*".[22] This seems a bit confused! It is not a struggle against *chaos*, yet *chaotic forces* are overcome; and it is not a struggle because we know the outcome! But this looks like special pleading. And the fact that in such conflicts it is simply a walkover for Yahweh in no way diminishes the mythic and dynamic power of its presentation as a conflict. We all know that the heroine will die in grand opera, or that Hamlet, Macbeth, Oedipus, *et al.* will come to a sticky end: it in no way diminishes the suspense. This dynamic is what I discern lurking behind the text of Genesis 1. In subsequent discussion of the metaphor of divine conflict in many biblical passages, such as Psalm 29, David denies any connection with the *Chaoskampf* motif. But let us ask this question: what is the source of the combat "metaphor", or as I would put it, "mythologem"? The ultimate answer is of course human conflict, but in its divinisation it is raised to a paradigmatic role (and I suggested above that the real paradigm for this is Zimri-Lim's oracle A1968 from Mari). Every conflict is from the psychological and ideological perspective a re-enact-

---

20 Above, p. 235 n. 90 in my paper.
21 See the commentary to point 3 of Table 3, pp. 246, 247–9.
22 Above, pp. 256–7; Klingbeil 1999, 306.

ment of the primordial conflict. The *Chaoskampf* symbol echoes down the labyrinthine ways of the literature, however attenuated it may become in some examples. This is true of the other conflict allusions which David discerns throughout the Old Testament (see further below). To dismiss allusions as debased, incidental, or mere metaphor is to miss the point.

We are in complete agreement over Richard Averbeck's account of Genesis 3. But David goes on from that discussion to claim that "indeed both [the Genesis serpent and Tiamat] are evil, but Tiamat is a frightfully powerful, world-ruling monster, whereas the serpent is cunning".[23] I see no statement in the texts that either is "evil". Furthermore, Tiamat cannot *rule* a world that is as yet uncreated,[24] and since she is both divine and the raw material of the world, it is best to regard her as in principle benign or neutral. As for the Genesis serpent, Zevit has given a very good account of it, which in my view redeems it.[25] We cannot blame the serpent for what tradition has done to besmirch its integrity.

In considering Psalm 29,[26] a theophany account, David notes all the implicit discontinuities with *Chaoskampf* material with regard to vocabulary and plot, but I see no reason not to recognise here an allusion to it. Failure to incorporate all the Ugaritic vocabulary would make sense if the argument were that this is effectively a "Canaanite" Psalm, as has been claimed, but we need go no further than speak of a cognate relationship between the two, as in my account of various recensions above (table). I agree that the psalm is not an account of a divine battle, but it is certainly a song of victory which presupposes that such a battle has taken place. Theophanies speak with two tongues. The language is of violence, storm, flood, the arrival of the warrior-god, and so on. On one level this is a grandiloquent way of describing the opening of a shrine-box, the processing of an image, and the accompanying incense, sacrifice, and cacophony of priestly chant and musical instruments, trumpets, lyres, drums ... On the other, it speaks of the irruption into human affairs of the divine, where one struggles to find the words, is breathless with the thrill and the terror of it all. Each theophany, experienced periodically in a temple's cultic and liturgical calendar and of which

---

[23] Above, p. 264, quoting Gunkel [1910] 1997, 16.
[24] A besetting problem in such discussion is the relative simplicity of the biblical world view, in distinction from Mesopotamian, Hittite and Greek (as well as Indo-Iranian and Indo-Āryan) examples, where an earlier precosmic dispensation, a "proto-world", has to give way to the present world of humans. Nothing of this is to be discerned in the relatively austere biblical corpus, though some very interesting material emerges or reemerges in the later Pseudepigrapha. We are *not* therefore comparing like with like.
[25] Zevit 2014, *passim*.
[26] Above, pp. 274–5.

texts are evocations, summaries or even the liturgies themselves, reenacts the archetype, so that there is always an implicit allusion to the *Chaoskampf*. And with regard to Psalm 46 and Habakkuk 3, it is again the extension of the primordial language to the present or futuristic expectation, not the mere borrowing of a worn-out metaphor. With regard to Psalm 46, David's observation[27] that "the flooding water was threatening Yahweh's people, not Yahweh himself" is a feint. The sharp distinction between people and their god is misleading, both because in flood stories it is the people who suffer, not the deity, yet it is the deity who fights an aqueous foe, in a conflict which is the mirror image of the *Chaoskampf*.[28]

David appears to have a problem with Isa 51:9.[29] Texts like this apparently "have nothing to do with cosmic origins".[30] I find this hard to follow. The passage clearly indicates that the listener (an exilic Jew) can now forget the old creation story, because a new one is even now taking place. Read at any level below the cosmogonic, the passage has little force. Read in this way (as a cosmogony revisited or, better, now re-experienced!), rather like the vision in Revelation 12 and 20,[31] it speaks of a complete world renewal.[32] Out of the chaos of history a new era will emerge. The ancient drakonomathy is alive and well and taking place afresh in Deutero-Isaiah's or John's vision. The whole point of the new world construction is that it makes sense only in contrast to the old-world construction. It seems perverse to deny this dimension to the text. And it is equally puzzling to read of these mythological allusions as fossilised. This is buying into the demythologisation scenario, which I think has been thoroughly discredited.

In turning to Psalm 74,[33] David's position appears to be as follows. He ignores the possibility that we have mythic material here. The parallel with the Ugaritic conflict myth, indicated by the names used in both traditions (Sea, Dragon, Leviathan, River), is not mentioned, and it *seems* that we have no more than a rather graphic account of the retreat of the sea (in the episode of the crossing of *Yam Sûp*):

---

27 Above, p. 272.
28 Wyatt 2003a.
29 Above, p. 278.
30 Above, p. 278.
31 See point 7 of Table 3, pp. 246, 250.
32 On the close relationship between creation and redemption see Stuhlmueller 1970 (cited with others in Wyatt 1996, 24).
33 Above, pp. 265–71.

> the sea dragons and their representative, Leviathan, are smashed/crushed ... on the heads over the waters ...[34]

Strangely, with the cross-reference to the *Yam Sûp* and therefore presumably with the exodus in mind, it looks as though this is to be understood soberly, presumably as a historical or legendary event, but with no admission that this is powerful mythology. The intertext Exodus 15 is not actually noted here, and there is no sense of the transformation by the incorporation of vv. 14b–15a into the victory feast that is to follow the new irruption of divine power in the making of a new world (cf. my treatment above). I am not sure how the hermeneutical gulf between us at this point is to be bridged. Furthermore, this view of David appears to be reductionist in the extreme, for it effectively denies any serious *religious* content in the account. Even the germ of a messianic feast is reduced to an observation about dead fish on the beach! His assessment of Psalm 74[35] is revealing:

> His salvation (*yšw'wt*) is a result of his victory as king in the battle against his and his people's enemies in the present world. There is no reason to connect it with his creation of the cosmos in the primordial time.

While this uses theological, even, in my view, mythological language, it effectively evacuates the psalm of religious content, because the whole force of the poem, the promise of restoration (sc. of that which has been destroyed: the original creation) is ignored. I appeal here to King Zimri-Lim! But in case I be accused here of overstating my case, let us see some further remarks on the same text:

> The sea dragons and Leviathan are to be compared with the seven-headed serpent or dragon in {the} ancient Near Eastern mythology ... It is probable that in Israel this multi-headed dragon was used as an idiom for strong enemies in general. Thus for the author of Ps 74 "to crush the heads of dragons or Leviathan" meant "to destroy the enemy completely".[36]

Here we have a clear case of the thought process I described above in referring to Cross. The acknowledged *myth* of the ancient Near East is reduced to the "*idiom*" (implicitly demythologised and even trivialised) of ancient Israel (Judah). Where is the warrant for this supposed reduction? I see no evidence for it. The fact that the idiom is drawn from the practice of warfare (immediate sequel, same page)

---

[34] Above, p. 266.
[35] Above, p. 269.
[36] Above, p. 269.

in no way requires that it no longer be myth. On the contrary, it shows how myth can derive many of its key symbols from the human context.

David's treatment of the relationship of Isa 27:1 and *KTU* 1.5 i 1–3, presumably alluded to in the phrase "the same literary tradition as the Canaanite mytho-poetic literature", is a further instance of reductionism:[37]

> Isa 27:1 is in the same literary tradition as the Canaanite mytho-poetic literature, though the author uses the similar expressions as a metaphor for the destruction of evil in an eschatological context.

There are two points here. Firstly, the expression "mytho-poetic" seems to me to mean something like "sub-mythic(al)", "dressed up in the language of myth, without the force", already impugning the vitality of the Ugaritic material; secondly, in the Bible it is more thoroughly reduced to (merely) metaphorical force. I think this does a disservice to both traditions. As for its eschatological reference, I think this has been seriously overrated (pretty well universally by biblical scholars: "eschatological" is a current buzz-word for anything futuristic), and the power of the biblical text is surely all the greater if it has to do, not with some end-of-the-world wishful thinking on the level of a cargo cult, but an assertion of the impending irruption of Yahweh into the real present of the psalmist's contemporaries?

This may appear to the reader to be a very negative response to David's paper. Given our different backgrounds I think that this only to be expected. But the sharpness of the encounter, reciprocated in his response to me, shows that the topic is a lively one, and has already had very diverse treatments throughout the history of scholarship.

---

[37] Above, p. 279.

Part III: **Final Reflections**

Nicolas Wyatt
Some Observations on David Tsumura's Response

When David[1] writes that "Wyatt is therefore *more interested* in the usage of terms in their context than in etymology" (my emphasis), I think he overstates my view, or rather emphasises one aspect against the other, where I have tried to maintain a balance. It suggests that I am not really interested in philological exactitude, preferring "the usage of terms in their context", that is, the contextual and above all intertextual aspects, and implicitly involving paronomasia. I think that I have taken good account of the serious philological issues involved (I have insisted that they are not to be ignored, or overridden by theological imperatives), and we should remember that theories are seldom universally accepted. The precise sense of the key words of Genesis 1, for example, is a hotly contested issue, as can be seen by the various views I have summarised in my initial paper, and David's own discussion. What I was trying to do, while taking full account of philological and etymological issues, was to show that the ancient writers (who would have had little knowledge of philological principles) played with words, and in particular their sounds (as described in connection with the mutually evocative words, *bārā'*, *bərē'šît*, *bərît*, *bərešet*[2]) and wrung meanings out of their supposed relationships. It may be described as a form of punning, or free association. It is typical of the *pesher* mode of exegesis which typifies DSS and rabbinic treatment of ancient texts. As modern readers, we would often find the associations forced or implausible: to ancient minds, God had put clues to intertextuality in the shapes the words used in a text, for those with ears to hear. A nice inner-biblical example occurs in Jeremiah 1:11–2. Even God plays with words! David concedes this in part, but continues, "I think each text should first be interpreted in its own immediate context, with a rigorous philological, literary and rhetorical understanding, taking note of all the linguistic aspects, before widening one's perspective and digging deeper".[3] I think he introduces a false dichotomy here, because I agree with everything he writes, and yet note that the term "rhetorical", not to be separated from the other elements in analysis, is precisely the technical term which serves as umbrella for the further discussion of individual passages which I have undertaken. To

---
[1] Above, p. 285.
[2] Above, pp. 218–9.
[3] Above, p. 285.

make it a *second stage* in analysis risks missing the point, because rigorous philology can get in the way of what I called the "poetic" understanding of a text. Some philologists cannot advance beyond philology. And to demand that philology be the first port of call in analysing *Finnegan's Wake* would be a short cut to a nervous breakdown! The various emphases belong together and will generally cooperate quite unconsciously in the scholar's mind. We may present an argument in stages for logical reasons, but this is always a rationalisation of a previous intuitive process.

But when all is said and done, I do not see an insurmountable clash between us here, but am happy to recognise a different emphasis, which emerges from our backgrounds and the way we have written our respective papers. David begins with "a rigorous philological ... understanding", in which philology is the first stage in analysis. I begin rather from an overview of the broader cultural scene, thinking more as a historian of religion, and turning to philology as a necessary implement in my toolbox. The two flies in the ointment here are firstly, that I refuse to privilege the Bible, not an accusation I lay at David's door, but one of which some of the authorities I cite are manifestly guilty (von Rad, Waltke openly, and some others without declaring their interest); and secondly, that we should not discuss "metaphorisation"[4] as a sufficient literary classification of the material, which is, I would insist, mythical. Myth is a much more concentrated idiom than metaphor, which also covers banal language. Of course, if myth is to be excluded as a category, as for many biblical scholars,[5] there is unlikely to be a meeting of minds here.

With regard to my discussion on the historical setting of the relationship between Genesis 1 and *Enuma Elish*,[6] David writes, "such a view [as Wyatt offers] means we have to assume that the Israelites were ignorant of the story of *Enuma Elish* until the time of the Babylonian exile".[7] Not so: I explicitly noted[8] that the Babylonian classics were known in the west in the Bronze Age (Amarna references EA 356–9 can be added to my list) and David notes the presence in principle of a "cuneiform culture".[9] My point was not a question of first contact (and many now argue anyway that *Enuma Elish* derives from an Amorite setting—sc. in northwest Syria—though no western copy of this particular composition has so far been found), but rather of the context for a parody or subversion of the

---

4 Above, pp. 277–8, 286, 293.
5 See my critique of this position in Wyatt 2001b, 2008a, both cited in my paper.
6 Above, pp. 242–3.
7 Above, p. 286.
8 Above, p. 242 n. 115.
9 See Horowitz, Oshima and Sanders 2006.

poem by the author of Genesis, by a writer undoubtedly already familiar with the western tradition.

The question of the scope of the *Chaoskampf* trope is the next point of disagreement. My view of it, as David writes,[10] is "much wider" than his. I think that a careful reading of my paper rather qualifies this assessment. My point is not that the trope is to be found wherever we look, but that it constitutes a particular version of the theomachy motif, and because of its ideological significance, inspired a wide range of derivatives, as illustrated in my table, which traced various possible stages in which development took place. Concerning Psalm 74, I argued that the verses isolated for examination "could be almost a translation of a digest of the Ugaritic tradition".[11] I suggested that the Baal cycle from Ugarit tends to a *Chaoskampf* account because it works towards the climax of the temple construction in *KTU* 1.4 v–vii, which is to be viewed as a microcosmic account of creation, since temples were precisely construed as microcosms. There is also a *Chaoskampf* dimension to Psalm 74, because the psalmist looks beyond the destruction of the temple to a new, restored world, which in effect will replicate the old *in a new creation*. I suggest that the mythic dimension is to be discerned by the percipient reader. The view that neither of our two main texts are versions of the *Chaoskampf* trope, because one has no conflict and the other no creation is to underestimate the allusive power of mythic language (indeed, all literary language), which can evoke a whole world in one telling phrase, just as a couple of bars in a musical score brings the whole work into the listener's mind. I think my argument gives an adequate account of both "missing" motifs, though the Genesis story has become a walkover ("This 'contest' is a walkover, but it remains a contest",[12] by virtue of the resonances of *bārā'*).

David remains unhappy with what he considers my excessive extension of the *Chaoskampf* trope (even to include Gospel episodes!).[13] I suspect that we are doomed to remain divided on this issue, since he appears to insist on strict etymological rules and their application, and the strict separation of *Gattungen* (when is a theomachy not a *Chaoskampf* ?), while I insist on the importance of resonances, as exemplified by my discussion above of the evocative words *bārā'*, *bərē'šît*, *bərît*, *bərešet* etc.,[14] but pervading my treatment of both texts.

---

[10] Above, p. 287.
[11] Above, p. 240.
[12] Above, p. 228.
[13] See my coverage of different versions, including New Testament ones, in Wyatt 2001a, 95–113.
[14] Pp. 218–21.

The paragraph in David's paper[15] beginning "Since Wyatt takes both Gen 1 and Ps 74 ..." and criticising my account, errs in my view precisely because it fails to recognise the "poetic" dimension I am attempting to take seriously. Whether or not conflict appears *explicitly* in the first, or creation in the second, is immaterial. We have to recognise the allusive nature of both texts: they evoke a whole nexus of associated motifs. They use a kind of unspoken shorthand. To spell out all the thoughts going through the authors' minds would take them forever. But their choice of vocabulary points the perceptive reader in the right direction with far greater economy. My discussion of *bārā'* well illustrates my point: even if the word does not mean "to cut" or something similar in the context of Genesis 1—and it may be argued that the jury is still out over what precisely it does mean, as the arguments I summarise above indicate—it hints at such a sense, and thus the author chooses it to evoke the dragon-killing trope. The same goes for my claim to which David alludes concerning the episodes of Jesus walking on the sea and stilling the storm. The first evokes victory over the dragon (cf. Job 9:8), the second points to Jesus as the deity taming the primaeval ocean. It is a question not of "broaden[ing my] definition of this myth too widely",[16] but rather of recognising allusions where they occur.

On the issues of *tōhû wābōhû* and *ḥōšek*, I am not sure that we are really as much at odds as it seems. I have no quarrel with the way David describes these,[17] and consider his account to be broadly complementary to mine. However, when we turn to the issue of *təhôm* and *ti'āmat*,[18] I must take issue. I am not asserting that the Hebrew is derived from the Akkadian, as he appears to be saying that I am saying; and I agree with Pardee on this philological point—one good reason to cite him!—so that I can hardly be accused of misunderstanding him. Rather the terms have a common root.[19] So we really have no quarrel on this issue. But he goes on to reject my argument that the biblical writer is deliberately choosing his word in order to allude to the Akkadian term. I do not see the force of his argument. I do not see how the point can be ultimately proved or disproved. But if I am right, the choice of word has the greater force. Of course the Old Testament is thoroughly familiar with the West Semitic theomachic tradition; all I am saying is that in this text the author is parodying the other, babylonianised version *Enuma Elish*, and choosing the term *təhôm* to highlight the point, not because it is really the same term as *ti'āmat*, but because it evokes it,

---

15 Above, p. 287.
16 Above, p. 288.
17 Above, pp. 289–91.
18 See David's "Response" above, pp. 291–95.
19 See above, pp. 234–5.

and indeed perhaps even pokes fun at it in the parody. Parody can be serious, and here results in a profound, magisterial and moving account of creation. David queries my "speculation" regarding the Babylonian setting for Genesis 1 as a literary composition.[20] I do not think that this requires a defence. It is pretty well the consensus of scholars, and Heidel's list of close parallels between the text and *Enuma Elish* is good evidence. Again, it is of course not the kind of thing that can be finally proved, one way or the other. But it seems to me a far likelier proposition than that it is set entirely within a West Semitic, non-Babylonian historical context. Were it to be read in such a context, the problem would arise as to why it is so different from other western versions and allusions, perhaps most clearly Psalm 74. So it is speculation with a good foundation in the evidence before us. I am not arguing that it is entirely "oriental" (that is, Babylonian in inspiration). It is a telling by an author entirely familiar with the western tradition, but adapted to the new, exilic, context. Incidentally, I claim no direct link between Psalm 74 and *Enuma Elish*, as apparently alleged.[21] Indeed, I wrote that the passage in the psalm I discuss is "almost a translation ...".[22] But lest this citation be misconstrued yet again, let us be clear, that I am not claiming that the psalm is directly derived from the Ugaritic tradition, only that it is remarkably close to it with regard to the common vocabulary, extending to the five terms used for the enemy. And by contrast with it, Genesis 1 is best read as rising within the exilic community.

An interesting point in this discussion is David's characterising *təhôm* as fresh water, over against *yām*, the salt sea.[23] It seems to me that this is a half-truth (in which case we half agree), in that the term may well denote fresh water, or simply water unspecified as to salinity. But there are a number of biblical passages where it is difficult to believe that this is the sense. Such are Exod 15:4–5 (*yām* || *yam-sûp*; *təhōmōt* || *məṣôlōt*), Isa 51:10 (*yām* || *təhôm rabbāh*), where the two terms, *təhôm* and *yām*, refer to the same body of water. Psalm 106:9 uses the same parallelism (*yam-sûp* || *təhōmôt*). The Ugaritic passage *KTU* 1.23.30 (*ym* || *thm*) is comparable. Not dissimilar is the Ugaritic usage *ym* || *nhr(m)*, as found frequently in Yam's titles (*zbl ym* || *ṭpṭ nhr*), where the "river" is best construed as the world-encircling ocean.[24]

---

20 Above, p. 293.
21 See above, pp. 242–3.
22 My paper, p. 238, and cited above, p. 317.
23 Above, pp. 259–60.
24 Thus Yam was god of the salt sea. His daughters were in control of fresh water, respectively Pidray (rain), Ṭaliy (dew) and Arṣiyu (springs, ground-water). On the river as the sea, see Wyatt

David objects to my seemingly sloppy reference to the verb *prr* in connection with Psalm 74:13.[25] In terms of philology, I am not at all opposed to him. I did not offer a translation of the word there, however,[26] but drew attention to words of similar phonology in the material, which is suggestive. I wrote "The whole point here is the evocative, 'triggering' nature of the term or idea: one word or even idea evokes a whole mythic nexus".[27] I stand by this. It seems to me that if we ignore the poetic dimension in these mythic traditions, with its suggestivity (also nicely exemplified in the materials I discussed above on pp. 218–21), we may as well give up, for we have revealed our insensitivity to the whole enterprise. We have to leave strict philology behind at this point (attempting to catalogue the evocative connection between the words *bārā'*, *bərē'šît*, *bərît*, *rešet*, *'ăšērāh*, *bārak* and *bāraq* is philological nonsense!), but it is how the ancient mind perceived these ideas. They thrived on ambiguity, innuendo and the similar shape of dissimilar terms, which drew concepts together. God (or in Egypt, for example, where the ritual texts are saturated with it, the gods) has (or have) put these words into the poets' minds.

In turning to the problem of Chaos, David writes "the 'chaos' in Wyatt's understanding is not so much a confusion or disorder, as often advocated by modern scholars, as an undifferentiated 'void'".[28] He then goes on to appeal to a semantic shift in the history of the term, suggesting that I am anachronistic in my usage. We are concerned not so much with the history of the word in European languages over the last two millennia as with the presence or absence of the concept in ancient Hebrew. It seems to me that all the qualities he lists as having been identified by me, that is, "not yet differentiated", "uncosmicised", "inchoate", "not yet organised", "precosmic"—the list could go on—are approximations to what the author of Genesis 1 was trying to express with his use of *tōhû wābōhû*.

And if we are to consider the subsequent history of the term, in order to try to capture something of its sense, then its literary richness, which I thought I had fully explored above, invites the reader to see an accumulation of ideas. The term expresses an ever-enriching synthesis of meanings and overtones,[29] rather than

---

2001a, 118–9. The most recent view of the Baal Cycle as reflecting a tsunami destroying Ugarit ca 1250 (see Wyatt 2017a and references) clearly presupposes a *saline* body of water.

25 Above, p. 239; Tsumura 295.
26 See entry *prr* in *DUL*³ and *HALOT*.
27 Above, p. 238 n. 100.
28 Above, p. 296.
29 See my original footnote 90 (p. 235).

a strictly univocal sense, to be judged as either right or wrong, in an analytical, "either ... or ..." approach.

The later history of a word does not necessarily negate its earlier history, especially with a word like this, which will continue to evoke the Greek meaning (Hesiod in the sixth century BCE) in the mind of a sophisticated twenty-first century AD speaker. Negation leads to a flat, unidimensional understanding of the text, which betrays and denies its poetic vigour. So I stand by everything I wrote above.

In the final analysis, the controversy here boils down to the problem of the doctrine of *creatio ex nihilo*. If there is no preexistent substance out of which the world is formed, then obviously *tōhû wābōhû* represent(s) vacuity: a non-existent state. If the doctrine is not present, then these terms denote the primordial precosmic raw substance about to be transformed. The latter represents my position, as outlined in my paper. David and I disagree on the issue.

While on the subject of *tōhû wābōhû*, let me respond to David's problem with my connection of Genesis 1 and Jeremiah 4:23–8.[30] In the narrowest sense, perhaps he is right. But he completely misses the whole poetic and mythological dimension of my citation of the latter. Jeremiah, or whoever wrote the poem,[31] is surely describing the dissolution of the world. He does so by evoking the chaos (I use the term advisedly!) which will ensue in the breakdown of all that holds the late preexilic monarchical world together. Given the intertextual nature of this material, it is even possible that the author of Genesis knows the Jeremiah passage, as I suggested, and constructs his narrative as an assertion of its reversal. Compare the wording of Genesis 1:2 and Jeremiah 4:23:

| Genesis: | wəhā'āreṣ | hāyətāh | tōhû wābōhû |
| Jeremiah: | hā'āreṣ | wəhinnēh- | tōhû wābōhû |

This is all done in suggestion, with a strongly allusive quality, and involving an almost *verbatim* citation of one text by the other. As R. Carroll remarked, the poem in Jeremiah has expanded the enemy from the north trope "so that it has become the figure of a return to chaos".[32] Such a concept also lies behind the P flood story. To fail to see the link here, or to suggest that imagined inconsistencies somehow disprove the connection, strikes me as an instance of ignoring the whole theological thrust of both passages. And my invocation of the

---

30 Above, p. 237; Tsumura 297.
31 Carroll (1986, 168) also detected (later) apocalyptic qualities in the poem in ch. 4. If the poem is later, then Genesis is the primary source, cited by the later poet.
32 Carroll 1986, 168.

Priestly flood story (especially Genesis 7:11),[33] which David seems to find irrelevant here, is part of the same mythological complex of ideas, on which all three sources are drawing, selecting those motifs which fit the immediate context.

Scholarship never stands still, and our debate is in danger of being overtaken by Noga Ayali-Darshan's new paper[34] which offers further discussion on the transmission and recensions of the myth of the storm-god's combat with the sea, including a detailed account of the Hurrian and Egyptian witnesses. However, this too has problematic aspects, such as lumping Psalm 74 (and other psalms) and implicitly Genesis 1 in one camp, orientated toward the Babylonian tradition (her "version B"), over against the West Semitic tradition exemplified by Ugaritic material, and by extension, the Egyptian and Hurro-Hittite material (her "version A"). As I have indicated, Psalm 74 is evidently familiar with the Ugaritic material (or at least a source common to the two recensions) since it shares some of its key vocabulary elements regarding the identity of the Sea. It does *not* share these with the Babylonian version.

Yet another can of worms would open up if we were to grant space for an adequate discussion of what we may call the "Egyptian option", to which my attention has only belatedly been drawn after the completion of all my contributions so far. This is to see the key motifs and thought structures of Genesis 1 as dependent on Egyptian cosmological and theological influences.[35] The arguments for such a view are by no means nonsensical, but since it finally has to boil down to the balance of probabilities, I think that a Mesopotamian and exilic framework offers the better overall explanation of the materials we have discussed, though it would be wrong to deny on principle that Egyptian metaphysics could have at least a catalytic effect on the development of some of the biblical tropes at issue.

David's characterisation of my work at the end of his response offers a *modus vivendi* between us. I have described my interests as being in the field of History of Religions, and consequently look at my sources with a historian's and a comparatist's eye. David sees himself primarily as a linguist. Naturally, he sees the weaknesses in my approach when it leads to an impasse between us, while I cheerfully reciprocate in return. Readers should not be either surprised or dismayed at this. A total consensus between us should probably cause greater surprise. I for one am relaxed about the situation, and see our approaches as broadly complementary, since each of them has much to offer in in-

---

33 Above, pp. 237–8.
34 Ayali-Darshan 2015, especially 48.
35 See in particular Hoffmeier 1983 and Johnston 2008, together with the references they cite.

creasing appreciation of the richness of the texts with which we engage. Perhaps, as with the rabbis, further insights may emerge from our disagreements.

Now, with the arrival of David's third piece, corresponding to this, my final response, I can perhaps sum up from my perspective. I quite understand his reluctance to go along with me in my appeals to word-play and so on. I quite appreciate his call for philological rigour. I think I can defend myself, however, by appealing to what we may call "the pesher mentality", to which I alluded above. This is to use language associations as the ancients did. The associative and evocative use of language discussed on pages 218–21 of my initial paper illustrate this very well. As philology, it is of course all complete nonsense. *But it is how the ancient theologians and mythographers thought.* I appeal to my background, teaching both Indian (Vedic and Hindu) and Egyptian religion in my previous life at Glasgow University. A glance at the *Śatapatha Brāhmaṇa* from India and the *Book of the Dead* from Egypt (together with endless temple-wall ritual inscriptions) gives ample, even tedious, evidence of just the kind of thinking I am trying to describe (as do the DSS *pesharim* and other Qumran documents), which Julius Eggeling (who edited and translated *ŚB* in Sacred Books of the East—five volumes of the stuff!) described as full of "flimsy symbolism".[36] Much of it is entirely trivial. But that is our perspective. I am convinced that my approach is as faithful as it can be to the concerns of ancient writers. In my paper "The Mythic Mind" I cited flags and musical chords (from say a hymn or a national anthem) as triggers to evoke ("conjure up"!) a whole symbolic world closed to the outsider. I submit that he is at least as much outside as I am to these ancient modes of thinking. But we can nevertheless see and appreciate the thought processes in the literature I am citing.

---

36 Eggeling 1882, ix. The phrase is best seen in the full glory of its expansive context:

> For wearisome prolixity of exposition, characterised by dogmatic assertion and a flimsy symbolism rather than by serious reasoning, these works are perhaps not equalled anywhere; unless, indeed, it be by the speculative vapourings of the Gnostics, than which, in the opinion of the learned translators of Irenaeus [A. Roberts and W. A. Rambast], "nothing more absurd has probably ever been imagined by rational beings".

One could readily parody this, or even apply it elsewhere, but it would be unkind. And the phenomenon Eggeling criticises is not far removed from the thought-forms mentioned in my original discussion on pp. 218–21. I remain more sympathetic to this way of thinking than he evidently was.

David Toshio Tsumura
Some Observations on Nicolas Wyatt's Response

I do not intend to respond N. Wyatt's response to my criticism of his paper in detail, but rather present several comments on the overall differences between his approach and mine.

In his response NW categorised me as a reductionist, who demythologises any mytho-poetic literature into simply a metaphor. However, I did not argue for, or even refer to, the practice of *demythologisation* in my paper. What I am interested in is not so much a "myth and history" approach of G. von Rad, G. E. Wright and F. M. Cross (to name a few) as in the use of mythological expressions for literary effects. I did not suggest even possibility of *historicisation* in my arguments.

NW said that my "main problem is the precision, that is, the over-precision, of some of [my] arguments".[1] I, however, am concerned about NW's loose and somewhat too free attitude to linguistic forms, including sound symbolism. NW seems to think that if there is any possibility of echo it is certain. His attitude is quite understandable because as a comparative mythologist he is more interested in the impact and influence of the mythopoetic literatures than exact form of linguistic phenomena. Yet, any study of religion or myth should be based on a sober philological analysis of the religious and mythological texts. Such analysis should include both phonology and phonetic *association*.

One should note that any interpretation of text must begin with words, including the etymology and use in each immediate context, and after that move on to the larger context. Theology, however profound, should be based on an adequate grasp of the texts' meaning. Even for the interpretation of poetic texts, especially of those not in one's native language, one should first apply a rigorous analysis of the phonology and grammar of parallelism, as Jakobson suggested.[2]

As for the matter of word play, ancient authors certainly "play with words, deliberately choose words that are ambiguous, or echo other ideas or words of similar sound or form".[3] But on what basis can a non-native modern scholar identify them? I am more sceptical than NW with regard to the phenomenon

---

1 Above, p. 299.
2 See, for examples, Tsumura 2009, 2017, 2018, 2019, and in press (a), (b).
3 Above, p. 300.

of word play or *paronomasia* in the ancient world since we often have no information of the phonic reality, especially of the prosody, of ancient written documents. Word play needs to be demonstrated, not simply assumed on an "anything goes" basis.

It is hard to see how Gen 1 is a parody of *Enuma Elish*. A parody is an imitation of a work which greatly exaggerates some aspects for humour or ridicule. But *Enuma Elish* centres around the battle between Marduk and Tiamat with her horde of grotesque creatures. Genesis has a passing reference to the deep (*təhôm*) and no mention of battle or even personification. One can certainly think that the author, if he was an exilic Jew, realised the difference between his work and *Enuma Elish*, but the works are just so different in style and especially in content, that it is hard to see how one could have been derived from the other.

I am not convinced either of NW's idea that the author of Gen 1 was "entirely familiar with the western [i.e. Canaanite (*my comment*)] tradition, but adapted to the new, exilic context".[4] A monotheistic author who lived in close proximity to a polytheistic culture would certainly notice how Gen 1 is distinct from the polytheistic and mythological world. The fact that there is no goddess involved in the creation of cosmos in Gen 1 was unique in its cultural and religious background. Specifically, I suspect that any Hebrew native who wanted to refer to an enemy sea would have used the Canaanite (i.e. western Semitic) term *yam*. Yet, in Gen 1:2 the author did not use *yam* but *təhom*, the West Semitic term for subterranean waters. Certainly, if the author was an exilic, the exilic Jews must have kept their native Hebrew language in midst of the Eastern and highly Westernised, i.e. Aramaicised, Semitic world of *Enuma Elish*.

NW says:

> We have to recognise the allusive nature of both texts [Gen 1 and Ps 74]: they evoke a whole nexus of associated motifs. They use a kind of unspoken shorthand. To spell out all the thoughts going through the authors' minds would take them forever. But their choice of vocabulary points the perceptive reader in the right direction with far greater economy.[5]

This well explains Nick's postmodern literary sensitive approach. However, it is not easy for a modern Western person to identify such *unspoken shorthand* in ancient literature, especially considering that what we have are only scraps of linguistic information of the language then used, both written and spoken.

Can we assume that the post-modern scholars' way of playing on words is identical to the ancients' way of playing on words in their native languages?

---

4 Above, p. 319.
5 Above, p. 318.

None of us moderners is a "perceptive reader" of the exilic time. How can a modern person attest an ancient author's "parodying" the other literature? To me, as a Japanese Christian monotheist who lives in a culture affected in every aspect by polytheism (e.g. ancestor worship, solar worship, and animism) and speaks a language filled with idioms based on, or originated in, ancient polytheistic and mythological expressions, NW's postmodern sensitivity toward ancient myths, including of Ugaritic and Hebrew traditions, sounds somewhat unrealistic and superficial.

Reading my review of Walton 2011,[6] NW comments that I am "critical of its attempt to contextualise Genesis 1 in the broader ancient Near Eastern cultural framework".[7] What I am concerned with about Walton's approach is his emphasis on similarities in sacrifice of differences between the ancient Near Eastern cosmologies and Gen 1. Placing the Bible in its ancient Near Eastern context one should not be surprised in finding many similarities, for it was written in one of the ancient Semitic languages. What surprises us is the uniqueness of Genesis' idea of creation, which is totally different, without goddess' involvement, from other creation stories. I would like to quote from Tsumura 2018 the following sentences:

> For the modern Western reader the similarities between the Bible and the ANE religions may be a problem. However, an ancient polytheistic reader would not be struck by the similarities, which he would take for granted. As Wenham declares, "It is the differences that would surprise him: its monotheism (only one God!), God's total sovereignty over the elements, his anger at sin, his rewarding of obedience, and so forth". [8] We can see this from the reactions of later polytheists upon hearing the Genesis creation story for the first time, such as the Japanese Jo Niijima and Kanzo Uchimura at the end of the nineteenth century, when the country was opened up to Western cultural and religious influence.[9]

* * *

One may note that the scholarly debate between NW and me began in 1977, when he responded to my 1974 article, where I identified the god *Mt w Šr* (*KTU* 1.23:8) as another form of the god Death. In his article he rejected my view (which has been well accepted by the majority of scholars[10]) and argued for the identification of the god as El. So our discussion was initiated early in the 1970s and still is continuing with a friendly spirit.

---

6 Tsumura 2015b.
7 Above, p. 234 n. 89.
8 See Wenham's Response to K.L. Sparks' article (2015, 101–9).
9 Tsumura 2018, 237.
10 See Healey 1999, 600.

This debate was a good opportunity for me to learn Nick Wyatt's view more thoroughly than before and to come to know the distinctive features in his scholarly approach, where my view and his remains different, and how our two approaches can help each other. I enjoyed this debate and am grateful to the editors, Rebecca Watson and Adrian Curtis, for inviting me to participate in this productive and exciting project.[11]

---

[11] For further discussion on this subject, see Tsumura 2020, in press (c).

Bibliography

Aaron, David H. 2001. *Biblical Ambiguities: Metaphor, Semantics, and Divine Imagery.* Leiden: Brill.
Albrektson, Bertil. 1967. *History and the Gods.* Lund: Gleerup.
Alter, Robert. 1996. *Genesis: Translation and Commentary.* New York: W. W. Norton.
Arbesman, Samuel. 2012. *The Half-Life of Facts: Why Everything We Know Has an Expiration Date.* New York: Penguin.
Arnaud, Daniel 2007. *Corpus des textes de la bibliothèque de Ras Shamra-Ougarit (1936–2000) en sumérien, babylonien et assyrien.* AuOrS 23. Sabadell: AUSA.
Atran, Scott. 2002. *In Gods We Trust: The Evolutionary Landscape of Religion.* Oxford: OUP.
Averbeck, Richard E. 2004. "Ancient Near Eastern Mythography as it Relates to Historiography in the Hebrew Bible: Genesis 3 and the Cosmic Battle". In T*he Future of Biblical Archaeology: Reassessing Methodologies and Assumptions,* edited by J. Hoffmeier and A. Millard, 328–56. Grand Rapids, MI: Eerdmans.
Averbeck, Richard E. 2013. "The Three 'Daughters' of Ba'al and Transformations of Chaoskampf in the Early Chapters of Genesis". In *Creation and Chaos: A Reconsideration of Hermann Gunkel's Chaoskampf Hypothesis,* edited by JoAnn Scurlock and Richard H. Beal, 237–56. Winona Lake, IN: Eisenbrauns.
Ayali-Darshan, Noga. 2015. "The Other Version of the Story of the Storm-God's Combat with the Sea in the Light of Egyptian, Ugaritic, and Hurro-Hittite Texts". *JANER* 15:20–51.
Baasten, Martin F. J. 2007. "First Things First: The Syntax of Gen 1:1–3 Revisited". In *Studies in Hebrew Literature and Jewish Culture Presented to Albert van der Heide on the Occasion of his Sixty-Fifth Birthday,* edited by M. F. J. Baasten and R. Munk, 169–87. Amsterdam Studies in Jewish Thought 12. Dordrecht: Springer.
Ballentine, Debra Scoggins. 2015. *The Conflict Myth and the Biblical Tradition.* Oxford: OUP.
Barr, James. 1961. *The Semantics of Biblical Language.* London: OUP.
Barr, James. 1982. "Jowett and the 'Original Meaning' of Scripture". *RS* 18: 433–7.
Barrett, Justin L. 2012. "The Naturalness of Religion and the Unnaturalness of Theology". In *Is Religion Natural?,* edited by Dirk Evers, Michael Fuller, Antje Jackelén and Taede A. Smedes, 3–23. Issues in Science and Theology. London: T. & T. Clark International.
Batto, Bernard F. 2013a. *In the Beginning: Essays on Creation Motifs in the Ancient Near East and the Bible.* Siphrut 9. Winona Lake, IN: Eisenbrauns.
Batto, Bernard F. 2013b. "The Combat Myth in Israelite Tradition Revisited". In *Creation and Chaos: A Reconsideration of Hermann Gunkel's Chaoskampf Hypothesis,* edited by JoAnn Scurlock and Richard H. Beal, 217–36. Winona Lake, IN: Eisenbrauns.
Beal, Timothy K. 2002. *Religion and its Monsters.* New York, London: Routledge.
Beauchamp, Paul (1969) 2005. *Création et séparation: Étude exégétique du chapitre premier de la Genèse. Bibliothèque de sciences religieuses.* Paris: Aubier-Montaigne. Reprinted as Lectio Divina 201. Paris: CERF.
Becking, Bob, and Marjo C. A. Korpel. 2010. "To Create, to Separate or to Construct: An Alternative for a Recent Proposal as to the Interpretation of ברא in Gen 1:1–2:4a". *JHebS* 10. https://doi.org/10.5508/jhs.2010.v10.a3.
Beckman, Gary M. 1997. "Mythologie. A. II. Bei den Hethitern". *RlA* 8: 564–72.

Berndt, Catherine H. 1975. Review of *When the Golden Bough Breaks*, by Peter Munz. In *IJCS* 16:311–2.
Blackmore, Susan. 1999. *The Meme Machine*. Oxford: OUP.
Blenkinsopp, Joseph. 2011a. *Creation, Un-Creation, Re-Creation: A Discursive Commentary on Genesis 1–11*. London: T. & T. Clark.
Blenkinsopp, Joseph. 2011b. "The Cosmological and Protological Language of Deutero-Isaiah". *CBQ* 73: 493–510.
Bockmuehl, Markus. 2012. "Creatio ex nihilo in Palestinian Judaism and Early Christianity". *SJT* 65: 253–70.
Bonting, Sjoerd L. 2002. *Chaos Theology: A Revised Creation Theology*. Ottawa: Saint Paul University.
Bonting, Sjoerd L. 2005. *Creation and Double Chaos: Science and Theology in Discussion*. Minneapolis, MN: Fortress.
Boyer, James L. 1962. "Semantics in Biblical Interpretation". *Grace Journal* 3: 25–34.
Boyer, Pascal. 1993. *The Naturalness of Religious Ideas: A Cognitive Theory of Religion*. Berkeley, CA: University of California Press.
Boyer, Pascal. 2001. *Religion Explained: The Evolutionary Origins of Religious Thought*. New York: Basic Books.
Brandon, S. G. F. 1963. *Creation Legends of the Ancient Near East*. London: Hodder and Stoughton.
Bratcher, Robert G., and William D. Reyburn. 1991. *A Translator's Handbook on the Book of Psalms*. UBS Handbook Series. New York: United Bible Societies.
Burkert, Walter. 1992. *The Orientalizing Revolution: Near Eastern Influence on Greek Culture in the Early Archaic Age*. Cambridge, MA: Harvard University Press.
Burrell, David B., Carlo Cogliati, Janet M. Soskice and William R. Stoeger, eds. 2010. *Creation and the God of Abraham*. New York: CUP.
Callot, Olivier. 1986. "La région nord du palais royal d'Ugarit". *CRAI* 130: 735–55.
Callot, Olivier. 1994. *La tranchée "Ville Sud": études d'architecture domestique*. RSO 10. Paris: ERC.
Callot, Olivier. 2011. *Les sanctuaires de l'acropole d'Ougarit: Les temples de Baal et de Dagan*. RSO 19. Lyon: Publications de la Maison de l'Orient et de la Méditerranée.
Carroll, Robert P. 1986. *Jeremiah, a Commentary*. OTL. London: SCM Press.
Cassuto, Umberto. 1961. *A Commentary on the Book of Genesis. Part 1*. Jerusalem: Magnes Press.
Cauvin, Jacques. 1997. *Naissance des Divinités, Naissance de l'Agriculture*. Paris: CNRS éditions.
Charles, J. Daryl, ed. 2013. *Reading Genesis 1–2: An Evangelical Conversation*. Peabody, MA: Hendrikson.
Charlesworth, James H. 1983–5. *The Old Testament Pseudepigrapha*. 2 vols. New York: Doubleday.
Childs, Brevard S. 1959. "The Enemy from the North and the Chaos Tradition". *JBL* 78:187–98.
Cho, Paul K.-K. 2014. "The Sea in the Hebrew Bible: Myth, Metaphor, and Muthos". PhD diss., Harvard University. http://nrs.harvard.edu/urn-3:HUL.InstRepos:12269820.
Churchill, Winston S. 1958. *A History of the English-Speaking Peoples*. Vol. 4. London: Cassell.

Clark, Richard T. 2006. *The Multiple Origins of Religion*. New York: Peter Lang.
Clifford, Richard J. 1994. *Creation Accounts in the Ancient Near East and in the Bible*. CBQMS 26. Washington DC: Catholic Biblical Association of America.
Clifford, Richard J. 2007. Review of *Creation and Destruction: A Reappraisal of the Chaoskampf Theory in the Old Testament*, by David T. Tsumura. In *CBQ* 69: 344–6.
Clifford, Richard J. 2014. Review of *Reading Genesis 1—2: An Evangelical Conversation*, edited by J. Daryl Charles. *TS* 75: 452–3.
Collins, C. John. 2006. *Genesis 1–4, a Linguistic, Literary, and Theological Commentary*. Phillipsburg, NJ: R. & R. Publishing.
Collins, John J. 1998. *The Apocalyptic Imagination: An Introduction to Jewish Apocalyptic Literature*. 2nd edition. Grand Rapids, MI: Eerdmans.
Collon, Dominique. 1987. *First Impressions: Cylinder Seals in the Ancient Near East*. London: British Museum Publications.
Connerton, Paul. 1989. *How Societies Remember*. Cambridge: CUP.
Craigie, Peter C. 1983. *Psalms 1–50*. WBC 19. Waco, TX: Word Books.
Crouch, Carly L. 2009. *War and Ethics in the Ancient Near East: Military Violence in Light of Cosmology and History*. BZAW 407. Berlin: de Gruyter.
Crouch, Carly L. 2011. "Ezekiel's Oracles Against the Nations in Light of a Royal Ideology of Warfare". *JBL* 130: 473–92.
Dahood, Mitchell J. 1972. "Ugaritic-Hebrew Parallel Pairs". In *Ras Shamra Parallels*. Vol. 1, edited by Loren. R. Fisher, 71–382. Rome: Pontifical Biblical Institute.
Dalley, Stephanie. 1991. *Myths from Mesopotamia*. World's Classics. Oxford: OUP.
Dantinne, E. 1961. "Création et Séparation". *Le Muséon* 74: 441–51.
Davies, Philip R. 1995. "Method and Madness: Some Remarks on Doing History with the Bible". *JBL* 114: 699–705.
Davies, Philip R., and Thomas Römer, eds. 2013. *Writing the Bible: Scribes, Scribalism and Script*. Bible World. Durham: Acumen.
Davis, Marjorie Hall, and Karl E. Peters. 2012. "Are Religious Experiences Natural? Biological Capacities for Religion". In *Is Religion Natural?*, edited by Dirk Evers, Michael Fuller, Antje Jackelén and Taede Smedes, 25–34. Edinburgh: T. & T. Clark.
Day, John. 1985. *God's Conflict with the Dragon and the Sea: Echoes of a Canaanite Myth in the Old Testament*. UCOP 35. Cambridge: CUP.
Day, John. 1992. "Dragon and Sea, God's Conflict with". *ABD* 2: 228–31.
Day, John. 1994. "Ugarit and the Bible: Do They Presuppose the Same Canaanite Mythology and Religion?" In *Ugarit and the Bible: Proceedings of the International Symposium on Ugarit and the Bible, Manchester, September 1992*, edited by George J. Brooke, Adrian H. W. Curtis and John F. Healey, 35–52. Münster: Ugarit-Verlag.
Day, John. 2013. *From Creation to Babel: Studies in Genesis 1–11*. LHBOTS 592. London: T. & T. Clark, Bloomsbury.
Deacon, Terrence. 1997. *The Symbolic Species: The Co-evolution of Language and the Human Brain*. London: Allen Lane, The Penguin Press.
Del Olmo Lete, Gregorio and Joaquin Sanmartín. 2003. *A Dictionary of the Ugaritic Language in the Alphabetic Tradition*. Leiden: Brill.
Dietrich, Manfred, and Oswald Loretz. 1999. "Baal, Leviathan und der siebenköpfige Drache Šlyṭ in der Rede des Todesgottes Môt (KTU 1.5 i 1–8 // 27a–31). *AuOr* 17: 55–80.

Durand, Jean-Marie. 1993. "Le mythologème du combat entre le dieu de l'orage et la mer en Mésopotamie", *MARI* 7: 41–61.
Edzard, Dietz-Otto. 1993. "Meer. A". In *RlA* 8: 1–3.
Eggeling, Julius. 1882. *The Śatapatha Brāhmaṇa According to the Text of the Mādhyandina School*. Part 1, Books I and II. SBE 12. Oxford: Clarendon.
Enns, Peter. 2012. *The Evolution of Adam: What the Bible Does and Doesn't Say About Human Origins*. Grand Rapids, MI: Brazos Press.
Fishbane, Michael. 1971. "Jeremiah IV 23–6 and Job III 13: A Recovered Use of the Creation Pattern". *VT* 21: 151–67.
Fishbane, Michael. 1979. *Text and Texture: Close Readings of Selected Biblical Texts*. New York: Schocken.
Fisher, Loren R. 1963. "The Temple Quarter". *JSS* 8: 34–41.
Fisher, Loren R. 1965. "Creation at Ugarit and in the Old Testament". *VT* 15: 313–24.
Fisher, Loren R. 2011. *Genesis, a Royal Epic: Introduction, Translation, and Notes*. 2nd edition. Eugene, OR: Cascade.
Flynn, Shawn W. 2014. *YHWH is King: The Development of Divine Kingship in Ancient Israel*. VTSup 159. Leiden: Brill.
Forsyth, Neil. 1987. *The Old Enemy: Satan and the Combat Myth*. Princeton NJ: Princeton University Press.
Foster, Benjamin R. 1997. "The Epic of Creation (Enūma Elish)". In *The Context of Scripture*, edited by W. W. Hallo. Vol 1: 390–402. Leiden: Brill.
Frankfort, Henri. (1954) 1970. *The Art and Architecture of the Ancient Orient*. Pelican History of Art. Middlesex: Penguin Books.
Frankfort, Henri, Henriette Antonia Frankfort, John A. Wilson, Thorkeld Jacobsen and William A. Irwin. 1946. *The Intellectual Adventure of Ancient Man: An Essay on Speculative Thought in the Ancient Near East*. Chicago: University of Chicago Press. Cambridge: CUP. Republished in part as Before Philosophy. Harmondsworth: Penguin, 1949.
Garr, W. Randall. 2003. *In His Own Image and Likeness: Humanity, Divinity, and Monotheism*. CHANE 15. Leiden: Brill.
Garr, W. Randall. 2004. "God's creation: ברא in The Priestly Source". *HTR* 97: 83–91.
George, Andrew R. 2003. *The Babylonian Gilgamesh Epic. Introduction, Critical Edition and Cuneiform Texts*. 2 vols. Oxford: OUP.
George, Andrew R. 2007. "The Gilgameš Epic at Ugarit". *AuOr* 25: 237–54.
Gibson, Arthur. 1981. *Biblical Semantic Logic: A Preliminary Analysis*. Oxford: Basil Blackwell.
Giere, Samuel D. 2009. *A New Glimpse of Day One: Intertextuality, History of Interpretation, and Genesis 1:1–5*. Berlin: Walter de Gruyter.
Goren, Yuval, Hans Mommsen, Israel Finkelstein and Nadav Na'aman. 2009. "A Provenance Study of the Gilgamesh Fragment from Megiddo". *Archaeometry* 51: 763–73.
Grayson, Albert K. 1969. "The Creation Epic". In *Ancient Near Eastern Texts Relating to the Old Testament*, edited by J. B. Pritchard, 501–3. 3rd edition. Princeton, NJ: Princeton University Press.
Green, Douglas J. 2010. *"I Undertook Great Works": The Ideology of Domestic Achievements in West Semitic Royal Inscriptions*. FAT 2/41. Tübingen: Mohr Siebeck.
Greenfield, Jonas C. 1994. "ʾattā pōrartā bĕʿozkā yam (Psalm 74:13a)". In *Language, Theology, and the Bible: Essays in Honour of James Barr*, edited by Samuel E. Balentine and John Barton, 113–9. Oxford: Clarendon Press.

Grossfeld, Bernard, trans. 1988. *The Targum Onqelos to Genesis*. The Aramaic Bible 6. Edinburgh: T. & T. Clark.
Gunkel, Hermann. (1910) 1997. *Genesis*. Translated by W.H. Carruth. Mercer Library of Biblical Studies. Macon, GA: Mercer University Press.
Gunkel, Hermann. 2006. *Creation and Chaos in the Primeval Era and the Eschaton. A Religio-Historical Study of Genesis 1 and Revelation 12*. Translated by K. W. Whitney Jr. Grand Rapids, MI: Eerdmans. Originally published *as Schöpfung und Chaos. Eine religionsgeschichtliche Untersuchung über Gen 1 und Ap Joh 12* (Göttingen: Vandenhoek und Ruprecht, [1895] 1921).
Guthrie, Stewart E. 1993. *Faces in the Clouds: A New Theory of Religion*. Oxford: OUP.
Habel, Norman C. 1972. "He who Stretches out the Heavens". *CBQ* 34: 417–30.
Hasel, Gerhard F. 1974. "The Polemic Nature of the Genesis Cosmology". *EQ* 46: 81–102.
Headland, Thomas. N., Kenneth L. Pike and Marvin Harris. 1990. *Emics and Etics: The Insider/Outsider Debate*. Frontiers of Anthropology 7. Newbury Park, London: Sage.
Healey, John F. 1999. "MOT מות". In *DDD*, 598–603.
Heidel, Alexander. 1963. *The Babylonian Genesis*. 2nd edition. Chicago, IL: Chicago University Press.
Heltne, P. G. 2014. Review of *The Faith of Biology and the Biology of Faith: Order, Meaning, and Free Will in Modern Medical Science*, by Robert Pollack. In *Zygon* 49: 264–5.
Hendel, Ronald S. 1995. "The Shape of Utnapishtim's Ark". *ZAW* 107: 128–9.
Hoffmeier, James. 1983. "Some Thoughts on Genesis 1 and 2 and Egyptian Cosmology". *JANES* 15: 39–49.
Hoffmeyer, Jesper. 1996. *Signs of Meaning in the Universe*. Translated by Barbara J. Haveland. Bloomington, IN: Indiana University Press.
Holloway, Stephen W. 1991. "What Ship Goes There: The Flood Narratives in the Gilgamesh Epic and Genesis Considered in Light of Ancient Near Eastern Temple Ideology". *ZAW* 103: 328–55.
Holloway, Stephen W. 1998. "The Shape of Utnapishtim's Ark: A Rejoinder". *ZAW* 110: 617–26.
Holmstedt, Robert D. 2008. "The Restrictive Syntax of Genesis i 1". *VT* 58: 56–67.
Horowitz, Wayne. 1998. *Mesopotamian Cosmic Geography*. Mesopotamian Civilizations 8. Winona Lake, IN: Eisenbrauns.
Horowitz, Wayne, Takayoshi Oshima and Seth Sanders. 2006. *Cuneiform in Canaan: Cuneiform Sources from the Land of Israel in Ancient Times*. Jerusalem: Israel Exploration Society, Hebrew University of Jerusalem.
Hossfeld, Frank-Lothar, and Erich Zenger. 2005. *Psalms 2: A Commentary on Psalms 51–100*. Hermeneia. Minneapolis, MN: Fortress Press.
Huehnergard, J. 1987/2008. *Ugaritic Vocabulary in Syllabic Transcription*. Harvard Semitic Studies 32. Atlanta, GA: Scholars Press.
Hutter, Manfred. 1985. "*ammatu*: Unterwelt in Enuma Eliš I 2". *RA* 79: 187–8.
Irwin, William A. 1946. "The Hebrews." In *The Intellectual Adventure of Ancient Man*, chap. 8–11, edited by Henri Frankfort and Henriette Antonia Frankfort. Chicago, IL: Chicago University Press. Baltimore, MD: Penguin.
Jacob, Benno. 1934. *Das erste Buch der Tora: Genesis*. Berlin: Schocken.
Jacobsen, Thorkild. 1968. The Battle between Marduk and Tiamat. *JAOS* 88: 104–8.

Jacobsen, Thorkild. 1976. *The Treasures of Darkness. A History of Mesopotamian Religion.* New Haven, CT. London: Yale University Press.

Jaynes, Julian. (1976) 1982. *The Origin of Consciousness in the Breakdown of the Bicameral Mind.* Boston: Houghton Mifflin.

Johnston, Gordon H. 2008. "Genesis 1 and Ancient Egyptian Creation Myths". *BS* 165: 178–94.

Jones, Scott. C. 2011. "Lions, Serpents, and Lion-serpents in Job 28:8 and Beyond". *JBL* 130: 663–86.

Jowett, Benjamin. 1860. "On the Interpretation of Holy Scripture". In *Essays and Reviews*, edited by John W. Parker, 330–433. London: John W. Parker. https://archive.org/stream/a578549600unknuoft#page/n9/mode/2up

Kämmerer, Thomas. R., and Kai. A. Metzler. 2012. *Das babylonische Weltschöpfungsepos Enūma elîš.* AOAT 375. Münster: Ugarit-Verlag.

Kaplan, Aryeh. 1979. *The Bahir. An Ancient Kabbalistic Text Attributed to Rabbi Nehunia ben haKana, First Century C.E.* New York: Weiser.

Kazmi, Yedullah. 2000. "Historical Consciousness and the Notion of the Authentic Self in the Qur'ān: Towards an Islamic Critical Theory". *Islamic Studies* 39: 375–98.

Keller, Catherine. 2003. *The Face of the Deep: A Theology of Becoming.* London: Routledge.

Kerr, Robert M. 2013. "Once upon a time … Gn 1:1 Reconsidered: Some Remarks on an Incipit problem". In *"Schrift und Sprache": Papers Read at the 10th Mainz International Colloquium on Ancient Hebrew (MICAH), Mainz 28–30 October 2011*, edited by Reinhard G. Lehmann and Anna Elise Zernecke, 33–47. KUSATU 15. Kamen: Hartmut Spenner.

Kister, Menahem. 2007. "*Tohu wa-Bohu*, Primordial Elements and *Creatio ex Nihilo*". *JSQ* 14: 229–56.

Klingbeil, Martin G. 1999. *Yahweh Fighting from Heaven: God as Warrior and as God of Heaven in the Hebrew Psalter and Ancient Near Eastern Iconography.* OBO 169. Freiburg: Universitätsverlag. Göttingen: Vandenhoeck and Ruprecht.

Kloos, Carola. 1986. *Yhwh's Combat with the Sea: A Canaanite Tradition in the Religion of Ancient Israel.* Amsterdam: van Oorschot. Leiden: Brill.

Knudsen, Ebbe Egede. 1981. *A Targum Aramaic Reader.* SSS NS 5; Leiden: Brill.

Kooten, Geurt Hendrik van. 2005. *The Creation of Heaven and Earth: Re-interpretations of Genesis 1 in the Context of Judaism, Ancient Philosophy, Christianity, and Modern Physics.* TBN 8. Leiden: Brill.

Korpel, Marjo C. A., and Johannes C. de Moor. 2014. *Adam, Eve, and the Devil: A New Beginning.* HBM 65. Sheffield: Phoenix.

Kraus, Hans-Joachim. 1978. *Psalmen.* BKAT 15/2. Neukirchen-Vluyn: Neukirchener.

Lambert, Wilfred. G. 2013a. *Babylonian Creation Myths.* Mesopotamian Civilizations 16. Winona Lake, IN: Eisenbrauns.

Lambert, Wilfred G. 2013b. "Creation in the Bible and the Ancient Near East". In *Creation and Chaos: A Reconsideration of Herman Gunkel's Chaoskampf Hypothesis*, edited by Joann Scurlock and Richard H. Beal, 44–7. Winona Lake, IN: Eisenbrauns.

Lambert, Wilfred G., and Alan R. Millard. 1969. *Atra Hasīs: The Babylonian Story of the Flood.* Oxford: Clarendon.

Lee, Stephen 1993. "Power not Novelty: The Connotations of ברא in the Hebrew Bible". In *Understanding Poets and Prophets: Essays in Honour of George Wishart Anderson*, edited by A. Graeme Auld, 199–212. JSOTS 152. Sheffield: Sheffield Academic Press.

Leeuwen, Raymond C. van. 2010. "Cosmos, Temple, House: Building and Wisdom in Ancient Mesopotamia and Israel". In *From the Foundations to the Crenellations: Essays on Temple Building in the Ancient Near East and Hebrew Bible*, edited by Mark J. Boda and Jamie Novotny, 399–421. AOAT 366. Münster: Ugarit-Verlag.
Lewis, Theodore J. 1989. *Cults of the Dead in Ancient Israel and Ugarit*. HSM 39. Atlanta, GA: Scholars Press.
Lewis, Theodore J. 1996. "CT 13.33–4 and Ezekiel 32: Lion-Dragon Myths". *JAOS* 116: 28–47.
Lewis-Williams, David. 2002. *The Mind in the Cave: Consciousness and the Origins of Art*. London: Thames and Hudson.
Lewis-Williams, David. 2010. *Conceiving God: The Cognitive Origin and Evolution of Religion*. London: Thames and Hudson.
Lewis-Williams, David, and David Pearce. 2005. *Inside the Neolithic Mind: Consciousness, Cosmos and the Realm of the Gods*. London: Thames and Hudson.
Lindberger, James M. 1983. *The Aramaic Proverbs of Aḥiqar*. Johns Hopkins Near Eastern Studies. Baltimore, MD: Johns Hopkins University Press.
Lindström, Fredrik. 1983. *God and the Origin of Evil: A Contextual Analysis of Alleged Monistic Evidence in the Old Testament*. Lund: Gleerup.
López-Ruiz, Carolina. 2010. *When the Gods were Born: Greek Cosmogonies and the Near East*. Cambridge, MA: Harvard University Press.
López-Ruiz, Carolina. 2012. "How to Start a Cosmogony: On the Poetics of Beginnings in Greece and the Near East". *JANER* 12: 30–48.
Loretz, Oswald. 1984. *Psalm 29: Kanaanäische El- und Baaltraditionen in jüdischer Sicht*. UBL 2: 49–51. Soest: CIS.
Loretz, Oswald. 1987. "KTU 1.101:1–3a und 1.2 IV 10 als Parallelen zu Ps 29,10". *ZAW* 99: 415–21.
Lowery, Daniel deWitt. 2013. *Toward a Poetics of Genesis 1–11: Reading Genesis 4:17–22 in its Near Eastern Context*. BBRSup 7. Winona Lake, IN: Eisenbrauns.
Luckenbill, Daniel D. 1926–7. *Ancient Records of Assyria and Babylonia*, 2 vols. Chicago: Chicago University Press.
Maher, Michael. 1992. *Targum Pseudo-Jonathan: Genesis*. The Aramaic Bible 1b. Edinburgh: T. & T. Clark.
Malamat, Abraham. 1988. "The Amorite Background of Psalm 29". *ZAW* 100: 156–60.
May, Gerhard. 1994. *Creatio ex Nihilo: The Doctrine of 'Creation out of Nothing' in Early Christian Thought*. Edinburgh: T. & T. Clark.
Mazar, Eilat, Takayoshi Oshima, Wayne Horowitz and Yuval Goren. 2010. "A Cuneiform Tablet from the Ophel in Jerusalem". *IEJ* 60: 4–21.
McCauley, Robert N., and Emma Cohen. 2010. "Cognitive Science and the Naturalness of Religion". *Philosophy Compass* 5/9: 779–92. https://doi.org/10.1111/j.1747-9991.2010.00326.x.
McCutcheon, Russell T. 1999. *Insider/Outsider Problem in the Study of Religion: A Reader*. Controversies in the Study of Religion. London: Cassell.
McKenzie, John L. 1950. "A Note on Psalm 73(74):13–5". *TS* 2: 281–2.
McNamara, Martin. 1992. *Targum Neofiti I: Genesis*. The Aramaic Bible 1a. Edinburgh: T. & T. Clark.
Mills, Donald H. 2002. *The Hero and the Sea: Patterns of Chaos in Ancient Myth*. Waucunda, IL: Bolchazy-Carducci.

Mithen, Stephen. 1996. *The Prehistory of the Mind: A Search for the Origins of Art, Religion and Science*. London: Thames and Hudson.
Mowinckel, Sigmund. 1962. *The Psalms in Israel's Worship*. Vol. 1. New York: Abingdon Press.
Munz Peter. 1973. *When the Golden Bough Breaks*. London: Routledge and Kegan Paul.
Murray, Robert. 1992. *The Cosmic Covenant*. Heythrop Monographs. London: Sheed and Ward.
Neve, Lloyd. 1975. "The Common Use of Traditions by the Author of Psalm 46 and Isaiah". *ExpTim* 86/8: 243–6.
Neville, Richard 2011. "Differentiation in Genesis 1: An Exegetical Creation *ex nihilo*". *JBL* 130: 209–26.
Newberg, Andrew B., Eugene G. D'Aquili and Vince Rause. 2002. *Why God Won't Go Away: Brain Science and the Biology of Belief*. New York: Ballantine.
Niditch, Susan. 1985. *Chaos to Cosmos: Studies in Biblical Patterns of Creation*. Atlanta, GA: Scholars Press.
Niditch, Susan. 1996. *Oral World and Written Word: Ancient Israelite Literature*. Library of Ancient Israel. Louisville, KY: Westminster John Knox Press.
Nilson, Tina D. 2013. "Creation in Collision? Isaiah 40–8 and Zoroastrianism, Babylonian Religion and Genesis 1". *JHebS* 13. https://doi.org/10.5508/jhs.2013.v13.a8.
Noegel, Scott B. 1998. "The Aegean Ogygos of Boeotia and the Biblical Og of Bashan: Reflections of the Same Myth". *ZAW* 110: 411–26.
Noegel, Scott B. 2014. "Kirtu's Allusive Dream". *AuOr* 32: 299–316.
Noegel, Scott B. 2017. "God of Heaven and She'ol: The 'Unearthing' of Creation". *HS* 58: 119–44.
Noort, E. 2005. "The Creation of Light in Genesis 1:1–5: Remarks on the Function of Light and Darkness in the Opening Verses of the Hebrew Bible, 3–20". In *The Creation of Heaven and Earth: Re-interpretations of Genesis 1 in the Context of Judaism, Ancient Philosophy, Christianity, and Modern Physics*, edited by Geurt Hendrik van Kooten. 2005. TBN 8. Leiden: Brill.
Olmo Lete, Gregorio del. 1992. "The Divine Panoply (KTU 1.65: 12–4)". *AuOr* 10: 254–6.
Olmo Lete, Gregorio del, and Joaquin Sanmartín. 2003. *A Dictionary of the Ugaritic Language in the Alphabetic Tradition*. Leiden: Brill.
O'Neill, John C. 2002. "How Early is the Christian Doctrine of *Creatio ex Nihilo*?" *JTS* 53: 449–65.
Orel, Vladimir E., and Olga V. Stolbova. 1994. *Hamito-Semitic Etymological Dictionary: Materials for a Reconstruction*. Leiden: Brill.
Ortlund, Eric Nels. 2010. *Theophany and Chaoskampf: The Interpretation of Theophanic Imagery in the Baal Epic, Isaiah, and the Twelve*. GUS 5. Piscataway, NJ: Gorgias Press.
Osborne, Grant R. 1991. *The Hermeneutical Spiral: A Comprehensive Introduction to Biblical Interpretation*. Downers Grove, IL: Inter-Varsity Press.
Otzen, Benedikt. 1980. "The Use of Myth in Genesis". In *Myths in the Old Testament*, edited by Benedikt Otzen, Hans Gottlieb and Knud Jeppesen, 22–61. London: SCM.
Otzen, Benedikt, Hans Gottlieb and Knud Jeppesen, eds. 1980. *Myths in the Old Testament*. London: SCM. Translated by Frederick Cryer from *Myter i det gamle Testamente*. Copenhagen: Gad, 1976.

Pardee, Dennis. 1988. *Les Textes Paramythologiques de la 24ᵉ Campagne (1961)*. RSO 4, Paris: ERC.
Pardee, Dennis. 1997. "West Semitic Canonical Compositions". In *The Context of Scripture*. Volume 1 *Canonical Compositions of the Biblical World*, edited by W. W. Hallo, 239–375. Leiden: Brill.
Pardee, Dennis. 2012. *The Ugaritic Texts and the Origins of West-Semitic Literary Composition*. Schweich Lectures on Biblical Archaeology 2007. London: OUP.
Pearce, Laurie, and E. Cornelia Wunsch. 2014. *Documents of Judean Exiles and West Semites in Babylonia in the Collection of David Sofer*. Cornell University Studies in Assyriology and Sumerology 28. Bethesda ML: CDL.
Penglase, Charles. 1994. *Greek Myths and Mesopotamia: Parallels and Influence in the Homeric Hymns and Hesiod*. London: Routledge.
Peters, Kurtis. 2014. "What's Cooking in Biblical Hebrew? A Study in the Semantics of Daily Life". PhD diss., University of Edinburgh.
Peterson, Jordan B. 1999. *Maps of Meaning: The Architecture of Belief*. London, New York: Routledge.
Pitard, Wayne. T. 2002. "Voices from the Dust: The Tablets from Ugarit and the Bible". In *Mesopotamia and the Bible: Comparative Explorations*, edited by Mark W. Chavalas and K. Lawson Younger, Jr., 262–3. JSOTSup 341. Sheffield: Sheffield Academic Press.
Polak, Frank. H. 2002. "Poetic Style and Parallelism in the Creation Account (Genesis 1.1–2.3)". In *Creation in Jewish and Christian Tradition*, edited by Henning Graf Reventlow and Yair Hoffmann, 2–31. JSOTS 319. Sheffield: Sheffield Academic Press.
Pollack, Robert. 2000. *The Faith of Biology and the Biology of Faith: Order, Meaning, and Free Will in Modern Medical Science*. New York: Columbia University Press.
Pollock, Sheldon. 1989. "Mimamsa and the Problem of History in Traditional India". *JAOS* 109: 603–10.
Pope, Marvin H. 1973. *Job: A New Translation with Introduction and Commentary*. 3rd edition. AB 15. New York: Doubleday.
Provan, Iain W. 1995. "Ideologies, Literary and Critical: Reflections on Recent Writing on the History of Israel". *JBL* 114: 585–606.
Pyysiäinen, Ilkka. 2003. *How Religion Works: Toward a New Cognitive Science of Religion*. Boston, MA: Brill.
Rad, Gerhard von. 1961. *Genesis*. Translated by John H. Marks. Philadelphia, PA: Westminster Press.
Rad, Gerhard von. 1962–5. *Old Testament Theology*. 2 vols. Edinburgh: Oliver and Boyd.
Rad, Gerhard von. 1963. *Genesis*. 2nd edition. OTL. London: SCM.
Robinson, Andrew, and Christopher Southgate. 2010. "God and the World of Signs: Semiotics and the Emergence of Life". *Zygon* 45: 339–44; 685–8.
Roche-Hawley, Carole. 2016. "La reconstruction du temple de Baʻlu à Ougarit au XIIIe siècle av. J.-C.: entre mythe et réalité". In *Espaces sacrés dans la méditerranée antique*, edited by Yves Lafond and Vincent Michel, 83–93. Rennes: Presses universitaires de Rennes.
Rollston, Christopher A. 2006. "Scribal Education in Ancient Israel: The Old Hebrew Epigraphic Evidence". *BASOR* 344: 47–74.
Rollston, Christopher A. 2010. *Writing and Literacy in the World of Ancient Israel: Epigraphic Evidence from the Iron Age*. Atlanta, GA: SBL.

Ruiten, Jacques T. A. G. M. van. 2005. "Back to Chaos: The Relationship between Jeremiah 4: 23–6 and Genesis 1: 21–30". In *The Creation of Heaven and Earth: Re-interpretations of Genesis 1 in the Context of Judaism, Ancient Philosophy, Christianity, and Modern Physics*, edited by Geurt Hendrik van Kooten. TBN 8. Leiden: Brill.

Scurlock, JoAnn. 2013. "Searching for Meaning in Genesis 1:2: Purposeful Creation out of Chaos without Kampf". In *Creation and Chaos: A Reconsideration of Herman Gunkel's Chaoskampf Hypothesis*, edited by JoAnn Scurlock and Richard H. Beal, 52–61. Winona Lake, IN: Eisenbrauns.

Scurlock, JoAnn, and Richard H. Beal, eds. 2013. *Creation and Chaos: A Reconsideration of Herman Gunkel's Chaoskampf Hypothesis*. Winona Lake, IN: Eisenbrauns.

Simkins, Ronald A. 2011. "Biblical Studies as a Secular Discipline: The Role of Faith and Theology". *JRS* 13: 1–17.

Sjöberg, Åke. 1973. "Miscellaneous Sumerian Hymns". *ZA* 63: 1–13.

Skinner, John. 1910. *Genesis*. ICC. Edinburgh: T. & T. Clark.

Smith, Mark S. 1994. *The Ugaritic Baal Cycle*. Volume 1, *Introduction with Text, Translation and Commentary of KTU 1.1–1.2*. VTSup 55. Leiden: Brill.

Smith, Mark S. 2001. *The Origins of Biblical Monotheism: Israel's Polytheistic Background and the Ugaritic Texts*. Oxford: OUP.

Smith, Mark S. 2010. *The Priestly Vision of Genesis 1*. Minneapolis, MN: Fortress.

Smith, Mark S. and Wayne T. Pitard. 2009. *The Ugaritic Baal Cycle*. Volume 2, *Introduction with Text, Translation and Commentary of KTU/CAT 1.3–1.4*. VTSup 114. Leiden, Boston: Brill.

Smith, Morton, trans. 2013. *Hekhalot Rabbati: The Greater Treatise Concerning the Palaces of Heaven*, corrected by Gershom Scholem, edited by Don Karr. http://www.digital-brilliance.com/kab/karr/HekRab/HekRab.pdf

Soldt, Wilfred H. van. 2013. "The Extent of Literacy in Syria and Palestine During the Second Millennium BCE". In *Time and History in the Ancient Near East. Proceedings of the 56th Rencontre Assyriologique Internationale at Barcelona, 26–30 July 2010*, edited by Lluis Feliu, J. Llop, A. Millet Albà and Joaquin Sanmartín, 19–31. Winona Lake, IN: Eisenbrauns.

Sonik, Karen. 2013. "Chaos and Cosmos in the Babylonian 'Epic of Creation'". In *Creation and Chaos: A Reconsideration of Herman Gunkel's Chaoskampf Hypothesis*, edited by JoAnn Scurlock and Richard H. Beal, 1–25. Winona Lake, IN: Eisenbrauns.

Sparks, Kenton L. 2007. "*Enūma Elish* and Priestly Mimesis: Elite Emulation in Nascent Judaism". *JBL* 126:625–48.

Speiser, Ephraim A. 1964. *Genesis*. AB 1. New York: Doubleday.

Speiser, Ephraim A. 1969. "The Creation Epic". In *Ancient Near Eastern Texts Relating to the Old Testament*, edited by J. B. Pritchard, 60–72. 3rd edition. Princeton, NJ: Princeton University Press.

Spronk, Klaas 1999. "RAHAB רהב". In *DDD*, 684–6.

Strine, Casey A., and Carly. L. Crouch. 2013. "Yhwh's Battle against Chaos in Ezekiel: the Transformation of Judahite Mythology for a New Situation". *JBL* 132: 883–903.

Stuhlmueller, Carroll. 1970. *Creative Redemption in Deutero-Isaiah*. Rome: Pontifical Biblical Institute.

Tate, Marvin E. 2002. *Psalms 51–100*. WBC 20. Dallas: Word.

Teske, John A. 2006. "Neuromythology: Brains and Stories". *Zygon* 41: 169–96.

Teske, John A. 2010. "Narrative and Meaning in Science and Religion". *Zygon* 45: 91–104.
Thompson, Thomas L. 1995. "Neo-Albrightean School in History and Biblical Scholarship?" *JBL* 114: 683–98.
Tsumura, David T. 1974. "A Ugaritic God, *Mt w Šr*, and his Two Weapons (UT 52:8–11)". *UF* 6:407–13.
Tsumura, David T. 1983a. "Janus Parallelism in Nah 1:8". *JBL* 102: 109–11.
Tsumura, David T. 1983b. "Literary Insertion (AXB Pattern) in Biblical Hebrew". *VT* 33: 468–82.
Tsumura, David T. 1988. "A 'Hyponymous' Word Pair, *'rṣ* and *thm(t)*, in Hebrew and Ugaritic". *Bib* 69: 258–69.
Tsumura, David T. 1989. *The Earth and the Waters in Genesis 1 and 2: A Linguistic Investigation*. JSOTSup 83. Sheffield: Sheffield Academic Press.
Tsumura, David T. 1994a. "Genesis and Ancient Near Eastern Stories of Creation and Flood: an Introduction". In *I Studied Inscriptions from before the Flood: Ancient Near Eastern, Literary, and Linguistic Approaches to Genesis 1–11*, edited by Richard S. Hess and David T. Tsumura, 58–72. SBTS 4. Winona Lake, IN: Eisenbrauns.
Tsumura, David T. 1994b. "The Earth in Genesis 1". In *I Studied Inscriptions from before the Flood: Ancient Near Eastern, Literary, and Linguistic Approaches to Genesis 1–11*, edited by Richard S. Hess and David T. Tsumura, 310–28. SBTS 4. Winona Lake, IN: Eisenbrauns.
Tsumura, David T. 1996a. "The 'Word Pair', *qšt and *mṭ, in Habakkuk 3:9 in the Light of Ugaritic and Akkadian". *In Go to the Land I Will Show You: Studies in Honor of Dwight W. Young*, edited by Joseph Coleson and Victor Mathews, 357–65. Winona Lake, IN: Eisenbrauns.
Tsumura, David T. 1996b. "Coordination Interrupted, or Literary Insertion AX&B Pattern, in the Books of Samuel". In *Literary Structure and Rhetorical Strategies in the Hebrew Bible*, edited by L. J. de Regt, Jan de Waard and J. P. Fokkelman, 117–32. Assen: Van Gorcum.
Tsumura, David T. 1997. "Vowel *sandhi* in Biblical Hebrew". *ZAW* 109: 575–88.
Tsumura, David T. 1998. "'The Breath of God' (Gen 1:2c) in Creation". *Exegetica* 9: 21–30. (In Japanese with an English summary).
Tsumura, David T. 1999. "Scribal Errors or Phonetic Spellings? Samuel as an Aural Text". *VT* 49: 390–411.
Tsumura, David T. 2004. "Janus Parallelism in Hab. III 4". *VT* 54: 124–8. Reprinted in *VT IOSOT* 2013: 113–6.
Tsumura, David T. 2005a. *Creation and Destruction: A Reappraisal of the Chaoskampf Theory in the Old Testament*. Winona Lake, IN: Eisenbrauns.
Tsumura, David T. 2005b. "'Misspellings' in Cuneiform Alphabetic Texts from Ugarit: Some Cases of Loss or Addition of Signs". In *Writing and Ancient Near Eastern Society: Papers in Honour of Alan R. Millard*, edited by Piotr Bienkowski, Christopher Mee and Elilzabeth Slater, 143–53. LHBOTS 426. London: T. & T. Clark International.
Tsumura, David T. 2007a. "The 'Chaoskampf' Motif in Ugaritic and Hebrew Literatures". In *Le Royaume d'Ougarit de la Crète à l'Euphrate: Nouveaux axes de Recherche*, edited by J.-M. Michaud, 473–99. Proche-Orient et Littérature Ougaritique 2. Sherbrooke: GGC.
Tsumura, David T. 2007b. *The First Book of Samuel*. NICOT. Grand Rapids, MI: Eerdmans.
Tsumura, David T. 2008. "Polysemy and Parallelism in Hab 1,8–9". *ZAW* 120: 194–203.

Tsumura, David T. 2009. "Vertical Grammar of Parallelism in Hebrew Poetry". *JBL* 128: 167–81.

Tsumura, David T. 2010. "Tense and Aspect of Hebrew Verbs in 2 Samuel 7:8–16 from the Point of View of Discourse Grammar". *VT* 60: 641–54.

Tsumura, David T. 2012. "The Doctrine of Creation *ex nihilo* and the Translation of *tōhû wābōhû*". In *Pentateuchal Traditions in the Late Second Temple Period: Proceedings of the International Workshop in Tokyo, August 28–31, 2007*, edited by Akio Moriya and Gohei Hata, 3–21. JSJSup 158. Leiden: Brill.

Tsumura, David T. 2014. "Textual Corruptions, or Linguistic Phenomena? The Cases in 2 Samuel (MT)". *VT* 64: 135–45.

Tsumura, David T. 2015a. "The Creation Motif in Psalm 74:12–4? A Reappraisal of the Theory of the Dragon Myth". *JBL* 134: 547–55.

Tsumura, David T. 2015b. Review of *Genesis 1 as Ancient Cosmology*, by John H. Walton. In *JAOS* 135: 356–7.

Tsumura, David T. 2016. "Temporal Consistency and Narrative Cohesion in 2 Sam. 7:8–11". In *The Books of Samuel: Stories—History—Reception History*, edited by Walter Dietrich, Cynthia Edenburg and Philippe Hugo, 385–92. BETL 284. Leuven: Peeters.

Tsumura, David T. 2017. "Verticality in Biblical Hebrew Parallelism". In *Advances in Biblical Hebrew Linguistics: Data, Methods, and Analyses*, edited by Adina Moshavi and Tania Notarius, 189–206. Winona Lake, IN: Eisenbrauns.

Tsumura, David T. 2018. "Rediscovery of the Ancient Near East and Its Implications for Genesis 1–2". In *Since the Beginning: Interpreting Genesis 1 and 2 Through the Ages*, edited by Kyle R. Greenwood, 215–38. Grand Rapids, MI: Baker Academic.

Tsumura, David T. 2019. "Vertical Grammar of Biblical Hebrew Parallelism: The AXX'B Pattern in Tetracolons". *VT* 69/3: 447–59.

Tsumura, David T. 2020. "The *Chaoskampf* Myth in the Biblical Tradition". *JAOS* 140: 963–9.

Tsumura, David T. In press (a). "Metaphor, Grammar and Parallelism in the Song of Songs 5: A Linguistic-Based Analysis of the Interdependence Between Metaphor and Parallelism". In *Poetic Approaches to the Song of Songs*, edited by Kevin Chau and Sarah Zhang. Winona Lake, IN: Eisenbrauns.

Tsumura, David T. In press (b). "Vertical Grammar of Parallelism in Ugaritic Poetry". In *"Like 'Ilu Are You Wise": Studies in Northwest Semitic Languages and Literatures in Honor of Dennis G. Pardee*, edited by H. H. Hardy, Joseph Lam and Eric D. Reymond. Chicago: Oriental Institute Press.

Tsumura, David T. In press (c). "Creation out of Conflict? The *Chaoskampf* motif in the Old Testament—Cosmic dualism or *creatio ex nihilo*—" *Congress Volume, 2019*. SVT. Leiden: Brill, forthcoming.

Tugendhaft, Aaron. 2012a. "Politics and Time in the Baal Cycle". *JANER* 12: 145–57.

Tugendhaft, Aaron. 2012b. "Unsettling Sovereignty: Politics and Poetics in the Baal Cycle". *JAOS* 132: 367–84.

Tur-Sinai, Naphtali H. 1967. *The Book of Job: A New Commentary*. Jerusalem: Kiryath Sepher.

Unger, Eckhard 1938. "Drachen und Drachenkampf". *RlA* 2: 231–5.

Vail, Eric M. 2012. *Creation and Chaos Talk: Charting a Way Forward*. Princeton Theological Monograph Series 185. Eugene, OR: Pickwick.

Vail, Eric M. 2015. "Creation out of Nothing Remodeled". In *Theologies of Creation: Creatio ex Nihilo and Its New Rivals*, edited by Thomas Jay Oord, 55–67. New York: Routledge.

Van der Horst, Pieter W. 1999. "CHAOS χάος". In *DDD*, 85–6.
Van der Ploeg, Johannes P. M. 1946. "Le sens du verbe hébreu ברא bārā': Étude sémasiologique. *Le Muséon* 59: 143–57.
Van der Toorn, Karel. 2007. *Scribal Culture and the Making of the Hebrew Bible*. Cambridge, MA: Harvard University Press.
Van der Veer, Peter. 1994. *Religious Nationalism. Hindus and Muslims in India*. Berkeley, CA: University of California Press.
Vidal, Jordi. 2011a. "Ugarit at War (4): Weapons in Sanctuaries". *UF* 43: 449–57.
Vidal, Jordi. 2011b. "Prestige Weapons in an Amorite Context". *JNES* 70: 247–52.
Waltke, Bruce K. 1975. "The Creation Account in Genesis 1:1–3". *BS* 132: 25–36, 136–44, 216–28.
Waltke, Bruce K. 2001. *Genesis: A Commentary*. Grand Rapids, MI: Zondervan.
Walton, John H. 2009. *The Lost World of Genesis One: Ancient Cosmology and the Origins Debate*. Downers Grove, IL: InterVarsity Press.
Walton, John H. 2011. *Genesis 1 as Ancient Cosmology*. Winona Lake, IN: Eisenbrauns.
Wardlaw, Terramce R., Jr., 2014. "The meaning of ברא in Genesis 1:1–2:3". *VT* 64: 502–13.
Watson, Rebecca S. 2005. *Chaos Uncreated. A Reassessment of the Theme of "Chaos" in the Hebrew Bible*. BZAW 341. Berlin: de Gruyter.
Watson, Wilfred G. E. 1994. *Traditional Techniques in Classical Hebrew Verse*. JSOTSup 170. Sheffield: Sheffield Academic press.
Watson, Wilfred G. E., and Nicolas Wyatt. 1997. "De nouveau sur les armes cérémonielles". *NABU* 1: 27–8.
Weiser, Artur. (1959) 1962. *The Psalms: A Commentary*. Philadelphia, PA: Westminster Press.
Wenham, Gordon J. 1987. *Genesis 1–15*. WBC 1. Waco, TX: Word Books.
Wenham, Gordon J. 2015. Response to K. L. Spark's article "Genesis 1–11 as Ancient Historiography". In *Genesis: History, Fiction, or Neither? Three Views on the Bible's Earliest Chapters*, edited by Charles Halton, 101–9. Grand Rapids, MI: Zondervan.
Wensinck, Arent J. 1918. *The Ocean in the Literature of the Western Semites*. Verhandelingen der Koninkliijke Akademie van Wetenschappen te Amsterdam n.s. 19/ 2. Amsterdam: J. Müller.
West, Martin L. 1997. *The East Face of Helicon: West Asiatic Elements in Greek Poetry and Myth*. Oxford: OUP.
Westermann, Claus. (1974) 1984. *Genesis 1–11: A Commentary*. Translated by J. J. Scullion. Minneapolis, MN: Augsburg Publishing House. London: SPCK.
Wiebe, Donald. 2009. "A Scientific Account of Meaning: Deflationary but not Disenchanting". *Zygon* 44: 31–40.
Wiggerman, Frans A. M. 1989. "Tišpak, his Seal, and the Dragon *mušḫuššu*". In *To the Euphrates and Beyond: Archaeological Studies in Honour of Maurits van Loon*, edited by Odette M. C. Haex, Hans H. Curvers and Peter M. M. G. Akkermans, 117–33. Rotterdam: A. A. Balkema.
Williams, Tyler F. 1996. "פרד" (#7296/7297). In *NIDOTTE*, Vol. 3.
Winther-Nielsen, Nicolai. 1992. "'In the Beginning' of Biblical Hebrew Discourse: Genesis 1:1 and the Fronted Time Expression". In *Language in Context: Essays for Robert E. Longacre*, edited by Shin Ja K. Hwang and William R. Merrifield, 67–80. Dallas, TX: SIL and University of Texas at Arlington.

Wolde, Ellen J. van. 2009. "Why the Verb ברא Does Not Mean 'To Create' in Genesis 1.1–2.4a". *JSOT* 34 :3–23.
Wolde, Ellen J. van, and Robert Rezetko. 2011. "Semantics and the Semantics of ברא: A Rejoinder to the Arguments Advanced by B. Becking and M. Korpel". *JHebS* 11: article 9.
Wyatt, Nicolas. 1977. "The identity of *Mt w Šr*". *UF* 9: 379–81.
Wyatt, Nicolas. 1985. "Killing and Cosmogony in Canaanite and Biblical Thought". *UF* 17: 375–81.
Wyatt, Nicolas. 1993. "The Darkness of Genesis i 2". *VT* 43: 543–54. Reprinted in Wyatt 2005a, 92–101.
Wyatt, Nicolas. 1994. "The Theogony Motif in Ugarit and the Bible". In *Ugarit and the Bible: Proceedings of the International Symposium on Ugarit and the Bible, Manchester, September 1992*, edited by George J. Brooke, Adrian H. W. Curtis and John F. Healey, 395–419. UBL 11. Münster: Ugarit-Verlag. Reprinted in Wyatt 2005b, 85–101.
Wyatt, Nicolas. 1995b. "The Liturgical Context of Psalm 19 and its Mythical and Ritual Origins". *UF* 27: 559–96. Reprinted in Wyatt 2005b, 103–31.
Wyatt, Nicolas. 1996. *Myths of Power. A Study of Royal Myth and Ideology in Ugaritic and Biblical Tradition*. UBL 13. Münster: Ugarit-Verlag.
Wyatt, Nicolas. 1998. "Arms and the King: the Earliest Allusions to the Chaoskampf Motif and their Implications for the Interpretation of the Ugaritic and Biblical Traditions". In *"Und Mose schrieb dieses Lied auf …". Studien zum Alten Testament und zum Alten Orient. Festschrift für O. Loretz zur Vollendung seines 70. Lebensjahres mit Beiträgen von Freunden, Schülern und Kollegen*, edited by Manfried Dietrich and Ingo Kottsiepier, 833–82. AOAT 250. Münster: Ugarit-Verlag. Reprinted in Wyatt 2005b, 151–89.
Wyatt, Nicolas. 1999. "The Religion of Ugarit: An Overview". In *Handbook of Ugaritic Studies*, edited by Wilfred G. E. Watson and Nicolas Wyatt, 529–85. HOS. Leiden: Brill.
Wyatt, Nicolas. 2001a. *Space and Time in the Religious Life of the Ancient Near East*. BS 85. Sheffield: Sheffield Academic Press.
Wyatt, Nicolas. 2001b. "The Mythic Mind". *SJOT* 15 : 3–56. Reprinted in Wyatt 2005a, 151–88.
Wyatt, Nicolas. 2002. *Religious Texts from Ugarit*. BS 53. 2nd edition. London: Continuum.
Wyatt, Nicolas. 2003a. "'Water, Water Everywhere …': Musings on the Aqueous Myths of the Near East". In *De la Tablilla a la Inteligencia Artificial. Homenaje al Prof. Jesús Luis Cunchillos en su 65 aniversario*, edited by D. A. González Blanco, J. P. Vita and J. A. Zamora, 211–59. Próximo Oriente Antiguo. Zaragoza: Instituto de estudios Islámicos y del Oriente Próximo. Reprinted in Wyatt 2005a, 189–237.
Wyatt, Nicolas. 2003b. Review of *Religion and its Monsters*, by Timothy K. Beal. In *SWC* 9: 128–34.
Wyatt, Nicolas. 2005a. *The Mythic Mind: Essays on Cosmology in Ugaritic and Old Testament Literature*. Bible World. London: Equinox.
Wyatt, Nicolas. 2005b *"There's Such Divinity Doth Hedge a King": Selected Essays of Nicolas Wyatt on Royal Ideology in Ugaritic and Old Testament Literature*. SOTSMS. London: Ashgate.
Wyatt, Nicolas. 2007a. "A la recherche des Rephaïm perdus". In *Le royaume d'Ougarit de la Crète à l'Euphrate: Nouveaux axes de recherche*, edited by Jean-Marc Michaud, 579–613. Proche-Orient et Littérature Ougaritique 2. Sherbrooke, QC: Éditions GGC. Reprinted in Wyatt 2010, 43–68.

Wyatt, Nicolas. 2007b. "Making Sense of the Senseless: Correcting Scribal Errors in Ugaritic". *UF* 39:757–72.

Wyatt, Nicolas. 2008a. "The Mythic Mind Revisited: Myth and History, or Myth versus History, a Continuing Problem in Biblical Studies". *SJOT* 22: 161–75. Reprinted in Wyatt 2010, 83–93.

Wyatt, Nicolas. 2008b. Review of *Chaos Uncreated: A Reassessment of the Theme of "Chaos" in the Hebrew Bible,* by Rebecca S. Watson. *JSS* 53: 338–40.

Wyatt, Nicolas. 2010. *The Archaeology of Myth: Papers on Old Testament Tradition*. Bible World. London: Equinox.

Wyatt, Nicolas. 2012. "After Death has us Parted: Encounters Between the Living and the Dead in the Ancient Semitic World". In *The Perfumes of Seven Tamarisks: Studies in Honour of Wilfred G. E. Watson*, edited by Gregorio del Olmo Lete, Jordi Vidal and Nicolas Wyatt, 259–92. AOAT 394. Münster: Ugarit-Verlag.

Wyatt, Nicolas. 2014a. "A Royal Garden: the Ideology of Eden". *SJOT* 28: 1–35.

Wyatt, Nicolas. 2014b. Review of *Toward a Poetics of Genesis 1–11: Reading Genesis 4:17–22 in its Near Eastern Context,* by Daniel DeWitt Lowery. In *SOTS Book List 2014, JSOT* 38/5: 66.

Wyatt, Nicolas. 2015. "The Evidence of the Colophons in the Assessment of Ilimilku's Scribal and Authorial Role". *UF* 46: 399–446.

Wyatt, Nicolas. 2017a. "National Memory, Seismic Activity at Ras Shamra and the Composition of the Baal Cycle". *UF* 48: 551–91.

Wyatt, Nicolas. 2017b. "The Problem of 'Dying and Rising' Gods: The Case of Baal". Paris Colloque Proceedings. *UF* 48: 811–38.

Wyatt, Nicolas. 2018. "The Baal au Foudre Stela and its Historical Context". *UF* 49: 329–37.

Wyatt, Nicolas. 2019. "A Ritual Response to a Natural Disaster: KTU 1.119.31 = RS 24.266.31 Revisited". *UF* 50: 453–69.

Wyatt, Nicolas. In press. "War in Heaven: the Ugaritian Ideology of Warfare as Reflected in the Composition of Ilimilku's Baal Cycle". ASOR-EPHE Conference paper, Paris September 2018: to be published in proceedings.

Wyatt, Simon, and Nicolas Wyatt. 2013. "The Longue Durée in the Beef Business". In *Ritual, Religion and Reason: Studies in the Ancient World in Honour of Paolo Xella*, edited by Oswald Loretz, Sergio Ribichini, Wilfred G. E. Watson and José-A. Zamora, 417–50. AOAT 404. Münster: Ugarit-Verlag.

Young, Frances. 1991. "'Creatio ex nihilo': A Context for the Emergence of the Christian Doctrine of Creation". *SJT* 44: 139–52.

Zadok, Ran. 1984. "Some Jews in Babylonian Documents". *JQR* 74: 294–7.

Zevit, Ziony. 2013. *What Really Happened in the Garden of Eden?* New Haven, CT: Yale University Press.

Zornberg, Avivah G. 1995. *Genesis: The Beginning of Desire*. Jerusalem: Jewish Publication Society.

Index of Hebrew words and phrases discussed in the text

ʾāb   147
ʾādām   226
ʾôr, wayəhî   212
ʾeḥād   167
ʾim   26, 41, 89, 109–25
ʾāmar   205, 262
ʾap   55, 63
ʾereṣ   55, 225, 231, 232, 289, 321
ʾăšērāh   163, 190, 219, 320

bādal   see hibdîl
bōhû   221, 231, 261
bwʾ   55
bayit   163
bāmāh, -ôt   61–2, 140
bqʿ   45, 46, 239, 270, 295
bārāʾ (brʾ, bôrēʾ)   205, 216–17, 218, 219, 222–4, 225, 226–7, 231, 234, 239, 247, 258, 262, 285, 288, 295, 315, 317, 318, 320
bərēʾšît   see rēʾšît
bārak   205, 219, 320
bāraq   219, 320
bərešet   see rešet
bərît   218, 219, 285, 315, 317, 320

gôyim   55
gayʾ   281
gʿr   239

deber (dbr)   19, 23, 24, 31, 32
dûš   54, 84
dārak (drk)   54, 55, 56–7, 60, 61, 62, 84
derek (drk)   56–57, 60–61

hă-   26, 41, 43, 82–3, 89, 103, 109–25
hălōʾ   82, 110, 112, 123, 124
hibdîl   205, 216, 222
hêkāl   163

zerem   47

ḥûl   318
ḥăzāqāh (ḥzq)   52
ḥayil   61
ḥll   65, 278
ḥēmāh   55, 65
ḥiṣṣîm   33
ḥārāh   63
ḥōšek   290–1

ṭmʾ   162

yabbāšāh   232
yhwh ṣəbāʾôt   172
yām (ym)   14, 18, 22, 29, 31, 34, 36, 37, 38, 39–42, 43, 54, 57, 71, 79, 265, 271, 272, 293–4, 319
yṣʾ   161, 163
yāṣar (yṣr)   204, 216, 258
yārēaḥ   16, 51
yšʿ   55
yəšûʿâ (yšwʿwt)   55, 269

kōhănîm   161
kālāh   277
kəmārîm   138, 159, 161, 162

lōʾ   see hălōʾ
lipnê   237

mabbûl   275
māwet   81
mizbəḥôt   139, 172
mḥṣ   237
maṭṭeh, -ôt   33, 44, 63, 66, 67, 100
mayim rabbîm   17, 34, 56, 57, 58–60, 75
mîn   222, 247
maktēš   46
melek   294
maʿălôt   139
mippənê   237

maṣṣēbôt 138
mišbərê-yām 36

nəhārôt 24, 89
nəhārîm 34, 37, 38–9, 45, 54, 89, 101, 272
naḥal 52
nēkār, bənê 17
nissaktî (nsk) 220
nqb 64, 65, 84
nātan qôl 46, 48, 49, 50, 53

selah 15
saʻar 65

ʻebrāh 63
ʻîr 162
ʻam 147
ʻāmad (ʻmd) 51, 55, 62
ʻrh 84
ʻāśāh (ʻśh) 204, 205, 216, 224, 226, 258

pānîm see lipnê, mippěnê etc.
prr 239, 265–8, 269, 271, 295, 320

ṣûr 46
ṣāʻad 54

qədēšîm (qādēš) 138, 163
qôl see nātan qôl

qûm 52
qānāh 223
qn'rṣ 142
qārāʼ 205, 216
qešet (qšt) 44, 64, 100

rēʼšît 218, 219, 285, 315, 317, 320
rōʼš 65
rûaḥ 262
rôm 51, 53
rāmas 55
rāqîaʻ 232, 233
rešep 23, 32
rāšāʻ 35, 64–5
rešet (ršt) 218, 219, 285, 315, 317

śrp 163

šwp 264
šeṭep 277
šemeš 51
šty 239

tōhû 221, 229, 230–1, 237, 251, 261, 281, 285, 289–90
təhôm (thwm) 34, 36, 46, 48–9, 50, 223, 228, 230–1, 232, 234, 235, 259, 260, 271, 285, 291–5, 300, 318, 319, 326
tannîn (tannînîm) 79, 222, 240, 278, 294

Biblical reference index

Genesis
- 1:1   214, 218, 221, 224, 225, 239, 271, 297
- 1:1–2   280
- 1:1–3   214, 257–9, 262, 288, 298
- 1:1–2:4a   216
- 1:2   225, 229, 233, 234, 251, 253, 254, 257, 259–62, 271, 273, 281, 285, 288, 294, 295–6, 297, 305, 321, 325
- 1:2–3   290
- 1:2–31   297
- 1:3   262–3
- 1:3, 6, 9, 11, 14, 20, 24, 26, 29   205
- 1:4   216
- 1:4, 7, 14, 18   205
- 1:6–10   224
- 1:7, 16, 25, 26, 31   204
- 1:20, 22, 28   205
- 1:26–27   205, 222
- 2:2   204
- 2:3   205
- 2:4b   204
- 2:5a   258
- 2:5–6   288
- 2:7   204, 216
- 3:15   264
- 3:24   236
- 4:7   109
- 6–8   246
- 7:11   46, 233, 237, 297, 322
- 9   246, 247, 250
- 13:9   109
- 14:19, 22   224
- 17:17   42, 114
- 18:21   109
- 18:28   109
- 24:21   112
- 27:21   112
- 37:8   115
- 37:32   112
- 42:16   112
- 49:25   45, 48

Exodus
- 3:19   52
- 7:20   239
- 13:3   52
- 14:21   265, 239, 265
- 15   102, 246, 249, 250, 310
- 15:1–18   17
- 15:4–5   319
- 15:8–10   271
- 15:17   249
- 16:4   112
- 17:7   112
- 19   87
- 20:4   141
- 20:11   224
- 20:22–23:33   158
- 20:25   158
- 24:1–11   180
- 24:7   157
- 32:11   52

Leviticus
- 11   247
- 21   161
- 26:1   141

Numbers
- 6:24–6   142
- 10:35   52
- 11:12   42, 115
- 11:22   115
- 11:23   112
- 13:18–20   41, 113
- 16:30   225, 226
- 24:7   65

Deuteronomy
- 1:36   56
- 4:16   141
- 4:34   52
- 4:35, 39   168
- 5:15   52
- 6:4   152, 167
- 8:2   113
- 11:24   56
- 11:25   56

– 12–18   167
– 20:1   138
– 20:2   152
– 24:16   158
– 28:61   157
– 29:20   157
– 30:10   157
– 31:26   157
– 32:13   62
– 32:24   32
– 33:2   36
– 33:2–3   32
– 33:13   48
– 33:23   221
– 33:28   44
– 33:29   62
Joshua
– 1:3   56
– 1:8   157
– 2:10   239
– 5:13   113
– 7:1   36
– 8:31   158
– 8:34   157
– 14:9   56
– 17:15, 18   217, 224
– 24:17   138–9
Judges
– 2:1   139
– 2:22   113
– 5   17
– 5:2–21   69
– 5:4   36, 44, 45, 54, 87
– 5:20   52
– 5:26   65
– 6:8, 13   139
– 6:31   42, 115
– 9:2   113
– 11:25   115
– 15:19   46
– 20:28   41, 113
1 Samuel
– 8:8   139
– 10:18   139
– 12:6   139
– 14:45   111
– 15:17   110

– 30:15   111
2 Samuel
– 7   168
– 7:22   168
– 14:19   111
– 17:6   110
– 19:14   41, 110
– 19:36   115
– 19:43   116
– 22:5–6   59
– 22:12   44
– 22:17   59
– 22:18   59
– 22:33b   61
– 22:33–4   60
– 22:34b   62
– 24:13   113
1 Kings
– 6:38   248
– 8:12   291
– 8:27   248
– 8:60   168
– 11:7   162
– 12:28   138
– 18:19   180
– 18:21, 24, 39   168
– 18:39   168
– 20:23   61
– 22:6   114
– 22:15   114
– 22:18   111
2 Kings
– 7:19   233
– 12:5   156
– 12:5–6   157
– 12:14   157
– 12:18–19   157
– 14:6   158
– 19:15, 19   168
– 20:11   139
– 21:3   139
– 21:5   164
– 22:1–23:3   136
– 22:1–2   153
– 22:2, 21   178
– 22:3–7   156, 157, 178
– 22:3–9   180

– 22:3–20   179, 189
– 22:8, 11   158, 178
– 22:9   156, 178
– 22:10   156
– 22:10–20   178
– 22:15–20   168
– 23:4   161, 186
– 23:4–15   137–8, 171, 174, 185
– 23:4–20   159, 168, 174, 178, 180, 181, 191
– 23:5, 8–9, 10, 13–4, 15–20   160–1
– 23:8a   153, 161
– 23:8, 10, 13, 16   162
– 23:9   161
– 23:10   162
– 23:12   137–8, 139, 140
– 23:15   140
– 23:15–20   159, 162
– 23:16–30   137
– 23:21   158
– 23:24   158
– 23:24   158
– 23:25   160
– 25:27–30   175

Isaiah
– 5:25   36
– 10:8–11   124
– 10:15   116
– 19:5   38
– 27:1   239, 241, 243
– 27:7   116
– 28:25   110
– 35:6   46
– 40:21   89
– 40:21a, 28a   103
– 40:26   89
– 40:28   42, 89, 122
– 42:15   239
– 43:1, 15   216, 258
– 44:27   239
– 45:6–7   225
– 45:7   215–16, 216
– 45:18   258, 261
– 48:21   46
– 49:24–5   116
– 50:2   116, 239
– 51:9–10   224

– 51:11   65
– 58:14   62
– 59:8   56
– 63:1   55
– 63:3   55
– 65:17   226
– 66:8–9   116
– 66:15   34

Jeremiah
– 1:11–12   315
– 2:14   117
– 2:31   117
– 3:4–5   117
– 4:23–8   237, 297, 306, 321
– 4:24–6   297
– 4:27   297
– 5:9   122
– 5:22   122
– 5:29   123
– 7:30–1   162
– 7:31   160
– 8:2   20
– 8:4   90, 123
– 8:19   123
– 8:22   123
– 9:8   123
– 14:19   117
– 14:22   117
– 18:14–15   118
– 19:6, 11–14   162
– 19:13   139, 164
– 22:28   118
– 23:19   65
– 30:23   65
– 31:20   118, 226
– 31:22   226
– 32:29   139
– 49:1   123
– 51:36   239

Ezekiel
– 1:4–28   32
– 13:11, 13   45
– 15:3–4   118
– 20:3   111
– 21:24   217, 224
– 21:36   36
– 22:14   118

– 23:47   217
Hosea
– 8:5   36
Joel
– 1:2   118
– 3:4   110
– 3:18   44
Amos
– 3:3   41
– 4:13   258, 291
– 3:5–7   119, 124
– 6:2   119
– 6:12   119
Obadiah
– 1:5   110
Micah
– 1:6   281
– 2:7   119
– 4:9   119
– 5:4–5   56
Nahum
– 1:4   239
Habakkuk
– 1:4, 13   65
– 2:12–20   81
– 3:3–7   47
– 3:3–15   17
– 3:8   18, 22, 30–43, 55, 83, 88, 90, 101, 121, 272–3
– 3:8–15   34, 43–53, 67, 90, 98
– 3:9   44–6
– 3:9–10   45, 87
– 3:10   46–53
– 3:12   54–5, 57
– 3:13–14   63–72, 91
– 3:15   56–60, 90, 273
– 3:17   62
– 3:19   60–2
Zephaniah
– 1:4–5   161
– 1:5   164
Zechariah
– 9:14   36
– 10:11   239
– 14:4   281
Psalms
– 2:1–3   245

– 7:7   36
– 9:6, 17   65
– 10:12   52
– 18:5–6   59
– 18:8, 12–17   46
– 18:12   44
– 18:13–15   45
– 18:16   59
– 18:17   59
– 18:18   59
– 18:33   61
– 18:33–4   60
– 18:34   62
– 28:2   53
– 29:3   274
– 29:10   274–5
– 42:8   49
– 46:1–4   271–2, 273
– 46:2–3   58
– 65:6–7   58
– 66:6   38
– 68:2   52
– 68:8–9   54
– 68:9–10   44–5
– 68:17   36
– 68:22   65
– 69:35   14
– 72:8   38
– 74:12–14   265–71, 273
– 74:13   320
– 74:13–14a   87, 97, 224, 239
– 74:14   65
– 74:14b–15a   240
– 74:15   24, 46
– 76:4   32
– 77:15–20   17
– 77:16–19   58
– 77:17   47, 50
– 77:17–18   33, 46
– 77:17–20   46, 50
– 77:18   44–5, 47, 48, 49, 50
– 77:18–19   87
– 77:20   56–7, 59
– 78:15   45, 46
– 78:48   32
– 80:12   38
– 88:11   42

- 89:11   14, 65
- 89:15   32
- 91:6   32
- 93:3–4   58
- 96:11   14, 49
- 97:4   47
- 98:7   14, 49
- 98:7–8   38
- 98:8   14
- 104:5–6   58
- 104:6–7   239
- 104:24   220
- 104:26   236
- 104:30   226
- 106:9   319
- 111:10   221
- 114:7–8   44–5
- 132:8   52
- 136:12   52
- 148:7   224

Job
- 4:17–18   120
- 5:7   32
- 6:5   90
- 6:5–6   120
- 6:30   124
- 7:1   90
- 7:12   43, 120
- 8:3   120
- 10:4–5   120
- 10:5–6   42
- 11:2   121
- 11:7   121
- 11:9   221
- 13:8–9   121
- 21:4   125
- 22:3   121
- 26:8   46
- 26:12   65
- 26:13   65
- 28:10   46
- 34:17   121
- 37:20   121
- 38:33   121
- 38:8–11   36
- 39:9–10   121
- 40:27   122

Proverbs
- 3:19   220
- 3:20   46
- 6:27–9   122
- 8:22   220
- 8:22–31   219
- 8:23   220
- 8:27–8   48

Song of Solomon
- 8:6

Daniel
- 9:15   52

Ezra
- 8:22   36

Nehemiah
- 1:10   52

2 Chronicles
- 18:5   114
- 18:14   114
- 18:17   112
- 34:3–7   178, 179
- 34:8–33   178

Ben Sira (Sirach)
- 6:24   219
- 6:29   218
- 6:18–33   218

Index of Ancient Near Eastern Texts and Inscriptions

Texts from Ugarit
Cuneiform Alphabetic Texts from Ugarit (CAT)
– 1.14 iii.52–iv.9a   140
– 1.14 iv. 1–9   140 n.17
– 1.41   139
– 1.41.50   140 n.15
Corpus des tablettes en cunéiformes alphabétiques découvertes à Ras Shamra-Ugarit de 1929 à 1939 (CTA)
– 13.33–4 obv. 17, 24, rev. 4, 7, 9   229 n.77
Corpus des textes de la bibliothèque de Ras Shamra-Ougarit (ed. Arnaud)
– 128–38   242 n. 115 (fragments of *The Epic of Gilgamesh*)
Die Keilalphabetischen Texte aus Ugarit (KTU)
– 1.1.iii 27   65 n.159
– 1.2.i 7–8, 16, 21, 21–2, 23   41 n.53
– 1.2.i 24   239
– 1.2.ii 9   64
– 1.2.iv 8–15, 18–23   64 n.155
– 1.2.iv 9   65 n.159, 239
– 1.2.iv 11   88 n.9
– 1.2.iv 27   239
– 1.2.iv 28   239
– 1.2.iv 29   239, 274 n.96
– 1.2.iv 31   239
– 1.3.ii 15   64
– 1.3.ii 15–6   67
– 1.3.iii 28–30   238 n.99, 249
– 1.3.iii 38–45   239 n.104
– 1.3.iii 38–46   241
– 1.3 iii 37– iv 3   278
– 1.3.iii 39–42   97, 105
– 1.3.iv 19–20   238 n.99, 249
– 1.3.vi 5–6   38 n.47, 39, 88
– 1.3.vi 10   41 n.52
– 1.3.vi 13–6   41 n.52
– 1.4.ii 6–7   88
– 1.4.ii 24   65 n.159
– 1.4.ii 31   41 n.52
– 1.4.ii 32   219, 220
– 1.4.ii   41 n.52
– 1.4.ii 6–7   38 n.47, 39
– 1.4 v–vii   317
– 1.4.vi 24–35   248, 256
– 1.4.vii 25–31   279
– 1.4.vii 27–31   274, 275
– 1.4.vii 52–60   53 n.117
– 1.5.i 1   65 n.159
– 1.5.i 1–3   96, 105, 241, 243, 278
– 1.5.i 14   232
– 1.5.i   14–6   229, 230 n.77, 289
– 1.5.i 1–3   269, 311
– 1.6.ii 32   239
– 1.6.vi 16–22   64 n.155, 78
– 1.14.i 19   31 n.15
– 1.15.ii 6   31 n.15
– 1.19.iii 14, 28   266
– 1.19.iii 47   65
– 1.19.iii 49, 56   64 n.154
– 1.19.iv 7   64 n.154
– 1.19.iv 34   65
– 1.23   204, 219
– 1.23.8   327
– 1.23.30   229 n.77, 319
– 1.23.33–5   277 n.107
– 1.23:37–8, 40, 44, 47   64 n.154
– 1.100.1   229 n.77
– 1.100.31   31 n.15
– 1.101.1–2   275
– 1.101:2   277
– 1.133.2–5   229 n.77, 230n.77
– 9.432.18   278 n.113
Ras Shamra (RS)
– 24.245   275
– 22.421 (fragments of *Atraḫasis*)   242 n.115
– 94.2066 (fragments of *The Epic of Gilgamesh*)   242 n.115

– 94.2082 (fragments of *The Epic of Gilgamesh*)   242 n.115
– 94.2083 (fragments of *The Epic of Gilgamesh*)   242 n.115
– 94.2191 (fragments of *The Epic of Gilgamesh*)   242 n.115

Myths from Mesopotamia
Enuma Elish
– 1.1–2   258
– 1.2   214 n.32, 232 n.86
– 4.19–28   214
– 4.49   275
– 4.103–12   267–8
– 4.137   239 n.107, 268
– 4.137–8   270
– 4.49   275
– 4.62   270
– 4.67–8   24
– 4:83–4   64
– 4.95   220
– 4.130   66
– 4.137   239 n.107
– 4.137–40, v 62   232
– 5.54–5   24
– 6.125   275
Gilgamesh
– XI 129–31   276
Atraḫasis
– III.iii 12   276
– III.iv:5–6   272 n.89
– III.viii 12   276

Dead Sea Scrolls
– 1QH 5:9–10   230 n.77
– 1QHª X 27   48 n.88
– 1QM 9:11   57 n.130
– 1QM 12:10   48 n.88
– 1QM 14:5   186
– 4Q424 1:4   47 n.86
– 4QpIsaᶜ 25:3   48 n.88
– 4QSamª   60 n.139
– 11QPsª   56 n.127
– CD   1.11

Other Texts, Tablets and Inscriptions
Ahiqar
– §28   229 n.77
– §34   229 n.77
Amarna tablets
– EA 227   242 n.115
– EA 270   242 n.115
– EA 271.   242 n.115
– EA 273   242 n.115
– EA 285–290   242 n.115
– EA 356–9   316
Archives royales de Mari (ARMT)
– A 1968 (Zimri-Lim Text)   244, 246, 307
Corpus of Ammonite Inscriptions (ed. Aufrecht)
– Amman Citadel Inscription and the Amman Theatre Inscription   143 n.32
Echoes from the Past: Hebrew and Cognate Inscriptions (ed. Aḥituv)
– Ostracon from the Upper City of Jerusalem   142 n.23
– Lachish Letters: ostraca 2, 3, 4, 5, 6, 9   142 n.25
'Inscriptions' in *Kuntillet 'Ajrud* (ed. Aḥituv et al.)
– Kuntillet 'Ajrud and Khirbet el-Qom inscriptions   139 n.12
Royal Inscriptions of Esarhaddon (ed. Leichty), vol. 4
– Assur Temple inscription   179
Vorderasiatische Abteilung Tontafel   (VAT)
– VAT 9307   214 n.32
– VAT 9805 + 9808 14 ff   214 n.32

Index of authors

Ahlström, Gösta W.   136, 172, 173, 174, 185
Albertz, Rainer   144–8, 152, 153, 154, 166–7
Albrektson, Bertil   286
Albright, W. F.   15, 16
Averbeck, R.   250, 251, 264, 308
Ayali-Darshan, Noga   322

Barker, Margaret   218, 220
Barrick, W. Boyd   159
Barth, Karl   254
Becking, Bob   223–4, 226
Bonting, Sjoerd L.   254, 305

Carroll, R.   321
Cassuto, Umberto   15
Cho, P. K.-K.   294
Cogan, Mordechai   175
Collins, John   221
Cross, Frank M.   17, 96, 305, 310, 325

Day, John   18–19, 261, 281
Deutsch, Robert   145
Dietrich, Manfred   230
Durand, Jean-Marie   244

Eaton, John   16–17, 24
Eggeling, Julius   323

Foster, B. R.   233, 267

Gibson, Arthur   26, 83, 89
Greenfield, Jonas C.   226
Gunkel, Herman   211, 243, 246, 253, 254, 259, 264, 265–6, 271, 287

Heidel, Alexander   213, 319
Heltzer, Michael   145
Hiebert, Theodore   15, 19–20, 24, 27
Hutton, James   140

Jacobsen, Thorkild   100, 260, 292, 325
Jowett, Benjamin   302

Keel, Othmar   57–8
Keller, Catherine   254
Kitchen, Kenneth   21
Klingbeil, M.   256–7
Korpel, Marjo   223–4, 225, 226

Lambert, W. G.   144, 212, 255, 267
Layton, Scott   146
Lee, Stephen   228
Lemaire, André   144, 145
Levin, Christoph   153, 173
Loretz, Oswald   230

Margulis, Baruch   18
May, H. G.   58, 75
Mowinckel, Sigmund   76, 77
Murray, Robert   227

Naudé, Jacobus   186, 190
Niditch, Susan   226
Niehr, Herbert   136, 152, 153, 154, 172–3, 185, 189
Noort, E.   231
Noth, Martin   145

O'Brien, Juliet   25, 86
Ortlund, Eric Nels   253, 256, 272, 277, 280, 305

Pakkala, Juha   163, 167
Pardee, Dennis   139, 145, 230, 279, 289, 291–2, 318
Peters, Kurtis   221
Pitard, Wayne   248

Redditt, P. L.   15, 26
Rezetko, Robert   224, 225, 228, 233
Roberts, J. J. M.   24, 25, 91

Sanmartín, Joaquin   230
Scurlock, JoAnn   246
Smith, Mark   96, 105, 167, 207, 248, 280, 297

Smith, Ralph L.   90–1
Sparks, Kenton L.   213, 242, 291, 292
Stavrakopoulou, Francesca   136, 172, 173, 174, 185, 189

Tadmor, Hayim   175
Tate, Marvin E.   266

Uehlinger, Christoph   159

Vail, Eric M.   253
Van Bekkum, Koert   98
Van Selms   43
Van Wolde, Ellen   222–3, 224, 225, 228, 233, 258

Von Rad, Gerhard   227–8, 232, 251, 254, 286, 316, 325

Wakeman, Mary K.   76, 77
Waltke, Bruce K.   222, 254, 305, 316
Walton, John H.   258, 327
Wardlaw, Terence   226, 228
Wenham, Gordon J.   327
Wensinck, Arent J.   231
Westermann, Claus   217

Yardeni, Ada   145

Zevit, Ziony   308
Zuckerman, Bruce   297

Subjects Index

Abraham   42, 114, 219
Adad (deity)   22, 244
Adonai (divine name)   34n35, 61
Ahaz, king   139, 171n5
Akkadian   33n22, 40n52, 64, 65, 66 – 7, 209n16, 210, 211n22, 212, 214, 222n55, 229n76, 234n89, 235, 236n92, 242n115, 259, 260n32, 267, 268, 272n89, 275, 276, 291 – 2, 293, 294, 318
Alexander the Great   175
alloforms   96
altars   137 – 9, 149, 161, 162, 164, 165, 171, 172, 199
Amman Citadel Inscription   143
Amman Theatre Inscription   143
Amarna texts   179, 203, 287, 316
Ammonites   123, 143, 145, 148
Amon, king   153, 155
Amos   147
amulets   142
Amun (deity)   204
analogy   24, 53, 54n119, 76, 304
Anat (deity)   64, 66, 105, 147, 175, 186, 239n104, 240, 278 see also Anat-Yahu
Anat-Yahu (deity)   149, 175
Anatolia   236n92, 279
Anu (deity)   214
anger, divine   26, 29, 33, 34, 36, 38, 40, 41, 43, 54 – 5, 56n127, 63, 84, 91, 98, 104, 327
anthropomorphism   14, 33, 87, 100, 223, 262
Anunitu (deity)   64
Apollo (deity)   23
apologetics   167
Apsû (deity)   212, 293, 295
Aqhat texts   64, 65, 266
Aram   61
Ararat, Mount   301
archaeology   2, 4, 135, 141, 151, 159, 171, 177, 186
ark, Noah's   248n130
Ark of the Covenant   52

arrows   14, 23, 30n6, 33 – 4, 52, 63, 67, 83, 87 – 8, 217
Asherah (deity)   138, 139, 140, 141, 149, 160, 161, 163 – 4, 166, 177, 181, 190
– Asherah poles   138, 161, 163 – 4, 165, 180, 190
Ashurbanipal, king of Assyria   69n178, 154
Assur (deity)   23, 179, 214, 257
Astarte   162
Assyrians   39n48, 67, 68, 80n21, 81, 144, 152 – 5, 164n33, 165 – 6, 172, 175, 178, 180, 213n30, 262, 268, 276 – 7
astral cults (host of heaven)   17, 32, 138, 139, 157, 161, 163 – 4, 165, 166, 172, 180
Athirat (deity)   39, 40n52, 88, 220
Aṭiratu (deity)   219
Atraḫasis   242, 246, 276, 300

Baal (deity)   16, 20, 42, 58, 77, 80n19, 115, 138, 139, 143, 147, 148, 149, 161, 163, 168, 234, 239n102, 245, 249, 255, 257, 260, 271, 277n107, 292, 294
– Baal cycle, Ugaritic   24 – 5, 64, 243, 246, 269, 270, 274 – 5, 279 – 80, 317, 320n24
– Baal stele   64, 88, 100
– Baal-Mot conflict   65n159, 78, 97, 228 – 9, 248
– Baal-Yam cycle   14, 22, 23, 38, 64, 64n154, 79, 85, 88, 96, 100, 105, 139n107, 247 – 8, 256, 272 – 3, 278, 307
Babylon   24, 27, 34, 37n46, 71, 86, 91, 149, 154, 175, 186, 215n34, 234n39, 242, 300
– Tel Aviv   242
Babylonians   13, 19, 25, 26, 27, 39n49, 71, 75, 81, 83, 85 – 6, 91, 135, 141, 142, 144, 148, 153, 154, 155, 204, 206, 212, 213, 234, 254, 260, 276, 286, 292, 293 – 4, 305, 316, 319, 322
Babylonian Chronicles   144
Bēl (deity)   214
Ben Hinnom, valley of   138

Bethel   138–9, 140, 149, 159, 162, 163, 174, 180, 185–6, 191
birth oracles   146
blessings   36, 45, 48, 51, 52n109, 53n116, 142, 150, 181, 221
Book of Dead, Egyptian   323
Book of the Law, discovery of   136, 155–9, 166, 168, 174, 177–80, 185
Britain   68
bullae   144, 148

Caesar, Julius   68
Canaanites   3, 4, 13, 15–16, 19, 20, 24, 25, 27, 29, 33n21, 40n54, 43, 75, 80, 85, 86, 95, 152, 165, 215n34, 234n89, 255, 257, 259–60, 272, 274, 279–80, 291–2, 293, 294, 295, 301n5, 308, 311, 326
captivity, Babylonian   21, 144, 149, 150, 151, 175, 181, 215, 219, 242, 286, 316
Chadic   220
chaos   3, 4, 13, 14, 16, 18, 19, 24–5, 34, 37, 43, 58, 66, 77, 78, 79, 91, 211, 221, 227n70, 228–38, 253–81, 288, 291, 295–7, 299, 305–6, 320, 321
Chaoskampf   13, 63, 64, 66, 99, 204, 213, 243–51, 253–81, 288, 297, 298, 306–7, 309
chariot, divine   23, 24, 33n21, 34, 59
chariots   22, 26, 33, 55, 67, 68–9, 71n182, 98, 138, 164, 165, 272
charms   141
Chemosh (deity)   138, 162
cherubs   236
cosmogony   204n4, 225n66, 246, 287–8, 309
council, divine   173, 225n66
covenant   155, 158, 168, 218
creatio continua   4
creatio ex nihilo   3, 4, 5, 13, 78, 85, 97, 208–28, 253, 259n28, 288–9, 299, 302, 321
cuneiform   144, 146, 287, 301n5, 316
Cushan   31, 36
cylinder-seals   301
Cyrus, emperor   175

darkness   49n96, 53n117, 68, 117, 211, 217n34, 216, 225, 231, 232, 260, 261, 262, 277, 288, 290–1, 297
David, king   52n111, 111, 113, 168
Davidic dynasty   152, 168
Dead Sea Scrolls   189
Death, personification of   16, 32n18, 81, 82n27, 327
Deber (deity)   19, 23, 31, 32
deification   100, 277
demiurge   212
demons   19, 24, 32n20
demythologisation   3, 23, 32n20, 58, 206, 207n11, 234n89, 236n95, 286, 292, 293, 301, 305, 309, 310, 325
Deutero-Isaiah   82, 168, 215, 217, 223, 225n67, 242, 309
Deuteronomistic History   104, 136, 160, 161, 162, 164, 166, 167–8, 175, 180, 190
ditransitivity   226
dragons, primordial   15, 16, 18, 20, 64, 65, 66, 72n183, 78, 79, 87, 97, 105, 134, 204, 222, 229n77, 240–1, 247, 250, 255–6, 264, 265–6, 267, 269, 271, 273, 275, 277–8, 279, 281, 287, 295, 310, 318
dualism   57, 256, 257, 278, 281, 296

Ea (deity)   214, 295
Edom   36, 87
Egypt   37n46, 39, 40, 45, 67, 69n176, 89, 101, 102, 138, 153, 154, 173, 177–8, 186, 204, 206, 230n77, 246, 249, 268, 278, 300, 301n5, 320, 322, 323
Egyptians   20, 36n41, 68, 102, 149, 152, 322
Ekron   143
El (divine name)   147, 148, 219, 233, 294, 327
Elam   69n178, 154, 268n77
Elephantine, Egypt   149, 175, 186
Eliashib   142, 146
Elijah   168
Eloah (divine name)   47
Elohim (divine name)   220, 236, 263n51, 295

Enkidu (deity)   205
Enlil (deity)   22, 214
Enuma Elish   24, 27, 64, 66, 71, 85,
    212–13, 214, 220, 232, 233–4, 242–3,
    246, 247, 249, 250, 255, 256, 257, 258,
    260, 267–8, 270, 271, 273, 275, 278,
    286–7, 292–3, 295, 300, 306, 316,
    318, 319, 326
epithets, divine   22, 138, 141–2
eschatology   19, 21, 237n97, 246, 250, 279,
    311
Esharra   179, 189
etymology   4, 6, 145, 150, 213, 218, 223,
    231–2, 235, 243, 253, 258–9, 262n46,
    264, 265–6, 267, 271, 285, 288, 293,
    294, 295, 298, 299–300, 306, 315, 317,
    325
evil   35, 37n46, 64, 65, 66, 117, 142,
    215n34, 216n34, 231, 250–1, 253–4,
    264, 277, 279, 280, 281, 296, 305, 306,
    308, 311
exegesis   1, 2, 3, 29, 36, 77, 106, 221, 228,
    257, 315
Exile, Judean see captivity, Babylonian
exodus, the   39, 45, 48, 58–9, 71, 90, 104,
    145, 151, 309

fertility   19, 48, 142, 146, 150, 262n46
festivals   50n102, 179, 189
– Autumn Festival   16, 17
– New Wine Festival   139
– Passover   158, 180
figurines, clay   141, 150, 171, 172
Flood, the   23, 48, 222n55, 237–8, 242,
    244n119, 246, 247, 264, 275, 276–7,
    290n31, 297, 300, 301, 309, 321–2
Fortschreibung   161, 175

Gilgamesh, Epic of   242, 276, 286, 300
griffins   236
Gattungen   317

Hadad see Baal
Hades (deity)   248
hapax legomenon   35n38, 51
Hazael of Damascus   157
Hazor   244n115, 287

Hekhalot Rabbati   220
Heliopolis, Egypt   204
hermeneutics   2, 285, 310
Hesiod   235, 236, 307, 321
heterodoxy   137, 186
Hezekiah, king   146, 155, 168
high places   138, 153, 160–2, 164, 165–6,
    180
Hilkiah   152, 156, 157, 158
Hinduism   207n12, 323
Hinnom, Valley of   138, 142
historicity   136, 151–2, 172, 174, 186, 189,
    191, 207
Holy Spirit   218
Horus (deity)   147
Hosea   147
Hoshayahu   142
Huldah   136, 168
Hurrians   322
Hydra   240

Ibbi-Sin   276
iconoclasm   139, 156, 301
iconography   24, 57–8, 67, 88, 141, 237,
    301
Ilu (deity)   140, 147
Incarnation   207
incense, burning of   138, 139, 161, 308
intertextuality   27, 285, 297, 310, 315, 321
Irenaeus of Lyons   254, 323n36
Israel, kingdom of (Northern Kingdom)   36,
    37n46, 77, 80, 95, 116, 147–8, 301n5,
    310

Japan   327
Jeroboam II, king   138, 147, 165
Jerusalem   104, 124, 137, 140, 158, 162,
    165, 171, 173, 177, 191, 287
– City of David   142, 144, 148
– fall of (c. 587 BCE)   21, 135, 141, 142,
    144, 148, 186, 242
– Temple   80n21, 81, 96, 105, 138, 139,
    156, 157, 161, 163, 166, 248, 249
Jesus   318
Joash, king   115, 156, 157, 178
Jordan, river   20, 50, 79

Josiah, reform of 4, 81n22, 135–91, 234n89
Josianic reform see Josiah, reform of
Judah (Yehud), kingdom of (Southern Kingdom) 3, 18, 27, 36, 37n46, 47n81, 77, 80–1, 95, 99, 105, 116, 117, 135–44, 148, 149, 150, 152–3, 154, 155, 159, 160, 161, 162, 164, 165, 166, 167, 171, 173, 174, 175, 177, 181, 185, 186, 205–6, 219, 242, 243, 286, 300, 301n5, 302, 310

ka 205
Kabbalah 220
kashrut 222, 247, 306
Kemosh (deity) 138, 162, 257
Ketef Hinnom 142
Khasis (deity) 64n155
Khirbet Beit Lei 142
Khirbet el-Qom 139, 140, 181
Khnum (deity) 205
Kidron Valley 165
kingship 13, 30n9, 31n12, 36, 64n155, 91, 96, 165, 275
Kirta, king of Ugarit 140
Kishon 52, 54n119, 69n178
Kothar (deity) 64n155
Kumarbi 236n93, 248
Kuntillet 'Ajrud 139, 140, 181

Lachish letters 142
land, possession of 56–7, 61
Leviathan 14, 65, 72n183, 79, 87, 96, 97, 236, 240, 241, 245, 264, 265, 266, 269, 279, 294, 309–10
linguistics, comparative 292
Litanu 241
Lotan (deity) 79, 96–7, 105, 269
Louis XV, king of France 245

maces 33n22, 66, 67, 68, 88, 268, 269n79, 272, 274
Makkedah 142
Manasseh, king 138n10, 139, 155, 164, 165
Marduk (deity) 20, 24–5, 27, 66, 71, 85, 86, 91, 204, 213n30, 214–15, 220, 232, 233, 234, 236, 239n107, 242, 245, 255, 260, 263n51, 264, 267, 268, 270, 271, 273, 275, 292, 293, 296, 326
Mari oracle 246, 249–50, 307
Masoretes 163, 209n18, 210, 227
Medes 153
Megiddo 286
Memphis, Egypt 39, 40n52
metaphor, use of 6, 22–3, 52, 56, 82, 97, 205, 240, 261, 268–9, 272, 275, 277, 278, 279, 280, 286, 293, 298, 300, 303, 307, 308, 309, 311, 316, 325
meteors 23
Midian 31, 36
Milkom (deity) 123, 143, 148, 162
miracles 139, 207
Moab 71n182, 115, 139n14, 145, 148, 158
Molek (deity) 138
monolatry 152, 166, 172, 173, 185
monotheism, definitions of 104, 135, 166–8, 327
Moses 112, 115, 157, 158, 160, 168, 215
Mot (deity) 31n15, 64, 65n159, 78, 81–2, 147, 149, 228, 239n107, 248
mythology 17, 56, 100, 221, 236, 269, 272, 274–5, 278, 279, 281, 285, 287, 293, 298, 302, 305, 307, 309, 310, 321–2, 325, 326, 327
 Babylonian 19, 25, 88, 91
 Canaanite 13, 14, 15, 16, 18, 19–20, 22, 24, 25, 43, 75, 80, 85, 96, 260
 comparative 4, 297
 – Chinese 253, 255, 296
 – Greek 235–6, 253, 255, 296, 308n24

Nahar (deity) 14, 18, 38, 40, 88, 97, 105, 240, 241, 275
names, personal 141, 144–9, 150
natural disasters 254
Nehunya ben Hakkanah, rabbi 220
Neo-Assyrian empire see Assyrians
Nergal (deity) 23, 273
Niijima, Jo 327
Nile, river 39, 89, 102
Nineveh 69n178, 277
Ninurta (deity) 22, 240, 269n80
Nur-Sin 244

Odysseus   304
orthodoxy   82, 104, 207
ostraca   141–2, 147, 148

Padi, king of the Philistines   143
Paran, mount   30n6, 36
pantheism   254
paronomasia   219, 315, 326
Passover see festivals
personification   14, 16, 18, 19, 20, 25, 32, 50, 78n14, 79, 81, 82n27, 100, 277, 326
Philistines   61, 110, 119, 143
philology   15, 217, 218, 235, 293, 298, 306–7, 315–16, 318, 320, 323
phonology   234n89, 291, 293, 320, 325
plague   16, 17, 19, 23, 24, 32, 102
poetry   21, 26, 82, 211n25, 214, 217n37, 242, 280
– epic   15
Polyphemus   304
polytheism   136n6, 148, 185, 256, 326–7
Poseidon (deity)   248
post-exilic period   15, 19, 105, 136, 137, 140, 149, 153, 168, 171, 172–5, 181, 186, 189, 190, 286
postmodernism   285, 297, 326, 327
potter, God as
pre-exilic period   3, 105, 137, 140, 144, 147, 148, 149, 171, 173–5, 177, 185, 321
pregnancy   146
priests   80n21, 152, 153, 156, 158, 160, 161, 162, 163, 178, 203, 206, 217, 237, 242, 297, 302, 322
prophecy   19, 27, 34, 46, 136, 151, 161, 162, 168, 237, 297, 301
prostitution   163
Proteus   247
Psammetichus I, pharaoh   154
Ptah (deity)   205
Ptgyh (deity)   143

Qumran   180, 186, 190, 228n72, 323

Ra (deity)   204
Rahab   14, 65, 72n183, 79, 87, 215n34, 229n77, 230n77, 241n111, 246, 249, 277–8

rain   17, 19, 33, 36n39, 44–5, 47, 48, 53, 54, 55n123, 58, 84
Rashi   210
Reception Criticism   210n19, 304
Reed Sea   17, 20, 39, 89, 102
Resheph (deity)   18, 19, 23, 24, 31, 34n20
rhetoric   1, 29, 37, 38, 41, 71, 77, 81, 82, 89, 98, 102, 107, 114–25, 167–8, 172, 173, 179, 211, 285, 315
rooftop rituals   138–40, 149, 185

Sahar (deity)   147
salvation   17, 18, 20, 36, 55, 145, 146, 265, 269, 270, 271, 280, 310
Samaria   80n21, 81, 124, 147, 148, 165
Samaria ostraca   147, 148
sea, personification of see Rahab
sea monsters see dragons, primordial; Leviathan; Rahab
seals   141, 144, 301
Second Temple Period   189
Sefer Bahir   220–1
Seir   30n6, 36, 87
Sennacherib, Annals of   23
Septuagint (LXX)   189, 219, 264, 265, 281, 296
Shabako stone   204–5
Shalem (deity)   147
Shaphan   152, 156, 178, 179
Shemesh (deity)   16, 164
Shephelah   61
Sheol   49, 50n103, 59, 81, 82n27 see also underworld
Sin-shar-ishkun, king of Assyria   154
Sinai   17, 18, 30n6, 34n35, 36, 87, 91,
Sisera   52, 67n166
Solomon, king   138, 162, 165, 168, 248, 291
spirit, divine   208, 211, 231, 262, 289, 290, 295 see also Holy Spirit
springs   14, 48, 237, 240, 270, 271, 319n24
storm gods   16, 18, 20, 22–3, 24, 30n9, 50, 61, 84, 86, 88, 204, 239n102, 245, 255, 260, 274, 275, 279, 292, 294, 322
Sumer   273, 276
sun gods   138, 164
Sun Tzu   67

Susa 276
syncretism 80n21, 149, 171, 173, 186

Targum Neofiti 219
Targum Onqelos 219
Targum Pseudo-Jonathan 219
Tehom (deity) 16, 18, 259, 260, 290
Tehom theology 254
Tell ed-Duweir 142
Tell en-Nasbeh 141
temple-building 4
teraphim 158, 159n20
theomachy 38, 43, 64, 65, 66, 72, 236n92, 256–7, 260, 261, 264, 273, 274–5, 277, 279, 281, 287, 306, 307, 317, 318
theophany 16, 17, 18, 19, 20, 25, 26, 30, 32–3, 33n35, 36, 44, 46, 47, 48, 49, 50, 51, 53, 56, 57, 58, 59, 61, 62, 63, 70, 80, 86, 87, 88, 100, 231, 232, 274, 308
theriomorphism 64
Tiamat (deity) 24, 25, 64, 66, 71, 85, 91, 204, 220, 229, 232–3, 234n89, 244, 255, 259–60, 264, 267, 268, 270, 271, 273, 275, 277, 291–5, 301, 306, 308, 326
ti'āmat, relation to təhôm 223, 233, 235, 291, 293, 294, 300, 318
Timaeus, Plato's 296
Tišpak-Labbu conflict 246, 250
Titanomachy 306
tophets 138, 160, 162
tsunamis 254, 320n24
Twelve, Book of the 15

Uchimura, Kanzo 327
Ugarit 13, 14, 20, 40, 85, 86, 140, 145, 147, 175, 204, 219, 229, 234n89, 235n92, 242n115, 243, 248, 318, 320n24
Ugaritic language 15, 16, 21–3, 25, 39, 63–4, 65, 75, 76, 79, 82, 83n32, 88, 96, 97, 100, 105, 139, 206, 210n22, 211n22, 220, 232, 233, 235, 238, 239, 240–1, 246, 249, 256, 259, 260, 266, 269, 270, 272, 274–5, 278, 279, 280, 281, 285, 289, 291, 292–4, 295, 297, 298, 300, 305, 307, 308, 309, 311, 319, 322, 327
underworld 36n41, 59, 210–11, 212n26, 214, 225, 288 see also Sheol
'Ur-Mythus' 246

vineyards 140

warrior, divine 3, 14, 17, 18, 19–20, 23, 24–5, 26, 30n10, 32, 34, 43, 44, 45, 50, 51, 55, 63, 71, 80, 83–4, 86–8, 97, 102, 213n30, 257n19, 268, 269, 273, 308
weaponry 16, 24, 32, 33, 34, 43, 44, 45, 46, 48n88, 61, 63–4, 66–8, 71, 83, 86, 87–8, 100, 245, 268, 274–5
weaving 138, 163, 219–20, 232n86
weqatal forms, use of 159, 160, 162, 180, 186, 190

Wisdom (personification) 218, 219, 220, 221

Yahweh
anger of see anger, divine
as divine warrior see warrior, divine
– chariot of see chariot, divine
– cult of see Yahwism
– epithets see epithets, divine
– kingship of see kingship
– names of see Adonai (divine name); Elohim (divine name)
Yahwism 37, 81n22, 82, 104, 140, 161
Yam (deity) 14, 18, 22, 23, 25, 31, 38, 40–1, 42, 43, 64, 71, 79, 85, 88, 96, 97, 100, 101, 105, 215n34, 233, 239n102, 241, 246, 247, 248, 255, 256, 259, 260, 268, 271, 272, 273, 274, 275, 278, 292, 294, 307, 309, 326
Yam Sûp 310, 319
Yareah (deity) 16

Zeus (deity) 248
Zimri-Lim of Mari 244, 248, 250, 307, 310
Zoroastrianism 215, 306

www.ingramcontent.com/pod-product-compliance
Lightning Source LLC
Chambersburg PA
CBHW020218170426
43201CB00007B/247